PostgreSQL 10 Administration Cookbook

Over 165 effective recipes for database management and
maintenance in PostgreSQL 10

Simon Riggs
Gianni Ciolli

BIRMINGHAM - MUMBAI

PostgreSQL 10 Administration Cookbook

Copyright © 2018 Packt Publishing

Commissioning Editor: Amey Varangaonkar
Acquisition Editor: Namrata Patil
Content Development Editor: Amrita Noronha
Technical Editor: Sneha Hanchate
Copy Editor: Safis
Project Coordinator: Shweta Birwatkar
Proofreader: Safis Editing
Indexer: Pratik Shirodkar
Graphics: Jisha Chirayil
Production Coordinator: Shraddha Falebhai

First published: April 2017

Production reference: 1070518

Published by Packt Publishing Ltd.
Livery Place
35 Livery Street
Birmingham
B3 2PB, UK.

ISBN 978-1-78847-492-4

www.packtpub.com

`mapt.io`

Mapt is an online digital library that gives you full access to over 5,000 books and videos, as well as industry leading tools to help you plan your personal development and advance your career. For more information, please visit our website.

Why subscribe?

- Spend less time learning and more time coding with practical eBooks and Videos from over 4,000 industry professionals

- Improve your learning with Skill Plans built especially for you

- Get a free eBook or video every month

- Mapt is fully searchable

- Copy and paste, print, and bookmark content

PacktPub.com

Did you know that Packt offers eBook versions of every book published, with PDF and ePub files available? You can upgrade to the eBook version at `www.PacktPub.com` and as a print book customer, you are entitled to a discount on the eBook copy. Get in touch with us at `service@packtpub.com` for more details.

At `www.PacktPub.com`, you can also read a collection of free technical articles, sign up for a range of free newsletters, and receive exclusive discounts and offers on Packt books and eBooks.

Contributors

About the authors

Simon Riggs is the CTO of 2ndQuadrant, having contributed to PostgreSQL as a major developer and committer for 14 years. He has written and designed features for replication, performance, BI, management, and security. Under his guidance, 2ndQuadrant is now a leading developer of open source PostgreSQL, serving hundreds of clients in USA, Europe, and worldwide. Simon is a frequent speaker at many conferences on PostgreSQL Futures. He has worked as a database architect for 30 years.

Gianni Ciolli is the head of professional services at 2ndQuadrant. PostgreSQL consultant, trainer, and speaker at many PostgreSQL conferences in Europe and abroad since the last 10 years. He has a PhD in Mathematics from the University of Florence. He has worked with free and open source software since the 1990s and is active in the community (Prato Linux User Group and Italian PostgreSQL Users Group). He lives in London with his son. His other interests include music, drama, poetry, and athletics.

About the reviewer

Sheldon Strauch is a 23-year veteran of software consulting at IBM, Sears, Ernst & Young, and Kraft Foods. Having a bachelor's degree in business administration, he leverages his technical skills to improve business' self-awareness. He is interested in data gathering, management, and mining; maps and mapping; business intelligence; and application of data analysis. He is currently focusing on the development of data management and mining at Enova International at Chicago. At his leisure, he enjoys performing arts, music, and traveling with his wife, Marilyn.

Packt is searching for authors like you

If you're interested in becoming an author for Packt, please visit `authors.packtpub.com` and apply today. We have worked with thousands of developers and tech professionals, just like you, to help them share their insight with the global tech community. You can make a general application, apply for a specific hot topic that we are recruiting an author for, or submit your own idea.

Table of Contents

Preface

PostgreSQL is an advanced SQL database server, available on a wide range of platforms and is fast becoming one of the world's most popular server databases with an enviable reputation for performance, stability, and an enormous range of advanced features. PostgreSQL is one of the oldest open source projects, completely free to use, and developed by a very diverse worldwide community. Most of all, it just works!

One of the clearest benefits of PostgreSQL is that it is open source, meaning that you have a very permissive license to install, use, and distribute PostgreSQL without paying anyone any fees or royalties. On top of that, PostgreSQL is well-known as a database that stays up for long periods, and requires little or no maintenance in many cases. Overall, PostgreSQL provides a very low total cost of ownership.

PostgreSQL Administration Cookbook offers the information you need to manage your live production databases on PostgreSQL. The book contains insights direct from the main author of the PostgreSQL replication and recovery features and the rest of the team at 2ndQuadrant. This hands-on guide will assist developers working on live databases, supporting web or enterprise software applications using Java, Python, Ruby, and .Net from any development framework. It's easy to manage your database when you've got PostgreSQL 10 Administration Cookbook at hand.

This practical guide gives you quick answers to common questions and problems, building on the author's experience as trainers, users, and core developers of the PostgreSQL database server.

Each technical aspect is broken down into short recipes that demonstrate solutions with working code, and then explain why and how that works. The book is intended to be a desk reference for both new users and technical experts.

The book covers all the latest features available in PostgreSQL 10. Soon you will be running a smooth database with ease!

Who this book is for

This book is for system administrators, database administrators, architects, developers, and anyone with an interest in planning for or running live production databases. This book is most suited to those who have some technical experience.

What this book covers

Chapter 1, *First Steps*, covers topics such as an introduction to PostgreSQL 10, downloading and installing PostgreSQL 10, connecting to a PostgreSQL server, enabling server access to network/remote users, using graphical administration tools, using psql query and scripting tools, changing your password securely, avoiding hardcoding your password, using a connection service file, and troubleshooting a failed connection.

Chapter 2, *Exploring the Database*, helps you identify the version of the database server you are using and also the server uptime. It helps you locate the database server files, database server message log, and database's system identifier. It lets you list a database on the database server, contains recipes that let you know the number of tables in your database, how much disk space is used by the database and tables, which are the biggest tables, how many rows a table has, how to estimate rows in a table, and how to understand object dependencies.

Chapter 3, *Configuration*, covers topics such as reading the fine manual (RTFM), planning a new database, changing parameters in your programs, the current configuration settings, parameters that are at non-default settings, updating the parameter file, setting parameters for particular groups of users, basic server configuration checklist, adding an external module into the PostgreSQL server, and running the server in power saving mode.

Chapter 4, *Server Control*, provides information about starting the database server manually, stopping the server quickly and safely, stopping the server in an emergency, reloading the server configuration files, restarting the server quickly, preventing new connections, restricting users to just one session each, and pushing users off the system. It contains recipes that help you decide on a design for multi-tenancy, how to use multiple schemas, giving users their own private database, running multiple database servers on one system, and setting up a connection pool.

Chapter 5, *Tables and Data*, guides you through the process of choosing good names for database objects, handling objects with quoted names, enforcing same name, same definition for columns, identifying and removing duplicate rows, preventing duplicate rows, finding a unique key for a set of data, generating test data, randomly sampling data, loading data from a spreadsheet, and loading data from flat files.

`Chapter 6`, *Security,* provides recipes on revoking user access to a table, granting user access to a table, creating a new user, temporarily preventing a user from connecting, removing a user without dropping their data, checking whether all users have a secure password, giving limited super user powers to specific users, auditing DDL changes, auditing data changes, integrating with LDAP, connecting using SSL, and encrypting sensitive data.

`Chapter 7`, *Database Administration,* provides recipes on useful topics such as writing a script wherein either all succeed or all fail, writing a psql script that exits on the first error, performing actions on many tables, adding/removing columns on tables, changing the data type of a column, adding/removing schemas, moving objects between schemas, adding/removing tablespaces, moving objects between tablespaces, accessing objects in other PostgreSQL databases, and making views updateable.

`Chapter 8`, *Monitoring and Diagnosis,* provides recipes that answer questions such as is the user connected?, what are they running?, are they active or blocked?, who is blocking them?, is anybody using a specific table?, when did anybody last use it?, how much disk space is used by temporary data?, and why are my queries slowing down? It also helps you in investigating and reporting a bug, producing a daily summary report of logfile errors, killing a specific session, and resolving an in-doubt prepared transaction.

`Chapter 9`, *Regular Maintenance,* provides useful recipes on controlling automatic database maintenance, avoiding auto freezing and page corruptions, avoiding transaction wraparound, removing old prepared transactions, actions for heavy users of temporary tables, identifying and fixing bloated tables and indexes, maintaining indexes, finding unused indexes, carefully removing unwanted indexes, and planning maintenance.

`Chapter 10`, *Performance and Concurrency,* covers topics such as finding slow SQL statements, collecting regular statistics from pg_stat* views, finding what makes SQL slow, reducing the number of rows returned, simplifying complex SQL, speeding up queries without rewriting them, why is my query not using an index?, how do I force a query to use an index?, using optimistic locking, and reporting performance problems. And of course, the new parallel query features.

Chapter 11, *Backup and Recovery*, insists that backups are essential, though they also devote only a very small amount of time to thinking about the topic. So, this chapter provides useful information about backup and recovery of your PostgreSQL database through recipes on understanding and controlling crash recovery, planning backups, hot logical backup of one database, hot logical backup of all databases, hot logical backup of all tables in a tablespace, backup of database object definitions, standalone hot physical database backup, hot physical backup and continuous archiving. It also includes topics such as recovery of all databases, recovery to a point in time, recovery of a dropped/damaged table, recovery of a dropped/damaged database, recovery of a dropped/damaged tablespace, improving performance of backup/recovery, and incremental/differential backup and restore.

Chapter 12, *Replication and Upgrades*, explains that replication isn't magic, though it can be pretty cool. It's even cooler when it works, and that's what this chapter is all about. This chapter covers replication concepts, replication best practices, setting up file-based log shipping replication, setting up streaming log replication, managing log shipping replication, managing Hot Standby, synchronous replication, upgrading to a new minor release, in-place major upgrades, major upgrades online, plus logical replication and Postgres-BDR.

To get the most out of this book

In order for this book to be useful, you need at least access to a PostgreSQL client that is allowed to execute queries on a server. Ideally, you'll also be the server administrator. Full client and server packages for PostgreSQL are available for most popular operating systems at http://www.postgresql.org/download/. All the examples here are executed at a Command Prompt, usually running the psql program. This makes them applicable to most platforms. It's straightforward to do many of these operations instead using a GUI tool for PostgreSQL, such as pgAdmin or OmniDB.

Download the example code files

You can download the example code files for this book from your account at www.packtpub.com. If you purchased this book elsewhere, you can visit www.packtpub.com/support and register to have the files emailed directly to you.

You can download the code files by following these steps:

1. Log in or register at `www.packtpub.com`.
2. Select the **SUPPORT** tab.
3. Click on **Code Downloads & Errata**.
4. Enter the name of the book in the **Search** box and follow the onscreen instructions.

Once the file is downloaded, please make sure that you unzip or extract the folder using the latest version of:

- WinRAR/7-Zip for Windows
- Zipeg/iZip/UnRarX for Mac
- 7-Zip/PeaZip for Linux

The code bundle for the book is also hosted on GitHub at `https://github.com/PacktPublishing/PostgreSQL-10-Administration-Cookbook`. In case there's an update to the code, it will be updated on the existing GitHub repository.

We also have other code bundles from our rich catalog of books and videos available at `https://github.com/PacktPublishing/`. Check them out!

Download the color images

We also provide a PDF file that has color images of the screenshots/diagrams used in this book. You can download it here: `http://www.packtpub.com/sites/default/files/downloads/PostgreSQL10Administratio nCookbook_ColorImages.pdf`.

Conventions used

There are a number of text conventions used throughout this book.

`CodeInText`: Indicates code words in text, database table names, folder names, filenames, file extensions, pathnames, dummy URLs, user input, and Twitter handles. Here is an example: "Mount the downloaded `WebStorm-10*.dmg` disk image file as another disk in your system."

A block of code is set as follows:

```
CREATE USER repuser
        SUPERUSER
        LOGIN
        CONNECTION LIMIT 1
        ENCRYPTED PASSWORD 'changeme';
```

When we wish to draw your attention to a particular part of a code block, the relevant lines or items are set in bold:

```
SELECT *FROM mytable
  WHERE   (col1, col2, ... ,colN) IN
  (SELECT col1, col2, ... ,colN
   FROM mytable
   GROUP BY col1, col2, ... ,colN
   HAVING count(*) > 1);
```

Any command-line input or output is written as follows:

```
$ postgres --single -D /full/path/to/datadir postgres
```

Bold: Indicates a new term, an important word, or words that you see onscreen. For example, words in menus or dialog boxes appear in the text like this. Here is an example: "Select **System info** from the **Administration** panel."

Warnings or important notes appear like this.

Tips and tricks appear like this.

Sections

In this book, you will find several headings that appear frequently (*Getting ready, How to do it..., How it works..., There's more...,* and *See also*).

To give clear instructions on how to complete a recipe, use these sections as follows:

Getting ready

This section tells you what to expect in the recipe and describes how to set up any software or any preliminary settings required for the recipe.

How to do it...

This section contains the steps required to follow the recipe.

How it works...

This section usually consists of a detailed explanation of what happened in the previous section.

There's more...

This section consists of additional information about the recipe in order to make you more knowledgeable about the recipe.

See also

This section provides helpful links to other useful information for the recipe.

Get in touch

Feedback from our readers is always welcome.

General feedback: Email `feedback@packtpub.com` and mention the book title in the subject of your message. If you have questions about any aspect of this book, please email us at `questions@packtpub.com`.

Errata: Although we have taken every care to ensure the accuracy of our content, mistakes do happen. If you have found a mistake in this book, we would be grateful if you would report this to us. Please visit `www.packtpub.com/submit-errata`, selecting your book, clicking on the Errata Submission Form link, and entering the details.

Piracy: If you come across any illegal copies of our works in any form on the internet, we would be grateful if you would provide us with the location address or website name. Please contact us at `copyright@packtpub.com` with a link to the material.

If you are interested in becoming an author: If there is a topic that you have expertise in and you are interested in either writing or contributing to a book, please visit `authors.packtpub.com`.

Reviews

Please leave a review. Once you have read and used this book, why not leave a review on the site that you purchased it from? Potential readers can then see and use your unbiased opinion to make purchase decisions, we at Packt can understand what you think about our products, and our authors can see your feedback on their book. Thank you!

For more information about Packt, please visit `packtpub.com`.

1
First Steps

In this chapter, we will cover the following recipes:

- Getting PostgreSQL
- Connecting to the PostgreSQL server
- Enabling access for network/remote users
- Using graphical administration tools
- Using the psql query and scripting tool
- Changing your password securely
- Avoiding hardcoding your password
- Using a connection service file
- Troubleshooting a failed connection

Introduction

PostgreSQL is a feature-rich, general-purpose, database management system. It's a complex piece of software, but every journey begins with the first step.

We'll start with your first connection. Many people fall at the first hurdle, so we'll try not to skip that too swiftly. We'll quickly move on to enabling remote users, and from there we will move on to access through GUI administration tools.

We will also introduce the `psql` query tool, which is the tool used to load our sample database, as well as many other examples in the book.

For additional help, we've included a few useful recipes that you may need for reference.

Introducing PostgreSQL 10

PostgreSQL is an advanced SQL database server, available on a wide range of platforms. One of the clearest benefits of PostgreSQL is that it is open source, meaning that you have a very permissive license to install, use, and distribute PostgreSQL, without paying anyone any fees or royalties. On top of that, PostgreSQL is well-known as a database that stays up for long periods and requires little or no maintenance, in most cases. Overall, PostgreSQL provides a very low total cost of ownership.

PostgreSQL is also noted for its huge range of advanced features, developed over the course of more than 30 years of continuous development and enhancement. Originally developed by the Database Research Group at the University of California, Berkeley, PostgreSQL is now developed and maintained by a huge army of developers and contributors. Many of these contributors have full-time jobs related to PostgreSQL, working as designers, developers, database administrators, and trainers. Some, but not many, of these contributors work for companies that specialize in support for PostgreSQL, like we (the authors) do. No single company owns PostgreSQL, nor are you required (or even encouraged) to register your usage.

PostgreSQL has the following main features:

- Excellent SQL standards compliance, up to SQL: 2016
- Client-server architecture
- Highly concurrent design, where readers and writers don't block each other
- Highly configurable and extensible for many types of applications
- Excellent scalability and performance, with extensive tuning features
- Support for many kinds of data models, such as relational, post-relational (arrays, nested relations via record types), document (JSON and XML), and key/value

What makes PostgreSQL different?

The PostgreSQL project focuses on the following objectives:

- Robust, high-quality software with maintainable, well-commented code
- Low maintenance administration for both embedded and enterprise use
- Standards-compliant SQL, interoperability, and compatibility
- Performance, security, and high availability

What surprises many people is that PostgreSQL's feature set is more comparable with Oracle or SQL Server than it is with MySQL. The only connection between MySQL and PostgreSQL is that these two projects are open source; apart from that, the features and philosophies are almost totally different.

One of the key features of Oracle, since Oracle 7, has been snapshot isolation, where readers don't block writers and writers don't block readers. You may be surprised to learn that PostgreSQL was the first database to be designed with this feature, and it offers a complete implementation. In PostgreSQL, this feature is called **Multiversion Concurrency Control** (**MVCC**), and we will discuss this in more detail later in the book.

PostgreSQL is a general-purpose database management system. You define the database that you would like to manage with it. PostgreSQL offers you many ways to work. You can either use a normalized database model, augmented with features such as arrays and record subtypes, or use a fully dynamic schema with the help of JSONB and an extension named `hstore`. PostgreSQL also allows you to create your own server-side functions in any of a dozen different languages.

PostgreSQL is highly extensible, so you can add your own data types, operators, index types, and functional languages. You can even override different parts of the system, using plugins to alter the execution of commands, or add a new optimizer.

All of these features offer a huge range of implementation options to software architects. There are many ways out of trouble when building applications and maintaining them over long periods of time. Regrettably, we simply don't have space in this book for all the cool features for developers; this book is about administration, maintenance, and backup.

In the early days, when PostgreSQL was still a research database, the focus was solely on the cool new features. Over the last 20 years, enormous amounts of code have been rewritten and improved, giving us one of the largest and most stable software servers available for operational use.

You may have read that PostgreSQL was, or is, slower than *My Favorite DBMS*, whichever that is. It's been a personal mission of mine over the last ten years to improve server performance, and the team has been successful in making the server highly performant and very scalable. That gives PostgreSQL enormous headroom for growth.

Who is using PostgreSQL? Prominent users include Apple, BASF, Genentech, Heroku, IMDB, Skype, McAfee, NTT, the UK Met Office, and the U. S. National Weather Service. Early in 2010, PostgreSQL received well in excess of one million downloads per year, according to data submitted to the European Commission, which concluded, *PostgreSQL is considered by many database users to be a credible alternative.*

We need to mention one last thing. When PostgreSQL was first developed, it was named Postgres, and therefore many aspects of the project still refer to the word *Postgres*; for example, the default database is named `postgres`, and the software is frequently installed using the postgres user ID. As a result, people shorten the name PostgreSQL to simply Postgres, and in many cases use the two names interchangeably.

PostgreSQL is pronounced as *post-grez-q-l*. Postgres is pronounced as *post-grez*.

Some people get confused and refer to it as *Postgre*, which is hard to say and likely to confuse people. Two names are enough, so don't use a third name!

The following sections explain the key areas in more detail.

Robustness

PostgreSQL is robust, high-quality software, supported by automated testing for both features and concurrency. By default, the database provides strong disk-write guarantees, and the developers take the risk of data loss very seriously in everything they do. Options to trade robustness for performance exist, though they are not enabled by default.

All actions on the database are performed within transactions, protected by a transaction log that will perform automatic crash recovery in case of software failure.

Databases may optionally be created with data block checksums to help diagnose hardware faults. Multiple backup mechanisms exist, with full and detailed **Point-in-time recovery (PITR)**, in case of the need for detailed recovery. A variety of diagnostic tools are available as well.

Database replication is supported natively. Synchronous Replication can provide greater than *5 nines* (99.999 percent) availability and data protection, if properly configured and managed or even higher with appropriate redundancy.

Security

Access to PostgreSQL is controllable via host-based access rules. Authentication is flexible and pluggable, allowing for easy integration with any external security architecture. The latest Salted Challenge Response Authentication Mechanism (SCRAM) provides full 256-bit protection.

Full SSL-encrypted access is supported natively for both user access and replication. A full featured cryptographic function library is available for database users.

PostgreSQL provides role-based access privileges to access data, by command type.

PostgreSQL also provides Row Level Security for privacy, medical and military grade security.

Functions may execute with the permissions of the definer, while views may be defined with security barriers to ensure that security is enforced ahead of other processing.

All aspects of PostgreSQL are assessed by an active security team, while known exploits are categorized and reported at http://www.postgresql.org/support/security/.

Ease of use

Clear, full, and accurate documentation exists as a result of a development process where documentation changes are required. Hundreds of small changes occur with each release that smooth off any rough edges of usage, supplied directly by knowledgeable users.

PostgreSQL works on small and large systems in the same way, and across operating systems.

Client access and drivers exist for every language and environment, so there is no restriction on what type of development environment is chosen now, or in the future.

The SQL standard is followed very closely; there is no weird behavior, such as silent truncation of data.

Text data is supported via a single data type that allows storage of anything from 1 byte to 1 gigabyte. This storage is optimized in multiple ways, so 1 byte is stored efficiently, and much larger values are automatically managed and compressed.

PostgreSQL has the clear policy of minimizing the number of configuration parameters, and with each release, we work out ways to auto-tune the settings.

Extensibility

PostgreSQL is designed to be highly extensible. Database extensions can be easily loaded by using CREATE EXTENSION, which automates version checks, dependencies, and other aspects of configuration.

PostgreSQL supports user-defined data types, operators, indexes, functions, and languages.

Many extensions are available for PostgreSQL, including the PostGIS extension, which provides world-class **Geographical Information System (GIS)** features.

Performance and concurrency

PostgreSQL 10 can achieve more than one million reads per second on a four socket server, and it benchmarks at more than 30,000 write transactions per second with full durability. With advanced hardware even higher levels of performance are possible.

PostgreSQL has an advanced optimizer that considers a variety of join types, utilizing user data statistics to guide its choices. PostgreSQL provides the widest range of index types of any commonly available database server, fully supporting all data types.

PostgreSQL provides MVCC, which enables readers and writers to avoid blocking each other.

Taken together, the performance features of PostgreSQL allow a mixed workload of transactional systems and complex search and analytical tasks. This is important because it means we don't always need to unload our data from production systems and reload it into analytical data stores just to execute a few ad hoc queries. PostgreSQL's capabilities make it the database of choice for new systems, as well as the right long-term choice in almost every case.

Scalability

PostgreSQL 10 scales well on a single node up to four CPU sockets. PostgreSQL scales well up to hundreds of active sessions, and up to thousands of connected sessions when using a session pool. Further scalability is achieved in each annual release.

PostgreSQL provides multi-node read scalability using the **Hot Standby** feature. Multi-node write scalability is under active development. The starting point for this is *Bi-Directional Replication* (discussed in `Chapter 12`, *Replication and Upgrades*).

SQL and NoSQL

PostgreSQL follows the SQL standard very closely. SQL itself does not force any particular type of model to be used, so PostgreSQL can easily be used for many types of models at the same time, in the same database.

With PostgreSQL acting as a relational database, we can utilize any level of denormalization, from the full third normal form (3NF), to the more normalized Star Schema models. PostgreSQL extends the relational model to provide arrays, row types, and range types.

A document-centric database is also possible using PostgreSQL's text, XML, and binary JSON (JSONB) data types, supported by indexes optimized for documents and by full text search capabilities.

Key/value stores are supported using the `hstore` extension.

Popularity

When MySQL was taken over by a commercial database vendor some years back, it was agreed in the EU monopoly investigation that followed that PostgreSQL was a viable competitor. That's certainly been true, with the PostgreSQL user base expanding consistently for more than a decade.

Various polls have indicated that PostgreSQL is the favorite database for building new, enterprise-class applications. The PostgreSQL feature set attracts serious users who have serious applications. Financial services companies may be PostgreSQL's largest user group, though governments, telecommunication companies, and many other segments are strong users as well. This popularity extends across the world; Japan, Ecuador, Argentina, and Russia have very large user groups, and so do USA, Europe, and Australasia.

Amazon Web Services' chief technology officer Dr. Werner Vogels described PostgreSQL as *"An amazing database,"* going on to say that *"PostgreSQL has become the preferred open source relational database for many enterprise developers and start-ups, powering leading geospatial and mobile applications. AWS have more recently revealed that PostgreSQL is their fastest growing service."*

Commercial support

Many people have commented that strong commercial support is what enterprises need before they can invest in open source technology. Strong support is available worldwide from a number of companies.

The authors work for 2ndQuadrant, which provides commercial support for open source PostgreSQL, offering 24/7 support in English and Spanish with bug-fix resolution times.

Many other companies provide strong and knowledgeable support to specific geographic regions, vertical markets, and specialized technology stacks.

PostgreSQL is also available as a hosted or cloud solution from a variety of companies, since it runs very well in cloud environments.

A full list of companies is kept up to date at
http://www.postgresql.org/support/professional_support/.

Research and development funding

PostgreSQL was originally developed as a research project at the University of California, Berkeley, in the late 1980s and early 1990s. Further work was carried out by volunteers until the late 1990s. Then, the first professional developer became involved. Over time, more and more companies and research groups became involved, supporting many professional contributors. Further funding for research and development was provided by the NSF. The project also received funding from the EU FP7 Programme in the form of the 4CaaST project for cloud computing and the AXLE project for scalable data analytics. AXLE deserves a special mention because it was a three year project aimed at enhancing PostgreSQL's business intelligence capabilities, specifically for very large databases. The project covered security, privacy, integration with data mining, and visualization tools and interfaces for new hardware.

Further details are available at http://www.axleproject.eu.

Other funding for PostgreSQL development comes from users who directly sponsor features and companies selling products and services based around PostgreSQL.

Getting PostgreSQL

PostgreSQL is 100 % open source software.

PostgreSQL is freely available to use, alter, or redistribute in any way you choose. Its license is an approved open source license, very similar to the **Berkeley Software Distribution (BSD)** license, though only just different enough that it is now known as **The PostgreSQL License (TPL)**.

How to do it...

PostgreSQL is already being used by many different application packages, so you may find it already installed on your servers. Many Linux distributions include PostgreSQL as part of the basic installation, or include it with the installation disk.

One thing to be wary of is that the included version of PostgreSQL may not be the latest release. It would typically be the latest major release that was available when that operating system release was published. There is usually no good reason to stick to that level—there is no increased stability implied there—and later production versions are just as well supported by the various Linux distributions as the earlier versions.

If you don't have a copy yet, or you don't have the latest version, you can download the source code or binary packages for a wide variety of operating systems from `http://www.postgresql.org/download/`.

Installation details vary significantly from platform to platform, and there aren't any special tricks or recipes to mention. Just follow the installation guide, and away you go! We've consciously avoided describing the installation processes here to make sure we don't garble or override the information published to assist you.

If you would like to receive email updates of the latest news, then you can subscribe to the PostgreSQL announce mailing list, which contains updates from all the vendors that support PostgreSQL. You'll get a few emails each month about new releases of core PostgreSQL, related software, conferences, and user group information. It's worth keeping in touch with these developments.

> For more information about the PostgreSQL announce mailing list, visit `http://archives.postgresql.org/pgsql-announce/`.

How it works...

Many people ask questions such as *How can this be free?*, *Are you sure I don't have to pay someone?*, or *Who gives this stuff away for nothing?*

Open source applications such as PostgreSQL work on a community basis, where many contributors perform tasks that make the whole process work. For many of these people, their involvement is professional, rather a hobby, and they can do this because there is generally great value for both the contributors and their employers alike.

You might not believe it. You don't have to, because it *just works!*

There's more...

Remember that PostgreSQL is more than just the core software. There is a huge range of websites offering add-ons, extensions, and tools for PostgreSQL. You'll also find an army of bloggers describing useful tricks and discoveries that will help you in your work.

Besides these, a range of professional companies can offer you help when you need it.

Connecting to the PostgreSQL server

How do we access PostgreSQL?

Connecting to the database is the first experience of PostgreSQL for most people, so we want to make it a good one. Let's do it now, and fix any problems we have along the way. Remember that a connection needs to be made securely, so there may be some hoops for us to jump through to ensure that the data we wish to access is secure.

Before we can execute commands against the database, we need to connect to the database server, giving us a session.

Sessions are designed to be long-lived, so you connect once, perform many requests, and eventually disconnect. There is a small overhead during connection. It may become noticeable if you connect and disconnect repeatedly, so you may wish to investigate the use of connection pools. Connection pools allow pre-connected sessions to be quickly served to you when you wish to reconnect.

Getting ready

First, catch your database. If you don't know where it is, you'll probably have difficulty accessing it. There may be more than one database, and you'll need to know the right one to access, and also have the authority to connect to it.

How to do it...

You need to specify the following parameters to connect to PostgreSQL:

- Host or host address
- Port
- Database name
- User
- Password (or other means of authentication, if any)

To connect, there must be a PostgreSQL server running on host, listening to port number port. On that server, a database named dbname and a user named user must also exist. The host must explicitly allow connections from your client (this is explained in the next recipe), and you must also pass authentication using the method the server specifies; for example, specifying a password won't work if the server has requested a different form of authentication.

Almost all PostgreSQL interfaces use the libpq interface library. When using libpq, most of the connection parameter handling is identical, so we can discuss that just once.

If you don't specify the preceding parameters, PostgreSQL looks for values set through environment variables, which are as follows:

- PGHOST or PGHOSTADDR
- PGPORT (set this to 5432 if it is not set already)
- PGDATABASE
- PGUSER
- PGPASSWORD (this is definitely not recommended)

If you somehow specify the first four parameters, but not the password, then PostgreSQL looks for a password file, discussed in the *Avoiding hardcoding your password* recipe.

Some PostgreSQL interfaces use the client-server protocol directly, so the ways the defaults are handled may differ. The information we need to supply won't vary significantly, so check the exact syntax for that interface.

Connection details can also be specified using a **Uniform Resource Identifier (URI)** format, as follows:

```
psql postgresql://myuser:mypasswd@myhost:5432/mydb
```

This specifies that we will connect the psql client application to the PostgreSQL server at myhost host, 5432 port, mydb database name, myuser user, and mypasswd password.

How it works...

PostgreSQL is a client-server database. The system it runs on is known as the host. We can access the PostgreSQL server remotely, through the network. However, we must specify host, which is a hostname, or hostaddr, which is an IP address. We can specify a host as localhost if we wish to make a TCP/IP connection to the same system. It is often better to use a Unix socket connection, which is attempted if the host begins with a slash (/) and the name is presumed to be a directory name (the default is /tmp).

On any system, there can be more than one database server. Each database server listens to exactly one well-known network port, which cannot be shared between servers on the same system. The default port number for PostgreSQL is 5432, which has been registered with the **Internet Assigned Numbers Authority (IANA)** and is uniquely assigned to PostgreSQL (you can see it used in the /etc/services file on most *nix servers). The port number can be used to uniquely identify a specific database server, if many exist.
The IANA (http://www.iana.org) is the organization that coordinates the allocation of available numbers for various internet protocols.

A database server is also sometimes known as a database cluster, because the PostgreSQL server allows you to define one or more databases on each server. Each connection request must identify exactly one database, identified by its dbname. When you connect, you will only be able to see only the database objects created within that database.

A database user is used to identify the connection. By default, there is no limit on the number of connections for a particular user; in a later recipe, we will cover how to restrict that. In the more recent versions of PostgreSQL, users are referred to as login roles, though many clues remind us of the earlier nomenclature, and that still makes sense in many ways. A login role is a role that has been assigned the CONNECT privilege.

Each connection will typically be authenticated in some way. This is defined at the server level: client authentication will not be optional at connection time, if the administrator has configured the server to require it.

Once you've connected, each connection can have one active transaction at a time and one fully active statement at any time.

The server will have a defined limit on the number of connections it can serve, so a connection request can be refused if the server is oversubscribed.

There's more...

If you are already connected to a database server with `psql` and you want to confirm that you've connected to the right place and in the right way, you can execute some, or all, of the following commands. Here is the command that shows the `current_database`:

```
SELECT current_database();
```

The following command shows the `current_user` ID:

```
SELECT current_user;
```

The next command shows the IP address and port of the current connection, unless you are using Unix sockets, in which case both values are `NULL`:

```
SELECT inet_server_addr(), inet_server_port();
```

A user's password is not accessible using general SQL, for obvious reasons.

You may also need the following:

```
SELECT version();
```

From PostgreSQL version `9.1` onwards, you can also use psql's new meta-command, `\conninfo`. It displays most of the preceding information in a single line:

```
postgres=# \conninfo
You are connected to database postgres, as user postgres, via socket in
/var/run/postgresql, at port 5432.
```

See also

There are many other snippets of information required to understand connections. Some of them are mentioned in this chapter, and others are discussed in `Chapter 6`, *Security*. For further details, refer to the PostgreSQL server documentation.

Enabling access for network/remote users

PostgreSQL comes in a variety of distributions. In many of these, you will note that remote access is initially disabled as a security measure.

How to do it...

By default, PostgreSQL gives access to clients who connect using Unix sockets, provided that the database user is the same as the system's username. Here, we'll show you how to enable other connections.

 In this recipe, we mention configuration files, which can be located as shown in the *Finding the current configuration settings* recipe in `Chapter 3`, *Configuration*.

The steps are as follows:

1. Add or edit this line in your `postgresql.conf` file:

    ```
    listen_addresses = '*'
    ```

2. Add the following line as the first line of `pg_hba.conf` to allow access to all databases for all users with an encrypted password:

# TYPE	DATABASE	USER	CIDR-ADDRESS	METHOD
host	all	all	0.0.0.0/0	md5

3. After changing `listen_addresses`, we restart the PostgreSQL server, as explained in the *Updating the parameter file* recipe in `Chapter 3`, *Configuration*.

 This recipe assumes that `postgresql.conf` does not include any other configuration file, which is the case in a default installation. If changing `listen_addresses` in `postgresql.conf` does not seem to work, perhaps that setting is overridden by another configuration file. Check out the *Updating the parameter file* recipe in `Chapter 3`, *Configuration*, for more details.

How it works...

The `listen_addresses` parameter specifies which IP addresses to listen to. This allows you to flexibly enable and disable listening on interfaces of multiple network cards (NICs) or virtual networks on the same system. In most cases, we want to accept connections on all NICs, so we use *, meaning *all IP addresses*.

The `pg_hba.conf` file contains a set of host-based authentication rules. Each rule is considered in sequence, until one rule fires or the attempt is specifically rejected with a `reject` method.

The preceding rule means that a remote connection that specifies any user or database on any IP address will be asked to authenticate using an MD5-encrypted password. Precisely, the following:

- **Type**: For this, `host` means a remote connection.
- **Database**: For this, `all` means *for all databases*. Other names match exactly, except when prefixed with a plus (+) symbol, in which case we mean a group role rather than a single user. You can also specify a comma-separated list of users, or use the @ symbol to include a file with a list of users. You can even specify `sameuser`, so that the rule matches when you specify the same name for the user and database.
- **User**: For this, `all` means *for all users*. Other names match exactly, except when prefixed with a plus (+) symbol, in which case we mean a group role rather than a single user. You can also specify a comma-separated list of users, or use the @ symbol to include a file with a list of users.
- **CIDR-ADDRESS**: This consists of two parts: IP address and subnet mask. The subnet mask is specified as the number of leading bits of the IP address that make up the mask. Thus, `/0` means 0 bits of the IP address, so that all IP addresses will be matched. For example, `192.168.0.0/24` would mean match the first 24 bits, so any IP address of the form 192.168.0.x would match. You can also use `samenet` or `samehost`.
- **Method**: For this, `md5` means that PostgreSQL will ask the client to provide a password encrypted with MD5. Another common setting is `trust`, which effectively means no authentication. Other authentication methods include GSSAPI, SSPI, LDAP, RADIUS, and PAM. PostgreSQL connections can also be made using SSL, in which case client SSL certificates provide authentication. See the *Using SSL certificates to authenticate the client* recipe in `Chapter 6`, *Security*, for more details about this.

Don't use the `password` setting, as this sends the password in plain text. This is not a real security issue if your connection is encrypted with SSL, and there are normally no downsides with MD5 anyway, and you have extra security for non-SSL connections.

There's more...

In earlier versions of PostgreSQL, access through the network was enabled by adding the – i command line switch when you started the server. This is still a valid option, but now it means the following:

```
listen_addresses = '*'
```

So, if you're reading some notes about how to set things up and this is mentioned, be warned that those notes are probably long out of date. They are not necessarily wrong, but it's worth looking further to see whether anything else has changed.

See also

Look at installer and/or operating system-specific documentation to find the standard location of the files.

Using graphical administration tools

Graphical administration tools are often requested by system administrators. PostgreSQL has a range of tool options. In this book, we'll cover pgAdmin4, and also OmniDB, which offers access to PostgreSQL and other databases.

Both of these tools are client applications that send and receive SQL to PostgreSQL, displaying the results for you. The admin client can access many databases servers, allowing you to manage a fleet of servers. Both tools work in standalone app mode and within web browsers.

How to do it...

pgAdmin 4 is usually named just pgAdmin. The "4" at the end has a long history, but isn't that important. It is not the release level; the release level at the time of writing this book is 3.0. **pgAdmin 4** replaces the earlier pgAdmin 3.

When you start pgAdmin, you will be prompted to register a new server.

Give your server a name on the **General** tab, then click **Connection** and fill in the five basic connection parameters, as well as the other information. You should uncheck the **Save password?** box:

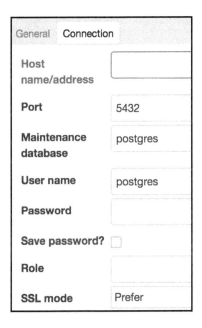

If you have many database servers, you can group them together. I suggest keeping any replicated servers together in the same Server Group. Give each server a sensible name.

Once you've added a server, you can connect to it and display information about it.

The default screen is the **Dashboard,** which presents a few interesting graphs based on the data it polls from the server. That's not very useful, so click on the **Statistics** tab.

You will then get access to the main browser screen, with the object tree view on the left and statistics on the right, as shown in the following screenshot:

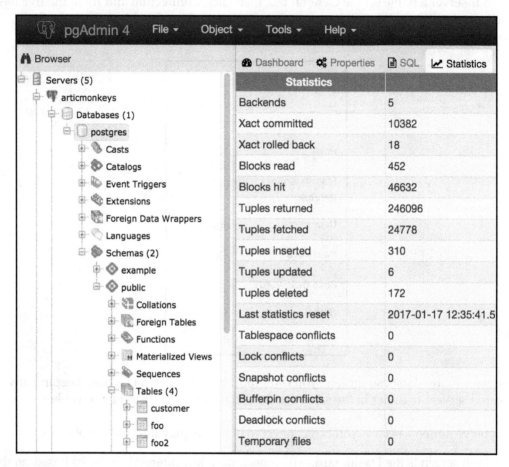

pgAdmin easily displays much of the data that is available from PostgreSQL. The information is context-sensitive, allowing you to navigate and see everything quickly and easily. The information is not dynamically updated; this will occur only when you click to refresh, so keep it in mind when using the application.

pgAdmin also provides **Grant Wizard**. This is useful for DBAs for review and immediate maintenance:

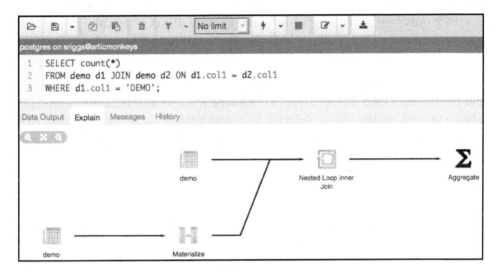

The pgAdmin query tool allows you to have multiple active sessions. The query tool has a good-looking Visual Explain feature, which displays the EXPLAIN plan for your query.

How it works...

pgAdmin provides a wide range of features, many of which are provided by other tools as well. This gives us the opportunity to choose which of those tools we want. For many reasons, it is best to use the right tool for the right job, and that is always a matter of expertise, experience, and personal taste.

pgAdmin submits SQL to the PostgreSQL server, and displays the results quickly and easily. As a browser, it is fantastic. For performing small DBA tasks, it is ideal. As you might've guessed from these comments, I don't recommend pgAdmin for every task.

Scripting is an important technique for DBAs. You keep a copy of the task executed, and you can edit and resubmit if problems occur. It's also easy to put all the tasks in a script into a single transaction, which isn't possible using the current GUI tools. pgAdmin provides pgScript, which only works with pgAdmin, so it is more difficult to port. For scripting, I strongly recommend the psql utility, which has many additional features that you'll increasingly appreciate over time.

Although I recommend psql as a scripting tool, many people find it convenient as a query tool. Some people may find this strange, and assume it is a choice for experts only. Two great features of psql are the online help for SQL and the tab completion feature, which allows you to build up SQL quickly without having to remember the syntax. See the *Using the psql query and scripting tool* recipe for more information.

pgAdmin also provides pgAgent, a task scheduler. Again, more portable schedulers are available, and you may wish to use those instead. Schedulers aren't covered in this book.

A quick warning! When you create an object in pgAdmin, the object will be created with a mixed case name if you use capitals anywhere in the object name. If I ask for a table named **MyTable**, then the only way to access that table is by referring to it in double quotes as "**MyTable**". See the *Handling objects with quoted names* recipe in Chapter 5, *Tables and Data*.

OmniDB

OmniDB is designed to access PostgreSQL, MySQL and Oracle in one interface, though makes sure it provides full features for the PostgreSQL database.

OmniDB is developing quickly, with monthly feature releases so I recommend you check out the latest information at https://omnidb.org/.

OmniDB provides a very responsive interface and is designed with full security in mind. It has the standard tree-view browsing interface, with multi-tab access for each database server you access. It's easy to be connected to multiple PostgreSQL, MySQL and Oracle database servers all at the same time:

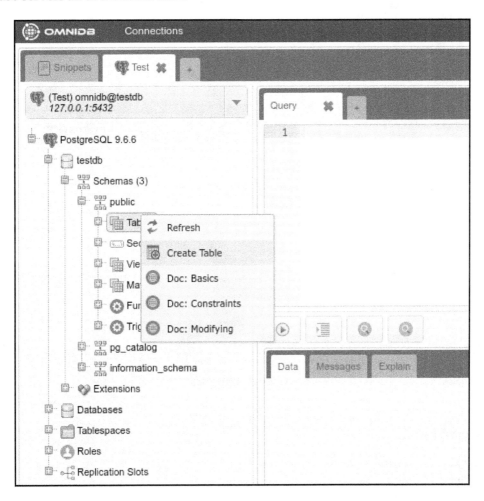

OmniDB has an SQL editor that has code completion and debugging. EXPLAIN ANALYZE output is colored to highlight the areas of the plan taking the most time:

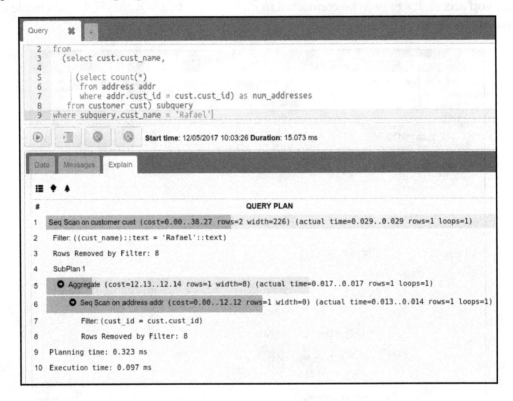

There are some very cool graphics features that are best seen using live data, so give it a try.

See also

You may also be interested in commercial tools of various kinds for PostgreSQL. A full listing is given in the PostgreSQL software catalog at http://www.postgresql.org/download/products/1.

Using the psql query and scripting tool

`psql` is the query tool supplied as a part of the core distribution of PostgreSQL, so it is available in all environments, and works similarly in them all. This makes it an ideal choice for developing portable applications and techniques.

`psql` provides features for use as both an interactive query tool and a a scripting tool.

Getting ready

From here on, we will assume that the `psql` command is enough to allow you access to the PostgreSQL server. This assumes that all your connection parameters are defaults, which may not be true.

Written in full, the connection parameters would be either of these options:

```
psql -h myhost -p 5432 -d mydb -U myuser
psql postgresql://myuser@myhost:5432/mydb
```

The default value for the port (`-p`) is `5432`. By default, `mydb` and `myuser` are both identical to the operating system's username. The default `myhost` on Windows is localhost, while on Unix, we use the default directory for Unix socket connections. The location of such directories varies across distributions and is set at compile time. However, note that you don't actually need to know its value, because on local connections both the server and the client are normally compiled together, so they use the same default.

How to do it...

The command that executes a single SQL command and prints the output is the easiest, as shown here:

```
$ psql -c "SELECT current_time"
     timetz
-----------------
 18:48:32.484+01
(1 row)
```

The `-c` command is non-interactive. If we want to execute multiple commands, we can write those commands in a text file and then execute them using the `-f` option. This command loads a very small and simple set of examples:

```
$ psql -f examples.sql
```

It produces the following output when successful:

```
SET
SET
SET
SET
SET
SET
DROP SCHEMA
CREATE SCHEMA
SET
SET
SET
CREATE TABLE
CREATE TABLE
COPY 5
COPY 3
```

The `examples.sql` script is very similar to a dump file produced by PostgreSQL backup tools, so this type of file and the output it produces are very common. When a command is executed successfully, PostgreSQL outputs a *command tag* equal to the name of that command; this is how the preceding output was produced.

The `psql` tool can also be used with both the `-c` and `-f` modes together; each one can be used multiple times. In this case, it will execute all the commands consecutively:

```
$ psql -c "SELECT current_time" -f examples.sql -c "SELECT current_time"
     timetz
-----------------
 18:52:15.287+01
(1 row)
   ...output removed for clarity...
     timetz
-----------------
 18:58:23.554+01
(1 row)
```

The `psql` tool can also be used in interactive mode, which is the default, so it requires no option:

```
$ psql
postgres=#
```

The first interactive command you'll need is the following:

```
postgres=# help
```

You can then enter SQL or other commands. The following is the last interactive command you'll need:

```
postgres=# \quit
```

Unfortunately, you cannot type `quit` on its own, nor can you type `\exit`, or other options. Sorry, just `\quit`, or `\q` for short!

How it works...

In psql, you can enter the following two types of commands:

- psql meta-commands
- SQL

A meta-command is a command for the psql client, whereas SQL is sent to the database server. An example of a meta-command is `\q`, which tells the client to disconnect. All lines that begin with \ (backslash) as the first nonblank character are presumed to be meta-commands of some kind.

If it isn't a meta-command, then it's SQL. We keep reading SQL until we find a semicolon, so we can spread SQL across many lines and format it any way we find convenient.

The `help` command is the only exception. We provide this for people who are completely lost, which is a good thought; so let's start from there ourselves.

There are two types of `help` commands, which are as follows:

- `\?`: This provides help on psql meta-commands
- `\h`: This provides help on specific SQL commands

Consider the following snippet as an example:

```
postgres=# \h DELETE
Command:     DELETE
Description: delete rows of a table
Syntax:
[ WITH [ RECURSIVE ] with_query [, ...] ]
DELETE FROM [ ONLY ] table [ [ AS ] alias ]
    [ USING usinglist ]
    [ WHERE condition | WHERE CURRENT OF cursor_name ]
    [ RETURNING * | output_expression [ AS output_name ] [,]]
```

I find this a great way to discover and remember options and syntax. You'll also like the ability to scroll back through the previous command history.

You'll get a lot of benefit from tab completion, which will fill in the next part of the syntax when you press the *Tab* key. This also works for object names, so you can type in just the first few letters and then press *Tab*; all the options will be displayed. Thus, you can type in just enough letters to make the object name unique, and then hit Tab to get the rest of the name.

One-line comments begin with two dashes, as follows:

```
-- This is a single-line comment
```

Multi-line comments are similar to those in C and Java:

```
/*
 * Multi-line comment
 */
```

You'll probably agree that psql looks a little daunting at first, with strange backslash commands. I do hope you'll take a few moments to understand the interface and keep digging for more information. The psql tool is one of the most surprising parts of PostgreSQL, and it is incredibly useful for database administration tasks when used alongside other tools.

There's more...

psql works across releases and works well with older versions. It may not work at all with newer server versions, so use the latest client whatever level of server you are accessing.

See also

Check out some other useful features of psql, which are as follows:

- Information functions
- Output formatting
- Execution timing using the \timing command
- Input/output and editing commands
- Automatic start up files, such as .psqlrc
- Substitutable parameters (variables)
- Access to the OS command line

Changing your password securely

If you are using password authentication, then you may wish to change your password from time to time.

How to do it...

The most basic method is to use the psql tool. The \password command will prompt you once for a new password and again to confirm. Connect to the psql tool and type the following:

```
\password
```

Enter a new password. This causes psql to send an SQL statement to the PostgreSQL server, which contains an already encrypted password string. An example of the SQL statement sent is as follows:

```
ALTER USER postgres PASSWORD 'md53175bce1d3201d16594cebf9d7eb3f9d';
```

Whatever you do, don't use postgres as your password. This will make you vulnerable to idle hackers, so make it a little more difficult than that!

Make sure you don't forget your password either. It may prove difficult to maintain your database if you can't get access to it later.

How it works...

As changing the password is just an SQL statement, any interface can do this. Other tools also allow this, such as the following:

- pgAdmin4
- phpPgAdmin

If you don't use one of the main routes to change the password, you can still do it yourself, using SQL from any interface. Note that you need to encrypt your password, because if you do submit a password in plain text, like the following, then it will be shipped to the server in plain text:

```
ALTER USER myuser PASSWORD 'secret'
```

Luckily, the password in this case will still be stored in an encrypted form. It will also be recorded in plain text in psql's history file, as well as in any server and application logs, depending on the actual log-level settings.

PostgreSQL doesn't enforce a password change cycle, so you may wish to use more advanced authentication mechanisms, such as GSSAPI, SSPI, LDAP, RADIUS, and so on.

Avoiding hardcoding your password

We all agree that hardcoding your password is a bad idea. This recipe shows you how to keep your password in a secure password file.

Getting ready

Not all database users need passwords; some databases use other means of authentication. Don't perform this step unless you know you will be using password authentication, and you know your password.

First, remove the hardcoded password from where you set it previously. Completely remove the `password = xxxx` text from the connection string in a program. Otherwise, when you test the password file, the hardcoded setting will override the details you are about to place in the file. Keeping the password hardcoded and in the password file is not any better. Using `PGPASSWORD` is not recommended either, so remove that also.

If you think someone may have seen the password, then change your password before placing it in the secure password file.

How to do it...

A password file contains the usual five fields that we require when connecting, as shown here:

```
host:port:dbname:user:password
```

Change this to the following:

```
myhost:5432:postgres:sriggs:moresecure
```

The password file is located using an environment variable named PGPASSFILE. If PGPASSFILE is not set, then a default filename and location must be searched for, as follows:

- On *nix systems, look for ~/.pgpass
- On Windows systems, look for %APPDATA%\postgresql\pgpass.conf, where %APPDATA% is the application data subdirectory in the path (for me, that would be C:\)

Don't forget to set the file permissions on the file, so that security is maintained. File permissions are not enforced on Windows, though the default location is secure. On *nix systems, you must issue the following: chmod 0600 ~/.pgpass.
If you forget to do this, the PostgreSQL client will ignore the .pgpass file. While the psql tool will issue a clear warning, many other clients will just fail silently, so don't forget!

How it works...

Many people name the password file .pgpass, whether or not they are on Windows, so don't get confused if they do this.

The password file can contain multiple lines. Each line is matched against the requested host:port:dbname:user combination until we find a line that matches. Then, we use that password.

Each item can be a literal value or *, a wildcard that matches anything. There is no support for partial matching. With appropriate permissions, a user can potentially connect to any database. Using the wildcard in the `dbname` and `port` fields makes sense, but it is less useful in other fields. Here are a few examples:

- `myhost:5432:*:sriggs:moresecurepw`
- `myhost:5432:perf:hannu:okpw`
- `myhost:*:perf:gianni:sicurissimo`

There's more...

This looks like a good improvement if you have a small number of database servers. If you have many different database servers, you may want to think about using a connection service file instead (see the next recipe), or perhaps even storing details on a **Lightweight Directory Access Protocol** (**LDAP**) server.

Using a connection service file

As the number of connection options grows, you may want to consider using a connection service file.

The connection service file allows you to give a single name to a set of connection parameters. This can be accessed centrally, to avoid the need for individual users to know the host and port of the database, and it is more resistant to future change.

You can set up a system-wide file as well as individual per-user files. The default file paths for these files are `/etc/pg_service.conf` and `~/.pg_service.conf` respectively.

A system-wide connection file controls service names for all users from a single place, while a per-user file applies only to that particular user. Keep in mind that the per-user file overrides the system-wide file—if a service is defined in both the files, then the definition in the per-user file will prevail.

How to do it...

First, create a file named `pg_service.conf` with the following content:

```
[dbservice1]
host=postgres1
port=5432
dbname=postgres
```

You can then copy it to either `/etc/pg_service.conf` or another agreed central location. You can then set the `PGSYSCONFDIR` environment variable to that directory location.

Alternatively, you can copy it to `~/.pg_service.conf`. If you want to use a different name, set `PGSERVICEFILE`. Either way, you can then specify a connection string like the following:

```
service=dbservice1 user=sriggs
```

The service can also be set using an environment variable named `PGSERVICE`.

How it works...

This feature applies to libpq connections only, so it does not apply to JDBC.

The connection service file can also be used to specify the user, though that would mean that the username would be shared.

The `pg_service.conf` and `.pgpass` files can work together, or you can use just one of the two as you choose. Note that the `pg_service.conf` file is shared, so it is not a suitable place for passwords. The per-user connection service file is not shared, but in any case, it seems best to keep things separate and confine passwords to `.pgpass`.

Troubleshooting a failed connection

This recipe is all about what you should do when things go wrong.

Bear in mind that 90 percent of problems are just misunderstandings, and you'll quickly be on track again.

How to do it...

Here we've made a checklist to be followed if a connection attempt fails:

- Check whether the database name and the username are accurate. You may be requesting a service on one system when the database you require is on another system. Recheck your credentials; ensure that you haven't mixed things up and that you are not using the database name as the username, or vice versa. If you receive too many connections, then you may need to disconnect another session before you can connect, or wait for the administrator to re-enable the connections.

- Check for explicit rejections. If you receive the **pg_hba.conf rejects connection for host...** error message, it means your connection attempt has been explicitly rejected by the database administrator for that server. You will not be able to connect from the current client system using those credentials. There is little point in attempting to contact the administrator, as you are violating an explicit security policy with what you are attempting to do.

- Check for implicit rejections. If the error message you receive is **no pg_hba.conf entry for...**, it means there is no explicit rule that matches your credentials. This is likely an oversight on the part of the administrator and is common in very complex networks. Contact the administrator and request a ruling on whether your connection should be allowed (hopefully) or explicitly rejected in the future.

- Check whether the connection works with psql. If you're trying to connect to PostgreSQL from anything other than the psql command-line utility, switch to that now. If you can make psql connect successfully but cannot make your main connection work correctly, then the problem may be in the local interface you are using.

- PostgreSQL 9.3 and later versions ship the `pg_isready` utility, which checks the status of a database server, either local or remote, by establishing a minimal connection. Only the hostname and port are mandatory, which is great if you don't know the database name, username, or password. The following outcomes are possible:
  - The server is running and accepting connections.
  - The server is running but not accepting connections (because it is starting up, shutting down, or in recovery).
  - A connection attempt was made, but it failed.
  - No connection attempt was made because of a client problem (invalid parameters, out of memory, and so on).

- Check whether the server is up. If a server is shut down, then you cannot connect. The typical problem here is simply mixing up the server to which you are connecting. You need to specify the hostname and port, so it's possible that you are mixing up those details.
- Check whether the server is up and accepting new connections. A server that is shutting down will not accept new connections, apart from superusers. Also, a standby server may not have the `hot_standby` parameter enabled, preventing you from connecting.
- Check whether the server is listening correctly, and check the port to which the server is actually listening. Confirm that the incoming request is arriving on the interface listed in the `listen_addresses` parameter. Check whether it is set to `*` for remote connections and `localhost` for local connections.
- Check whether the database name and username exist. It's possible that the database or user no longer exists.
- Check the connection request, that is, check whether the connection request was successful and was somehow dropped after the connection. You can confirm this by looking at the server log when the following parameters are enabled:

```
log_connections = on
log_disconnections = on
```

- Check for other reasons for disconnection. If you are connecting to a standby server, it is possible that you have been disconnected because of Hot Standby conflicts.
  See `Chapter 12`, *Replication and Upgrades*, for more information.

There's more...

Client authentication and security are the rapidly changing areas over subsequent major PostgreSQL releases. You will also find differences between maintenance release levels. The PostgreSQL documents on this topic can be viewed at
`http://www.postgresql.org/docs/current/interactive/client-authentication.html`.

Always check which release level you are using before consulting the manual or asking for support. Many problems are caused simply by confusing the capabilities between release levels.

Exploring the Database

2

In this chapter, we'll cover the following recipes:

- What version is the server?
- What is the server uptime?
- Locating the database server files
- Locating the database server's message log
- Locating the database's system identifier
- Listing databases on this database server
- How many tables are there in a database?
- How much disk space does a database use?
- How much disk space does a table use?
- Which are my biggest tables?
- How many rows in a table?
- Quickly estimating the number of rows in a table
- Listing extensions in this database
- Understanding object dependencies

Introduction

To understand PostgreSQL, you need to see it in use. An empty database is like a ghost town without houses.

For now, we will assume that you already have a database. There are over a thousand books on how to design your own database from nothing. So here we aim to help people who already have access to a PostgreSQL database, but are still learning to use the PostgreSQL database management system.

The best way to start is by asking some simple questions to orient yourself and begin the process of understanding. Incidentally, these are also questions you'll need to answer if you ask someone else for help.

What version is the server?

If you experience problems, then you'll need to double-check which version of the server you have. This will help you to report a fault or to consult the correct version of the manual.

How to do it...

We will find out the version by directly querying the database server:

1. Connect to the database and issue the following command:

```
postgres # SELECT version();
```

2. You'll get a response that looks something like this:

```
PostgreSQL 10.2 on x86_64-apple-darwin16.7.0,
 compiled by Apple LLVM version 9.0.0 (clang-900.0.39.2), 64-
bit
```

That's probably too much information all at once!

How it works...

The current PostgreSQL server version format is Major.Maintenance, from 10 onward. The first release was 10.0, and subsequent maintenance releases will be 10.1, 10.2, 10.3, and so on.

Prior to release 10, PostgreSQL used a three-part numbering series, meaning that the feature set and compatibility related to the **Major.Minor** release level. What this means is that version 9.4 contains more additional features and compatibility changes when compared to version 9.3. There is also a separate version of the manual, so if something doesn't work exactly the way you think it should, you must consult the correct version of the manual. Maintenance software releases were identified by the full three-part numbering scheme. Version 9.4.0 was the initial release of 9.4, and version 9.4.1 was a later maintenance release.

The release support policy for PostgreSQL is available at `http://www.postgresql.org/support/versioning/`. This article explains that each release will be supported for a period of five years. Since we release one major version per year, this means five major releases.

All releases, up to and including 9.2, were de-supported in September 2017. So, by the time you're reading this book, only the PostgreSQL 9.3 and higher versions will be supported. The earlier versions are still robust, though many performance and enterprise features are missing from those releases. The later de-support dates are as follows:

Version	Last supported date
PostgreSQL 9.3	September 2018
PostgreSQL 9.4	December 2019
PostgreSQL 9.5	January 2021
PostgreSQL 9.6	September 2021
PostgreSQL 10	September 2022

There's more...

Some other ways of checking the version number are as follows:

```
bash # psql --version
psql (PostgreSQL) 10.2
```

However, be wary that this shows the client software version number, which may differ from the server software version number. You should check the server version directly by using the following command:

```
bash # cat $PGDATA/PG_VERSION
```

Here, you must set PGDATA to the actual data directory. Refer to the *Locating the database server files* recipe for more information.

Notice that the preceding command does not show the maintenance release number.

Why is the database version important?
PostgreSQL has internal version numbers for the data file format, database catalog layout, and crash recovery format. Each of these is checked as the server runs to ensure that the data doesn't become corrupt. PostgreSQL doesn't change these internal formats for a single release; they only change across releases.
From a user's perspective, each release differs in terms of the way the server behaves. If you know your application well, then it should be possible to assess the differences simply by reading the release notes for each version. In many cases, a retest of the application is the safest thing to do.

What is the server uptime?

You may wonder, *How long has it been since the server started?*

As mentioned in the previous recipe, we will find this out by asking the database server.

How to do it...

Issue the following SQL from any interface:

```
postgres=# SELECT date_trunc('second',
current_timestamp - pg_postmaster_start_time()) as uptime;
```

You should get output as follows:

```
    uptime
------------------------------------
 2 days 02:48:04
```

How it works...

Postgres stores the server start time, so we can access it directly, as follows:

```
postgres=# SELECT pg_postmaster_start_time();
pg_postmaster_start_time
------------------------------------
2018-01-01 19:37:41.389134+00
```

Then, we can write a SQL query to get the uptime, like this:

```
postgres=# SELECT current_timestamp - pg_postmaster_start_time();
        ?column?
----------------------------------------------------------
 2 days 02:50:02.23939
```

Finally, we can apply some formatting:

```
postgres=# SELECT date_trunc('second',
  current_timestamp - pg_postmaster_start_time()) as uptime;
        uptime
---------------------------
 2 days 02:51:18
```

See also

This is simple stuff. Further monitoring and statistics are covered in Chapter 8, *Monitoring and Diagnosis*.

Locating the database server files

Database server files are initially stored in a location referred to as the **data directory**. Additional data files may also be stored in tablespaces, if any exist.

In this recipe, you will learn how to find the location of these directories on a given database server.

Getting ready

You'll need to get operating system access to the database system, which is what we call the platform on which the database runs.

How to do it...

On Debian or Ubuntu systems, the default data directory location is: /var/lib/postgresql/R.r/main.

Here, R.r represents the major and minor release numbers of the database server software, respectively; for example, 9.6. The configuration files are located in /etc/postgresql/R.r/main/.

Note that for release 10 onwards, it will just be 10, not 10.0.

In both cases, main is just the name of a database server. Other names are also possible. For the sake of simplicity, we assume that you only have a single installation, although the point of including the release number and database server name as components of the directory path is to allow multiple database servers to coexist on the same host.

The pg_lsclusters utility is specific to Debian/Ubuntu, and displays a list of all the available database servers, including information, such as the following, for each server:
1. Major release number.
2. Port.
3. Status (for example, online, down, and so on).
4. Data directory.
5. Log file.
The pg_lsclusters utility is part of the postgresql-common Debian/Ubuntu package, which provides a structure under which multiple versions of PostgreSQL can be installed, and multiple clusters can be maintained, at one time.

On Red Hat RHEL, CentOS, and Fedora, the default data directory location is /var/lib/pgsql/data/. This also contains the configuration files (*.conf) by default.

Again, that is just the default location. You can create additional data directories using the initdb utility.

On Windows, the default data directory location is: C:\Program Files\PostgreSQL\R.r\data.

The initdb utility populates the given data directory with the initial content. The directory will be created for convenience if it is missing, but for safety, the utility will stop if the data directory is not empty. The initdb utility will read the data directory name from the PGDATA environment variable, unless the -d command-line option is used.

How it works...

Even though the Debian/Ubuntu and Red Hat file layouts are different, they both follow the Linux **Filesystem Hierarchy Standard** (**FHS**), so neither layout is *wrong*.

The Red Hat layout is simpler and easier to understand. The Debian/Ubuntu layout is more complex, but it has different and more adventurous goals. The Debian/Ubuntu layout is similar to the **Optimal Flexible Architecture** (**OFA**) of other database systems. As pointed out earlier, the goals are to provide a file layout that will allow you to have multiple PostgreSQL database servers on one system, and to allow many versions of the software to exist in the filesystem at once.

Again, the layout for the Windows and OS X installers is different. Multiple database clusters are possible, but they are also more complex than on Debian/Ubuntu.

I recommend that you follow the Debian/Ubuntu layout on whichever platform you are using. It doesn't really have a name, so I call it the **PostgreSQL Flexible Architecture** (**PFA**). Clearly, if you are using Debian or Ubuntu, then the Debian/Ubuntu layout is already being used. If you do this on other platforms, you'll need to lay things out yourself, but it does pay off in the long run. To implement PFA, you can set the following environment variables to name parts of the file layout:

```
export PGROOT=/var/lib/pgsql/
export PGRELEASE=10
export PGSERVERNAME=mamba
export PGDATA=$PGROOT/$PGRELEASE/$PGSERVERNAME
```

In this example, PGDATA is /var/lib/pgsql/10/mamba.

Finally, you must run initdb to actually initialize the data directory, as noted earlier, and custom administration scripts should be prepared to automate actions such as starting or stopping the database server when the system undergoes similar procedures.

Note that server applications such as initdb can only work with one major PostgreSQL version. On distributions that allow several major versions, such as Debian or Ubuntu, these applications are placed in dedicated directories, which are not put in the default command path. This means that if you just type initdb, the system will not find the executable, and you will get an error message.

This may look like a bug, but in fact it is the desired behavior. Instead of directly accessing initdb, you are supposed to use the pg_createcluster utility from postgresql-common, which will select the right initdb depending on the major version you specify.

 If you plan to run more than one database server on the same host, you must set the preceding variables differently for each server, as they mandate the name of the data directory. For instance, you can set them in the script that you use to start or stop the database server, which would be enough because PGDATA is mostly used only by the database server process.

There's more...

Once you've located the data directory, you can look for the files that comprise the PostgreSQL database server. The layout is as follows:

Subdirectory	Purpose
base	This is the main table storage. Beneath this directory, each database has its own directory, within which are the files for each database table or index.
global	Here are the tables that are shared across all databases, including the list of databases.
pg_commit_ts	Here we store transaction commit timestamp data (from 9.5 onwards).
pg_dynshmem	This includes dynamic shared memory information (from 9.4 onwards).
pg_logical	This includes the logical decoding status data.
pg_multixact	This includes files used for shared row-level locks.
pg_notify	This includes the LISTEN/NOTIFY status files.
pg_replslot	This includes information about replication slots (from 9.4 onwards).
pg_serial	This includes information on committed serializable transactions.
pg_snapshots	This includes exported snapshot files.
pg_stat	This includes permanent statistics data.
pg_stat_tmp	This includes transient statistics data.
pg_subtrans	This includes subtransaction status data.
pg_tblspc	This includes symbolic links to tablespace directories.

pg_twophase	This includes state files for prepared transactions.
pg_wal	This includes the transaction log or **Write-Ahead Log (WAL)** (formerly pg_xlog).
pg_xact	This includes the transaction status files (formerly pg_clog).

None of the aforementioned directories contain user-modifiable files, nor should any of the files be manually deleted in order to save space, or for any other reason. *Don't touch it, because you'll break it, and you may not be able to fix it!* It's not even sensible to copy files in these directories without carefully following the procedures described in Chapter 11, *Backup and Recovery*. Keep off the grass!

We'll talk about tablespaces later in the book. We'll also discuss a performance enhancement that involves putting the transaction log on its own set of disk drives in Chapter 10, *Performance and Concurrency*.

The only things you are allowed to touch are configuration files, which are all *.conf files, and server message log files. Server message log files may or may not be in the data directory. For more details on this, refer to the next recipe *Locating the database server's message log*.

Locating the database server's message log

The database server's message log is a record of all messages recorded by the database server. This is the first place to look if you have server problems, and a good place to check regularly.

This log will include messages that look something like the following:

```
2016-09-01 19:37:41 GMT [2507-1] LOG:  database system was shut down at
2016-09-01 19:37:38 GMT

2016-09-01 19:37:41 GMT [2506-1] LOG:  database system is ready to accept
connections
```

We'll explain some more about these logs once we've located the files.

Getting ready

You'll need to get operating system access to the database system, which is what we call the platform on which the database runs.

How to do it...

The server log can be in a few different places, so let's list all of them first, so that we can locate the log or decide where we want it to be placed:

- The server log may be in a directory beneath the data directory.
- It may be in a directory elsewhere on the filesystem.
- It may be redirected to `syslog`.
- There may be no server log at all. Then it's time to add a log soon.

If not redirected to `syslog`, the server log consists of one or more files. You can change the names of these files, so it may not always be the same on every system.

On Debian or Ubuntu systems, the default server log location is `/var/log/postgresql`. The current server log file is named `postgresql-R.r-main.log`, where `R.r` represents the major and minor release numbers of the server, for example, 9.6. From release 10 onwards, there will be just one number. The older log files are numbered as `postgresql-10-main.log.1`. The higher the final number, the older the file, since they are being rotated by the `logrotate` utility.

On Red Hat, RHEL, CentOS, and Fedora, the default server log location is a subdirectory of the `data` directory, that is, `/var/lib/pgsql/data/pg_log`.

On Windows systems, the messages are sent to the Windows Event Log by default.

How it works...

The server log is just a file that records messages from the server. Each message has a severity level, the most typical of them being LOG, though there are others, as shown in the following table:

PostgreSQL severity	Meaning	Syslog severity	Windows Event Log
DEBUG 1 to DEBUG 5	This comprises the internal diagnostics	DEBUG	INFORMATION
INFO	This is the command output for the user	INFO	INFORMATION
NOTICE	This is helpful information	NOTICE	INFORMATION
WARNING	This warns of likely problems	NOTICE	WARNING
ERROR	This is the current command that is aborted	WARNING	ERROR
LOG	This is useful for sysadmins	INFO	INFORMATION
FATAL	This is the event that disconnects one session only	ERR	ERROR
PANIC	This is the event that crashes the server	CRIT	ERROR

Watch out for FATAL and PANIC. This shouldn't happen in most cases during normal server operation, apart from certain cases related to replication; so check out Chapter 12, *Replication and Upgrades*, also.

You can adjust the number of messages that appear in the log by changing the log_min_messages server parameter. You can also change the amount of information that is displayed for each event by changing the log_error_verbosity parameter. If the messages are sent to a standard log file, then each line in the log will have a prefix of useful information that can also be controlled by the system administrator, with a parameter named log_line_prefix.

You can also alter the *what* and the *how much* that goes into the logs by changing other settings such as log_statements, log_checkpoints, log_connections/log_disconnections, log_verbosity, log_lock_waits, and so on.

There's more...

The `log_destination` parameter controls where the log messages are stored. The valid values are `stderr`, `csvlog`, `syslog`, and `eventlog` (the latter only on Windows).

The logging collector is a background process that writes to a log file everything that the PostgreSQL server outputs to `stderr`. This is probably the most reliable way to log messages in case of problems, since it depends on fewer services.

Log rotation can be controlled with settings such as `log_rotation_age` and `log_rotation_size` if you are using the logging collector. Alternatively, it is possible to configure the `logrotate` utility to perform log rotation, which is the default on Debian and Ubuntu systems.

In general, monitoring activities are covered in `Chapter 8`, *Monitoring and Diagnosis*, and examining the message log is just one part of it. Refer to the *Producing a daily summary of log file errors* recipe in `Chapter 8`, *Monitoring and Diagnosis*, for more details.

Locating the database's system identifier

Each database server has a system identifier assigned when the database is initialized (created). The server identifier remains the same if the server is backed up, cloned, and so on.

Many actions on the server are keyed to the system identifier, and you may be asked to provide this information when you report a fault.

In this recipe, you will learn how to display the system identifier.

Getting ready

Connect as the postgres OS user, or another user with execute privileges on the server software.

How to do it...

We just need to launch the following command:

```
pg_controldata <data-directory> | grep "system identifier"
Database system identifier:          5558338346489861223
```

Note that the preceding syntax will not work on Debian or Ubuntu systems, for the same reasons explained for initdb in the *Locating the database server files* recipe. However, in this case, there is no postgresql-common alternative, so if you must run pg_controldata, you need to specify the full path to the executable, as in this example:

```
/usr/lib/postgresql/10/bin/pg_controldata $PGDATA
```

Don't use -D in front of the data directory name. This is the only PostgreSQL server application where you don't need to do that.

How it works...

The pg_controldata utility is a PostgreSQL server application that shows the content of a server's control file. The control file is located within the data directory of a server, and it is created at database initialization time. Some of the information within it is updated regularly, and some when certain major events occur.

The full output of pg_controldata looks like the following (the bold values are those that may change over time as the server runs):

```
pg_control version number: 1002
Catalog version number: 201707211
Database system identifier: 6320137769675861859
Database cluster state: in production
pg_control last modified: Sun 31 Dec 2017 16:17:41 PM GMT
Latest checkpoint location: 0/19000728
Prior checkpoint location: 0/19000648
Latest checkpoint's REDO location: 0/190006F0
Latest checkpoint's REDO WAL file: 000000010000000000000019
Latest checkpoint's TimeLineID: 1
Latest checkpoint's PrevTimeLineID: 1
Latest checkpoint's full_page_writes: on
Latest checkpoint's NextXID: 0/703
Latest checkpoint's NextOID: 24978
Latest checkpoint's NextMultiXactId: 1
Latest checkpoint's NextMultiOffset: 0
Latest checkpoint's oldestXID: 616
```

```
Latest checkpoint's oldestXID's DB: 1
Latest checkpoint's oldestActiveXID: 703
Latest checkpoint's oldestMultiXid: 1
Latest checkpoint's oldestMulti's DB: 1
Latest checkpoint's oldestCommitTsXid:0
Latest checkpoint's newestCommitTsXid:0
Time of latest checkpoint: Sun 31 Dec 2017 16:17:41 PM GMT
Fake LSN counter for unlogged rels: 0/1
Minimum recovery ending location: 0/0
Min recovery ending loc's timeline: 0
Backup start location: 0/0
Backup end location: 0/0
End-of-backup record required: no
wal_level setting: replica
wal_log_hints setting: off
max_connections setting: 100
max_worker_processes setting: 8
max_prepared_xacts setting: 0
max_locks_per_xact setting: 64
track_commit_timestamp setting: off
Maximum data alignment: 8
Database block size: 8192
Blocks per segment of large relation: 131072
WAL block size: 8192
Bytes per WAL segment: 16777216
Maximum length of identifiers: 64
Maximum columns in an index: 32
Maximum size of a TOAST chunk: 1996
Size of a large-object chunk: 2048
Date/time type storage: 64-bit integers
Float4 argument passing: by value
Float8 argument passing: by value
Data page checksum version: 0
Mock authentication nonce    a6b19bbbd477... (not shown in full
```

Never edit the PostgreSQL control file. If you do, the server probably won't start correctly, or you may mask other errors. And if you do that, people will be able to tell, so fess up as soon as possible!

Listing databases on this database server

When we connect to PostgreSQL, we always connect to just one specific database on any database server. If there are many databases on a single server, it can get confusing, so sometimes you may just want to find out which databases are parts of the database server.

This is also confusing because we can use the word database in two different, but related, contexts. Initially, we start off by thinking that PostgreSQL is a database in which we put data, referring to the whole *database server* by just the word *database*. In PostgreSQL, a database server (also known as, *cluster*) is potentially split into multiple, individual databases, so, as you get more used to working with PostgreSQL, you'll start to separate the two concepts.

How to do it...

If you have access to `psql`, you can type the following command:

```
bash $ psql -l
                           List of databases
    Name     | Owner  | Encoding |   Collate   |    Ctype    | Access
privileges
-----------+--------+----------+-------------+-------------+---------------
----
 postgres  | sriggs | UTF8     | en_GB.UTF-8 | en_GB.UTF-8 |
 template0 | sriggs | UTF8     | en_GB.UTF-8 | en_GB.UTF-8 | =c/sriggs
+
           |        |          |             |             |
sriggs=CTc/sriggs
 template1 | sriggs | UTF8     | en_GB.UTF-8 | en_GB.UTF-8 | =c/sriggs
+
           |        |          |             |             |
sriggs=CTc/sriggs
(3 rows)
```

You can also get the same information while running `psql` by simply typing `\l`.

The information that we just looked at is stored in a PostgreSQL catalog table named `pg_database`. We can issue a SQL query directly against that table from any connection to get a simpler result, as follows:

```
postgres=# select datname from pg_database;
datname
-----------
template1
template0
postgres
 (3 rows)
```

How it works...

PostgreSQL starts with three databases: `template0`, `template1`, and `postgres`. The main user database is `postgres`.

You can create your own databases as well, like this:

```
CREATE DATABASE my_database;
```

You can do the same from the command line, using the following expression:

```
bash $ createdb my_database
```

After you've created your databases, make sure to secure them properly, as discussed in Chapter 6, *Security*.

When you create another database, it actually takes a copy of an existing database. Once it is created, there is no further link between the two databases.

The `template0` and `template1` databases are known as template databases. The `template1` database can be changed to allow you to create a localized template for any new databases that you create. The `template0` database exists so that, when you alter `template1`, you still have a pristine copy on which to fall back on. In other words, if you break `template1`, then you can drop it and recreate it from `template0`.

You can drop the database named `postgres`. But don't, okay? Similarly, don't try to touch `template0`, because you won't be allowed to do anything with it, except use it as a template. On the other hand, the `template1` database exists to be modified, so feel free to change it.

There's more...

The information that we just saw is stored in a PostgreSQL catalog table named `pg_database`. We can look at this directly to get some more information. In some ways, the output is less useful as well, as we need to look up some of the code in other tables:

```
postgres=# \x
postgres=# select * from pg_database;
-[ RECORD 1 ]-+-------------------------------
datname       | template1
datdba        | 10
encoding      | 6
datcollate    | en_GB.UTF-8
datctype      | en_GB.UTF-8
datistemplate | t
datallowconn  | t
datconnlimit  | -1
datlastsysoid | 11620
datfrozenxid  | 644
dattablespace | 1663
datacl        | {=c/sriggs,sriggs=CTc/sriggs}
-[ RECORD 2 ]-+-------------------------------
datname       | template0
datdba        | 10
encoding      | 6
datcollate    | en_GB.UTF-8
datctype      | en_GB.UTF-8
datistemplate | t
datallowconn  | f
datconnlimit  | -1
datlastsysoid | 11620
datfrozenxid  | 644
dattablespace | 1663
datacl        | {=c/sriggs,sriggs=CTc/sriggs}
-[ RECORD 3 ]-+-------------------------------
datname       | postgres
datdba        | 10
encoding      | 6
datcollate    | en_GB.UTF-8
datctype      | en_GB.UTF-8
datistemplate | f
datallowconn  | t
datconnlimit  | -1
datlastsysoid | 11620
datfrozenxid  | 644
dattablespace | 1663
datacl        |
```

First of all, look at the use of the \x command. It makes the output in psql appear as one column per line, rather than one row per line.

This output raises many questions, I know. We've already discussed templates. The other interesting things are that we can turn connections on and off for a database, and we can set connection limits for them as well.

Also, you can see that each database has a default tablespace. Therefore, data tables get created inside one specific database, and the data files for that table get placed in one tablespace.

You can also see that each database has a collation sequence, which is the way various language features are defined. We'll cover more on that in the *Choosing good names for database objects* recipe in Chapter 5, *Tables and Data*.

How many tables are there in a database?

The number of tables in a relational database is a good measure of the complexity of a database, so it is a simple way to get to know any database.

In this recipe, we will show you how to compute the number of tables.

How to do it...

From any interface, type the following SQL command:

```
SELECT count(*) FROM information_schema.tables
WHERE table_schema NOT IN ('information_schema',
'pg_catalog');
```

You can also look at the list of tables directly, and judge whether the list is a small or large number.

In psql, you can see your own tables by using the following command:

```
postgres@ebony:~/10.2/main$ psql -c "\d"
          List of relations
  Schema |   Name    | Type  |  Owner
 --------+-----------+-------+----------
  public | accounts  | table | postgres
  public | branches  | table | postgres
```

In **pgAdmin 4**, you can see the tables in the tree view on the left-hand side, as shown in the following screenshot:

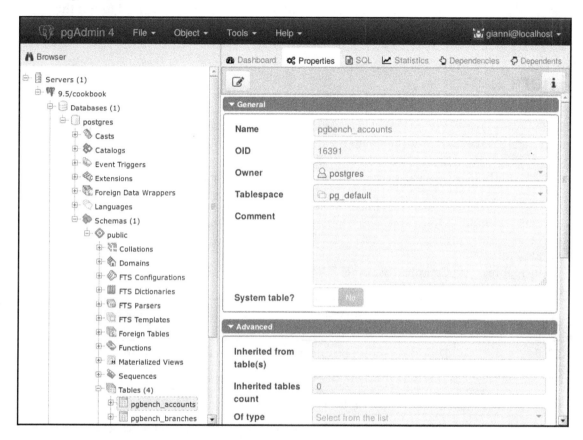

How it works...

PostgreSQL stores information about the database in catalog tables. They describe every aspect of the way the database has been defined. There is a main set of catalog tables stored in a schema, called `pg_catalog`. There is a second set of catalog objects called the Information Schema, which is the SQL standard way of accessing information in a relational database.

We want to exclude both of these schemas from our query. Otherwise, we'll get too much information. We excluded them in the preceding query using the NOT IN phrase in the WHERE clause.

Note that this query shows only the number of tables in one of the databases on the PostgreSQL server. You can only see the tables in the database to which you are currently connected, so you'll need to run the same query on each database in turn.

There's more...

As I said, the number of tables in a relational database is a good measure of the complexity. But the complexity of what? Well, a complex database may have been designed to be deliberately flexible in order to cover a variety of business situations, or, a complex business process may have a limited portion of its details covered in the database. So, a large number of tables might likely reveal a complex business process or just a complex piece of software.

The highest number of distinct, major tables I've ever seen in a database is 20,000, not counting partitions, views, and work tables. That clearly rates as a very complex system:

Number of distinct tables (entities)	Complexity rating
20,000	This is incredibly complex. You're either counting wrong or you have a big team to manage this.
2,000	This is a complex business database. Usually, not many of these are seen.
200	This is a typical modern business database.
20	This is a simple business database.
2	This is a database with a single, clear purpose, strictly designed for performance or some other goal.
0	This tells you that you haven't loaded any data yet!

Of course, you can't always easily tell which tables are entities, so we just need to count the tables. Some databases use a lot of partitions or similar tables, so the numbers can grow dramatically. I've seen databases with up to 200,000 tables (of any kind). That's not recommended, however, as the database catalog tables then begin to become awfully large.

How much disk space does a database use?

For planning or space monitoring, we often need to know how big the database is.

How to do it...

We can do this in the following ways:

- Look at the size of the files that make up the database server
- Run a SQL request to confirm the database size

If you look at the size of the actual files, you'll need to make sure that you include the data directory and all subdirectories, as well as all other directories that contain tablespaces. This can be tricky, and it is also difficult to break out all the different pieces.

The easiest way is to ask the database a simple query, like this:

```
SELECT pg_database_size(current_database());
```

However, this is limited to only the current database. If you want to know the size of all the databases together, then you'll need a query such as the following:

```
SELECT sum(pg_database_size(datname)) from pg_database;
```

How it works...

The database server knows which tables it has loaded. It also knows how to calculate the size of each table, so the `pg_database_size()` function just looks at the file sizes.

How much disk space does a table use?

How big is a table? What is the total size of all the parts of a table?

How to do it...

We can see the size of a table by using this command:

```
postgres=# select pg_relation_size('pgbench_accounts');
```

The output of this command is as follows:

```
pg_relation_size
------------------
        13582336
(1 row)
```

We can also see the total size of a table, including indexes and other related spaces, as follows:

```
postgres=# select pg_total_relation_size('pgbench_accounts');
```

The output is as follows:

```
pg_total_relation_size
------------------------
        15425536
(1 row)
```

We can also use a `psql` command, like this:

```
postgres=# \dt+ pgbench_accounts
                    List of relations
 Schema |       Name       | Type  | Owner  | Size  | Description
--------+------------------+-------+--------+-------+-------------
 gianni | pgbench_accounts | table | gianni | 13 MB |
(1 row)
```

How it works...

In PostgreSQL, a table is made up of many relations. The main relation is the data table. In addition, there are a variety of additional data files. Each index created on a table is also a relation. Long data values are placed in a secondary table named TOAST, so in most cases, each table also has a TOAST table and a TOAST index.

Each relation consists of multiple data files. The main data files are broken into 1 GB pieces. The first file has no suffix; others have a numbered suffix (such as .2). There are also files marked _vm and _fsm, which represent the visibility map and free space map, respectively. They are used as part of maintenance operations. They stay fairly small, even for very large tables.

There's more...

The preceding functions, which measure the size of a relation, output the number of bytes, which is normally too large to be immediately clear. You can apply the pg_size_pretty() function to format that number nicely, as shown in the following example:

```
SELECT pg_size_pretty(pg_relation_size('pgbench_accounts'));
```

This yields the following output:

```
pg_size_pretty
-----------------
13 MB
(1 row)
```

TOAST stands for **The Oversize Attribute Storage Technique**. As the name implies, this is a mechanism used to store long column values. PostgreSQL allows many data types to store values up to 1 GB in size. It transparently stores large data items in many smaller pieces, so the same data type can be used for data ranging from 1 byte to 1 GB. When appropriate, values are automatically compressed and decompressed before they are split and stored, so the actual limit will vary, depending on compressibility.

You may also see files ending in _init; they are used by unlogged tables, and their indexes, for restoring them after a crash. Unlogged objects are called this way because they do not produce WAL. So they support faster writes, but in the event of a crash they must be truncated, that is, restored to an empty state.

Which are my biggest tables?

We've looked at getting the size of a specific table, so now it's time to widen the problem to related areas. Rather than having an absolute value for a specific table, let's look at the relative sizes.

How to do it...

The following basic query will tell us the 10 biggest tables:

```
SELECT table_name
,pg_relation_size(table_schema || '.' || table_name) as size
FROM information_schema.tables
WHERE table_schema NOT IN ('information_schema', 'pg_catalog')
ORDER BY size DESC
LIMIT 10;
```

The tables are shown in descending order of size, with at the most 10 rows displayed. In this case, we look at all the tables in all the schemas, apart from the tables in `information_schema` or `pg_catalog`, like we did in the *How many tables are in the database?* recipe.

How it works...

PostgreSQL provides a dedicated function, `pg_relation_size`, to compute the actual disk space used by a specific table or index. We just need to provide the table name. In addition to the main data files, there are other files (called forks) that can be measured by specifying an optional second argument. These include the **Visibility Map (VM)**, the **Free Space Map (FSM)**, and the **Initialization Fork** for unlogged objects.

How many rows are there in a table?

Counting is one of the easiest SQL statements, so it is also many people's first experience of a PostgreSQL query.

How to do it...

From any interface, the SQL command used to count rows is as follows:

```
SELECT count(*) FROM table;
```

This will return a single integer value as the result.

In `psql`, the command looks like the following:

```
postgres=# select count(*) from orders;
 count
--------
   345
(1 row)
```

How it works...

PostgreSQL can choose between two techniques available to compute the SQL count (*) function. Both are available in all the currently supported versions.

The first is called **sequential scan**. We access every data block in the table one after the other, reading the number of rows in each block. If the table is on the disk, it will cause a beneficial disk access pattern, and the statement will be fairly fast.

The other technique is known as **index-only scan**. It requires an index on the table, and it covers a more general case than optimizing SQL queries with count (*), so we will cover it in more detail in Chapter 10, *Performance and Concurrency*.

Some people think that the count SQL statement is a good test of the performance of a DBMS. Some DBMS have specific tuning features for the count SQL statement, and Postgres optimizes this using index-only scans. The PostgreSQL project has talked about this many times, but few people thought we should try to optimize this. Yes, the count function is frequently used within applications, but without any WHERE clause it is not that useful. Therefore, the index-only scans feature has been implemented which applies to more real-world situations, as well as this recipe.

We scan every block of the table because of a major feature of Postgres named **Multiversion Concurrency Control (MVCC)**. MVCC allows us to run the count SQL statement at the same time that we are inserting, updating, or deleting data from the table. That's a very cool feature, and we went to a lot of trouble in Postgres to provide it for you.

MVCC requires us to record information on each row of a table, stating when that change was made. If the changes were made after the SQL statement began to execute, then we just ignore those changes. This means that we need to carry out visibility checks on each row in the table to allow us to work out the results of the count SQL statement. The optimization provided by index-only scans is the ability to skip such checks on the table blocks that are already known to be visible to all current sessions. Rows in these blocks can be counted directly on the index, which is normally smaller than the table, and hence faster.

If you think a little deeper about this, you'll see that the result of the count SQL statement is just the value at a moment in time. Depending on what happens to the table, that value could change a little or a lot while the count SQL statement is executing. So, once you've executed this, all you really know is that, at a particular point in the past, there were exactly x rows in the table.

Quickly estimating the number of rows in a table

We don't always need an accurate count of rows, especially on a large table that may take a long time to execute. Administrators often need to estimate how big a table is so that they can estimate how long other operations may take.

How to do it...

We can get a quick estimate of the number of rows in a table using roughly the same calculation that the Postgres optimizer uses:

```
SELECT (CASE WHEN reltuples > 0 THEN
pg_relation_size(oid)*reltuples/(8192*relpages)
ELSE 0
END)::bigint AS estimated_row_count
FROM pg_class
WHERE oid = 'mytable'::regclass;
```

This gives us the following output:

```
estimated_count
--------------------
             293
(1 row)
```

It returns a row count very quickly, no matter how large the table that we are examining is.

How it works...

We saw the `pg_relation_size()` function earlier, so we know it brings back an accurate value for the current size of the table.

When we vacuum a table in Postgres, we record two pieces of information in the `pg_class` catalog entry for the table. These two items are the number of data blocks in the table (`relpages`) and the number of rows in the table (`reltuples`). Some people think they can use the value of `reltuples` in `pg_class` as an estimate, but it could be severely out of date. You will also be fooled if you use information in another table named `pg_stat_user_tables`, which is discussed in more detail in `Chapter 10`, *Performance and Concurrency*.

The Postgres optimizer uses the `relpages` and `reltuples` values to calculate the average rows per block, which is also known as the average tuple density.

If we assume that the average tuple density remains constant over time, then we can calculate the number of rows using this formula: *Row estimate = number of data blocks * rows per block*.

We include some code to handle cases where the `reltuples` or `relpages` fields are zero. The Postgres optimizer actually works a little harder than we do in that case, so our estimate isn't very good.

The `WHERE oid = 'mytable'::regclass;` syntax introduces the concept of object identifier types. They just use a shorthand trick to convert the name of an object to the object identifier number for that object. The best way to understand this is to think of that syntax as meaning the same as a function named `relname2relid()`.

There's more...

The good thing about the aforementioned recipe is that it returns a value in about the same time, no matter how big the table is. The bad thing about it is that `pg_relation_size()` requests a lock on the table, so if any other user has an `AccessExclusiveLock` lock on the table, then the table size estimate will wait for the lock to be released before returning a value.

Err... so what is an `AccessExclusiveLock` lock? While performing a SQL maintenance action, such as changing the data type of a column, PostgreSQL will lock out all other actions on that table, including `pg_relation_size`, which takes a lock in the `AccessShareLock` mode. For me, a typical case is when I issue some form of SQL maintenance action, such as `ALTER TABLE`, and the statement takes much longer than I thought it would. At that point, I think, *Oh, was that table bigger than I thought? How long will I be waiting?* Yes, it's better to calculate that beforehand, but hindsight doesn't get you out of the hole you are in right now. So, we need a way to calculate the size of a table without needing the lock.

My solution is to look at the operating system files that Postgres uses to store data, and figure out how large they are.

Now, this can get somewhat difficult. If the table is locked, PostgreSQL is probably doing something to the table, so trying to look at the files might well be fruitless or give wrong answers. The following are the steps we need to perform:

1. First, get some details on the table from `pg_class`:

   ```
   SELECT reltablespace, relfilenode FROM pg_class
   WHERE oid = 'mytable'::regclass;
   ```

2. Then, confirm the `databaseid` in which the table resides:

   ```
   SELECT oid as databaseid FROM pg_database
   WHERE datname = current_database();
   ```

Together, `reltablespace`, `databaseid`, and `relfilenode` are the three things we need to locate the underlying data files within the `data` directory.

If `reltablespace` is zero, then the files will be at the following location:

`$PGDATADIR/base/{databaseid}/{relfilenode}*`

The bigger the table, the more files you see. If `reltablespace` is not zero, then the files will be at the following location:

`$PGDATADIR/pg_tblspc/{reltablespace}/{databaseid}/{relfilenode}*`

Every file should be 1 GB in size, apart from the last file.

The preceding discussion glossed over a few other points, as follows:

- Postgres uses the terms data blocks and pages to refer to the same concept. Postgres also does that with the terms tuple and row.
- A data block is 8,192 bytes in size, by default. You can change that if you recompile the server yourself, and create a new database.

You may want to create SQL functions for the preceding calculations, so you won't need to retype the SQL code every now and then.

Function 1 – Estimating the number of rows

The following function estimates the total number of rows using a mathematical procedure called **extrapolation**. In other words, we take the average number of bytes per row resulting from the last statistics collection, and we apply it to the current table size:

```sql
CREATE OR REPLACE FUNCTION estimated_row_count(text)
RETURNS bigint
LANGUAGE sql
AS $$
SELECT (CASE WHEN reltuples > 0 THEN
                pg_relation_size($1)*reltuples/(8192*relpages)
             ELSE 0
             END)::bigint
FROM pg_class
WHERE oid = $1::regclass;
$$;
```

Function 2 – Computing the size of a table without locks

Here is a function that does what `pg_relation_size` does, more or less, without taking any locks. Because of this, it is always fast, but it may give an incorrect result if the table is being heavily altered at the same time:

```sql
CREATE OR REPLACE FUNCTION pg_relation_size_nolock(tablename regclass)
RETURNS BIGINT
LANGUAGE plpgsql
AS $$
DECLARE
    classoutput RECORD;
    tsid        INTEGER;
    rid         INTEGER;
    dbid        INTEGER;
```

```
        filepath    TEXT;
        filename    TEXT;
        datadir     TEXT;
        i           INTEGER := 0;
        tablesize   BIGINT;
BEGIN
    --
    -- Get data directory
    --
    EXECUTE 'SHOW data_directory' INTO datadir;
    --
    -- Get relfilenode and reltablespace
    --
    SELECT
     reltablespace as tsid
    ,relfilenode as rid
    INTO classoutput
    FROM pg_class
    WHERE oid = tablename
    AND relkind = 'r';
    --
    -- Throw an error if we can't find the tablename specified
    --
    IF NOT FOUND THEN
       RAISE EXCEPTION 'tablename % not found', tablename;
    END IF;
    tsid := classoutput.tsid;
    rid := classoutput.rid;
    --
    -- Get the database object identifier (oid)
    --
    SELECT oid INTO dbid
    FROM pg_database
    WHERE datname = current_database();
    --
    -- Use some internals knowledge to set the filepath
    --
    IF tsid = 0 THEN
filepath := datadir || '/base/' || dbid || '/' || rid;
    ELSE
filepath := datadir || '/pg_tblspc/' || tsid || '/'
              || dbid || '/' || rid;
    END IF;
    --
    -- Look for the first file. Report if missing
    --
    SELECT (pg_stat_file(filepath)).size
    INTO tablesize;
```

```
    --
    -- Sum the sizes of additional files, if any
    --
    WHILE FOUND LOOP
i := i + 1;
filename := filepath || '.' || i;
        --
        -- pg_stat_file returns ERROR if it cannot see file
        -- so we must trap the error and exit loop
        --
      BEGIN
      SELECT tablesize + (pg_stat_file(filename)).size
          INTO tablesize;
      EXCEPTION
          WHEN OTHERS THEN
          EXIT;
      END;
    END LOOP;
    RETURN tablesize;
  END;
  $$;
```

This function can also work on Windows with a few minor changes, which are left as an exercise for you.

Listing extensions in this database

Every PostgreSQL database contains some objects that are automatically brought in when the database is created. Every user will find a `pg_database` system catalog that lists databases, as shown in the *Listing databases on this database server* recipe. There is little point in checking whether these objects exist, because even superusers are not allowed to drop them.

On the other hand, PostgreSQL comes with tens of collections of optional objects, called **modules**, or equivalently **extensions**. The database administrator can install or uninstall these objects, depending on the requirements. They are not automatically included in a newly created database, because they might not be required by every use case. Users will install only the extensions they actually need, when they need them; an extension can be installed while a database is up and running.

In this recipe, we will explain how to list extensions that have been installed on the current database. This is important to get to know the database better, and also because certain extensions affect the behavior of the database.

Getting ready

To get an idea of which extensions are available, you can browse the list of additional modules shipped together with PostgreSQL, which are almost all extensions, at `https://www.postgresql.org/docs/current/static/contrib.html`.

How to do it...

In PostgreSQL, there is a catalog table recording the list of installed extensions, so this recipe is quite simple. Issue the following command:

```
cookbook=> SELECT * FROM pg_extension;
```

This results in the following output (note that the format is expanded, as if the `\x` metacommand has been previously issued):

```
-[ RECORD 1 ]--+---------
extname        | plpgsql
extowner       | 10
extnamespace   | 11
extrelocatable | f
extversion     | 1.0
extconfig      |
extcondition   |
```

To get the same list with fewer technical details, you can use the metacommand `\dx`, like when listing databases.

How it works...

A PostgreSQL extension is represented by a control file, `<extension name>.control`, located in the `SHAREDIR/extension` directory, plus one or more files containing the actual extension objects. The control file specifies the extension name, version, and other information that is useful for the extension infrastructure. Each time an extension is installed, uninstalled, or upgraded to a new version, the corresponding row in the `pg_extension` catalog table is inserted, deleted, or updated, respectively.

There's more...

In this recipe, we only mentioned extensions distributed with PostgreSQL, and solely for the purpose of listing which ones are being used in the current database. The infrastructure for extensions will be described in greater detail in `Chapter 3`, *Configuration*. We will talk about the version number of an extension, and we will show you how to install, uninstall, and upgrade extensions, including those distributed independently of PostgreSQL.

Understanding object dependencies

In most databases, there will be dependencies between objects in the database. Sometimes, we need to understand these dependencies to figure out how to perform certain actions. Let's look at this in detail.

Getting ready

We'll use the following simple database to understand and investigate them. There are two tables, as follows:

```
CREATE TABLE orders (
orderid integer PRIMARY KEY
);
CREATE TABLE orderlines (
orderid integer
,lineid smallint
,PRIMARY KEY (orderid, lineid)
);
```

Now, we add a link between them to enforce what is known as **Referential Integrity**, as follows:

```
ALTER TABLE orderlines ADD FOREIGN KEY (orderid)
REFERENCES orders (orderid);
```

If we try to drop the referenced table, we get the following message:

```
DROP TABLE orders;
ERROR: cannot drop table orders because other objects depend on it
DETAIL: constraint orderlines_orderid_fkey on table orderlines depends on
table orders
HINT: Use DROP ... CASCADE to drop the dependent objects too.
```

Be very careful! If you follow the hint, you may accidentally remove all the objects that have any dependency on the `orders` table. You might think that this would be a great idea, but to me it seems lazy and foolish. It might work, but we need to ensure that it will work.

Therefore, you need to know what dependencies are present on the `orders` table, and then review them. Then, you can decide whether it is okay to issue the `CASCADE` version of the command, or whether you should reconcile the situation manually.

How to do it...

You can use the following command from `psql` to display full information about a table the constraints that are defined upon it, and the constraints that reference it:

```
\d+ orders
```

You can also get specific details of the constraints by using the following query:

```
SELECT * FROM pg_constraint
WHERE confrelid = 'orders'::regclass;
```

Unfortunately, this is not the end of the story, so read the *There's more...* section.

How it works...

When we create a foreign key, we add a constraint to the catalog table known as `pg_constraint`. Therefore, the query shows us how to find all the constraints that depend upon the `orders` table.

There's more...

With Postgres, there's always a little more when you look beneath the surface. In this case, there's a lot more, and it's important.

The aforementioned queries only covered constraints between tables. We didn't discuss dependencies with other kinds of objects. Two important types of object that might have dependencies to tables are views and functions.

Consider the following command:

```
DROP TABLE orders;
```

If you issue this, the dependency on any of the views will prevent the table from being dropped. Thus, you need to remove those views and then drop the table.

The story with function dependencies is not as useful. Relationships between functions and tables are not recorded in the catalog, nor is the dependency information between functions and functions. This is partly due to the fact that most PostgreSQL procedural languages allow dynamic query execution, so you wouldn't be able to tell which tables or functions a function would access until it executes. That's only partly the reason, because most functions clearly reference other tables and functions, so it should be possible to identify and store those dependencies. However, right now, we don't do that. So, make a note that you need to record the dependency information for your functions manually, so that you'll know if and when it's okay to remove or alter a table or other objects that the functions depend on.

3
Configuration

In this chapter, we will cover the following recipes:

- Reading the fine manual
- Planning a new database
- Changing parameters in your programs
- Finding the current configuration settings
- Which parameters are at non-default settings?
- Updating the parameter file
- Setting parameters for particular groups of users
- The basic server configuration checklist
- Adding an external module to PostgreSQL
- Using an installed module
- Managing installed extensions

Introduction

I get asked many questions about parameter settings in PostgreSQL. Everybody's busy, and most people want a 5-minute tour of how things work. That's exactly what a cookbook does, so we'll do our best.

Some people believe that there are some magical parameter settings that will improve their performance, spending hours combing the pages of books to glean insights. Others feel comfortable because they have found a website somewhere that *explains everything*, and they *know* they have their database configured OK.

For the most part, the settings are easy to understand. Finding the best setting can be difficult, and the optimal setting may change over time. This chapter is mostly about knowing how, when, and where to change parameter settings.

Reading the fine manual

Reading the fine manual (**RTFM**) is often (rudely) used to mean *don't bother me, I'm busy*; or it is used as a stronger form of abuse. The strange thing is that asking you to read a manual is most often very good advice. Don't flame the advisors back; take the advice! The most important point to remember is that you should refer to a manual whose release version matches that of the server on which you are operating.

The PostgreSQL manual is very well written and comprehensive in its coverage of specific topics. However, one of its main failings is that the documents aren't organized in a way that helps somebody who is trying to learn PostgreSQL. They are organized from the perspective of people checking specific technical points so that they can decide whether their difficulty is a user error or not. It sometimes answers *What?* but seldom *Why?* Or *How?*

I've helped write sections of the PostgreSQL documents, so I'm not embarrassed to steer you toward reading them. There are, nonetheless, many things to read here that are useful.

How to do it...

The main documents for each PostgreSQL release are available at
`http://www.postgresql.org/docs/manuals/`.

The most frequently accessed parts of the documents are as follows:

- SQL command reference, as well as client and server tools reference:
  `http://www.postgresql.org/docs/current/interactive/reference.html`
- Configuration:
  `http://www.postgresql.org/docs/current/interactive/runtime-config.html`
- Functions:
  `http://www.postgresql.org/docs/current/interactive/functions.html`

You can also grab yourself a PDF version of the manual, which can allow easier searching in some cases. Don't print it! The documents are more than 2,000 pages of A4-sized sheets.

How it works...

The PostgreSQL documents are written in SGML, which is similar to, but not the same as, XML. These files are then processed to generate HTML files, PDFs, and so on. This ensures that all the formats have exactly the same content. Then you can choose the format you prefer, and you can even compile it in other formats, such as EPUB, INFO, and so on.

Moreover, the PostgreSQL manual is actually a subset of the PostgreSQL source code, so it evolves together with the software. It is written by the same people who make PostgreSQL. Even more reasons to read it!

There's more...

More information is also available at `http://wiki.postgresql.org`.

Many distributions offer packages that install static versions of the HTML documentation. For example, on Debian and Ubuntu, the docs for the most recent stable PostgreSQL version are named `postgresql-10-docs` (unsurprisingly).

Planning a new database

Planning a new database can be a daunting task. It's easy to get overwhelmed by it, so here we present some planning ideas. It's also easy to charge headlong at the task, thinking that whatever you know is all you'll ever need to consider.

Getting ready

You are ready. Don't wait to be told what to do. If you haven't been told what the requirements are, then write down what you think they are, clearly labeling them as *assumptions* rather than *requirements*; you must not confuse the two things.

Iterate until you get some agreement, and then build a prototype.

How to do it...

Write a document that covers the following items:

- Database design - plan your database design
- Calculate the initial database sizing
- Transaction analysis - How will we access the database?
- Look at the most frequent access paths
- What are the requirements for response times?
- Hardware configuration
- Initial performance thoughts - Will all of the data fit into the RAM?
- Choose the operating system and filesystem types
- How do we partition the disk?
- Localization plan
- Decide the server encoding, locale, and time zone
- Access and security plan
- Identify client systems and specify the required drivers
- Create roles according to a plan for access control
- Specify `pg_hba.conf`
- Maintenance plan - Who will keep it working? How?
- Availability plan - consider the availability requirements
- `checkpoint_timeout` (for more details on this parameter, see the *Understanding and controlling crash recovery* recipe in `Chapter 11`, *Backup and Recovery*)
- Plan your backup mechanism, and test it
- High-availability plan
- Decide which form of replication you'll need, if any

How it works...

One of the most important reasons for planning your database ahead of time is that retrofitting some things is difficult. This is especially true of server encoding and locale, which can cause much downtime and exertion if we need to change them later. Security is also much more difficult to set up after the system is live.

There's more...

Planning always helps. You may know what you're doing, but others may not. Tell everybody what you're going to do before you do it, to avoid wasting time. If you're not sure yet, then build a prototype to help you decide. Approach the administration framework as if it were a development task. Make a list of things you don't know yet, and work through them one by one.

This is deliberately a very short recipe. Everybody has their own way of doing things, and it's very important not to be too prescriptive about how to do things. If you already have a plan, great! If you don't, think about what you need to do, make a checklist, and then do it.

Changing parameters in your programs

PostgreSQL allows you to set some parameter settings for each session or transaction.

How to do it...

1. You can change the value of a setting during your session, like this:

```
SET work_mem = '16MB';
```

2. This value will then be used for every future transaction. You can also change it only for the duration of the current transaction:

```
SET LOCAL work_mem = '16MB';
```

3. The setting will last until you issue this command:

```
RESET work_mem;
```

4. Alternatively, you can issue the following command:

```
RESET ALL;
```

The SET and RESET commands are SQL commands that can be issued from any interface. They apply only to PostgreSQL server parameters, but this does not mean that they affect the entire server. In fact, the parameters you can change with SET and RESET apply only to the current session. Also, note that there may be other parameters, such as JDBC driver parameters, that cannot be set in this way. Refer to the *Connecting to the PostgreSQL server* recipe in Chapter 1, *First Steps*, for help with those parameters.

How it works...

Suppose you change the value of a setting during your session, for example, by issuing this command:

```
SET work_mem = '16MB';
```

Then, the following will show up in the pg_settings catalog view:

```
postgres=# SELECT name, setting, reset_val, source
                    FROM pg_settings WHERE source = 'session';
    name    | setting | reset_val | source
----------+---------+-----------+---------
 work_mem | 16384   | 1024      | session
```

This will show until you issue this command:

```
RESET work_mem;
```

After issuing it, the setting returns to reset_val and the source returns to default:

```
    name    | setting | reset_val | source
---------+---------+-----------+---------
 work_mem | 1024    | 1024      | default
```

There's more...

You can change the value of a setting during your transaction as well, like this:

```
SET LOCAL work_mem = '16MB';
```

This results in the following output:

```
WARNING:  SET LOCAL can only be used in transaction blocks
SET
```

In order to understand what the warning means, we look that `setting` up in the `pg_settings` catalog view:

```
postgres=# SELECT name, setting, reset_val, source
                    FROM pg_settings WHERE source = 'session';
    name    | setting | reset_val | source
-----------+---------+-----------+---------
 work_mem  |  1024   |   1024    | session
```

Huh? What happened to your parameter setting? The `SET LOCAL` command takes effect only for the transaction in which it was executed, which was just the `SET LOCAL` command in our case. We need to execute it inside a transaction block to be able to see the setting take hold, as follows:

```
BEGIN;
SET LOCAL work_mem = '16MB';
```

Here is what shows up in the `pg_settings` catalog view:

```
postgres=# SELECT name, setting, reset_val, source
                    FROM pg_settings WHERE source = 'session';
    name    | setting | reset_val | source
-----------+---------+-----------+---------
 work_mem  |  16384  |   1024    | session
```

You should also note that the value of `source` is `session` rather than `transaction`, as you might have been expecting.

Finding the current configuration settings

At some point, it will occur to you to ask, *What are the current configuration settings?*

Most settings can be changed in more than one way, and some ways do not affect all users or all sessions, so it is quite possible to get confused.

How to do it...

Your first thought is probably to look in `postgresql.conf`, which is the configuration file, described in detail in the *Updating the parameter file* recipe. That works, but only as long as there is only one parameter file. If there are two, then maybe you're reading the wrong file! How would you know? So, the cautious and accurate way is to not trust a text file, but to trust the server itself.

Moreover, you learned in the previous recipe, *Changing parameters in your programs*, that each parameter has a scope that determines when it can be set. Some parameters can be set through `postgresql.conf`, but others can be changed afterwards. So, the current values of configuration settings may have been subsequently changed.

We can use the `SHOW` command like this:

```
postgres=# SHOW work_mem;
```

Its output is as follows:

```
work_mem
----------
1MB
(1 row)
```

However, remember that it reports the current setting at the time it is run, and that can be changed in many places.

Another way of finding the current settings is to access a PostgreSQL catalog view named `pg_settings`:

```
postgres=# \x
Expanded display is on.
postgres=# SELECT * FROM pg_settings WHERE name = 'work_mem';
[ RECORD 1 ] ------------------------------------------------------------
name        | work_mem
setting     | 1024
unit        | kB
category    | Resource Usage / Memory
short_desc  | Sets the maximum memory to be used for query workspaces.
extra_desc  | This much memory can be used by each internal sort operation
and hash table before switching to temporary disk files.
context     | user
vartype     | integer
source      | default
min_val     | 64
max_val     | 2147483647
enumvals    |
boot_val    | 1024
reset_val   | 1024
sourcefile  |
sourceline  |
```

Thus, you can use the `SHOW` command to retrieve the value for a setting, or you can access the full details via the catalog table.

There's more...

The actual location of each configuration file can be asked directly to the PostgreSQL server, as shown in this example:

```
postgres=# SHOW config_file;
```

This returns the following output:

```
                    config_file
-------------------------------------------
 /etc/postgresql/10/main/postgresql.conf
(1 row)
```

The other configuration files can be located by querying similar variables: `hba_file` and `ident_file`.

How it works...

Each parameter setting is cached within each session, so that we can get fast access to the parameter settings. This allows us to access the parameter settings with ease.

Remember that the values displayed are not necessarily settings for the server as a whole. Many of those parameters will be specific to the current session. That's different from what you experience with many other types of database software, and is also very useful.

Which parameters are at non-default settings?

Often, we need to check which parameters have been changed, or whether our changes have taken effect correctly.

In the previous two recipes, we have seen that parameters can be changed in several ways, and with different scopes. You learned how to inspect the value of one parameter or get the full list of parameters.

In this recipe, we will show you how to use SQL capabilities to list only those parameters whose value in the current session differs from the system-wide default value.

This list is valuable for several reasons. First, it includes only a few of the 200-plus available parameters, so it is more immediate. Also, it is difficult to remember all our past actions, especially in the middle of a long or complicated session.

Version 9.4 introduces the ALTER SYSTEM syntax, which we will describe in the next recipe, *Updating the parameter file*. From the viewpoint of this recipe, the behavior of this syntax is quite different from all the other setting-related commands: you run it from within your session, and it changes the default value, but not the value in your session.

How to do it...

We write an SQL query that lists all parameter values, excluding those whose current value is either the default or set from a configuration file:

```
postgres=# SELECT name, source, setting
                  FROM pg_settings
                  WHERE source != 'default'
                  AND source != 'override'
                  ORDER by 2, 1;
```

The output is as follows:

```
            name             |       source         |      setting
-----------------------------+----------------------+-------------------
 application_name            | client               | psql
 client_encoding             | client               | UTF8
 DateStyle                   | configuration file   | ISO, DMY
 default_text_search_config  | configuration file   | pg_catalog.english
 dynamic_shared_memory_type  | configuration file   | posix
 lc_messages                 | configuration file   | en_GB.UTF-8
 lc_monetary                 | configuration file   | en_GB.UTF-8
 lc_numeric                  | configuration file   | en_GB.UTF-8
 lc_time                     | configuration file   | en_GB.UTF-8
 log_timezone                | configuration file   | Europe/Rome
 max_connections             | configuration file   | 100
 port                        | configuration file   | 5460
 shared_buffers              | configuration file   | 16384
 TimeZone                    | configuration file   | Europe/Rome
 max_stack_depth             | environment variable | 2048
```

How it works...

From `pg_settings`, you can see which parameters have non-default values, and what the source of the current value is.

The `SHOW` command doesn't tell you whether a parameter is set at a non-default value. It just tells you the value, which isn't of much help if you're trying to understand what is set and why.

If the source is a configuration file, then the `sourcefile` and `sourceline` columns are also set. These can be useful in understanding where the configuration came from.

There's more...

The `setting` column of `pg_settings` shows the current value, but you can also look at the `boot_val` and `reset_val` parameters. The `boot_val` parameter shows the value assigned when the PostgreSQL database cluster was initialized (`initdb`), while `reset_val` shows the value that the parameter will return to if you issue the `RESET` command.

The `max_stack_depth` parameter is an exception, because `pg_settings` says it is set by the environment variable, though it is actually set by `ulimit -s` on Linux and Unix systems. The `max_stack_depth` parameter just needs to be set directly on Windows.

The timezone settings are also picked up from the OS environment, so you shouldn't need to set those directly. In older releases, `pg_settings` showed them as command-line settings. From version 9.1 onward, they are written to `postgresql.conf` when the `data` directory is initialized, so they show up as configuration files.

Updating the parameter file

The parameter file is the main location for defining parameter values for the PostgreSQL server. All the parameters can be set in the parameter file, which is known as `postgresql.conf`.

There are also two other parameter files: `pg_hba.conf` and `pg_ident.conf`. Both of these relate to connections and security, so we'll cover them in the appropriate chapters that follow.

Getting ready

First, locate `postgresql.conf`, as described previously.

How to do it...

Some of the parameters take effect only when the server is first started. A typical example might be `shared_buffers`, which defines the size of the shared memory cache.

Many of the parameters can be changed while the server is still running. After changing the required parameters, we issue a `reload` command to the server, forcing PostgreSQL to reread the `postgresql.conf` file (and all other configuration files). There are a number of ways to do that, depending on your distribution and OS. The most common is to issue the following command, with the same OS user that runs the PostgreSQL server process:

```
pg_ctl reload
```

This assumes the default data directory; otherwise, you have to specify the correct data directory with the `-D` option.

As previously noted, Debian and Ubuntu have a different multiversion architecture, so you should issue the following command instead:

```
pg_ctlcluster 10 main reload
```

On modern distributions, you can also use `systemd`, as follows:

```
sudo systemctl reload postgresql@10-main
```

See the *Starting the database server manually* recipe, in Chapter 4, *Server Control*, for more details on how to manage PostgreSQL via `systemd`; the *Reloading the server configuration files* recipe, also in Chapter 4, *Server Control*, shows more ways to reload configuration files.

Some other parameters require a restart of the server for changes to take effect; for instance, `max_connections`, `listen_addresses`, and so on. The syntax is very similar to a `reload` operation, as shown here:

```
pg_ctl restart
```

For Debian and Ubuntu, use this command:

```
pg_ctlcluster 10 main restart
```

With system, use this command:

```
sudo systemctl restart postgresql@10-main
```

Of course, a restart also has some impact on existing connections. See the *Restarting the server quickly* recipe in Chapter 4, *Server Control*, for further details.

The postgresql.conf file is a normal text file that can be simply edited. Most of the parameters are listed in the file, so you can just search for them and then insert the desired value in the right place.

How it works...

If you set the same parameter twice in different parts of the file, the last setting is what applies. This can cause lots of confusion if you add settings to the bottom of the file, so you are advised against doing it.

The best practice is to version-control this by using git alongside any other code or config changes.

There's more...

The postgresql.conf file also supports an include directive. This allows the postgresql.conf file to reference other files, which can then reference other files, and so on. That may help you organize your parameter settings better, if you don't make it too complicated.

For more on reloading, see the *Reloading the server configuration files* recipe in Chapter 4, *Server Control*.

If you are working with PostgreSQL version 9.4 or later, you can change the values stored in the parameter files directly from your session, with syntax such as the following:

```
ALTER SYSTEM SET shared_buffers = '1GB';
```

This command will not actually edit `postgresql.conf`. Instead, it writes the new setting to another file named `postgresql.auto.conf`. The effect is equivalent, albeit in a safer way. The original configuration is never written, so it cannot be damaged in the event of a crash. If you mess up with too many `ALTER SYSTEM` commands, you can always delete `postgresql.auto.conf` manually, and reload the configuration or restart PostgreSQL, depending on what parameters you changed.

PostgreSQL 10 now supports up to 7 TB of cache, if you have that much memory.

Setting parameters for particular groups of users

PostgreSQL supports a variety of ways of defining parameter settings for various user groups. This is very convenient, especially to manage user groups that have different requirements.

How to do it...

1. For all users in the `saas` database, use the following commands:

```
ALTER DATABASE saas
SET configuration_parameter = value1;
```

2. For a user named `simon` connected to any database, use this:

```
ALTER ROLE simon
SET configuration_parameter = value2;
```

3. Alternatively, you can set a parameter for a user only when connected to a specific database, as follows:

```
ALTER ROLE simon
IN DATABASE saas
SET configuration_parameter = value3;
```

The user won't know that these have been executed specifically for them. These are default settings, and in most cases they can be overridden if the user requires non-default values.

How it works...

You can set parameters for each of the following:

- Database
- User (which is named role by PostgreSQL)
- Database/user combination

Each of the parameter defaults is overridden by the one following it.

In the preceding three SQL statements:

- If user hannu connects to the saas database, then value1 will apply
- If user simon connects to a database other than saas, then value2 will apply
- If user simon connects to the saas database, then value3 will apply

PostgreSQL implements this in exactly the same way as if the user had manually issued the equivalent SET statements immediately after connecting.

The basic server configuration checklist

PostgreSQL arrives configured for use on a shared system, though many people want to run dedicated database systems. The PostgreSQL project wishes to ensure that PostgreSQL will play nicely with other server software, and will not assume that it has access to the full server resources. If you, as the system administrator, know that there is no other important server software running on the system, then you can crank the values up much higher.

Getting ready

Before we start, we need to know two sets of information:

- We need to know the size of the physical RAM that will be dedicated to PostgreSQL
- We need to know something about the types of applications for which we will use PostgreSQL

How to do it...

If your database is larger than 32 MB, then you'll probably benefit from increasing `shared_buffers`. You can increase this to a much larger value, but remember that running out of memory induces many problems.

For instance, PostgreSQL is able to store information to the disk when the available memory is too small, and it employs sophisticated algorithms to treat each case differently and to place each piece of data on the disk or in memory, depending on each use case.

On the other hand, overstating the amount of available memory confuses such abilities and results in suboptimal behavior. For instance, if the memory is swapped to disk, then PostgreSQL will inefficiently treat all data as if it were the RAM. Another unfortunate circumstance is when the Linux **Out-Of-Memory** (**OOM**) killer terminates one of the various processes spawned by the PostgreSQL server. So, it's better to be conservative. It is a good practice to set a low value in your `postgresql.conf` and increment slowly, to ensure that you get the benefits from each change.

If you increase `shared_buffers` and you're running on a non-Windows server, you will almost certainly need to increase the value of the `SHMMAX` OS parameter (and on some platforms, other parameters as well).

On Linux, Mac OS, and FreeBSD, you will need to either edit the `/etc/sysctl.conf` file or use `sysctl -w` with the following values:

- For Linux, use `kernel.shmmax=value`
- For Mac OS, use `kern.sysv.shmmax=value`
- For FreeBSD, use `kern.ipc.shmmax=value`

There's more...

For more information, you can refer to
`http://www.postgresql.org/docs/9.6/static/kernel-resources.html#SYSVIPC`.

For example, on Linux, add the following line to `/etc/sysctl.conf`:

```
kernel.shmmax=value
```

Don't worry about setting `effective_cache_size`. It is much less important a parameter than you might think. There is no need for too much fuss selecting the value.

If there is heavy write activity, you may want to set `wal_buffers` to a much higher value than the default. In fact, `wal_buffers` is automatically set from the value of `shared_buffers`, following a rule that fits most cases. However, it is always possible to specify an explicit value that overrides the computation for the very few cases where the rule is not good enough.

If you're doing heavy write activity and/or large data loads, you may want to set `max_wal_size` and `min_wal_size` higher than the default to avoid wasting I/O in excessively frequent checkpoints. You may also wish to set `checkpoint_timeout` and `checkpoint_completion_target`.

If your database has many large queries, you may wish to set `work_mem` to a value higher than the default. However, remember that such a limit applies to *each* node separately in the query plan, so there is a real risk of over-allocating memory, with all the problems discussed earlier.

Ensure that `autovacuum` is turned on, unless you have a very good reason to turn it off; most people don't. See later chapters for more information on `autovacuum`; in particular, see `Chapter 9`, *Regular Maintenance*.

Leave the settings as they are for now. Don't fuss too much about getting the settings right. You can change most of them later, so you can take an iterative approach to improving things.

And remember, don't touch the `fsync` parameter. It's keeping you safe.

Adding an external module to PostgreSQL

Another strength of PostgreSQL is its extensibility. Extensibility was one of the original design goals, going back to the late 1980s. Now, in PostgreSQL 10, there are many additional modules that plug into the core PostgreSQL server.

There are many kinds of additional module offerings, such as the following:

- Additional functions
- Additional data types
- Additional operators
- Additional index types

Note that many tools and client interfaces work with PostgreSQL without any special installation. Here, we are discussing modules that extend and alter the behavior of the server beyond its normal range of SQL standard syntax, functions, and behavior.

The procedure that makes a module usable is actually a two-step process. First, you install the module's files on your system so that they become available to the database server. Next, you connect to the database (or databases) where you want to use the module, and create the required objects. The first step is discussed in this recipe. For the second step, refer to the next recipe, *Using an installed module*.

In this book, we will use the words *extension* and *module* as synonyms, like in the PostgreSQL documentation. Note, however, that the SQL commands that manage extensions, which we'll describe in the next recipe, are as follows:

- `CREATE EXTENSION myext;`
- `ALTER EXTENSION myext UPDATE;`

In particular, commands such as `CREATE MODULE` won't work at all!

Getting ready

First, you'll need to select an appropriate module to install.

The journey toward a complete, automated package management system for PostgreSQL is not over yet, so you need to look in more than one place for the available modules, such as the following:

- **Contrib**: The PostgreSQL core includes many functions. There is also an official section for add-in modules, known as contrib modules. They are always available for your database server, but are not automatically enabled in every database, because not all users might need them. In PostgreSQL version 10, we have 59 such modules. These are documented at `http://www.postgresql.org/docs/10/static/contrib.html`.
- **PGXN**: This is the PostgreSQL Extension Network, a central distribution system dedicated to sharing PostgreSQL extensions. The website started in 2010 as a repository dedicated to the sharing of extension files. By 2017 there were more than 220 extensions from 239 different authors. You can learn more about it at `http://pgxn.org/`.

- **Separate projects**: These are large external projects, such as PostGIS, offering extensive and complex PostgreSQL modules. For more information, take a look at `http://www.postgis.org/`.

How to do it...

There are several ways to make additional modules available for your database server, as follows:

- Using a software installer
- Installing from PGXN
- Installing from a manually downloaded package
- Installing from source code

Often, a particular module will be available in more than one way, and users are free to choose their favorite, exactly like PostgreSQL itself, which can be downloaded and installed through many different procedures.

Installing modules using a software installer

Certain modules are available exactly like any other software packages that you may want to install in your server. All main Linux distributions provide packages for the most popular modules, such as PostGIS, SkyTools, procedural languages other than those distributed with the core, and so on.

Modules can sometimes be added during installation if you're using a standalone installer application; for example, the OneClick installer, or tools such as `rpm`, `apt-get`, and `YaST` on Linux distributions. The same procedure can also be followed after the PostgreSQL installation, when the need for a certain module arrives. We will actually describe this case, which is very common.

For example, let's say that you need to manage a collection of Debian package files and that one of your tasks is to be able to pick the latest version of one of them. You start by building a database that records all package files. Clearly, you need to store the version number of each package. However, Debian version numbers are much more complex than what we usually call "numbers". For instance, on my Debian laptop, I currently have version `10.3-1.pgdg90+1` of the PostgreSQL client package. Despite being complicated, that string follows a clearly defined specification, which includes many bits of information, including how to compare two versions to establish which of them is older.

Since this recipe discusses extending PostgreSQL with custom data types and operators, you might have already guessed that I will now consider a custom data type for Debian version numbers that is capable of tasks such as understanding the Debian version number format, sorting version numbers, choosing the latest version number in a given group, and so on. It turns out that somebody else already did the work of creating the required PostgreSQL data type, endowed with all the useful accessories: comparison operators, input/output functions, support for indexes, and maximum/minimum aggregates. All of this has been packaged as a PostgreSQL extension, as well as a Debian package (not a big surprise), so it is just a matter of installing the `postgresql-10-debversion` package with a Debian tool such as `apt-get`, `aptitude`, or `synaptic`. On my laptop, that boils down to the following command:

```
apt-get install postgresql-10-debversion
```

This will download the required package and unpack all the files in the right locations, making them available to my PostgreSQL server.

Installing modules from PGXN

The PostgreSQL Extension Network, PGXN for short, is a website (`http://pgxn.org`) launched in late 2010 with the purpose of providing a central distribution system for open source PostgreSQL extension libraries. Anybody can register and upload their own module, packaged as an extension archive. The website allows browsing available extensions and their versions, either via a search interface or from a directory of packages and usernames.

The simple way is to use a command-line utility called `pgxnclient`. It can be easily installed in most systems; see the PGXN website for how to do so. Its purpose is to interact with PGXN and take care of administrative tasks, such as browsing available extensions, downloading the package, compiling the source code, installing files in the proper places, and removing installed package files. Alternatively, you can download the extension files from the website and place them in the right place by following the installation instructions.

PGXN is different from official repositories because it serves another purpose. Official repositories usually contain only seasoned extensions, because they accept new software only after a certain amount of evaluation and testing. On the other hand, anybody can ask for a PGXN account and upload their own extensions, so there is no filter except requiring that the extension has an open source license and a few files that any extension must have.

Installing modules from a manually downloaded package

You might have to install a module that is correctly packaged for your system, but is not available from the official package archives. For instance, it could be the case that the module has not been accepted in the official repository yet, or you may have repackaged a bespoke version of that module with some custom tweaks, which are so specific that they will never become official. Whatever the case, you will have to follow the installation procedure for standalone packages specific to your system.

Here is an example with the Oracle compatibility module, described at `http://postgres.cz/wiki/Oracle_functionality_(en)`:

1. First, we get the package (say, for PostgreSQL 8.4 on a 64-bit architecture) from `http://pgfoundry.org/frs/download.php/2414/orafce-3.0.1-1.pg84.rhel5.x86_64.rpm`.

2. Then, we install the package in the standard way:

```
rpm -ivh orafce-3.0.1-1.pg84.rhel5.x86_64.rpm
```

If all the dependencies are met, we are done.

I mentioned dependencies because that's one more potential problem when installing packages that are not officially part of the installed distribution; you can no longer assume that all software version numbers have been tested, all requirements are available, and there are no conflicts. If you get error messages that indicate problems in these areas, you may have to solve them yourself, by manually installing missing packages and/or uninstalling conflicting packages.

Installing modules from source code

In many cases, useful modules may not have full packaging. In these cases, you may need to install the module manually. This isn't very hard, and it's a useful exercise that will help you understand what happens.

Each module will have different installation requirements. There are generally two aspects of installing a module. They are as follows:

- Building the libraries (only for modules that have libraries)
- Installing the module files in the appropriate locations

You need to follow the instructions for the specific module in order to build the libraries, if any are required. Installation will then be straightforward, and usually there will be a suitably prepared configuration file for the `make` utility, so that you just need to type the following command:

```
make install
```

Each file will be copied to the right directory. Remember that you normally need to be a system super user in order to install files on system directories.

Once a library file is in the directory expected by the PostgreSQL server, it will be loaded automatically as soon as requested by a function. Modules such as `auto_explain` do not provide any additional user-defined functions, so they won't be auto-loaded; that needs to be done manually by a super user with a `LOAD` statement.

How it works...

PostgreSQL can dynamically load libraries in the following ways:

- Using the explicit `LOAD` command in a session
- Using the `shared_preload_libraries` parameter in `postgresql.conf` at the server start
- At the session start, using the `local_preload_libraries` parameter for a specific user, as set using `ALTER ROLE`

PostgreSQL functions and objects can reference code in these libraries, allowing extensions to be bound tightly to the running server process. The tight binding makes this method suitable for use in even very high-performance applications, and there's no significant difference between additionally supplied features and native features.

Using an installed module

In this recipe, we will explain how to enable an installed module so that it can be used in a particular database. The additional types, functions, and so on will exist only in those databases where we have carried out this step.

Although most modules require this procedure, there are actually a couple of notable exceptions. For instance, the `auto_explain` module mentioned earlier, which is shipped together with PostgreSQL, does not create any function, type, or operator. To use it, you must load its object file using the `LOAD` command. From that moment, all statements longer than a configurable threshold will be logged together with their execution plan. In the rest of this recipe, we will cover all the other modules. They do not require a `LOAD` statement, because PostgreSQL can automatically load the relevant libraries when they are required.

As mentioned in the previous recipe, *Adding an external module to PostgreSQL*, specially packaged modules are called extensions in PostgreSQL. They can be managed with dedicated SQL commands.

Getting ready

Suppose that you have chosen to install a certain module among those available for your system (see the previous recipe, *Adding an external module to PostgreSQL*); all you need to know is the extension name.

How to do it...

Each extension has a unique name, so it is just a matter of issuing the following command:

```
CREATE EXTENSION myextname;
```

This will automatically create all the required objects inside the current database.

For security reasons, you need to do so as a database super user. For instance, if you want to install the `dblink` extension, type this:

```
CREATE EXTENSION dblink;
```

How it works...

When you issue a CREATE EXTENSION command, the database server looks for a file named EXTNAME.control in the SHAREDIR/extension directory. That file tells PostgreSQL some properties of the extension, including a description, some installation information, and the default version number of the extension (which is unrelated to the PostgreSQL version number). Then, a creation script is executed in a single transaction; thus, if it fails, the database is unchanged. The database server also notes in a catalog table the extension name and all the objects that belong to it.

Managing installed extensions

In the last two recipes, we showed you how to install external modules in PostgreSQL to augment its capabilities.

In this recipe, we will show you some more capabilities offered by the extension infrastructure.

How to do it...

1. First, we list all the available extensions:

```
postgres=# \x on
Expanded display is on.
postgres=# SELECT *
postgres-# FROM pg_available_extensions
postgres-# ORDER BY name;
-[ RECORD 1 ]-----+---------------------------------------------
------
name              | adminpack
default_version   | 1.0
installed_version |
comment           | administrative functions for PostgreSQL
-[ RECORD 2 ]-----+---------------------------------------------
------
name              | pg_stat statements
default_version   | 1.5
installed_version |
comment           | track execution statistics of all SQL
statements executed
(...)
```

In particular, if the `dblink` extension is installed, then we see a record like this:

```
-[ RECORD 10 ]----+-------------------------------------------
------
name              | dblink
default_version   | 1.0
installed_version | 1.0
comment           | connect to other PostgreSQL databases from
within a database
```

2. Now, we can list all the objects in the `dblink` extension, as follows:

```
postgres=# \x off
Expanded display is off.
postgres=# \dx+ dblink
                    Objects in extension "dblink"
                         Object Description
-----------------------------------------------------------------
------
 function
dblink_build_sql_delete(text,int2vector,integer,text[])
 function
dblink_build_sql_insert(text,int2vector,integer,text[],text[])
 function
dblink_build_sql_update(text,int2vector,integer,text[],text[])
 function dblink_cancel_query(text)
 function dblink_close(text)
 function dblink_close(text,boolean)
 function dblink_close(text,text)
(...)
```

3. Objects created as parts of extensions are not special in any way, except that you can't drop them individually. This is done to protect you from mistakes:

```
postgres=# DROP FUNCTION dblink_close(text);
ERROR:  cannot drop function dblink_close(text) because
extension dblink requires it
HINT:  You can drop extension dblink instead.
```

4. Extensions might have dependencies, too. The `cube` and `earthdistance` contrib extensions are a good example, since the latter depends on the former:

```
postgres=# CREATE EXTENSION earthdistance;
ERROR:  required extension "cube" is not installed
postgres=# CREATE EXTENSION cube;
CREATE EXTENSION
postgres=# CREATE EXTENSION earthdistance;
CREATE EXTENSION
```

5. As you can reasonably expect, dependencies are taken into account when dropping objects, just like for other objects:

```
postgres=# DROP EXTENSION cube;
ERROR:  cannot drop extension cube because other objects depend
on it
DETAIL:  extension earthdistance depends on extension cube
HINT:  Use DROP ... CASCADE to drop the dependent objects too.
postgres=# DROP EXTENSION cube CASCADE;
NOTICE:  drop cascades to extension earthdistance
DROP EXTENSION
```

How it works...

The `pg_available_extensions` system view shows one row for each extension control file in the `SHAREDIR/extension` directory (see the *Using an installed module* recipe). The `pg_extension` catalog table records only the extensions that have actually been created.

The `psql` command-line utility provides the `\dx` meta-command to examine the extensions. It supports an optional plus sign (+) to control verbosity, and an optional pattern for the extension name to restrict its range. Consider the following command:

```
\dx+ db*
```

This will list all extensions whose names start with db, together with all their objects.

The `CREATE EXTENSION` command creates all objects belonging to a given extension, and then records the dependency of each object on the extension in `pg_depend`. That's how PostgreSQL can ensure that you cannot drop one such object without dropping its extension.

The extension control file admits an optional line, `requires`, that names one or more extensions on which the current one depends. The implementation of dependencies is still quite simple. For instance, there is no way to specify a dependency on a specific version number of other extensions, and there is no command that installs one extension and all its prerequisites.

As a general PostgreSQL rule, the `CASCADE` keyword tells the `DROP` command to delete all objects that depend on `cube`, the `earthdistance` extension in this example.

There's more...

Another system view, `pg_available_extension_versions`, shows all the versions available for each extension. It can be valuable when there are multiple versions of the same extension available at the same time; for example when making preparations for an extension upgrade.

When a more recent version of an already installed extension becomes available to the database server, for instance, because of a distribution upgrade that installs updated package files, the super user can perform an upgrade by issuing the following command:

```
ALTER EXTENSION myext UPDATE TO '1.1';
```

This assumes that the author of the extension taught it how to perform the upgrade.

Extensions interact nicely with logical backup and restore nicely, a topic that will be fully discussed in Chapter 11, *Backup and Recovery*. As an example, if your database contains the `cube` extension, then you will surely want a single line (`CREATE EXTENSION cube;`) in the dump file instead of lots of lines recreating each object individually, which is inefficient and also dangerous.

The `CASCADE` option is accepted also by the `CREATE EXTENSION` syntax, with the meaning of "issue `CREATE EXTENSION` recursively to cover all dependencies." So, instead of creating an extension `cube` before creating the extension `earthdistance`, you could have issued the following command:

```
postgres=# CREATE EXTENSION earthdistance CASCADE;
NOTICE:  installing required extension "cube"
CREATE EXTENSION
```

Remember that `CREATE EXTENSION ... CASCADE` will only work if all the extensions it tries to install have already been placed in the appropriate location.

Server Control

4

In this chapter, we will cover the following recipes:

- Starting the database server manually
- Stopping the server safely and quickly
- Stopping the server in an emergency
- Reloading the server configuration files
- Restarting the server quickly
- Preventing new connections
- Restricting users to only one session each
- Pushing users off the system
- Deciding on a design for multitenancy
- Using multiple schemas
- Giving users their own private database
- Running multiple servers on one system
- Setting up a connection pool
- Accessing multiple servers using the same host and port

Introduction

PostgreSQL consists of a set of server processes, the group leader of which is named the **postmaster**. Starting the server is the act of creating these processes, and stopping the server is the act of terminating those processes.

Each postmaster listens for client connection requests on a defined port number. Multiple concurrently running postmasters cannot share that port number. The port number is often used to uniquely identify a particular postmaster and hence also the database server that it leads.

When we start a database server, we refer to a data directory, which contains the heart and soul—or at least the data—of our database. Subsidiary tablespaces may contain some data outside the main `data` directory, so the `data` directory is just the main central location, and not the only place where data for that database server is held. Each running server has one `data` directory, and one `data` directory can have, at the most, one running server (or instance).

To perform any action for a database server, we must know the `data` directory for that server. The basic actions we can perform on the database server are starting and stopping. We can also perform a restart, though that is just a stop followed by a start. In addition, we can reload the server, which means we can reread the server's configuration files.

We should also mention a few other points.

The default port number for PostgreSQL is `5432`. That has been registered with the **Internet Assigned Numbers Authority** (**IANA**), and so it should already be reserved for PostgreSQL's use in most places. Because each PostgreSQL server requires a distinct port number, the normal convention is to use subsequent numbers for any additional server; for example, `5433`, `5434`, and so on. Subsequent port numbers might not be as easily recognized by the network infrastructure, which might, in some cases, make life more difficult for you in large enterprises, especially in more security-conscious ones.

Port number `6432` has been registered with IANA for PgBouncer, the connection pooler that we will describe in the *Setting up a connection pool* recipe. This happened only recently, and many installations are using nonstandard port numbers such as `6543` only because they were deployed earlier.

A database server is also sometimes referred to as a database cluster. I don't recommend this term for normal usage because it makes people think about multiple nodes, not one database server on one system.

Starting the database server manually

Typically, the PostgreSQL server will start automatically when the system boots. You may have opted to stop and start the server manually, or you may need to start up or shut down for various operational reasons.

Getting ready

First, you need to understand the difference between the service and the server. The word *server* refers to the database server and its processes. The word *service* refers to the operating system wrapper by which the server gets called. The server works in essentially the same way on every platform, whereas each operating system and distribution has its own concept of a service.

Moreover, the way services are managed has changed recently: for instance, as of now (the beginning of 2018), most Linux distributions have adopted the systemd service manager. This means that you need to know which *distribution* and *release* you are using to find the correct variant of this recipe.

With systemd, a PostgreSQL server process is represented by a **service unit**, which is managed via the systemctl command. The systemd command syntax is the same on all distributions, but the name of the service unit unfortunately is not, for example, it will have to be adjusted depending on your distribution.

In other cases, you need to type the actual **data directory** path as part of the command line to start the server. More information on how to find out the data directory path is available in the *Locating the database server files* recipe in Chapter 2, *Exploring the Database*.

How to do it...

On each platform there is a specific command to start the server.

If you are using a modern Linux distribution, you are probably using systemd. In this case, PostgreSQL can be started with the following command:

```
systemctl start SERVICEUNIT
```

This must be issued with OS superuser privileges, after replacing SERVICEUNIT with the appropriate systemd service unit name.

> The systemctl command must always be issued with operating system superuser privileges. Remember, throughout this book we will always prepend systemctl invocations with sudo.

There are a couple of things to keep in mind:

- This will work only if the user executing the command has been previously granted appropriate `sudo` privileges by the system administrator
- If the command is executed from a superuser account, then the `sudo` keyword is unnecessary, although not harmful

As mentioned previously, the service unit name depends on what distribution you are using. Precisely:

- On Ubuntu and Debian there is a service unit called:

  `postgresql@RELEASE-CLUSTERNAME`

- For each database server instance, there is another service unit called just `postgresql`, that can be used to manage all the database servers at once. So you can issue, for example:

  `sudo systemctl start postgresql`

- To start all the available instances, and to start only the default version 10 instance:

  `sudo systemctl start postgresql@10-main`

- Default Red Hat/Fedora packages call the service unit simply `postgresql`, so the syntax is as follows:

  `sudo systemctl start postgresql`

- Red Hat/Fedora packages from the PostgreSQL Yum repository create a service unit called `postgresql--RELEASE`, so we can start version 10 as follows:

  `sudo systemctl start postgresql-10`

As noted previously, `systemctl` is part of `systemd`, which is only available on Linux and is normally used by most of the recent distributions.
The following commands can be used where `systemd` is not available:

- On Debian and Ubuntu releases, you must invoke the PostgreSQL-specific utility `pg_ctlcluster` as follows:

  `pg_ctlcluster 10 main start`

This command will also work when `systemd` is available; it will just redirect the start request to `systemctl` and print a message on the screen, so that the next time you will remember to use `systemctl` directly.

- For Red Hat/Fedora, you can use this command:

  `service postgresql start`

- For Windows, the command is as follows:

  `net start postgres`

- For Red Hat/Fedora, you can also use the following command:

  `pg_ctl -D $PGDATA start`

  where `PGDATA` is set to the data directory path.

In fact, this command works on most distributions, including **macOS**, **Solaris**, and **FreeBSD**, although:

- It is recommended to use, whenever possible, the distribution-specific syntax described previously.
- You may have to specify the full path to the `pg_ctl` executable if it's not in your path already. This is normally the case with multi-version directory schemes such as Debian/Ubuntu, where distribution-specific scripts pick the appropriate executable for your version.

How it works...

On Ubuntu/Debian, the `pg_ctlcluster` wrapper is a convenient utility that allows multiple servers to coexist more easily, which is especially good when you have servers with different versions. This capability is very useful, and is transposed on `systemd` as shown in the examples using @ in the name of the service unit, where @ denotes the usage of a service file template.

Another interesting `systemd` feature is the capability to `enable`/`disable` a service unit to specify whether it will be started automatically on the next boot, with a syntax such as:

```
sudo systemctl enable postgresql@10-main
```

This can be very useful to set the appropriate behavior based on the purpose of each instance.

A similar feature is implemented on Ubuntu and Debian by the `start.conf` file, located next to the other configuration files (that is, in the same directory). Apart from the informational comments, it contains only a single word, with the following meaning:

- `auto`: The server will be started automatically on boot. This is the default when creating a new server. It is suitable for frequently used servers, such as those powering live services or being used for everyday development activities.
- `manual`: The server will not be started automatically on boot, but can be started with `pg_ctlcluster`. This is suitable for custom servers that are seldom used.
- `disabled`: The server is not supposed to be started. This setting is only a protection from starting the server accidentally. The `pg_ctlcluster` wrapper won't let you start it, but a skilled user can easily bypass the protection.

If you need to reserve a port for a server not managed by `pg_ctlcluster`, for example, when compiling directly from the source code, then you can create a cluster with `start.conf` set to `disabled`, and then use its port. Any new servers will be allocated different ports.

Stopping the server safely and quickly

There are several modes to stop the server, depending on the level of urgency. We'll do a comparison in view of the effects in each mode.

How to do it...

We provide two variants: with and without `systemd`. This is similar to the previous recipe, *Starting the database server manually*, which we'll refer to for further information. For example, what is the exact name of the `systemd` service unit for a given database server on a given GNU/Linux distribution?

When using `systemd`, you can stop PostgreSQL using the *fast* mode by issuing the following after having replaced SERVICEUNIT with the appropriate `systemd` service unit name:

```
sudo systemctl stop SERVICEUNIT
```

If `systemd` is not available, and you are using Debian or Ubuntu, the command is as in the following example, which applies to the default version 10 instance:

```
pg_ctlcluster 10 main stop -m fast
```

The fast mode is the default since PostgreSQL 9.5; the previous default was to use the `smart` mode, meaning *wait for all users to finish before we exit*. This can take a very long time, and all the while new connections are refused.

On other Linux/Unix distributions, you can issue a database server `stop` command using the `fast` mode, as follows:

```
pg_ctl -D datadir -m fast stop
```

How it works...

When you do a `fast stop`, all users have their transactions aborted and all connections are disconnected. This is not very polite to users, but it still treats the server and its data with care, which is good.

PostgreSQL is similar to other database systems in that it does do a shutdown checkpoint before it closes. This means that the startup that follows will be quick and clean. The more work the checkpoint has to do, the longer it will take to shut down.

One difference between PostgreSQL and some other RDBMSes such as Oracle, DB2, or SQL Server is that the transaction rollback is very fast. On those other systems, if you shut down the server in a mode that rolls back transactions, it can cause the shutdown to take a while, possibly a very long time. This difference is for internal reasons, and isn't in any way unsafe. Debian and Ubuntu's `pg_ctlcluster` supports the `--force` option, which is rather nice because it first attempts a fast shutdown, and if that fails, it performs an immediate shutdown. After that, it kills the postmaster.

See also

- The technology that provides immediate rollback for PostgreSQL is called **Multiversion Concurrency Control (MVCC)**. More information on this is provided in the *Identifying and fixing bloated tables and indexes* recipe in `Chapter 9, Regular Maintenance`.

Stopping the server in an emergency

If nothing else is working, we may need to stop the server quickly, without caring about disconnecting the clients gently.

Break the glass in case of emergency!

How to do it...

1. The basic command to perform an emergency stop on the server is the following:

   ```
   pg_ctl -D datadir stop -m immediate
   ```

2. On Debian/Ubuntu, you can also use:

   ```
   pg_ctlcluster 10 main stop -m immediate
   ```

As mentioned in the previous recipe, this is just a wrapper around `pg_ctl`. From this example, we can see that it can pass through the `-m immediate` option.

 In the previous recipe, we have seen examples where the `systemctl` command was used to stop a server safely; however, that command cannot be used to perform an emergency stop.

How it works...

When you do an immediate stop, all users have their transactions aborted and all connections are disconnected. There is no clean shutdown, nor is there politeness of any kind.

An immediate mode stop is similar to a database crash. Some cached files will need to be rebuilt, and the database itself needs to undergo crash recovery when it comes back up.

Note that for DBAs with Oracle experience, the immediate mode is the same thing as a shutdown abort. The PostgreSQL immediate mode stop is *not* the same thing as `shutdown immediate` on Oracle.

Reloading the server configuration files

Some PostgreSQL configuration parameters can be changed only by reloading the entire configuration file(s).

How to do it...

There are two variants of this recipe, depending on whether you are using `systemd`. This is similar to the previous recipes in this chapter, and especially the *Starting the database server manually* recipe. More details are explained there, such as the exact names of `systemd` service units depending on which database server you want to reload, and which GNU/Linux distribution you are working on.

With `systemd`, configuration files can be reloaded with the following syntax:

```
sudo systemctl reload SERVICEUNIT
```

Here, `SERVICEUNIT` must be replaced with the exact name of the `systemd` service unit for the server(s) that you want to reload.

Otherwise, on each platform there is a specific command to reload the server without using `systemd`. All of these are listed as follows:

- On Ubuntu and Debian, you can issue:

```
pg_ctlcluster 10 main reload
```

- On older Red Hat/Fedora, the command is as follows:

```
service postgresql reload
```

- You can also use the following command:

```
pg_ctl -D /var/lib/pgsql/data reload
```

This also works on macOS, Solaris, and FreeBSD, replacing `/var/lib/pgsql/data` with your actual data directory if it's different.

On all platforms, you can also reload the configuration files while still connected to PostgreSQL. If you are a superuser, this can be done from the following command line:

```
postgres=# select pg_reload_conf();
```

The output is rather short:

```
pg_reload_conf
-----------------
t
```

This function is also often executed from an admin tool, such as **OmniDB**.

If you do this, you should realize that it's possible to implement a new authentication rule that is violated by the current session. It won't force you to disconnect, but when you do disconnect, you may not be able to reconnect.

 Any error in a configuration file will be reported in the message log, so we recommend to look there immediately after reloading. You will quickly notice (and fix!) syntax errors in the parameter file, because they prevent any login even before reloading. Other errors, such as typos in parameter names, or wrong units, will only be reported in the log; moreover, only some non-syntax errors will prevent reloading the whole file, so it's best to always check the log.

How it works...

To reload the configuration files, we send the SIGHUP signal to the postmaster, which then passes that to all connected backends. That's why some people call reloading the server *sigh-up-ing*.

If you look at the pg_settings catalog table, you'll see that there is a column named context. Each setting has a time and a place where it can be changed. Some parameters can only be reset by a server reload, and so the value of context for those parameters will be a sighup. Here are a few of the parameters you'd want to change sometimes during server operation (there are others, however):

```
postgres=#  SELECT name, setting, unit
                    , (source = 'default') as is_default
            FROM pg_settings
            WHERE context = 'sighup'
            AND (name like '%delay' or name like '%timeout')
            AND setting != '0';
            name                        | setting | unit | is_default
  ----------------------------------+---------+------+-----------
   authentication_timeout           | 60      | s    | t
   autovacuum_vacuum_cost_delay     | 20      | ms   | t
   bgwriter_delay                   | 10      | ms   | f
```

```
checkpoint_timeout             | 32      | s    | f
deadlock_timeout               | 1000    | ms   | t
max_standby_archive_delay      | 30000   | ms   | t
max_standby_streaming_delay    | 30000   | ms   | t
wal_receiver_timeout           | 60000   | ms   | t
wal_sender_timeout             | 60000   | ms   | t
wal_writer_delay               | 200     | ms   | t
(9 rows)
```

There's more...

Since reloading the configuration file is achieved by sending the SIGHUP signal, we can reload the configuration file only for a single backend using the kill command. As you might expect, you may get some strange results from doing this, so don't try it at home.

First, find the PID of the backend using pg_stat_activity. Then, from the OS prompt, issue the following:

```
kill -SIGHUP    pid
```

Alternatively, we can do both at once, as shown in this command:

```
kill -SIGHUP \
&& psql -t -c "select pid from pg_stat_activity limit 1";
```

This is only useful with a sensible WHERE clause.

Restarting the server quickly

Some of the database server parameters require you to stop and start the server again fully. Doing this as quickly as possible can be very important in some cases. The best time to do this is usually a quiet time, with lots of planning, testing, and forethought. Sometimes, not everything goes according to plan.

How to do it...

It's now become a habit for many recipes in this chapter to be presented in two forms, one with systemd and one without. This may look repetitive or boring, but it's unavoidable because the introduction of a new system does not automatically eliminate all existing alternatives, or migrate old installations to new ones.

Like before, the reader can find further `systemd` details, including details on service unit names, in the previous recipe, *Starting the database server manually*, of this chapter.

A PostgreSQL server managed by `systemd` can be restarted in the *fast* mode by issuing the following command:

```
sudo systemctl restart SERVICEUNIT
```

As before, change `SERVICEUNIT` to the appropriate service unit name, for example, `postgresql@10-main` for a PostgreSQL 10 cluster running in Debian or Ubuntu.

If `systemd` is not available, then you can use the following syntax:

```
pg_ctlcluster 10 main restart -m fast
```

The basic command to restart the server is the following:

```
pg_ctl -D datadir restart -m fast
```

A `restart` is just a stop followed by a start, so it sounds very simple. In many cases, it will be simple, but there are times when you'll need to restart the server while it is fairly busy. That's when we need to start performing some tricks to make that restart happen faster.

First, the stop performed needs to be a `fast stop`. If we do a default or `smart` stop, then the server will just wait for everyone to finish. If we do an immediate stop, then the server will crash, and we will need to crash-recover the data, which will be slower overall.

The running database server has a cache full of data blocks, many of them dirty. PostgreSQL is similar to other database systems in that it does a shutdown checkpoint before it closes. This means that the startup that follows will be quick and clean. The more work the checkpoint has to do, the longer it will take to shut down.

The actual shutdown will happen much faster if we issue a normal checkpoint first, as the shutdown checkpoint will have much less work to do. So, flush all the dirty shared buffers to disk with the following command, issued by a database superuser:

```
psql -c "CHECKPOINT"
```

The next consideration is that once we restart, the database cache will be empty again and will need to refresh itself. The larger the database cache, the longer it takes for the cache to get warm again, and 30 to 60 minutes is not uncommon before returning to full speed. So, what was a simple restart can actually have a large business impact if handled badly.

There's more...

There is an extension called `pgfincore` that implements a set of functions to manage PostgreSQL data pages in the operating system's file cache. One possible use is to preload some tables so that PostgreSQL will load them faster when requested. The general idea is that you can provide more detailed information for the operating system cache, which can therefore behave more efficiently.

The `pgfincore` extension is a stable project started in 2009. More details about it are available at `http://pgfoundry.org/projects/pgfincore`, including the source code. However, it should be noted that most distributions include a prebuilt `pgfincore` package, which makes installation easier.

There is also a contrib module called `pg_prewarm`, introduced in PostgreSQL 9.4, which addresses a similar problem. While there is some overlapping with `pgfincore`, the feature sets are not the same; for instance, `pgfincore` can operate on files not in the shared buffer cache, and can also preload full relations with only a few system calls, taking into account the existing cache; on the other hand, `pg_prewarm` can operate on the PostgreSQL shared buffer cache, and it also works on Windows.

Preventing new connections

In certain emergencies, you may need to lock down the server completely, or just prevent specific users from accessing the database. It's hard to foresee all the situations in which you might need to do this, so we will present a range of options.

How to do it...

Connections can be prevented in a number of ways, as follows:

- Pause and resume the session pool. See the *Setting up a connection pool* recipe later in this chapter on controlling connection pools.
- Stop the server! See the *Stopping the server safely and quickly* and *Stopping the server in an emergency* recipes, but this is not recommended.
- Restrict the connections for a specific database to zero, by setting the connection limit to zero:

```
ALTER DATABASE foo_db CONNECTION LIMIT 0;
```

- This will limit normal users from connecting to that database, though it will still allow superuser connections.

- Restrict the connections for a specific user to zero by setting the connection limit to zero (see the *Restricting users to only one session each* recipe):

    ```
    ALTER USER foo CONNECTION LIMIT 0;
    ```

- This will limit normal users from connecting to that database, but it will still allow connections if the user is a superuser, so luckily you cannot shut yourself out accidentally.
- Change the **host-based authentication (HBA)** file to refuse all incoming connections, and then reload the server:
    - Create a new file named `pg_hba_lockdown.conf`, and add the following two lines to the file. This puts in place rules that will completely lock down the server, including superusers. You should have no doubt that this is a serious and drastic action:

        ```
        # TYPE    DATABASE   USER            ADDRESS        METHOD
          local   all        all                            reject
          host    all        all             0.0.0.0/0      reject
        ```

    If you still want superuser access, then try something like the following:

    ```
    # TYPE    DATABASE   USER            ADDRESS        METHOD
      local   all        postgres                       peer
      local   all        all                            reject
      host    all        all             0.0.0.0/0      reject
    ```

    This will prevent connections to the database by any user except the `postgres` operating system user ID, which connects locally to any database. Be careful not to confuse the second and third columns—the second column is the database and the third column is the username. It's worth keeping the header line just for that reason. The `peer` method should be replaced by other authentication methods if a more complex configuration is in use.

- Copy the existing `pg_hba.conf` file to `pg_hba_access.conf` so that it can be replaced later, if required
- Copy `pg_hba_lockdown.conf` to `pg_hba.conf`
- Reload the server following the recipe earlier in this chapter

How it works...

The `pg_hba.conf` file is where we specify the host-based authentication rules. We do not specify the authentications themselves, but just specify which authentication mechanisms will be used. This is the top-level set of rules for PostgreSQL authentication. The rules are specified in a file and applied by the postmaster process when connections are attempted. To prevent denial-of-service attacks, the HBA rules never involve database access, so we do not know whether a user is a superuser or not. As a result, you can lock out all users, but note that you can always re-enable access by editing the file and reloading.

Restricting users to only one session each

If resources need to be closely controlled, you may wish to restrict users so that they can only connect to the server once, at most. The same technique can be used to prevent connections entirely for that user.

How to do it...

We can restrict users to only one connection using the following command:

```
postgres=# ALTER ROLE fred CONNECTION LIMIT 1;
ALTER ROLE
```

This will then cause any additional connections to receive the following error message:

```
FATAL: too many connections for role "fred".
```

You can eliminate this restriction by setting the value to -1.

It's possible to set the limit to zero or any positive integer. You can set this to a number other than `max_connections`, though it is up to you to make sense of that if you do.

Setting the value to zero will completely restrict normal connections. Note that even if you set the connection limit to zero for superusers, they will still be able to connect.

How it works...

The connection limit is applied during the session connection. Raising this limit will never affect any connected users. Lowering the limit doesn't have any effect either, unless they try to disconnect and reconnect.

So, if you lower the limit, you should immediately check to see whether there are more sessions connected than the new limit you just set. Otherwise, there may be some surprises in case there is a crash:

```
postgres=> SELECT rolconnlimit
            FROM pg_roles
            WHERE rolname = 'fred';
 rolconnlimit
--------------
            1
(1 row)
postgres=> SELECT count(*)
            FROM pg_stat_activity
            WHERE usename = 'fred';
 count
-------
     2
(1 row)
```

If you have more connected sessions than the new limit, you can ask users politely to disconnect, or apply the next recipe, *Pushing users off the system*.

Users can't raise or lower their own connection limit, just in case you are worried that they might be able to override this somehow.

Pushing users off the system

Sometimes, we may need to remove groups of users from the database server for various operational reasons. Here's how to do it.

How to do it...

You can terminate a user's session with the `pg_terminate_backend()` function included with PostgreSQL. That function takes the PID, or the process ID, of the user's session on the server. This process is known as the backend, and it is a different system process from the program that runs the client.

To find the PID of a user, we can look at the `pg_stat_activity` view. We can use it in a query, like this:

```
SELECT pg_terminate_backend(pid)
FROM pg_stat_activity
WHERE ...
```

There are a couple of things to note if you run this query. If the `WHERE` clause doesn't match any sessions, then you won't get any output from the query. Similarly, if it matches multiple rows, you will get a fairly useless result, that is, a list of Boolean `true` values. Unless you are careful enough to exclude your own session from the query, you will disconnect yourself! What's even funnier is that you'll disconnect yourself halfway through disconnecting the other users, as the query will run `pg_terminate_backend()` in the order in which sessions are returned from the outer query.

Therefore, I suggest a safer and more useful query that gives a useful response in all cases, which is as follows:

```
postgres=# SELECT count(pg_terminate_backend(pid))
FROM pg_stat_activity
WHERE usename NOT IN
(SELECT usename
 FROM pg_user
WHERE usesuper);
 count
--------
     1
```

This is assuming that superusers are performing administrative tasks.

Other good filters might be the following:

```
WHERE application_name = 'myappname'
WHERE wait_event_type IS NOT NULL AND wait_event_type != 'Activity'
WHERE state = 'idle in transaction'
WHERE state = 'idle'
```

How it works...

The `pg_terminate_backend()` function sends a signal directly to the operating system process for that session.

It's possible that the session may have closed by the time `pg_terminate_backend()` is named. As PID numbers are assigned by the operating system, it could even happen that you try to terminate a given session (call it "session A"), but you actually terminate another session (call it "session B").

Here is how it could happen. Suppose you take note of the PID of session A and decide to disconnect it. Before you actually issue `pg_terminate_backend()`, session A disconnects, and right after, a new session B is given exactly the same PID. So, when you terminate that PID, you hit session B instead.

On the one hand, you need to be careful. On the other hand, this case is really unlikely, and is only mentioned for completeness. For it to happen, *all* the following events must happen as well:

- One of the sessions you are trying to close must terminate independently in the very short interval between the moment `pg_stat_activity` is read and the moment `pg_terminate_backend()` is executed
- Another session on the same database server must be started in the even shorter interval between the old session closing and the execution of `pg_terminate_backend()`
- The new session must get exactly the same PID value as the old session, which is less than one chance in 32,000 on a 32-bit Linux machine

Nonetheless, probability theory is tricky, even for experts. Therefore, it's better to be aware that there is a tiny risk, especially if you use the query many times per day over a long period of time, in which case the probability of getting caught at least once builds up.

It's also possible that new sessions could start after we get the list of active sessions. There's no way to prevent this other than by following the *Preventing new connections* recipe.

Finally, remember that superusers can terminate any session, whilst a non-superuser can only terminate a session which belongs to the same user.

Deciding on a design for multitenancy

There are many reasons why we might want to split groups of tables or applications: security, resource control, convenience, and so on. Whatever the reason, we often need to separate groups of tables (I avoid saying the word *database*, just to avoid various kinds of confusion).

This topic is frequently referred to as **multitenancy**, though it is not a fully accepted term as of yet.

The purpose of this recipe is to discuss the options and lead to other, more detailed recipes.

How to do it...

If you want to run multiple physical databases on one server, then you have four main options, which are as follows:

- **Option 1**: Run multiple sets of tables in different schemas in one database of a PostgreSQL instance (covered in the *Using multiple schemas* recipe)
- **Option 2**: Run multiple databases in the same PostgreSQL instance (covered in the *Giving users their own private database* recipe)
- **Option 3**: Run multiple PostgreSQL instances on the same virtual/physical system (covered in the *Running multiple servers on one system* recipe)
- **Option 4**: Run separate PostgreSQL instances in separate virtual machines on the same physical server

Which is best? Well, that's certainly a question many people ask, and something on which many views exist. The answer lies in looking at the specific requirements, which are as follows:

- If our goal is the separation of physical resources, then *Option 3* or *Option 4* works best. Separate database servers can be easily assigned different disks, individual memory allocations can be assigned, and we can take the servers up or down without impacting the others.
- If our goal is security, then *Option 2* is sufficient.
- If our goal is merely the separation of tables for administrative clarity, then *Option 1* or *Option 2* can be useful.

Option 2 allows complete separation for security purposes. This does, however, prevent someone with privileges on both groups of tables from performing a join between those tables. So, if there is a possibility of future cross-analytics, it might be worth considering *Option 1*. However, it might also be argued that such analytics should be carried out on a separate data warehouse, not by co-locating production systems.

Option 3 has a difficulty in many of the PostgreSQL distributions: the default installation uses a single location for the database, making it a little harder to configure that option. Ubuntu/Debian handles that aspect particularly well, making it more attractive in that environment.

Option 4 can be applied using virtualization technology, but that is outside the scope of this book.

How it works...

I've seen people who use PostgreSQL with thousands of databases, but it is my opinion that the majority of people use only one database, such as `postgres` (or at least, only a few databases). I've also seen people with a great many schemas.

One thing you will find is that almost all admin GUI tools become significantly less useful if there are hundreds or thousands of items to display. In most cases, administration tools use a tree view, which doesn't cope gracefully with a large number of items.

Using multiple schemas

We can separate groups of tables into their own *namespaces*, referred to as *schemas* by PostgreSQL. In many ways, they can be thought of as being similar to directories, though that is not a precise description.

Getting ready

Make sure you've read the *Deciding on a design for multitenancy* recipe so that you're certain that this is the route you wish to take. Other options exist, and they may be preferable in some cases.

How to do it...

1. Schemas can be easily created using the following commands:

    ```
    CREATE SCHEMA finance;
    CREATE SCHEMA sales;
    ```

2. We can then create objects directly within those schemas using *fully qualified* names, like this:

    ```
    CREATE TABLE finance.month_end_snapshot (.....)
    ```

    The default schema in which an object is created is known as the current_schema. We can find out which is our current schema using the following query:

    ```
    postgres=# select current_schema;
    ```

    This returns an output like the following:

    ```
    current_schema
    -----------------
     public
    (1 row)
    ```

3. When we access database objects, we use the user-settable search_path parameter to identify the schemas to search for. The current_schema is the first schema in the search_path parameter. There is no separate parameter for the current_schema.

    So, if we want to let only a specific user look at certain sets of tables, we can modify their search_path parameter. This parameter can be set for each user so that the value will be set when they connect. The SQL queries for this would be something like the following:

    ```
    ALTER ROLE fiona SET search_path = 'finance';
    ALTER ROLE sally SET search_path = 'sales';
    ```

     The public schema is not mentioned on search_path, so it will not be searched. All tables created by fiona will go into the finance schema by default, whereas all tables created by sally will go into the sales schema by default.

4. The users for `finance` and `sales` will be able to see that the other schema exists and change `search_path` to use it, but we will be able to GRANT or REVOKE privileges so that they can neither create objects nor read data in other people's schemas:

```
REVOKE ALL ON SCHEMA finance FROM public;
GRANT ALL ON SCHEMA finance TO fiona;
REVOKE ALL ON SCHEMA sales FROM public;
GRANT ALL ON SCHEMA sales TO sally;
```

An alternate technique is to allow one user to create privileges on only one schema, but grant usage rights on all other schemas. We can set up that arrangement like this:

```
REVOKE ALL ON SCHEMA finance FROM public;
GRANT USAGE ON SCHEMA finance TO fiona;
GRANT CREATE ON SCHEMA finance TO fiona;
REVOKE ALL ON SCHEMA sales FROM public;
GRANT USAGE ON SCHEMA sales TO sally;
GRANT CREATE ON SCHEMA sales TO sally;
GRANT USAGE ON SCHEMA sales TO fiona;
GRANT USAGE ON SCHEMA finance TO sally
```

5. Note that you need to grant the privileges for usage on the schema, as well as specific rights on the objects in the schema. So, you will also need to issue specific grants for objects, as shown here:

```
GRANT SELECT ON month_end_snapshot TO public;
```

You can also set default privileges so that they are picked up when objects are created, using the following command:

```
ALTER DEFAULT PRIVILEGES FOR USER fiona IN SCHEMA finance
GRANT SELECT ON TABLES TO PUBLIC;
```

How it works...

Earlier, I said that schemas work like directories, or at least a little.

The PostgreSQL concept of `search_path` is similar to the concept of a PATH environment variable.

The PostgreSQL concept of the current schema is similar to the concept of the current working directory. There is no `cd` command to change the directory. The current working directory is changed by altering `search_path`.

A few other differences exist; for example, PostgreSQL schemas are not arranged in a hierarchy like filesystem directories.

Many people create a user of the same name as the schema to make this work in a way similar to other RDBMSes, such as Oracle.

> Both the `finance` and `sales` schemas exist within the same PostgreSQL database, and run on the same database server. They use a common buffer pool, and there are many global settings that tie the two schemas fairly close together.

Giving users their own private database

Separating data and users is a key part of administration. There will always be a need to give users a private, secure, or simply risk-free area (*sandpit*) to use the database. Here's how.

Getting ready

Again, make sure you've read the *Deciding on a design for multitenancy* recipe so that you're certain this is the route you wish to take. Other options exist, and they may be preferable in some cases.

How to do it...

1. We can create a database for a specific user with some ease. From the command line, as a superuser, these actions would be as follows:

```
postgres=# create user fred;
CREATE ROLE
postgres=# create database fred owner fred;
CREATE DATABASE
```

2. As the database owners, users have login privileges, so they can connect to any database by default. There is a command named ALTER DEFAULT PRIVILEGES, however, this does not currently apply to databases, tablespaces, or languages. The ALTER DEFAULT PRIVILEGES command also currently applies only to roles (that is, users) that already exist.

So, we need to revoke the privilege to connect to our new database from everybody except the designated user. There isn't a REVOKE ... FROM PUBLIC EXCEPT command. Therefore, we need to revoke everything and then just re-grant everything we need, all in one transaction, such as in the following:

```
postgres=# BEGIN;
BEGIN
postgres=# REVOKE connect ON DATABASE  fred FROM public;
REVOKE
postgres=# GRANT connect ON DATABASE fred TO fred;
GRANT
postgres=# COMMIT;
COMMIT
postgres=# create user bob;
CREATE ROLE
```

3. Then, try to connect as bob to the fred database:

```
os $ psql -U bob fred
psql: FATAL:  permission denied for database "fred"
DETAIL:  User does not have CONNECT privilege.
```

This is exactly what we wanted.

How it works...

If you didn't catch it before, PostgreSQL allows transactional DDL in most places, so either both of the REVOKE and GRANT commands in the preceding section work or neither works. This means that the fred user never loses the ability to connect to the database. Note that CREATE DATABASE cannot be performed as part of a transaction, though nothing serious happens as a result.

There's more...

Superusers can still connect to the new database, and there is no way to prevent them from doing so.

No other users can see the tables created in the new database, nor can they know the names of any of the objects.

The new database can be seen to exist by other users, and they can also see the name of the user who owns the database.

See also

- See Chapter 6, *Security*, for more details on these issues

Running multiple servers on one system

Running multiple PostgreSQL servers on one physical system is possible if it is convenient for your needs.

Getting ready

Once again, make sure you've read the *Deciding on a design for multitenancy* recipe so that you're certain this is the route you wish to take. Other options exist, and they may be preferable in some cases.

How to do it...

Core PostgreSQL easily allows multiple servers to run on the same system, but there are a few wrinkles to be aware of.

Some installer versions create a PostgreSQL data directory named data. It then gets a little difficult to have more than one data directory without using different directory structures and names.

Debian/Ubuntu packagers chose a layout specifically designed to allow multiple servers, potentially running with different software release levels. You might remember this from the *Locating the database server files* recipe in `Chapter 2`, *Exploring the Database*.

Starting from `/var/lib/postgresql`, which is the home directory of the Postgres user, there is a subdirectory for each major version, for example, `10` or `9.3`, inside which the individual data directories are placed. When installing PostgreSQL server packages, a data directory is created with the default name of `main`. Configuration files are separately placed in `/etc/postgresql/<version>/<name>`, and log files are created in `/var/log/postgresql/postgresql-<version>-<name>.log`.

Thus, not all files will be found in the `data` directory. As an example, let's create an additional `data` directory:

1. We start by running this command:

   `sudo -u postgres pg_createcluster 10 main2`

2. The new database server can then be started using the following command:

   `sudo -u postgres pg_ctlcluster 10 main2 start`

This is sufficient to create and start an additional database cluster in version `10`, named `main2`. The data and configuration files are stored inside the `/var/lib/postgresql/10/main2/` and `/etc/postgresql/10/main2/` directories respectively, giving the new database the next unused port number, for example `5433` if this is the second PostgreSQL server on that machine.

Local access to multiple PostgreSQL servers has been simplified as well. PostgreSQL client programs, such as `psql`, are wrapped by a special script that takes the cluster name as an additional parameter and automatically uses the corresponding port number. Hence, you don't really need the following command:

`psql --port 5433 -h /var/run/postgresql ...`

Instead, you can refer to the database server by name, as shown here:

`psql --cluster 10/main2 ...`

This has its advantages, especially if you wish (or need) to change the port in the future. I find this extremely convenient, and another reason is that it works with other utilities such as `pg_dump`, `pg_restore`, and so on.

With Red Hat systems, you will need to run `initdb` directly, selecting your directories carefully:

1. First, initialize your `data` directory with something like the following:

   sudo -u postgres initdb -D /var/lib/pgsql/datadir2

2. Then, modify the `port` parameter in the `postgresql.conf` file and start using the following command:

   sudo -u postgres pg_ctl -D /var/lib/pgsql/datadir2 start

   This will create an additional database server at the default server version, with files stored in `/var/lib/pgsql/datadir2`.

You can also set up the server with `chkconfig`, if your distribution supports it.

How it works...

PostgreSQL servers are controlled using `pg_ctl`. Everything else is a wrapper of some kind around this utility. The only constraints on running multiple versions of PostgreSQL come from file locations and naming conventions, assuming (of course) that you have enough resources such as disk space, memory, and so on. Everything else is straightforward. Having said that, the Debian/Ubuntu design is currently the only design that makes it actually easy to run multiple servers.

Setting up a connection pool

A connection pool is a term used for a collection of already connected sessions that can be used to reduce the overhead of connection and reconnection.

There are various ways by which connection pools can be provided, depending on the software stack in use. Probably, the best option is to look at the server-side connection pool software because that works for all connection types, not just within a single software stack.

Here, we're going to look at **PgBouncer**, which is designed as a very lightweight connection pool. The name comes from the idea that the pool can be paused and resumed to allow the server to be restarted, or *bounced*.

Getting ready

First of all, decide where you're going to store the PgBouncer parameter files, log files, and PID files. PgBouncer can manage more than one database server's connections at the same time, though that probably isn't wise for simple architectures. If you keep PgBouncer files associated with the database server, then it should be easy to manage.

How to do it...

Carry out the following steps to configure PgBouncer:

1. Create a `pgbouncer.ini` file, as follows:

```
;
; pgbouncer configuration example
;
[databases]
postgres = port=5432 dbname=postgres
[pgbouncer]

listen_addr = 127.0.0.1
listen_port = 6432
admin_users = postgres
;stats_users = monitoring userid
auth_type = any
; put these files somewhere sensible:
auth_file = users.txt
logfile = pgbouncer.log
pidfile = pgbouncer.pid

server_reset_query = DISCARD ALL;
; default values
pool_mode = session
default_pool_size = 20
log_pooler_errors = 0
```

2. Create a `users.txt` file. This must contain the minimum users mentioned in `admin_users` and `stats_users`. Its format is very simple: a collection of lines with a username and a password. Consider the following as an example:

```
"postgres"      ""
```

3. PgBouncer also supports MD5 authentication. To use that effectively, you need to copy the MD5 encrypted passwords from the database server into the `users.txt` file.

4. You may wish to create the `users.txt` file by directly copying the details from the server. This can be done by using the following `psql` script:

```
postgres=> \o users.txt
postgres=> \t
postgres=> SELECT '"'||rolname||'" "'||rolpassword||'"'
postgres-> FROM pg_authid;
postgres=> \q
```

5. Launch `pgbouncer`:

```
pgbouncer -d pgbouncer.ini
```

6. Test the connection; it should respond to `reload`:

```
psql -p 6432 -h 127.0.0.1 -U postgres pgbouncer -c "reload"
```

7. Finally, verify that PgBouncer's `max_client_conn` parameter does not exceed the `max_connections` parameter on PostgreSQL.

How it works...

PgBouncer is a great piece of software. Its feature set is very carefully defined to ensure that it is simple, robust, and very fast. PgBouncer is not multithreaded, so it runs in a single process, and thus, on a single CPU. It is very efficient, but very large data transfers will take more time and reduce concurrency, so create those data dumps using a direct connection.

PgBouncer provides connection pooling. If you set `pool_mode = transaction`, then PgBouncer will also provide connection concentration. This allows hundreds or even thousands of incoming connections to be managed, while only a few server connections are made.

As new connections, transactions, or statements arrive, the pool will increase in size up to the user-defined maximum values. Those connections will stay around for at most the `server_idle_timeout` value before the pool releases them.

PgBouncer also releases sessions every `server_lifetime`. This allows the server to free backends in rotation, to avoid issues with very long-lived session connections.

The earlier query that creates `users.txt` only includes database users that have a password. All other users will have a null `rolpassword` field, so the whole string evaluates to `NULL`, and the line is omitted from the password file. This is intentional; users without a password represent a security risk, unless they are closely guarded. An example of this is the `postgres` system user connecting from the same machine, which bypasses PgBouncer, and is used only for maintenance by responsible and trusted people.

It is possible to use an HBA file with the same syntax as `pg_hba.conf`. This allows for more flexibility enabling TLS encryption (which includes SSL) only for connections to remote servers, while using the more efficient peer authentication for local servers.

There's more...

Instead of retrieving passwords from the `userlist.txt` file, PgBouncer can retrieve them directly from PostgreSQL, using the optional `auth_user` and `auth_query` parameters. If `auth_user` is set, PgBouncer will connect to the database using that user and run `auth_query` every time it needs to retrieve the password of some user trying to login. The default value of `auth_query` is as follows:

```
SELECT usename, passwd FROM pg_shadow WHERE usename=$1
```

This default is just a minimal functioning example, which illustrates the idea of `auth_query`; however, it requires giving PgBouncer superuser access to PostgreSQL. Hence it is good practice to use the more sophisticated approach of creating a `SECURITY DEFINER` function which can retrieve username and password, possibly making some checks on the username to allow only applicative connections. This is a good restriction because database administration connections should not go through a connection pooler.

It's also possible to connect to PgBouncer itself to issue commands. This can be done interactively, as if you were entering `psql`, or it can be done using single commands or scripts.

To shut down PgBouncer, we can just type `SHUTDOWN` or enter a single command, as follows:

```
psql -p 6432 pgbouncer -c "SHUTDOWN"
```

You can also use the `RELOAD` command to make PgBouncer reload (which means reread) the parameter files, like we did to test that everything is working.

If you are using `pool_mode = transaction` or `pool_mode = statement`, then you can use the `PAUSE` command. This waits for the current transaction to complete before holding further work on that session. Thus, it allows you to perform DDL more easily or restart the server.

PgBouncer also allows you to use the `SUSPEND` mode, which waits for all server-side buffers to flush.

The `PAUSE` or `SUSPEND` modes should eventually be followed by `RESUME` when the work is done.

In addition to the PgBouncer control commands, there are many varieties of `SHOW` commands, as listed here:

`SHOW` **command**	**Result set.**
`SHOW STATS`	Traffic stats, total and average requests, query duration, bytes sent/received, and so on. See also `SHOW STATS_TOTALS` and `SHOW STATS_AVERAGES`.
`SHOW SERVERS`	One row per connection to the database server.
`SHOW CLIENTS`	One row per connection from the client.
`SHOW POOLS`	One row per pool of users.
`SHOW LISTS`	Gives a good summary of resource totals.
`SHOW USERS`	Lists users in `users.txt`.
`SHOW DATABASES`	Lists databases in `pgbouncer.ini`.
`SHOW CONFIG`	Lists configuration parameters.
`SHOW FDS`	Shows file descriptors.
`SHOW SOCKETS`	Shows file sockets.
`SHOW VERSION`	Shows the PgBouncer version.

Accessing multiple servers using the same host and port

We will now show you one simple, yet important, application of the previous recipe, *Setting up a connection pool*. In that recipe, you saw how to reuse connections with PgBouncer, and thus reduced the cost of disconnecting and reconnecting.

Here, we will demonstrate another way to use PgBouncer—one instance can connect to databases hosted by different database servers at the same time. The databases can be on separate hosts, and can even have different major versions of PostgreSQL!

Getting ready

Suppose we have three database servers, each one hosting one database. All you need to know beforehand is the connection string for each database server.

More complex arrangements are possible, but those are left to you as an exercise.

Before you try this recipe, you should have already gone through the previous recipe. These two recipes have many steps in common, but we've kept them separate because they have clearly different goals.

How to do it...

Each database is completely identified by its connection string. PgBouncer will read this information from its configuration file. The steps to be done are as follows:

1. All you need to do is to set up PgBouncer as you did in the previous recipe, replacing the databases section of pgbouncer.ini with the following:

```
[databases]
myfirstdb = port=5432 host=localhost
anotherdb = port=5437 host=localhost
sparedb = port=5435 host=localhost
```

2. Once you have started PgBouncer, you can connect to the first database:

```
$ psql -p 6432 -h 127.0.0.1 -U postgres myfirstdb
psql (9.6.1)
Type "help" for help.

myfirstdb=# show port;
port
------
5432
(1 row)

myfirstdb=# show server_version;
server_version
----------------
10.1
(1 row)
```

3. Now you can connect to the `anotherdb` database as if it were on the same server:

```
myfirstdb=# \c anotherdb
psql (10.1, server 9.6.5)
You are now connected to database "anotherdb" as user
"postgres".
```

4. The server's greeting message suggests that we have landed on a different server, so we check the port and version:

```
anotherdb=# show port;
 port
------
 5437
(1 row)

anotherdb=# show server_version;
server_version
----------------
   9.5.5
(1 row)
```

There's more...

The *Listing databases on this database server* recipe in `Chapter 2`, *Exploring the Database,* shows you how to list the available databases on the current database server, using either the \l meta-command or a couple of equivalent variations. Unfortunately, that doesn't work when using PgBouncer, for the very good reason that the current database server cannot know the answer.

We need to ask PgBouncer instead, and we do so by using the SHOW command when connected to the pgbouncer special administrative database:

```
myfirstdb=# \c pgbouncer
psql (10.1, server 1.8.1/bouncer)
You are now connected to database "pgbouncer" as user "postgres".
pgbouncer=# show databases;
    name    |    host    | port | database  | force_user | pool_size |
reserve_pool
------------+------------+------+-----------+------------+-----------+-------
--------
  anotherdb | localhost  | 5437 | anotherdb |            |        20 |
0
  myfirstdb | localhost  | 5432 | myfirstdb |            |        20 |
0
  pgbouncer |            | 6432 | pgbouncer | pgbouncer  |         2 |
0
  sparedb   | localhost  | 5435 | sparedb   |            |        20 |
0
(4 rows)
```

5
Tables and Data

This chapter covers a range of general recipes for your tables and for working with the data they contain. Many of the recipes contain general advice, though with specific PostgreSQL examples.

Some system administrators I've met work only on the external aspects of the database server. What's actually in the database is someone else's problem.

Look after your data, and your database will look after you. Keep your data clean, and your queries will run faster and cause fewer application errors. You'll also gain many friends in the business. Getting called in the middle of the night to fix data problems just isn't cool.

In this chapter, we will cover the following recipes:

- Choosing good names for database objects
- Handling objects with quoted names
- Enforcing the same name and definition for columns
- Identifying and removing duplicates
- Preventing duplicate rows
- Finding a unique key for a set of data
- Generating test data
- Randomly sampling data
- Loading data from a spreadsheet
- Loading data from flat files

Choosing good names for database objects

The easiest way to help other people understand a database is to ensure that all the objects have a meaningful name.

What makes a name meaningful?

Getting ready

Take some time to reflect on your database to make sure you have a clear view of its purpose and main use cases. This is because all the items in this recipe describe certain naming choices that you need to consider carefully in view of your specific circumstances.

How to do it...

Here are the points you should consider when naming your database objects:

1. The name follows the existing standards and practices in place. Inventing new standards isn't helpful; enforcing existing standards is.
2. The name clearly describes the role or table contents.
3. For major tables, use short, powerful names.
4. Name lookup tables after the table to which they are linked, such as `account_status`.
5. For associative or linked tables, use all the names of the major tables to which they relate, such as `customer_account`.
6. Make sure that the name is clearly distinct from other similar names.
7. Use consistent abbreviations.
8. Use underscores. Casing is not preserved by default, so using CamelCase names, such as `customerAccount`, as used in Java will just leave them unreadable. See the *Handling objects with quoted names* recipe.
9. Use consistent plurals, or don't use them at all.
10. Use suffixes to identify the content type or domain of an object. PostgreSQL already uses suffixes for automatically generated objects.
11. Think ahead. Don't pick names that refer to the current role or location of an object. So don't name a table `London` because it exists on a server in London. That server might get moved to Los Angeles.

12. Think ahead. Don't pick names that imply that an entity is the only one of its kind, such as a table named TEST, or a table named BACKUP_DATA. On the other hand, such information can be put in the database name, which is not normally used from within the database.
13. Avoid using acronyms in place of long table names. For example, money_allocation_decision is much better than MAD. This is especially important when PostgreSQL translates the names into lowercase, so the fact that it is an acronym may not be clear.
14. The table name is commonly used as the root for other objects that are created, so don't add the table suffix or similar ideas.

There's more...

The standard names for indexes in PostgreSQL are as follows:

```
{tablename}_{columnname(s)}_{suffix}
```

Here, the suffix is one of the following:

- pkey: This is used for a primary key constraint
- key: This is used for a unique constraint
- excl: This is used for an exclusion constraint
- idx: This is used for any other kind of index

The standard suffix for all sequences is seq.

Tables can have multiple triggers fired on each event. Triggers are executed in alphabetical order, so trigger names should have some kind of action name to differentiate them and to allow the order to be specified. It might seem a good idea to put INSERT, UPDATE, or DELETE in the trigger name, but that can get confusing if you have triggers that work on both UPDATE and DELETE, and all of this may end up as a mess.

The alphabetical order for trigger names always follows the C locale, regardless of your actual locale settings. If your trigger names use non-ASCII characters, then the actual ordering might not be what you expect.

The following example shows how the characters è and é are ordered in the C locale. You can change the locale and/or the list of strings to explore how different locales affect ordering:

```
WITH a(x) AS (
   VALUES ('è'),('é')
) SELECT *
FROM a
ORDER BY x
COLLATE "C";
```

A useful naming convention for triggers is as follows:

```
{tablename}_{actionname}_{after|before}_trig
```

If you do find yourself with strange or irregular object names, it will be a good idea to use the RENAME subcommands to get things tidy again. Here is an example of this:

```
ALTER INDEX badly_named_index RENAME TO tablename_status_idx;
```

Handling objects with quoted names

PostgreSQL object names can contain spaces and mixed case characters if we enclose the table names in double quotes. This can cause some difficulties, so this recipe is designed to help you if you get stuck with this kind of problem.

Case sensitivity issues can often be a problem for people more used to working with other database systems, such as MySQL, or for people who are facing the challenge of migrating code away from MySQL.

Getting ready

First, let's create a table that uses a quoted name with mixed cases, such as the following:

```
CREATE TABLE "MyCust"
AS
SELECT * FROM cust;
```

How to do it...

If we try to access these tables without the proper case, we get this error:

```
postgres=# SELECT count(*) FROM mycust;
ERROR:   relation "mycust" does not exist LINE 1: SELECT * FROM mycust;
```

So we write it in the correct case:

```
postgres=# SELECT count(*) FROM MyCust;
ERROR:   relation "mycust" does not exist
LINE 1: SELECT * FROM mycust;
```

This still fails, and in fact gives the same error.

If you want to access a table that was created with quoted names, then you must use quoted names, such as the following:

```
postgres=# SELECT count(*) FROM "MyCust";
```

The output is as follows:

```
 count
--------
     5
(1 row)
```

The usage rule is that if you create your tables using quoted names, then you need to write your SQL using quoted names. Alternatively, if your SQL uses quoted names, then you will probably have to create the tables using quoted names as well.

How it works...

PostgreSQL folds all names to lowercase when used within an SQL statement. Consider this command:

```
SELECT * FROM mycust;
```

This is exactly the same as the following command:

```
SELECT * FROM MYCUST;
```

It is also exactly the same as this command:

```
SELECT * FROM MyCust;
```

However, it is not the same thing as the following command:

```
SELECT * FROM "MyCust";
```

There's more...

If you are extracting values from a table that is being used to create object names, then you may need to use a handy function named `quote_ident()`. This function puts double quotes around a value if PostgreSQL requires that for an object name, as shown here:

```
postgres=# SELECT quote_ident('MyCust');
 quote_ident
--------------
 "MyCust"
(1 row)
postgres=# SELECT quote_ident('mycust');
 quote_ident
--------------
 mycust
(1 row)
```

The `quote_ident()` function may be especially useful if you are creating a table based on a variable name in a PL/pgSQL function, as follows:

```
EXECUTE 'CREATE TEMP TABLE ' || quote_ident(tablename) ||
                 '(col1           INTEGER);'
```

Enforcing the same name and definition for columns

Sensibly designed databases have smooth, easy-to-understand definitions. This allows all users to understand the meaning of data in each table. It is an important way of removing data quality issues.

Getting ready

If you want to run the queries in this recipe as a test, then use the following examples. Alternatively, you can just check for problems in your own database:

```
CREATE SCHEMA s1;
CREATE SCHEMA s2;
CREATE TABLE s1.X(col1 integer,col2 TEXT);
CREATE TABLE s2.X(col1 integer,col3 NUMERIC);
```

How to do it...

First, we will show you how to identify columns that are defined in different ways in different tables, using a query against the catalog. We use an information_schema query, as follows:

```
SELECT
 table_schema
,table_name
,column_name
,data_type
  ||coalesce(' ' || text(character_maximum_length), '')
  ||coalesce(' ' || text(numeric_precision), '')
  ||coalesce(',' || text(numeric_scale), '')
  as data_type
FROM information_schema.columns
WHERE column_name IN
 (SELECT
 column_name
FROM
 (SELECT
   column_name
  ,data_type
  ,character_maximum_length
  ,numeric_precision
  ,numeric_scale
  FROM information_schema.columns
  WHERE table_schema NOT IN ('information_schema', 'pg_catalog')
  GROUP BY
   column_name
  ,data_type
  ,character_maximum_length
  ,numeric_precision
  ,numeric_scale
 ) derived
```

```
GROUP BY column_name
HAVING count(*) > 1
)
AND table_schema NOT IN ('information_schema', 'pg_catalog')
ORDER BY column_name
;
```

The query gives an output as follows:

```
table_schema | table_name | column_name |    data_type
-------------+------------+-------------+-----------------
 s2          | x          | col1        | integer 32,0
 s1          | x          | col1        | smallint 16,0
(2 rows)
```

Comparing two given tables is more complex, as there are so many ways that the tables might be similar and yet a little different. The following query looks for all tables of the same name (and hence, in different schemas) that have different definitions:

```
WITH table_definition as
( SELECT table_schema
       , table_name
       , string_agg( column_name || ' ' || data_type
                   , ',' ORDER BY column_name
                   ) AS def
    FROM information_schema.columns
   WHERE table_schema NOT IN ( 'information_schema'
                             , 'pg_catalog')
   GROUP BY table_schema
          , table_name
)
   , unique_definition as
( SELECT DISTINCT table_name
       , def
    FROM table_definition
)
   , multiple_definition as
( SELECT table_name
    FROM unique_definition
   GROUP BY table_name
  HAVING count( * ) > 1
)
SELECT table_schema
     , table_name
     , column_name
     , data_type
  FROM information_schema.columns
 WHERE table_name
```

```
        IN ( SELECT table_name
                FROM multiple_definition )
    ORDER BY table_name
           , table_schema
           , column_name
  ;
```

Here is its output:

```
  table_schema | table_name | column_name | data_type
  -------------+------------+-------------+-----------
  s1           | x          | col1        | smallint
  s1           | x          | col2        | text
  s2           | x          | col1        | integer
  s2           | x          | col3        | numeric
  (4 rows)
```

How it works...

The definitions of tables are held within PostgreSQL, and can be accessed using the Information Schema catalog views.

There might be valid reasons why the definitions differ. We've excluded PostgreSQL's own internal tables because there are similar names between the two catalogs: PostgreSQL's implementation of the SQL Standard Information Schema and PostgreSQL's own internal pg_catalog schema.

Those queries are fairly complex. In fact, there is even more complexity that we could add to those queries to compare all sorts of things such as default values or constraints. The basic idea can be extended in various directions from here.

There's more...

We can compare the definitions of any two tables using the following function:

```
CREATE OR REPLACE FUNCTION diff_table_definition
(t1_schemaname text
,t1_tablename text
,t2_schemaname text
,t2_tablename text)
RETURNS TABLE
(t1_column_name text
,t1_data_type text
```

```
,t2_column_name text
,t2_data_type text
)
LANGUAGE SQL
as
$$
SELECT
 t1.column_name
,t1.data_type
,t2.column_name
,t2.data_type
FROM
  (SELECT column_name, data_type
   FROM information_schema.columns
   WHERE table_schema = $1
       AND table_name = $2
  ) t1
  FULL OUTER JOIN
  (SELECT column_name, data_type
   FROM information_schema.columns
   WHERE table_schema = $3
       AND table_name = $4
  ) t2
  ON t1.column_name = t2.column_name
  AND t1.data_type = t2.data_type
WHERE t1.column_name IS NULL OR t2.column_name IS NULL
;
$$;
```

Identifying and removing duplicates

Relational databases work on the idea that items of data can be uniquely identified. However hard we try, there will always be bad data arriving from somewhere. This recipe shows you how to diagnose that and clean up the mess.

Getting ready

Let's start by looking at our example table, cust. It has a duplicate value in customerid:

```
postgres=# SELECT * FROM cust;
 customerid | firstname | lastname | age
------------+-----------+----------+-----
          1 | Philip    | Marlowe  | 38
```

```
    2 | Richard  | Hannay   |  42
    3 | Holly    | Martins  |  25
    4 | Harry    | Palmer   |  36
    4 | Mark     | Hall     |  47
(5 rows)
```

Before you delete duplicate data, remember that sometimes it isn't the data that is wrong; it is your understanding of it. In those cases, it may be that you haven't properly normalized your database model, and that you need to include additional tables to account for the shape of the data. You might also find that duplicate rows are caused because of you deciding to exclude a column somewhere earlier in a data load process. Check twice, and delete once.

How to do it...

First, identify the duplicates using a query such as the following:

```
CREATE UNLOGGED TABLE dup_cust AS
SELECT *
FROM cust
WHERE customerid IN
  (SELECT customerid
   FROM cust
   GROUP BY customerid
   HAVING count(*) > 1);
```

We save the list of duplicates in a separate table because the query can be very slow if the table is big, so we don't want to run it more than once.

 An UNLOGGED table can be created with less I/O because it does not write WAL. It is better than a temporary table, because it doesn't disappear if you disconnect and then reconnect. The other side of the coin is that you lose its contents after a crash, but this is not too bad, because if you are using an unlogged table then you are telling PostgreSQL that you are able to recreate the contents of that table in the (unlikely) event of a crash.

The results can be used to identify the bad data manually, and you can resolve the problem by carrying out the following steps:

1. Merge the two rows to give the best picture of the data, if required. This might use values from one row to update the row you decide to keep, as shown here:

   ```
   UPDATE cust
   SET age = 47
   ```

```
                    WHERE customerid = 4
                    AND lastname = 'Palmer';
```

2. Delete the remaining undesirable rows:

```
            DELETE FROM cust
            WHERE customerid = 4
            AND lastname = 'Hall';
```

In some cases, the data rows might be completely identical, as in the new_cust table, which looks like the following:

```
postgres=# SELECT * FROM new_cust;
 customerid
------------
          1
          2
          3
          4
          4
(5 rows)
```

Unlike the preceding case, we can't tell the data apart at all, so we cannot remove duplicate rows without any manual process. SQL is a set-based language, so picking only one row out of a set is slightly harder than most people want it to be.

In these circumstances, we should use a slightly different procedure to detect duplicates. We will use a hidden column named ctid. It denotes the physical location of the row you are observing; for example, duplicate rows will all have different ctid values. The steps are as follows:

1. First, we start a transaction:

```
    BEGIN;
```

2. Then, we lock the table in order to prevent any INSERT, UPDATE, or DELETE operations, which would alter the list of duplicates and/or change their ctid values:

```
    LOCK TABLE new_cust IN SHARE ROW EXCLUSIVE MODE;
```

3. Now we locate all duplicates, keeping track of the minimum ctid value so that we don't delete that value:

```
        CREATE TEMPORARY TABLE dups_cust AS
        SELECT customerid, min(ctid) AS min_ctid
```

```
FROM new_cust
GROUP BY customerid
HAVING count(*) > 1;
```

4. Then we can delete each duplicate, with the exception of the duplicate with the minimum ctid value:

```
DELETE FROM new_cust
USING dups_cust
WHERE new_cust.customerid = dups_cust.customerid
AND new_cust.ctid != dups_cust.min_ctid;
```

5. We commit the transaction, which also releases the lock we previously took:

```
COMMIT;
```

6. Finally, we clean up the table after the deletions:

```
VACUUM new_cust;
```

How it works...

The first query works by grouping together the rows on the unique column and counting rows. Anything with more than one row must be caused by duplicate values. If we're looking for duplicates of more than one column (or even all columns), then we have to use an SQL of the following form:

```
SELECT *
FROM mytable
WHERE  (col1, col2, ... ,colN) IN
(SELECT col1, col2, ... ,colN
 FROM mytable
 GROUP BY  col1, col2, ... ,colN
 HAVING count(*) > 1);
```

Here, col1, col2, and so on until colN are the columns of the key.

Note that this type of query may need to sort the complete table on all the key columns. That will require sort space equal to the size of the table, so you'd better think first before running that SQL on very large tables. You'll probably benefit from a large work_mem setting for this query, probably 128 MB or more.

The `DELETE FROM ... USING` query that we showed only works with PostgreSQL because it uses the `ctid` value, which is the internal identifier of each row in the table. If you wanted to run that query against more than one column, as we did earlier in the chapter, you'd need to extend the queries in step 3, as follows:

```
SELECT customerid, customer_name, ..., min(ctid) AS min_ctid
FROM ...
GROUP BY customerid, customer_name, ...
...;
```

Then, extend the query in step 4, like this:

```
DELETE FROM new_cust
...
WHERE new_cust.customerid = dups_cust.customerid
AND new_cust.customer_name = dups_cust.customer_name
AND ...
AND new_cust.ctid != dups_cust.min_ctid;
```

The preceding query works by grouping together all the rows with similar values and then finding the row with the lowest `ctid` value. The lowest will mean closer to the start of the table, so duplicates will be removed from the far end of the table. When we run `VACUUM`, we may find that the table gets smaller, because we have removed rows from the far end.

The `BEGIN` and `COMMIT` commands wrap the `LOCK` and `DELETE` commands into a single transaction, which is required. Otherwise, the lock will be released immediately after being taken.

Another reason to use a single transaction is that we can always roll back if anything goes wrong, which is a good thing when we are removing data from a live table.

There's more...

Locking the table against changes for long periods may not be possible while we remove duplicate rows. That creates some fairly hard problems with large tables. In that case, we need to do things slightly differently:

1. Identify the rows to be deleted, and save them in a side table.
2. Build an index on the main table to speed up access to rows (maybe using the `CONCURRENTLY` keyword, as explained in the *Maintaining indexes* recipe in `Chapter 9`, *Regular Maintenance*).

3. Write a program that reads the rows from the side table in a loop, performing a series of smaller transactions.
4. Start a new transaction.
5. From the side table, read a set of rows that match.
6. Select those rows from the main table for updates, relying on the index to make those accesses happen quickly.
7. Delete the appropriate rows.
8. Commit, and then loop again.

The aforementioned program can't be written as a `database` function, as we can't have multiple transactions in a function. We need multiple transactions to ensure that we hold locks on each row for the shortest possible duration.

Preventing duplicate rows

Preventing duplicate rows is one of the most important aspects of data quality for any database. PostgreSQL offers some useful features in this area, extending beyond most relational databases.

Getting ready

Identify the set of columns that you wish to make unique. Does this apply to all rows, or just a subset of rows?

Let's start with our example table:

```
postgres=# SELECT * FROM newcust;
  customerid
-------------
           1
           2
           3
           4
(4 rows)
```

How to do it...

To prevent duplicate rows, we need to create a unique index that the database server can use to enforce uniqueness of a particular set of columns. We can do this in the following three similar ways for basic data types:

1. Create a primary key constraint on the set of columns. We are allowed only one of these per table. The values of the data rows must not be NULL, as we force the columns to be NOT NULL if they aren't already:

```
ALTER TABLE newcust ADD PRIMARY KEY(customerid);
```

2. This creates a new index named newcust_pkey.
3. Create a unique constraint on the set of columns. We can use these instead of/or with a primary key. There is no limit on the number of these per table. NULL values are allowed in the columns:

```
ALTER TABLE newcust ADD UNIQUE(customerid);
```

4. This creates a new index named newcust_customerid_key.
5. Create a unique index on the set of columns:

```
CREATE UNIQUE INDEX ON newcust (customerid);
```

6. This creates a new index named newcust_customerid_idx.

All of these techniques exclude duplicates, just with slightly different syntaxes. All of them create an index, but only the first two create a formal *constraint*. Each of these techniques can be used when we have a primary key or unique constraint that uses multiple columns.

The last method is important because it allows you to specify a WHERE clause on the index. This can be useful if you know that the column values are unique only in certain circumstances. The resulting index is then known as a partial index.

Suppose our data looked like this:

```
postgres=# SELECT * FROM partial_unique;
```

This gives the following output:

```
customerid | status | close_date
-----------+--------+------------
         1 | OPEN   |
         2 | OPEN   |
         3 | OPEN   |
         3 | CLOSED | 2010-03-22
(4 rows)
```

Then we can put a partial index on the table to enforce uniqueness of `customerid` only for `status = 'OPEN'`, like this:

```
CREATE UNIQUE INDEX ON partial_unique (customerid)
    WHERE status = 'OPEN';
```

If your uniqueness constraint needs to be enforced across more complex data types, then you may need to use a more advanced syntax. A few examples will help here.

Let's start with the simplest example: create a table of boxes and put sample data in it. This may be the first time you're seeing PostgreSQL's data type syntax, so bear with me:

```
postgres=# CREATE TABLE boxes (name text, position box);
CREATE TABLE
postgres=# INSERT INTO boxes VALUES
                          ('First', box '((0,0), (1,1))');
INSERT 0 1
postgres=# INSERT INTO boxes VALUES
                          ('Second', box '((2,0), (2,1))');
INSERT 0 1
postgres=# SELECT * FROM boxes;
  name   |   position
---------+--------------
 First   | (1,1),(0,0)
 Second  | (2,1),(2,0)
(2 rows)
```

We can see two boxes that neither touch nor overlap, based on their x and y coordinates.

To enforce uniqueness here, we want to create a constraint that will throw out any attempt to add a position that overlaps with any existing box. The overlap operator for the box data type is defined to be `&&`, so we use the following syntax to add the constraint:

```
postgres=# ALTER TABLE boxes ADD EXCLUDE USING gist
                          (position WITH &&);
NOTICE:  ALTER TABLE / ADD EXCLUDE will create implicit index
```

```
"boxes_position_excl" for table "boxes"
ALTER TABLE
```

This creates a new index named `boxes_position_excl`.

We can use the same syntax even with the basic data types. So a fourth way of performing our first example would be as follows:

```
ALTER TABLE newcust ADD EXCLUDE (customerid WITH =);
```

This creates a new index named `newcust_customerid_excl`.

How it works...

Uniqueness is always enforced by an index.

Each index is defined with a data type operator. When a new row is inserted or the set of column values is updated, we use the operator to search for existing values that conflict with the new data.

So, to enforce uniqueness, we need an index and a search operator defined on the data types of the columns. When we define normal UNIQUE constraints, we simply assume that we mean the equality operator (=) for the data type. The EXCLUDE syntax offers a richer syntax to allow us to express the same problem with different data types and operators.

There's more...

Unique and exclusion constraints can be marked as deferrable, meaning that the user can choose to postpone the check to the end of the transaction, a nice way to relax constraints without reducing data integrity. However, as of PostgreSQL 10, there are a few limitations that you should be aware of; the restrictions are as follows:

- You must define a constraint as DEFERRABLE when creating it, either in the CREATE TABLE statement or in the ALTER TABLE statement. You cannot change an existing constraint from NOT DEFERRABLE to DEFERRABLE, nor can you make it INITIALLY DEFERRED or INITIALLY IMMEDIATE. If you need to apply such a change on an existing constraint, you need to create a new constraint and then drop the old constraint. Optionally, you can rename the new constraint at the end.

- You cannot mix deferrable unique constraints with foreign keys. You will get an error message if you try to add a foreign key that refers to a unique constraint that is deferrable.

It's likely that these restrictions will be lifted in later releases.

Duplicate indexes

Note that PostgreSQL allows you to have multiple indexes with exactly the same definition. This is useful in some contexts, but can also be annoying if you accidentally create multiple indexes, as each index has its own cost in terms of writes. You can also have constraints defined using each of the aforementioned different ways. Each of these ways enforces essentially the same constraint, so take care.

Uniqueness without indexes

It's possible to have uniqueness in a set of columns without creating an index. That might be useful if all we want is to ensure uniqueness rather than allow index lookups.

To do that, you can do either of the following:

- Use a serial data type
- Manually alter the default to be the `nextval()` function of a sequence

Each of these will provide a unique value for use as a row's key. The uniqueness is not enforced, nor will there be a unique constraint defined. So there is still a possibility that someone might reset the sequence to an earlier value, which will eventually cause duplicate values.

Consider also that this method provides the unique value as a default, which is not used when the user specifies an explicit value. An example of this is as follows:

```
CREATE TABLE t(id serial, descr text);
INSERT INTO t(descr) VALUES ('First value');
INSERT INTO t(id,descr) VALUES (1,'Cheating!');
```

Finally, you might also wish to have mostly unique data, such as using the `clock_timestamp()` function to provide ascending times to microsecond resolution.

Real-world example – IP address range allocation

The problem is about assigning ranges of IP addresses, while at the same time ensuring that we don't allocate (or potentially allocate) the same addresses to different people or purposes. This is easy to do if we keep track of each individual IP address, and much harder to do if we want to deal solely with ranges of IP addresses.

Initially, you may think of designing the database as follows:

```
CREATE TABLE iprange
  (iprange_start inet
  ,iprange_stop inet
  ,owner text);
INSERT INTO iprange VALUES
        ('192.168.0.1','192.168.0.16', 'Simon');
INSERT INTO iprange VALUES
        ('192.168.0.17','192.168.0.24', 'Gianni');
INSERT INTO iprange VALUES
        ('192.168.0.32','192.168.0.64', 'Gabriele');
```

However, you'll realize that there is no way to create a unique constraint that enforces the model constraint of avoiding overlapping ranges. You could create an after trigger that checks existing values, but it's going to be messy.

PostgreSQL offers a better solution, based on *range types*. In fact, every data type that supports a btree operator class (that is, a way of ordering any two given values) can be used to create a range type. In our case, the SQL is as follows:

```
CREATE TYPE inetrange AS RANGE (SUBTYPE = inet);
```

This command creates a new data type that can represent ranges of inet values, that is, of IP addresses. Now we can use this new type when creating a table:

```
CREATE TABLE iprange2
(iprange inetrange
,owner text);
```

This new table can be populated as usual. We just have to group the extremes of each range into a single value, as follows:

```
INSERT INTO iprange2
VALUES ('[192.168.0.1,192.168.0.16]', 'Simon');
INSERT INTO iprange2
VALUES ('[192.168.0.17,192.168.0.24]', 'Gianni');
INSERT INTO iprange2
VALUES ('[192.168.0.32,192.168.0.64]', 'Gabriele');
```

Now we can create a *unique exclusion constraint* on the table, using the following syntax:

```
ALTER TABLE iprange2
  ADD EXCLUDE USING GIST (iprange WITH &&);
```

If we try to insert a range that overlaps with any of the existing ranges, then PostgreSQL will stop us:

```
INSERT INTO iprange2
VALUES ('[192.168.0.10,192.168.0.20]', 'Somebody else');
ERROR:  conflicting key value violates exclusion constraint
"iprange2_iprange_excl"
DETAIL:  Key (iprange)=([192.168.0.10,192.168.0.20]) conflicts with
existing key (iprange)=([192.168.0.1,192.168.0.16]).
```

Real-world example – range of time

In many databases, there will be historical data tables with data that has a START_DATE and an END_DATE value, or something similar. As in the previous example, we can solve this example elegantly with a range type. Actually, this example is even shorter—we don't need to create the range type since the most common cases are already built-in, and precisely—integers, decimal values, dates, and timestamps with and without a time zone.

Real-world example – prefix ranges

Another common problem involves assigning credit card numbers or telephone numbers. For example, with credit card numbers, we may need to perform additional checking for certain financial institutions, assuming that each institution is assigned a given range. In that case, we must check efficiently if a given credit card number belongs to a certain range.

The prefix range data type has been specifically designed to address this class of problems. This is available as a PostgreSQL extension at `http://github.com/dimitri/prefix`.

A warning—despite the similar name, prefix ranges cannot be implemented as range types.

Finding a unique key for a set of data

Sometimes, it can be difficult to find a unique set of key columns that describe the data.

Getting ready

Let's start with a small table, where the answer is fairly obvious:

```
postgres=# select * from ord;
```

We assume that the output is as follows:

```
 orderid | customerid |  amt
---------+------------+--------
   10677 |          2 |   5.50
    5019 |          3 | 277.44
    9748 |          3 |  77.17
(3 rows)
```

How to do it...

First of all, there's no need to do this through a brute-force approach. Checking all the permutations of columns to see which is unique might take you a long time.

Let's start by using PostgreSQL's own optimizer statistics. Run the following command on our table to get a fresh sample of statistics:

```
postgres=# analyze ord;
ANALYZE
```

This runs quickly, so we don't have to wait too long. Now we can examine the relevant columns of the statistics:

```
postgres=# SELECT attname, n_distinct
                  FROM pg_stats
                  WHERE schemaname = 'public'
                  AND tablename = 'ord';
```

```
  attname   | n_distinct
------------+------------
 orderid    |         -1
 customerid |  -0.666667
 amt        |         -1
(3 rows)
```

The preceding example was chosen because we have two potential answers. If the value of `n_distinct` is -1, then the column is thought to be unique within the sample of rows examined.

We would then need to use our judgment to decide whether one or both of these columns are unique by chance, or as part of the design of the database that created them.

It's possible that there is no single column that uniquely identifies the rows. Multiple column keys are fairly common. If none of the columns were unique, then we should start looking for unique keys that are combinations of the most unique columns. The following query shows a frequency distribution for the table such that a value occurs twice in one case, and another value occurs only once:

```
postgres=# SELECT num_of_values, count(*)
              FROM (SELECT customerid, count(*) AS num_of_values
                      FROM ord
                      GROUP BY customerid) s
            GROUP BY num_of_values
            ORDER BY count(*);
 num_of_values | count
---------------+-------
             2 |     1
             1 |     1
(2 rows)
```

We can change the query to include multiple columns, like this:

```
SELECT num_of_values, count(*)
FROM (SELECT    customerid, orderid, amt
              ,count(*) AS num_of_values
              FROM ord
              GROUP BY customerid, orderid, amt
              ) s
GROUP BY num_of_values
ORDER BY count(*);
```

This query will result in only one row once we find a set of columns that is unique.

As we get closer to finding the key, we will see that the distribution gets tighter and tighter.

So, the procedure is as follows:

1. Choose one column to start with.
2. Compute the corresponding frequency distribution.
3. If the outcome is multiple rows, then add one more column and repeat from step 2. Otherwise, it means you have found a set of columns satisfying a uniqueness constraint.

Now you must verify that the set of columns is minimal; for example, check whether it is possible to remove one or more columns without violating the unique constraint. This can be done using the frequency distribution as a test. Precisely, do the following:

1. Test each column by computing the frequency distribution on all the other columns.
2. If the frequency distribution has one row, then the column is not needed in the uniqueness constraint. Remove it from the set of columns and repeat from step *1*. Otherwise, you have found a minimal set of columns, which is also called a key for that table.

How it works...

Finding a unique key is possible for a program, but in most cases, a human can do this much faster by looking at things such as column names, foreign keys, or business understanding to reduce the number of searches required by the brute-force approach.

The ANALYZE command works by taking a sample of the table data, and then performing a statistical analysis of the results. The n_distinct value has two different meanings, depending on its sign: if positive, it is the estimate of the number of distinct values for the column; if negative, it is the estimate of the density of such distinct values, with the sign changed. For example, n_distinct = -0.2 means that a table of one million rows is expected to have 200,000 distinct values, while n_distinct = 5 means that we expect just five distinct values.

Generating test data

DBAs frequently need to generate test data for a variety of reasons, whether it's for setting up a test database or just for generating a test case for an SQL performance issue.

How to do it...

To create a table of test data, we need the following:

- Some rows
- Some columns
- Some order

The steps are as follows:

1. First, generate a lot of rows of data. We use something named a `set-returning` function. You can write your own, though PostgreSQL includes a couple of very useful ones.

2. You can generate a sequence of rows using a query like the following:

```
postgres=# SELECT * FROM generate_series(1,5);
 generate_series
-----------------
               1
               2
               3
               4
               5
(5 rows)
```

3. Alternatively, you can generate a list of dates, like this:

```
postgres=# SELECT date(t)
FROM generate_series(now(),
  now() + '1 week', '1 day') AS f(t);
     date
------------
 2018-04-24
 2018-04-25
 2018-04-26
 2018-04-27
 2018-04-28
 2018-04-29
 2018-04-30
 2018-05-01
(8 rows)
```

4. Then we want to generate a value for each column in the `test` table. We can break that down into a series of functions, using the following examples as a guide:

   - Either of these functions can be used to generate both rows and reasonable primary key values for them
   - For a random `integer` value, this is the function:

   ```
   (random()*(2*10^9))::integer
   ```

- For a random `bigint` value, the function is as follows:

```
(random()*(9*10^18))::bigint
```

5. For random `numeric` data, the function is the following:

```
(random()*100.)::numeric(5,2)
```

  - For a random-length string, up to a maximum length, this is the function:

```
repeat('1',(random()*40)::integer)
```

  - For a random-length substring, the function is as follows:

```
substr('abcdefghijklmnopqrstuvwxyz',1,
(random()*25)::integer)
```

  - Here is the function for a random string from a list of strings:

```
(ARRAY['one','two','three'])[0.5+random()*3]
```

6. Finally, we can put both techniques together to generate our table:

```
postgres=# SELECT key
                        , (random()*100.)::numeric(4,2)
                        , repeat('1', (random()*25)::integer)
FROM generate_series(1,10) AS f(key);
 key | numeric |            repeat
-----+---------+------------------------------
   1 |   83.05 | 1111
   2 |    5.28 | 11111111111111
   3 |   41.85 | 111111111111111111111111
   4 |   41.70 | 11111111111111111
   5 |   53.31 | 1
   6 |   10.09 | 111111111111111
   7 |   68.08 | 111
   8 |   19.42 | 111111111111111111
   9 |   87.03 | 11111111111111111111111
  10 |   70.64 | 11111111111111111
(10 rows)
```

7. Alternatively, we can use random ordering:

```
postgres=# SELECT key
                        , (random()*100.)::numeric(4,2)
                        , repeat('1', (random()*25)::integer)
```

```
                            FROM generate_series(1,10) AS f(key)
                            ORDER BY random() * 1.0;
     key | numeric |           repeat
    -----+---------+------------------------
       4 |   86.09 | 1111
      10 |   28.30 | 11111111
       2 |   64.09 | 111111
       8 |   91.59 | 111111111111111
       5 |   64.05 | 11111111
       3 |   75.22 | 1111111111111111
       6 |   39.02 | 1111
       7 |   20.43 | 1111111
       1 |   42.91 | 1111111111111111111
       9 |   88.64 | 1111111111111111111111
    (10 rows)
```

How it works...

To set returning functions, literally return a set of rows. That allows them to be used in either the FROM clause, as if they were a table, or the SELECT clause. The generate_series() set of functions returns either dates or integers, depending on the data types of the input parameters you use.

The :: operator is used to cast between data types. The *random string from a list of strings* example uses PostgreSQL arrays. You can create an array using the ARRAY constructor syntax, and then use an integer to reference one element in the array. In our case, we used a random subscript.

There's more...

There are also some commercial tools used to generate application-specific test data for PostgreSQL. They are available at http://www.sqlmanager.net/products/postgresql/datagenerator and http://www.datanamic.com/datagenerator/index.html.

The key features for any data generator are as follows:

- The ability to generate data in the right format for custom data types
- The ability to add data to multiple tables, while respecting foreign key constraints between tables
- The ability to add data to non-uniform distributions

The tools and tricks shown here are cool and clever, though there are some problems hiding here as well. Real data has so many strange things in it that it can be very hard to simulate. One of the most difficult things is generating data that follows realistic distributions. For example, if we had to generate data for people's heights, then we'd want to generate data to follow a normal distribution. If we were generating customer bank balances, we'd want to use a Zipf distribution, or for the number of reported insurance claims, perhaps a Poisson distribution (or perhaps not). Replicating the real quirks in data can take some time.

Finally, note that casting a float into an integer rounds it to the nearest integer, so the distribution of integers is not uniform on each extreme. For instance, the probability of `(random()*10)::int` being 0 is just 5%, as is its probability of being 10, while each integer between 1 and 9 occurs with a probability of 10%. This is why we put 0.5 in the last example, which is simpler than using the `floor()` function.

See also

- You can use existing data to generate test databases using sampling. That's the subject of our next recipe, *Randomly sampling data*.

Randomly sampling data

DBAs may be asked to set up a test server and populate it with test data. Often, that server will be old hardware, possibly with smaller disk sizes. So, the subject of data sampling raises its head.

The purpose of sampling is to reduce the size of the dataset and improve the speed of later analysis. Some statisticians are so used to the idea of sampling that they may not even question whether its use is valid or it can cause further complications.

The SQL standard way to perform sampling is by adding the `TABLESAMPLE` clause to the `SELECT` statement.

How to do it...

In this section, we will take a random sample of a given collection of data (for example, a given table). First, you should realize that there isn't a simple tool to slice off a sample of your database. It would be neat if there were, but there isn't. You'll need to read all of this to understand why:

1. We first consider using SQL to derive a sample. Random sampling is actually very simple because we can use the TABLESAMPLE clause. Consider the following example:

```
postgres=# SELECT count(*) FROM mybigtable;
 count
-------
 10000
(1 row)
postgres=# SELECT count(*) FROM mybigtable
                         TABLESAMPLE BERNOULLI(1);
 count
-------
   106
(1 row)
postgres=# SELECT count(*) FROM mybigtable
                         TABLESAMPLE BERNOULLI(1);
 count
-------
    99
(1 row)
```

2. Here the TABLESAMPLE clause applies to mybigtable, and tells SELECT to consider only a random sample, while the BERNOULLI keyword denotes the sampling method used, and the number 1 between parentheses represents the percentage of rows that we want to consider in the sample, that is, the 1%. Quite easy!

3. Now we need to get the sampled data out of the database, which is tricky for a few reasons. Firstly, there is no option to specify a WHERE clause for pg_dump. Secondly, if you create a view that contains the WHERE clause, pg_dump dumps only the view definition, not the view itself.

4. You can use pg_dump to dump all databases, apart from a set of tables, so you can produce a sampled dump like this:

```
pg_dump --exclude-table=mybigtable > db.dmp
pg_dump --table=mybigtable --schema-only > mybigtable.schema
psql -c '\copy (SELECT * FROM mybigtable
```

```
                      TABLESAMPLE BERNOULLI (1)) to
mybigtable.dat'
```

5. Then reload onto a separate database using the following commands:

```
psql -f db.dmp
psql -f mybigtable.schema
psql -c '\copy mybigtable from mybigtable.dat'
```

Overall, my advice is to use sampling with caution. In general, it is easier to apply it to a few very large tables only, in view of both the mathematical issues surrounding the sample design and the difficulty of extracting the data.

How it works...

The extract mechanism shows off the capabilities of the PostgreSQL command-line tools, psql and pg_dump, as pg_dump allows you to include or exclude objects and dump the entire table (or only its schema), whereas psql allows you to dump out the result of an arbitrary query into a file.

The BERNOULLI clause specifies the sampling method, that is, PostgreSQL takes the random sample by performing a full table scan, and then selecting each row with the required probability, here 1%.

Another built-in sampling method is SYSTEM, which reads a random sample of table pages, and then includes all rows in these pages; this is generally faster, given that samples are normally quite smaller than the original, but the randomness of the selection is affected by how rows are physically arranged on disk, which makes it suitable for some applications only.

Here is an example that shows what the problem is. Suppose you take a dictionary, rip out a few pages, and then select all the words in them; you will get a random sample composed by a few *clusters* of consecutive words. This is good enough if you want to estimate the average length of a word, but not for analyzing the average number of words for each initial letter. The reason is that the initial letter of a word is strongly correlated with how the words are arranged in pages, while the length of a word is not.

We haven't discussed how random the TABLESAMPLE clause is. This isn't the right place for such details; however, it is reasonably simple to extend PostgreSQL with extra functions or sampling methods, so if you prefer another mechanism, you can find an external random number generator, and create a new sampling method for the TABLESAMPLE clause. PostgreSQL includes two extra sampling methods, tsm_system_rows and tsm_system_time, as contrib extensions: they are excellent examples to start from.

The tsm_system_rows method does not work with percentages; instead, the numeric argument is interpreted as the number of rows to be returned. Similarly, the tsm_system_time method will regard its argument as the number of milliseconds to spend retrieving the random sample.

These two methods include the word system in their name because they use block-level sampling, like the built-in SYSTEM sampling method; hence, their randomness is affected by the same *clustering* limitation as described previously.

The sampling method shown earlier is a simple random sampling technique that has an **equal probability of selection (EPS)** design.

EPS samples are considered useful because the variance of the sample attributes is similar to the variance of the original dataset. However, bear in mind that this is useful only if you are considering variances.

Simple random sampling can make the eventual sample biased towards more frequently occurring data. For example, if you have a 1% sample of data on which some kinds of data occur only 0.001% of the time, you may end up with a dataset that doesn't have any of that outlying data.

What you might wish to do is to pre-cluster your data and take different samples from each group to ensure that you have a sampled dataset that includes many more outlying attributes. A simple method might be to do the following:

- Include 1% of all normal data
- Include 25% of outlying data

Note that if you do this, then it is no longer an EPS sample design.

Undoubtedly, there are statisticians who will be in apoplexy after reading this. You're welcome to use the facilities of the SQL language to create a more accurate sample. Just make sure that you know what you're doing and/or check out some good statistical literature, websites, or textbooks.

Loading data from a spreadsheet

Spreadsheets are the most obvious starting place for most data stores. Studies within a range of businesses consistently show that more than 50% of the smaller data stores are held in spreadsheets or small desktop databases. Loading data from these sources is a frequent and important task for many DBAs.

Getting ready

Spreadsheets combine data, presentation, and programs all into one file. That's perfect for power users wanting to work quickly. Like other relational databases, PostgreSQL is mainly concerned with the lowest level of data, so extracting just the data from these spreadsheets can present some challenges.

We can easily handle spreadsheet data if that spreadsheet's layout follows a very specific form, as follows:

- Each spreadsheet column becomes one column in one table
- Each row of the spreadsheet becomes one row in one table
- Data is only in one worksheet of the spreadsheet
- Optionally, the first row is a list of column descriptions/titles

This is a very simple layout, and more often there will be other things in the spreadsheet, such as titles, comments, constants for use in formulas, summary lines, macros, images, and so on. If you're in this position, the best thing to do is to create a new worksheet within the spreadsheet in the pristine form described earlier, and then set up cross-worksheet references to bring in the data. An example of a cross-worksheet reference would be =Sheet2.A1. You'll need a separate worksheet for each set of data that will become one table on PostgreSQL. You can load multiple worksheets into one table, however.

Some spreadsheet users will say that all of this is unnecessary, and is evidence of the problems of databases. The real spreadsheet gurus do actually advocate this type of layout—data in one worksheet and calculation and presentation in other worksheets. So it is actually best practice to design spreadsheets in this way; however, we must work with the world the way it is.

How to do it...

Here, we will show you an example where data in a spreadsheet is loaded into a database:

1. If your spreadsheet data is neatly laid out in a single worksheet, as shown in the following screenshot, then you can go to **File** | **Save As** and then select **CSV** as the file type to be saved:

2. This will export the current worksheet to a file, like the following:

```
"Key","Value"
1,"c"
2,"d"
```

3. We can then load it into an existing PostgreSQL table, using the following `psql` command:

```
postgres=# \COPY sample FROM sample.csv CSV HEADER
postgres=# SELECT * FROM sample;
 key | value
-----+-------
   1 | c
   2 | d
```

4. Alternatively, from the command line, this would be as follows:

```
psql -c '\COPY sample FROM sample.csv CSV HEADER'
```

5. Note that the file can include a full file path if the data is in a different directory. The `psql` `\COPY` command transfers data from the client system where you run the command through to the database server, so the file is on the client.

6. If you are submitting SQL through another type of connection, then you should use the following SQL statement:

```
COPY sample FROM '/mydatafiledirectory/sample.csv' CSV HEADER;
```

Note that the preceding SQL statement runs on the database server and can only be executed by a super user. So you need to ensure that the server process is allowed to read that file, then transfer the data yourself to the server, and finally load the file. The COPY statement shown in the preceding SQL statement uses an absolute path to identify data files, which is required.

The COPY (or \COPY) command does not create the table for you; that must be done beforehand. Note also that the HEADER option does nothing but ignore the first line of the input file, so the names of the columns from the .csv file don't need to match those of the Postgres table. If it hasn't occurred to you yet, this is also a problem. If you say HEADER and the file does not have a header line, then all it does is ignore the first data row. Unfortunately, there's no way for PostgreSQL to tell whether the first line of the file is truly a header or not. Be careful!

There isn't a standard tool to load data directly from the spreadsheet to the database. It's fairly simple to write a spreadsheet macro to automate the aforementioned tasks, but that's not a topic for this book.

How it works...

The \COPY command executes a COPY SQL statement, so the two methods described earlier are very similar. There's more to be said about COPY, so we'll cover that in the next recipe.

There's more...

There are many data extract and loading tools available out there, some cheap and some expensive. Remember that the hardest part of loading data from any spreadsheet is separating the data from all the other things it contains. I've not yet seen a tool that can help with that.

Loading data from flat files

Loading data into your database is one of the most important tasks. You need to do this accurately and quickly. Here's how.

Getting ready

You'll need a copy of `pgloader`, which is commonly available in all main software distribution.

At the time of writing, the current stable version is 3.4.1. The 3.x series is a major rewrite, with many additional features, and the 2.x series is now considered obsolete.

How to do it...

PostgreSQL includes a command named `COPY` that provides the basic data load/unload mechanism. The `COPY` command doesn't do enough when loading data, so let's skip the basic command and go straight to `pgloader`.

To load data, we need to understand our requirements, so let's break this down into a step-by-step process, as follows:

1. Identify the data files and where they are located. Make sure that `pgloader` is installed at the location of the files.
2. Identify the table into which you are loading, ensure that you have the permissions to load, and check the available space.Work out the file type (examples include fixed-size fields, delimited text, and CSV) and check the encoding.
3. Specify the mapping between columns in the file and columns on the table being loaded. Make sure you know which columns in the file are not needed—`pgloader` allows you to include only the columns you want. Identify any columns in the table for which you don't have data. Do you need them to have a default value on the table, or does `pgloader` need to generate values for those columns through functions or constants?
4. Specify any transformations that need to take place. The most common issue is date formats, though possibly there may be other issues.
5. Write the `pgloader` script.

6. `pgloader` will create a log file to record whether the load has succeeded or failed, and another file to store rejected rows. You need a directory with sufficient disk space if you expect them to be large. Their size is roughly proportional to the number of failing rows.

7. Finally, consider what settings you need for performance options. This is definitely last, as fiddling with things earlier can lead to confusion when you're still making the load work correctly.

8. You must use a script to execute `pgloader`. This is not a restriction; actually it is more like best practice, because it makes it much easier to iterate towards something that works. Loads never work the first time, except in the movies!

Let's look at a typical example from pgloader's documentation—the `example.load` file:

```
LOAD CSV
    FROM 'GeoLiteCity-Blocks.csv' WITH ENCODING iso-646-us
        HAVING FIELDS
        (
            startIpNum, endIpNum, locId
        )
    INTO postgresql://user@localhost:54393/dbname?geolite.blocks
        TARGET COLUMNS
        (
            iprange ip4r using (ip-range startIpNum endIpNum),
            locId
        )
    WITH truncate,
        skip header = 2,
        fields optionally enclosed by '"',
        fields escaped by backslash-quote,
        fields terminated by '\t'
      SET work_mem to '32 MB', maintenance_work_mem to '64 MB';
```

We can use the `load` script like this:

```
pgloader --summary summary.log example.load
```

How it works...

pgloader copes gracefully with errors. The COPY command loads all rows in a single transaction, so only a single error is enough to abort the load. pgloader breaks down an input file into reasonably sized chunks, and loads them piece by piece. If some rows in a chunk cause errors, then pgloader will split it iteratively until it loads all the good rows and skips all the bad rows, which are then saved in a separate "rejects" file for later inspection. This behavior is very convenient if you have large data files with a small percentage of bad rows; for instance, you can edit the rejects, fix them, and finally, load them with another pgloader run.

Versions 2.x of pgloader were written in Python and connected to PostgreSQL through the standard Python client interface. Version 3.x is written in Common Lisp. Yes, pgloader is less efficient than loading data files using a COPY command, but running a COPY command has many more restrictions: the file has to be in the right place on the server, has to be in the right format, and must be unlikely to throw errors on loading. pgloader has additional overhead, but it also has the ability to load data using multiple parallel threads, so it can be faster to use as well. pgloader's ability to reformat the data via user-defined functions is often essential; straight COPY is just too simple.

pgloader also allows loading from fixed-width files, which COPY does not.

There's more...

If you need to reload the table completely from scratch, then specify the -WITH TRUNCATE clause in the pgloader script.

There are also options to specify SQL to be executed before and after loading the data. For instance, you may have a script that creates the empty tables before, or you can add constraints after, or both.

After loading, if we have load errors, then there will be some junk loaded into the PostgreSQL tables. It is not junk that you can see, or that gives any semantic errors, but think of it more like fragmentation. You should think about whether you need to add a VACUUM command after the data load, though this will make the load take possibly much longer.

We need to be careful to avoid loading data twice. The only easy way of doing that is to make sure that there is at least one unique index defined on every table that you load. The load should then fail very quickly.

String handling can often be difficult, because of the presence of formatting or non-printable characters. The default setting for PostgreSQL is to have a parameter named `standard_conforming_strings` set to `off`, which means that backslashes will be assumed to be escape characters. Put another way, by default, the `\n` string means line feed, which can cause data to appear truncated. You'll need to turn `standard_conforming_strings` to `on`, or you'll need to specify an escape character in the load-parameter file.

If you are reloading data that has been unloaded from PostgreSQL, then you may want to use the `pg_restore` utility instead. The `pg_restore` utility has an option to reload data in parallel, `-j number_of_threads`, though this is only possible if the dump was produced using the custom `pg_dump` format. Refer to the recipes in Chapter 11, *Backup and Recovery*, for more details. This can be useful for reloading dumps, though it lacks almost all of the other `pgloader` features discussed here.

If you need to use rows from a read-only text file that does not have errors, then you may consider using the `file_fdw` contrib module. The short story is that it lets you create a *virtual* table that will parse the text file every time it is scanned. This is different from filling a table once and for all, either with `COPY` or `pgloader`; therefore, it covers a different use case. For example, think about an external data source that is maintained by a third party and needs to be shared across different databases.

6
Security

n this chapter, we will cover the following recipes:

- The PostgreSQL superuser
- Revoking user access to a table
- Granting user access to a table
- Granting user access to specific columns
- Granting user access to specific rows
- Creating a new user
- Temporarily preventing a user from connecting
- Removing a user without dropping their data
- Checking whether all users have a secure password
- Giving limited superuser powers to specific users
- Auditing database access
- Always knowing which user is logged in
- Integrating with LDAP
- Connecting using SSL
- Using SSL certificates to authenticate
- Mapping external usernames to database roles
- Encrypting sensitive data

Introduction

First set up access rules into the database server. PostgreSQL allows you to control access based upon the host that is trying to connect, using the pg_hba.conf file. You can specify SSL connections if needed, or skip that if the network is secure. You can specify the use of SCRAM authentication using 256 bit keys, as well as many other mechanisms.

Next set up the role and privileges for accessing your data. Databases are mostly used to store data with several restrictions on how it can be used. Some records or tables can only be seen by certain users, and even for those tables that are visible to everyone, there can be restrictions on who can insert new data or change the existing data. All of this is managed by a privilege system, where users are granted different privileges for different tables or other database objects, such as schemas or functions.

It is good practice not to grant these privileges directly to users, but to use an intermediate role to collect a set of privileges. Then, instead of granting all the same privileges to the actual user, this entire role is granted to users needing these privileges. For example, a clerk role may have rights to both insert data and update existing data in the `user_account` table, but may have rights to only insert data in the `transaction_history` table.

Fine grained control over access can be managed using the **Row Level Security** (**RLS**) feature, which allows a defined Policy on selected tables.

Another aspect of database security concerns the management of this access to the database; making sure that only the right people can access the database, and that one user can't see what other users are doing (unless you are an administrator or auditor); and deciding whether users can or cannot grant forward the roles granted to them.

You should consider auditing the actions of administrators using `pgaudit`.

Typical user role

The minimal production database setup contains at least two types of users, namely administrators and end users, where administrators can do everything (they are superusers), and end users can only do very little, usually just modify the data in only a few tables and read from a few more.

It is not a good idea to let ordinary users create or change database object definitions, meaning that they should not have the `CREATE` privilege on any schema, including `PUBLIC`.

There can be more roles for different types of end users, such as analysts, who can only select from a single table or view, or some maintenance script "users" who see no data at all and just have the ability to execute a few functions.

Alternatively, there can also be a manager role, which can grant and revoke roles for other users but is not supposed to do anything else.

The PostgreSQL superuser

In this recipe, you will learn how to grant right to a user to become a superuser.

A PostgreSQL **superuser** is a user that can do anything in the database, regardless of what privileges it has been granted. Many cloud databases do not allow this level of privilege to be granted. It is normal to place strict controls on users of this type.

How to do it...

1. A user becomes a superuser when it is created with the SUPERUSER attribute set:

       CREATE USER username SUPERUSER;

2. A user can be deprived of its superuser status by removing the SUPERUSER attribute, using this command:

       ALTER USER username NOSUPERUSER;

3. A user can be restored to superuser status later, using the following command:

       ALTER USER username SUPERUSER;

4. When neither SUPERUSER nor NOSUPERUSER is given in the CREATE USER command, then the default is to create a user who is not a superuser.

How it works...

Rights to some operations in PostgreSQL are not available by default and need to be granted specifically to users. They must be performed by a special user who has this special attribute set. The preceding commands set or reset this attribute for the user.

There's more...

The PostgreSQL system comes set up with at least one superuser. Most commonly, this superuser is named `postgres`, but occasionally it adopts the same name as the system user who owns the database directory and with whose rights the PostgreSQL server runs.

Other superuser-like attributes

In addition to `SUPERUSER`, there are two lesser attributes—`CREATEDB` and `CREATEUSER`—that give the user only some of the power reserved for superusers, namely creating new databases and users. See the *Giving limited superuser powers to specific users* recipe for more information on this.

Attributes are never inherited

Later, you will learn about granting one role to another user-role inheritance, and how privileges can be granted through these intermediate group roles. None of this applies to attributes—to perform superuser-only operations, you must be that user.

See also

Also check out the *Always knowing which user is logged in* recipe in this chapter.

 All of the following recipes assume a non-superuser unless it is explicitly mentioned that they apply to or need a superuser.

Revoking user access to a table

This recipe answers the question, *How do I make sure that user X cannot access table Y?*

Getting ready

The current user must either be a superuser, the owner of the table, or a user with a `GRANT` option for the table.

Also, bear in mind that you can't revoke rights from a user who is a superuser.

How to do it...

To revoke all rights on the `table1` table from the `user2` user, you must run the following SQL command:

```
REVOKE ALL ON table1 FROM user2;
```

However, if `user2` has been granted another role that gives them some rights on `table1`, say `role3`, this command is not enough; you must also choose one of the following options:

- Fix the user -that is, revoke `role3` from `user2`
- Fix the role - that is, revoke privileges on `table1` from `role3`

Both choices are imperfect because of their side-effects: The former will revoke all the privileges associated to `role3`, not just the privileges concerning `table1`; the latter will revoke the privileges on `table1` from all the other users that have been granted `role3`, not just from `user2`.

It is normally better to avoid damaging other legitimate users, so we opt for the first solution. The following is a worked example.

Using `psql`, display the list of roles that have been granted at least one privilege on `table1` by issuing `\z table1`. For instance, you can obtain the following output (an extra column about column privileges has been removed from the right-hand side because it was not relevant here):

```
                          Access privileges
 Schema |  Name  | Type  |      Access privileges      | ...
--------+--------+-------+-----------------------------+ ...
 public | table1 | table | postgres=arwdDxt/postgres+| ...
        |        |       | role3=r/postgres         +| ...
        |        |       | role5=a/postgres          | ...
(1 row)
```

Then we check whether `user2` is a member of any of those roles by typing `\du user2`:

```
                 List of roles
 Role name | Attributes |   Member of
-----------+------------+----------------
 user2     |            | {role3, role4}
```

From the previous step, we notice that `role3` had been granted the `SELECT` privilege (*r* for *read*) by the `postgres` user, so we must revoke it, as follows:

```
REVOKE role3 FROM user2;
```

We must also inspect `role4`. Even if it doesn't have privileges on `table1`, in theory it could be a member of one of the three roles that have privileges on that table. We issue `\du role4` and get the following output:

```
              List of roles
   Role name |   Attributes   | Member of
 ------------+----------------+-----------
   role4     | Cannot login   | {role5}
```

Our suspicion was well founded: `user2` can get the `INSERT` privilege (*a* for *append*) on `table1`, first via `role4` and then via `role5`. So we must break this two-step chain as follows:

```
REVOKE role4 FROM user2;
```

 This example may seem too unlikely to be true. We unexpectedly gain access to the table via a chain of two different role memberships, which was made possible by the fact that a non-login role, such as `role4`, was made a member of another non-login role, that is, `role5`. In most real-world cases, superusers will know very well whether such chains exist at all, so there will be no surprise; however, the goal of this recipe is to make sure that the user cannot access the table, meaning we cannot exclude less likely options.

How it works...

The `\z` command, as well as its synonym, `\dp`, displays all privileges granted on tables, views, and sequences. If the `Access privileges` column is empty, it means *default privileges*; that is, all privileges are given to the owner (and the superusers, as always).

The `\du` command shows attributes and roles that have been granted to roles.

Both commands accept an optional name or pattern to restrict the display.

There's more...

Here we'll cover some good practices on user and role management.

Database creation scripts

For production systems, it is usually a good idea to always include GRANT and REVOKE statements in the database creation script so that you can be sure that only the right set of users has access to the table. If this is done manually, it is easy to forget. Also, in this way, we are sure that the same roles are used in development and testing environments so that there are no surprises at deployment time.

The following is a sample extract from the database creation script:

```
CREATE TABLE table1(
...
);
GRANT SELECT ON table1 TO webreaders;
GRANT SELECT, INSERT, UPDATE, DELETE ON table1 TO editors;
GRANT ALL ON table1 TO admins;
```

Default search path

It is always good practice to use a fully qualified name when revoking or granting rights; otherwise, you may be inadvertently working with the wrong table.

To see the effective search path for the current database, run the following:

```
pguser=# show search_path ;
   search_path
-----------------
 "$user",public
(1 row)
```

To see which table will be affected if you omit the schema name, run the following in psql:

```
pguser=# \d x
      Table "public.x"
 Column | Type | Modifiers
--------+------+-----------
```

The public.x table name in the response contains the full name, including the schema.

Securing views

It is a common technique to use a view to disclose only some parts of a secret table; however, a clever attacker can use access to the view to display the rest of the table using log messages. For instance, consider the following example:

```
CREATE VIEW for_the_public AS
  SELECT * FROM reserved_data WHERE importance < 10;
GRANT SELECT ON for_the_public TO PUBLIC;
```

A malicious user could define the following function:

```
CREATE FUNCTION f(text)
RETURNS boolean
COST 0.00000001
LANGUAGE plpgsql AS $$
BEGIN
  RAISE INFO '$1: %', $1;
  RETURN true;
END;
$$;
```

Then, they could use it to filter rows from the view:

```
SELECT * FROM for_the_public x WHERE f(x :: text);
```

The PostgreSQL optimizer will then internally rearrange the query, expanding the definition of the view and then combining the two filter conditions into a single WHERE clause. The trick here is that the function has been told to be very cheap using the COST keyword, so the optimizer will choose to evaluate that condition first. In other words, the function will access all the rows in the table, as you will realize when you see the corresponding INFO lines on the console if you run the code yourself.

This security leak can be prevented using the security_barrier attribute:

```
ALTER VIEW for_the_public SET (security_barrier = on);
```

This means that the conditions that define the view will always be computed first, irrespective of cost considerations.

The performance impact of this fix has been mitigated by introducing the LEAKPROOF attribute for functions. In short, a function that cannot leak information other than its output value can be marked as LEAKPROOF by a superuser so the planner will know that it's secure enough to compute the function before the other view conditions.

Granting user access to a table

A user needs to have access to a table in order to perform any action on it.

Getting ready

Make sure that you have the appropriate roles defined, and that privileges are revoked from the PUBLIC role.

How to do it...

Grant access to the schema containing the table, as follows:

```
GRANT USAGE ON SCHEMA someschema TO somerole;
GRANT SELECT, INSERT, UPDATE, DELETE ON someschema.sometable TO somerole;
GRANT somerole TO someuser, otheruser;
```

How it works...

This sequence of commands first grants a role full access to all objects in that schema, then gives viewing (SELECT) and modifying (INSERT, UPDATE, and DELETE) rights on that table to the role, and finally grants membership in that role to two database users.

There's more...

There is no requirement in PostgreSQL to have some privileges in order to have others. This means that you may well have *write-only* tables, where you are allowed to insert but you can't select. This can be used to implement a mail-queue-like functionality, where several users post messages to one user, but they can't see what other users have posted.

Alternatively, you could set up a situation where you can write a record, but you can't change or delete it. This is useful for auditing log type tables, where all changes are recorded, but cannot be tampered with.

Access to the schema

We had to grant access to the schema in order to allow access to the table. This suggests that access to a given schema can be used as a fast and extreme way of preventing any access to any object in that schema. Otherwise, if you want to allow some access, you must use specific GRANT and REVOKE statements as needed.

Granting access to a table through a group role

It is often desirable to give a group of users similar permissions to a group of database objects. To do this, you first assign all the permissions to a proxy role (also known as a permission group), and then assign the group to selected users, as follows:

```
CREATE GROUP webreaders;
GRANT SELECT ON pages TO webreaders;
GRANT INSERT ON viewlog TO webreaders;
GRANT webreaders TO tim, bob;
```

Now both tim and bob have the SELECT privilege on the pages table and INSERT on the viewlog table. You can also add privileges to the group role after assigning it to users. Consider the following command:

```
GRANT INSERT, UPDATE, DELETE ON comments TO webreaders;
```

After running this command, both bob and tim have all of the aforementioned privileges on the comments table.

This assumes that both the bob and tim roles were created with the INHERIT default setting. Otherwise, they do not automatically inherit the rights of roles but need to explicitly set their role to the granted user to make use of the privileges granted to that role.

Granting access to all objects in a schema

Using this syntax, we can grant or revoke privileges on all objects of a certain kind in a specific schema:

```
GRANT SELECT ON ALL TABLES IN SCHEMA staging TO bob;
```

You still need to grant the privileges on the schema itself in a separate GRANT statement.

Granting user access to specific columns

A user can be given access to only some table columns.

Getting ready

We will continue the example in the previous recipe, so we assume that there is already a schema called someschema and a role called somerole with USAGE privileges on it. We create a new table on which we will grant column-level privileges:

```
CREATE TABLE someschema.sometable2(col1 int, col2 text);
```

How to do it...

We want to grant somerole the ability to view existing data and insert new data; we also want to give the ability to amend existing data, limited to column col2 only. We use the following self-evident statements:

```
GRANT SELECT, INSERT ON someschema.sometable2 TO somerole;
GRANT UPDATE (col2) ON someschema.sometable2 TO somerole;
```

Let us assume the identity of role somerole and test these privileges with the following commands:

```
SET ROLE TO somerole;
INSERT INTO someschema.sometable2 VALUES (1, 'One');
SELECT * FROM someschema.sometable2 WHERE col1 = 1;
```

As expected, we are able to insert a new row, and to view its contents. Let us now check our ability to update individual columns. We start with the second column, which we have authorized:

```
UPDATE someschema.sometable2 SET col2 = 'The number one';
```

This command returns the familiar output:

```
UPDATE 1
```

This means that we were able to successfully update that column in one row. Now we try to update the first column:

```
UPDATE someschema.sometable2 SET col1 = 2;
```

This time we get the following error message:

```
ERROR:  permission denied for relation sometable2
```

This confirms that, as planned, we only authorized updates to the second column.

How it works...

The GRANT command has been extended to allow specifying a list of columns, meaning that the privilege is granted on that list of columns, rather than on the whole table.

There's more...

Consider a table t with columns c1, c2, and c3; there are two different ways of authorizing user u to perform the following query:

```
SELECT * FROM t;
```

The first is by granting a table-level privilege as follows:

```
GRANT SELECT ON TABLE t TO u;
```

The alternative way is by granting column-level privileges as follows:

```
GRANT SELECT (c1, c2, c3) ON TABLE t TO u;
```

Despite these two ways having overlapping effects, table-level privileges are distinct from column-level privileges, which is correct since the meaning of each is different. Granting privileges on a table means *to all columns present and future*, while column-level privileges require the explicit indication of columns and, therefore, don't extend automatically to new columns.

The way privileges work in PostgreSQL means that a given role will be allowed to perform a given action if it matches one of its privileges. This creates some ambiguity in overlapping areas. For example, consider the following command sequence:

```
GRANT SELECT ON someschema.sometable2 TO somerole;
REVOKE SELECT (col1) ON someschema.sometable2 FROM
somerole;
```

The outcome, somehow surprisingly, will be that `somerole` is allowed to view all the columns of that table, using the table-level privilege granted by the first command. The second command was ineffective because it tried to revoke a column-level privilege (`SELECT` on `col1`) that was never granted in the first place.

Granting user access to specific rows

Recent PostgreSQL versions support granting users privileges on some rows only.

Getting ready

This recipe uses **row-level security (RLS)**, which is available only on PostgreSQL version 9.5 or later, so start by checking that you are not using an older version.

As for the previous recipe, we assume that there is already a schema called `someschema` and a role called `somerole` with `USAGE` privileges on it. We create a new table to experiment with row-level privileges:

```
CREATE TABLE someschema.sometable3(col1 int, col2 text);
```

Row-level security must also be enabled on that table:

```
ALTER TABLE someschema.sometable3 ENABLE ROW LEVEL SECURITY;
```

How to do it...

First, we grant `somerole` the privilege to view the contents of the table, as we did in the previous recipe:

```
GRANT SELECT ON someschema.sometable3 TO somerole;
```

Let us assume that the contents of the table are as shown by the following command:

```
SELECT * FROM someschema.sometable3;
 col1 |   col2
------+-----------
    1 | One
   -1 | Minus one
(2 rows)
```

In order to grant the ability to access some rows only, we create a policy specifying what is allowed and on which rows. For instance, this way we can enforce the condition that somerole is only allowed to select rows with positive values of col1:

```
CREATE POLICY example1 ON someschema.sometable3
FOR SELECT
TO somerole
USING (col1 > 0);
```

The effect of this command is that the rows that do not satisfy the policy are silently skipped, as shown when somerole issues the following command:

```
SELECT * FROM someschema.sometable3;
 col1 |    col2
------+-----------
    1 | One
(1 row)
```

What if we want to introduce a policy on the INSERT clause? The preceding policy shows how the USING clause specifies which rows are affected. There is also a WITH CHECK clause that can be used to specify which inserts are accepted. More generally, the USING clause applies to pre-existing rows, while WITH CHECK applies to rows that are generated by the statement being analyzed. So the former works with SELECT, UPDATE, and DELETE, while the latter works with INSERT and UPDATE.

Coming back to our example, we may want to allow only inserts where col1 is positive:

```
CREATE POLICY example2 ON someschema.sometable3
FOR INSERT
TO somerole
WITH CHECK (col1 > 0);
```

We must also remember to allow the INSERT commands on the table, as we did before with the SELECT:

```
GRANT INSERT ON someschema.sometable3 TO somerole;
SELECT * FROM someschema.sometable3;
 col1 |    col2
------+-----------
    1 | One
(1 row)
```

Now we are able to insert a new row, and to see it afterward:

```
INSERT INTO someschema.sometable3 VALUES (2, 'Two');
SELECT * FROM someschema.sometable3;
 col1 |   col2
------+-----------
    1 | One
    2 | Two
(2 rows)
```

How it works...

Row-level security policies are created and dropped on a given table using the CREATE POLICY syntax. The row-level security policy itself must also be enabled explicitly on the given table, because it is disabled by default.

In the previous example, we needed to grant privileges on the table or on the columns, in addition to creating the row-level security policy. This is because row-level security is not one more privilege to be added to the other; rather, it works like an additional check. In this sense, it is convenient that it is off by default, so that we have to create policies only on the tables where our access logic depends on the row contents.

There's more...

Row-level security can lead to very complex configurations for a variety of reasons. For instance:

- An UPDATE policy can specify both the rows on which we act and what changes can be accepted
- UPDATE and DELETE policies in some cases require visibility as granted by an appropriate SELECT policy
- UPDATE policies are also applied to INSERT ... ON CONFLICT DO UPDATE

We recommend reading the fine details at the following URL:

https://www.postgresql.org/docs/current/static/ddl-rowsecurity.html

Creating a new user

In this recipe, we will show you two ways of creating a new database user, one with a dedicated command-line utility, and one using SQL commands.

Getting ready

To create new users, you must either be a superuser or have the CREATEROLE or CREATEROLE privilege.

How to do it...

From the command line, you can run the createuser command:

```
pguser@hvost:~$ createuser bob
```

If you add the --interactive command-line option, you activate the interactive mode, which means you will be asked some questions, as follows:

```
pguser@hvost:~$ createuser --interactive alice
Shall the new role be a superuser? (y/n) n
Shall the new role be allowed to create databases? (y/n) y
Shall the new role be allowed to create more new roles? (y/n) n
```

Without --interactive, the preceding questions get no as the default answer; you can change that with the -s, -d, and -r command-line options.

In interactive mode, questions are asked only if they make sense. One example is when the user is a superuser; no other questions are asked because a superuser is not subject to privilege checks. Another example is when one of the preceding options is used to specify a non-default setting; the corresponding question will not be asked.

How it works...

The `createuser` program is just a shallow wrapper around the executing SQL against the database cluster. It connects to the `postgres` database and then executes SQL commands for user creation. To create the same users through SQL, you can issue the following commands:

```
CREATE USER bob;
CREATE USER alice CREATEDB;
```

There's more...

You can check the attributes of a given user in `psql` as follows:

```
pguser=# \du alice
```

This gives the following output:

```
             List of roles
  Role name | Attributes | Member of
 -----------+------------+-----------
  alice     | Create DB  | {}
```

The `CREATE USER` and `CREATE GROUP` commands are actually variations of `CREATE ROLE`. The `CREATE USER username;` statement is equivalent to `CREATE ROLE username LOGIN;`, and the `CREATE GROUP groupname;` statement is equivalent to `CREATE ROLE groupname NOLOGIN;`.

Temporarily preventing a user from connecting

Sometimes, you need to temporarily revoke a user's connection rights without actually deleting the user or changing the user's password. This recipe presents the ways of doing this.

Getting ready

To modify other users, you must either be a superuser or have the `CREATEROLE` privilege (in the latter case, only non-superuser roles can be altered).

How to do it...

1. To temporarily prevent the user from logging in, run this command:

```
pguser=# alter user bob nologin;
ALTER ROLE
```

2. To let the user connect again, run the following:

```
pguser=# alter user bob login;
ALTER ROLE
```

How it works...

This sets a flag in the system catalog, telling PostgreSQL not to let the user log in. It does not kick out already connected users.

There's more...

Here are some additional remarks.

Limiting the number of concurrent connections by a user

The same result can be achieved by setting the connection limit for that user to 0:

```
pguser=# alter user bob connection limit 0;
ALTER ROLE
```

To allow 10 concurrent connections for the bob user, run this command:

```
pguser=# alter user bob connection limit 10;
ALTER ROLE
```

To allow an unlimited number of connections for this user, run the following:

```
pguser=# alter user bob connection limit -1;
ALTER ROLE
```

Forcing NOLOGIN users to disconnect

In order to make sure that all users whose login privilege has been revoked are disconnected right away, run the following SQL statement as a superuser:

```
SELECT pg_terminate_backend(pid)
  FROM pg_stat_activity a
    JOIN pg_roles r ON a.usename = r.rolname AND NOT rolcanlogin;
```

This disconnects all users who no longer are allowed to connect by terminating the backends opened by these users.

Removing a user without dropping their data

When trying to drop a user who owns some tables or other database objects, you get the following error, and the user is not dropped:

```
testdb=# drop user bob;
ERROR:  role "bob" cannot be dropped because some objects depend on it
DETAIL:  owner of table bobstable
owner of sequence bobstable_id_seq
```

This recipe presents two solutions to this problem.

Getting ready

To modify users, you must either be a superuser or have the CREATEROLE privilege.

How to do it...

The easiest solution to this problem is to refrain from dropping the user and use the trick from a previous recipe to prevent the user from connecting:

```
pguser=# alter user bob nologin;
ALTER ROLE
```

This has the added benefit of the original owner of the table being available later, if needed, for auditing or debugging purposes (*Why is this table here? Who created it?*).

Then you can assign the rights of the deleted user to a new user, using the following code:

```
pguser=# GRANT bob TO bobs_replacement;
GRANT
```

How it works...

As noted previously, a user is implemented as a role with the login attribute set. This recipe works by removing that attribute from the user, which is then kept just as a role.

If you really need to get rid of a user, you have to assign all ownership to another user. To do so, run the following query, which is a PostgreSQL extension to standard SQL:

```
REASSIGN OWNED BY bob TO bobs_replacement;
```

It does exactly what it says: it assigns ownership of all database objects currently owned by the bob role to the bobs_replacement role.

However, you need to have privileges on both the old and the new roles to do that, and you need to do it in all databases where bob owns any objects, as the REASSIGN OWNED command works only on the current database.

After this, you can delete the original user, bob.

Checking whether all users have a secure password

PostgreSQL has no built-in facilities to make sure that you are using strong passwords.

The best you can do is to make sure that all user passwords are encrypted, and that your pg_hba.conf file does not allow logins with a plain password. That is, always use the SCRAM-SHA-256 the login method for users, which is new in PostgreSQL 10. Any servers upgrading from earlier versions should upgrade from md5 to SCRAM-SHA-256 password encryption.

For client applications connecting from trusted private networks, either real or virtual (VPN), you may use host-based access, provided you know that the machine on which the application is running is not used by some non-trusted individuals. For remote access over public networks, it may be a better idea to use SSL client certificates.

How to do it...

To see which users don't yet have SCRAM encrypted passwords, use this query:

```
test2=# select usename,passwd from pg_shadow where passwd
not like 'SCRAM%' or passwd is null;
 usename  |    passwd
----------+---------------
 tim      | weakpassword
 asterisk | md5chicken
(2 rows)
```

To enable SCRAM-SHA-256 for encrypted passwords, use the following:

```
test2=# SET password_encryption = 'scram-sha-256';
test2=# ALTER USER bob ENCRYPTED PASSWORD 'whatever';
 ALTER USER
```

How it works...

The password_encryption parameter decides how the ALTER USER statement will encrypt the password. This should be set globally in the postgresql.conf file.

Having the passwords encrypted in the database is just half of the equation. The bigger problem is making sure that users actually use passwords that are hard to guess that is, passwords such as password, secret, or test are out, and most common words are not good passwords either.

If you don't trust your users to select strong passwords, you can write a wrapper application that checks the password strength and make them use that when changing passwords. A contrib module lets you do this for a limited set of cases (the password is sent from client to server in plain text). Visit http://www.postgresql.org/docs/current/static/passwordcheck.html for more information on this.

Giving limited superuser powers to specific users

First, the superuser role has some privileges that can also be granted to non-superuser roles separately.

To give the bob role the ability to create new databases, run this:

```
ALTER ROLE BOB WITH CREATEDB;
```

To give the bob role the ability to create new users, run the following:

```
ALTER ROLE BOB WITH CREATEROLE;
```

However, it is also possible to give ordinary users more fine-grained and controlled access to an action reserved for superusers using security definer functions. The same trick can also be used to pass partial privileges between different users.

Getting ready

First, you must have access to the database as a superuser in order to delegate powers. Here, we assume the use of the default superuser named postgres.

We will demonstrate two ways to make some superuser-only functionality available to a selected ordinary user.

How to do it...

One thing that a superuser can do that ordinary user cannot tell PostgreSQL to copy table data from a file:

```
pguser@hvost:~$ psql -U postgres
test2
...
test2=# create table lines(line text);
CREATE TABLE
test2=# copy lines from '/home/bob/names.txt';
COPY 37
test2=# SET ROLE to bob;
SET
test2=> copy lines from '/home/bob/names.txt';
ERROR:  must be superuser to COPY to or from a file
HINT:  Anyone can COPY to stdout or from stdin. psql's \copy command also
works for anyone.
```

To let bob copy directly from the file, the superuser can write a special wrapper function for bob, as follows:

```
create or replace function copy_from(tablename text, filepath text)
returns void
security definer
as
$$
 declare
 begin
      execute 'copy ' || quote_ident(tablename)
                  || ' from ' || quote_literal(filepath) ;
 end;
$$ language plpgsql;
```

It is usually a good idea to restrict the use of such a function to the intended user only:

```
revoke all on function copy_from( text,  text) from public;
grant execute on function copy_from( text,  text) to bob;
```

You may also want to verify that bob imports files only from his home directory.

Unfortunately, this solution is not completely secure against superuser privilege escalation by a malicious attacker. This is because the execution of the COPY command inside the function will also cause the execution, as the postgres user, of all side-effects, such as the execution of any INSERT trigger, computation of any CHECK constraint, computation of any functional index, and more.

In other words, if the user wants to execute a given function as the superuser, it's enough to put that function inside any of the preceding functions.

There are a few workarounds for this security hole, none of which are optimal.

Require that the table has no triggers, CHECK constraints, and functional indexes.

Instead of running COPY on the given table, create a new table with the same structure using the CREATE newtable(LIKE oldtable) syntax. Run the COPY against the new table, drop the old table, and give the new table the same name as the old table.

How it works...

When a function defined with `security definer` is called, PostgreSQL changes the session's rights to those of the user who defined the function while that function is being executed.

So, when `bob` executes the `copy_from(tablename, filepath)` function, `bob` is effectively promoted to superuser for the time the function is running.

This behavior is similar to the `setuid` flag in Unix systems, where you can have a program that can be run by anybody (with execute access) as the owner of that program. It also carries similar risks.

There's more...

There are other operations that are reserved for PostgreSQL superusers, such as setting certain parameters.

Writing a debugging_info function for developers

Several of the parameters controlling logging are reserved for superusers.

If you want to allow some of your developers to set logging on, you can write a function for them to do exactly that:

```
create or replace function debugging_info_on()
returns void
security definer
as
$$
  begin
    set client_min_messages to 'DEBUG1';
    set log_min_messages to 'DEBUG1';
    set log_error_verbosity to 'VERBOSE';
    set log_min_duration_statement to 0;
  end;
$$ language plpgsql;
revoke all on function debugging_info_on() from public;
grant execute on function debugging_info_on() to bob;
```

You may also want to have a function go back to the default logging state by assigning
DEFAULT to all the variables involved:

```
create or replace function debugging_info_reset()
returns void
security definer
as
$$
  begin
    set client_min_messages to DEFAULT;
    set log_min_messages to DEFAULT;
    set log_error_verbosity to DEFAULT;
    set log_min_duration_statement to DEFAULT;
  end;
$$ language plpgsql;
```

There's no need for GRANT and REVOKE statements here, as setting them back to the default
does not pose a security risk. Instead of SET xxx to DEFAULT, you can also use a shorter
version of the same command, namely RESET xxx.

Alternatively, you can simply end your session, as the parameters are valid only for the
current session.

Auditing database access

Auditing database access is a much bigger topic than you might expect because it can cover
a whole range of requirements.

Getting ready

First decide which of these you want and look at the appropriate subsection

- What were the SQL statements executed? Auditing SQL
- What were the tables accessed? Auditing table access
- What were the data rows changed? Auditing data changes
- What were the data rows viewed? Not described here, usually too much data

Auditing just SQL produces the lowest volume of audit log information, especially if you
choose to log only DDL. Higher levels accumulate more information very rapidly, so you
may quickly decide not to do this in practice. Read each section to understand the benefits
and trade-offs.

Auditing SQL

There are two main ways to log SQL

- Using the PostgreSQL `log_statement` parameter
- Using the pgaudit extension's `pgaudit.log` parameter

The `log_statement` parameter can be set to one of the following options:

- ALL: logs all SQL statements executed at top-level
- MOD: logs all SQL statements for `INSERT`, `UPDATE`, `DELETE`, and `TRUNCATE`
- `ddl`: logs all SQL statements for DDL commands
- NONE: no statements logged

For example,to log all DDL commands, edit your `postgresql.conf` file to set the
following

```
log_statement  =  'ddl'
```

The `log_statement` SQL statements explicitly given in top-level commands. It is still
possible to perform SQL without it being logged by this setting if you use any of the PL
languages, either through DO statements or by calling a function that includes SQL
statements.

Was the change committed? It is possible to have some statements recorded in the log file
but not visible in the database structure. Most DDL commands in PostgreSQL can be rolled
back, so what is in the log is just a list of commands executed by PostgreSQL-not what was
actually committed. The log file is not transactional, and it keeps commands that were
rolled back. It is possible to display the transaction identifier on each log line by including
`%x` in the `log_line_prefix` setting, though that has some difficulties in usage.

Who made the changes? To be able to know which database user who made the DDL
changes, you have to make sure that this information is logged as well. In order to do so,
you may have to change the `log_line_prefix` parameter to include the `%u` format string.

A recommended minimal `log_line_prefix` format string for auditing DDL is `%t   %u
%d`, which tells PostgreSQL to log the timestamp, database user, and database name at the
start of every log line.

The `pgaudit` extension provides two levels of audit logging: session and object levels. Session level has been designed to solve some of the problems of `log_statement`. `pgaudit` will log all access, even if it is not executed as a top-level statement and it will log all dynamic SQL. `pgaudit.log` can be set to include zero or more of the following settings:

- READ: SELECT and COPY
- WRITE: INSERT, UPDATE, DELETE, TRUNCATE and COPY
- FUNCTION: Function calls and DO blocks
- ROLE: GRANT, REVOKE, CREATE/ALTER/DROP ROLE
- DDL: All DDL not already included in the ROLE category
- MISC: Miscelaneous – DISCARD, FETCH, CHECKPOINT, VACUUM, and so on

For example, to log all DDL commands, edit your `postgresql.conf` file to set the following:

```
pgaudit.log = 'role, ddl'
```

You should set these parameters to reduce the overhead of logging:

```
pgaudit.log_catalog = off
pgaudit.log_relation = off
pgaudit.log_statement_once = on
```

The pgaudit extension was originally written by Simon Riggs and Abhijit Menon-Sen of 2ndQuadrant as part of the AXLE project for the EU. The next version was designed by Simon Riggs and David Steele to provide object level logging. The original version has been deprecated and is no longer available. The new version is fully supported and has been adopted by the US DoD as the tool of choice for PostgreSQL audit logging.

`pgaudit` is available in binary form via `postgresql.org` repositories.

Auditing table access

pgaudit can log each access to each table. So if an SQL table touches three tables then it can generate three log records, one for each table. This is important because otherwise, you might have to try and parse the SQL to find out which tables it touched, which would be difficult without access to the schema and the `search_path` settings.

To make it easier to access the audit log per table, adjust these settings:

```
pgaudit.log_relation = on
pgaudit.log_statement_once = off
```

If you want even finer grained auditing, pgaudit allows you to control which tables are audited. The user cannot tell which tables are logged and which are not, so it is possible for investigators to quietly enhance the level of logging once they are alerted to a suspect or a potential attack.

First, set the role that will be used by the auditor:

```
pgaudit.role = 'investigator'
```

Then you can define logging through the privilege system, like the following command:

```
GRANT INSERT, UPDATE, DELETE on <vulnerable_table> TO investigator;
```

And remove it again when no longer required.

Privileges may be set at individual column level to protect **Personally Identifiable Information (PII)**.

Managing the audit log

Both `log_statement` and `pgaudit` output audit log records to the server log. This is the most flexible approach since the log can be routed in various ways to ensure it is safe and separate from normal log entries.

If you allow the log entries to go the normal server log you can find all occurrences of the CREATE, ALTER, and DROP commands in the log:

```
postgres@hvost:~$ egrep -i "create|alter|drop" \
/var/log/postgresql/postgresql-9.6-main.log
```

If log rotation is in effect, you may need to use grep on older logs as well.

If the available logs are too new, and you haven't saved the older logs in some other place, you are out of luck.

The default settings in the `postgresql.conf` file for log rotation are as follows:

```
log_filename = 'postgresql-%Y-%m-%d_%H%M%S.log'
log_rotation_age = 1d
log_rotation_size = 10MB
```

Log rotation can also be implemented with third-party utilities. For instance, the default behavior on Debian and Ubuntu distributions is to use the `logrotate` utility to compress or delete old log files, according to the rules specified in the `/etc/logrotate.d/postgresql-common` file.

To make sure you have the full history of DDL commands, you may want to set up a cron job that saves the DDL statements extracted from the main PostgreSQL log to a separate DDL audit log. You would still want to verify that the logs are not rotating too fast for this to catch all DDL statements.

If you use syslog, then you can route audit messages using various OS utilities.

Alternatively, you can use the pgaudit analyze extension to load data back into a special audit log databases. Various other options exist.

Auditing data changes

This recipe provides different ways of collecting changes to data contained in the tables for auditing purposes.

First, you must make the following decisions:

- Do you need to audit all changes or only some?
- What information about the changes do you need to collect? Only the fact that the data has changed?
- When recording the new value of a field or tuple, do you also need to record the old value?
- Is it enough to record which user made the change, or do you also need to record the IP address and other connection information?
- How secure (tamper-proof) must the auditing information be? For example, does it need to be kept separately, away from the database being audited?

Changes can be collected using triggers which collect new (and if needed, old) values from tuples, and save them to auditing table(s). Triggers can be added to whichever tables need to be tracked.

The Audit-Trigger Extension provides a handy universal audit trigger so you do not need to write your own. It logs both old and new values of rows in any table, serialized as `hstore` data type values. The latest version of the trigger and its documentation are both available at `https://github.com/2ndQuadrant/audit-trigger`.

The extension creates a schema called audit into which all the other components of the audit trigger code are placed, after which we can enable auditing on specific tables.

As an example, we create standard pgbench tables by running the pgbench utility:

```
pgbench -i
```

Next, we connect to PostgreSQL as a superuser, and issue the following SQL to enable auditing on the pgbench_account table:

```
SELECT  audit.audit_table('pgbench_accounts');
```

Now we perform some write activity to see how it is audited. The easiest choice is to run the pgbench utility again, this time to perform some transactions, as follows:

```
pgbench -t 1000
```

We expect the audit trigger to have logged the actions on pgbench_accounts, as we have enabled auditing on it. In order to verify this, we connect again with psql and issue the following SQL:

```
cookbook=# SELECT count(*) FROM audit.logged_actions;
count
-------
1000
(1 row)
```

This confirms that we have indeed logged 1000 actions. Let us inspect what information is logged by reading one row of the logged_actions table. First, we enable expanded mode, as the query produces a large number of columns:

```
cookbook=# \x on
```

Then we issue the following command:

```
cookbook=# SELECT * FROM audit.logged_actions LIMIT 1;
-[ RECORD 1 ]-----+---------------------------------------------------
------------
event_id          | 1
schema_name       | public
table_name        | pgbench_accounts
relid             | 246511
session_user_name | gianni
action_tstamp_tx  | 2017-01-18 19:48:05.626299+01
action_tstamp_stm | 2017-01-18 19:48:05.626446+01
action_tstamp_clk | 2017-01-18 19:48:05.628488+01
```

```
transaction_id      | 182578
application_name    | pgbench
client_addr         |
client_port         |
client_query        | UPDATE pgbench_accounts SET abalance = abalance + -758
WHERE aid = 86061;
action              | U
row_data            | "aid"=>"86061", "bid"=>"1", "filler"=>"   ",
"abalance"=>"0"
changed_fields      | "abalance"=>"-758"
statement_only      | f
```

Always knowing which user is logged in

In the preceding recipes, we just logged the value of the user variable in the current PostgreSQL session to log the current user role.

This does not always mean that this particular user was the user that was actually authenticated at the start of the session. For example, a superuser can execute the SET ROLE TO ... command to set its current role to any other user or role in the system. As you might expect, non-superusers can assume only those roles that they own.

It is possible to differentiate between the logged-in role and the assumed role using the current_user and session_user session variables:

```
postgres=# select current_user, session_user;
current_user | session_user
-------------+--------------
postgres     | postgres

postgres=# set role to bob;
SET
postgres=> select current_user, session_user;
current_user | session_user
-------------+--------------
bob          | postgres
```

Sometimes, it is desirable to let each user log in with their own username and just assume the role needed on a case-by-case basis.

Getting ready

Prepare the required group roles for different tasks and access levels by granting the necessary privileges and options.

How to do it...

The steps are as follows:

1. Create user roles with no privileges and with the NOINHERIT option:

```
postgres=# create user alice noinherit;
CREATE ROLE
postgres=# create user bob noinherit;
CREATE ROLE
```

2. Then, create roles for each group of privileges that you need to assign:

```
postgres=# create group sales;
CREATE ROLE
postgres=# create group marketing;
CREATE ROLE
postgres=# grant postgres to marketing;
GRANT ROLE
```

3. Now grant each user the roles it may need:

```
postgres=# grant sales to alice;
GRANT ROLE
postgres=# grant marketing to alice;
GRANT ROLE
postgres=# grant sales to bob;
GRANT ROLE
```

After you do this, the users alice and bob have no rights after login, but they can assume the sales role by executing SET ROLE TO sales, and alice can additionally assume the superuser role.

How it works...

If a role or user is created with the NOINHERIT option, this user will not automatically get the rights that have been granted to the other roles that have been granted to itself. To claim these rights from a specific role, it has to set its role to one of those other roles.

In some sense, this works a bit like the su (set user) command in Unix and Linux systems. That is, you (may) have the right to become that user, but you do not automatically have the rights of the aforementioned user.

This setup can be used to get better audit information, as it lets you know who the actual user was. If you just allow each user to log in as the role needed for a task, there is no good way to know later which of the users was really logged in as clerk1 when this $100,000 transfer was made.

There's more...

The SET ROLE command works both ways; that is, you can both gain and lose privileges. A superuser can set its role to any user defined in the system. To get back to your original login role, just use RESET ROLE.

Not inheriting user attributes

Not all rights come to users via GRANT commands. Some important rights are given via user attributes (SUPERUSER, CREATEDB, and CREATEROLE), and these are never inherited.

If your user has been granted a superuser role and you want to use the superuser powers of this granted role, you have to use SET ROLE To mysuperuserrole; before anything that requires the superuser attribute to be set.

In other words, the user attributes always behave as if the user had been a NOINHERIT user.

Integrating with LDAP

This recipe shows you how to set up your PostgreSQL system so that it uses the **Lightweight Directory Access Protocol (LDAP)** for authentication.

Getting ready

Ensure that the usernames in the database and your LDAP server match, as this method works for user authentication checks of users who are already defined in the database.

How to do it...

In the PostgreSQL authentication file, `pg_hba.conf`, we define some address ranges to use LDAP as an authentication method, and we configure the LDAP server for this address range:

```
host     all         all         10.10.0.1/16            ldap \
ldapserver=ldap.our.net ldapprefix="cn=" ldapsuffix=",
    dc=our,dc=net"
```

How it works...

This setup makes the PostgreSQL server check passwords from the configured LDAP server.

User rights are not queried from the LDAP server but have to be defined inside the database using the `ALTER USER`, `GRANT`, and `REVOKE` commands.

There's more...

We have shown how PostgreSQL can use an LDAP server for password authentication. It is also possible to use some more information from the LDAP server, as shown in the next two examples.

Setting up the client to use LDAP

If you are using the `pg_service.conf` file to define your database access parameters, you may define some to be queried from the LDAP server by including a line similar to the following in your `pg_service.conf` file:

```
ldap://ldap.mycompany.com/dc=mycompany,dc=com?uniqueMember?one?(cn=mydb)
```

Replacement for the User Name Map feature

Although we cannot use the User Name Map feature with LDAP, we can achieve a similar effect on the LDAP side. Use `ldapsearchattribute` and the *search + bind* mode to retrieve the PostgreSQL role name from the LDAP server.

See also

- For server setup, including the search + bind mode, visit `http://www.postgresql.org/docs/current/static/auth-methods.html#AUTH-LDAP`
- For client setup, visit `http://www.postgresql.org/docs/current/static/libpq-ldap.html`

Connecting using SSL

Here, we will demonstrate how to enable PostgreSQL to use SSL for the protection of database connections by encrypting all of the data passed over that connection. Using SSL makes it much harder to sniff the database traffic, including usernames, passwords, and other sensitive data. Otherwise, everything that is passed unencrypted between a client and the database can be observed by someone listening to a network somewhere between them. An alternative to using SSL is running the connection over a **virtual private network** (**VPN**).

Using SSL makes the data transfer on the encrypted connection a little slower, so you may not want to use it if you are sure that your network is safe. The performance impact can be quite large if you are creating lots of short connections, as setting up an SSL connection is quite CPU-heavy. In this case, you may want to run a local connection pooling solution, such as PgBouncer, to which the client connects without encryption, and then configure PgBouncer for server connections using SSL. Older versions of PgBouncer did not support SSL; the solution was to channel server connections through stunnel, as described in the PgBouncer FAQ at `https://pgbouncer.github.io/faq.html`.

Getting ready

Get, or generate, an SSL server key and certificate pair for the server, and store these in the `data` directory of the current database instance as the `server.key` and `server.crt` files.

On some platforms, this is unnecessary; the key and certificate pair may already be generated by the packager. For example, on Ubuntu, PostgreSQL is set up to support SSL connections by default.

How to do it...

1. Set `ssl = on` in `postgresql.conf` and restart the database

How it works...

If `ssl = on` is set, then PostgreSQL listens to both plain and SSL connections on the same port (`5432` by default) and determines the type of connection from the first byte of a new connection.

Then, it proceeds to set up an SSL connection if an incoming request asks for it.

There's more...

You can leave the choice of whether or not to use SSL to the client, or you can force SSL usage from the server's side.

To let the client choose, use a line of the following form in the `pg_hba.conf` file:

```
host database  user  IP-address/IP-mask  auth-method
```

If you want to allow only SSL clients, use the `hostssl` keyword instead of `host`.

The contents of `pg_hba.conf` can be seen using the view `pg_hba_file_rules`.

The following fragment of `pg_hba.conf` enables both non-SSL and SSL connections from the `192.168.1.0/24` local subnet, but requires SSL from everybody accessing the database from other networks:

```
host      all      all      192.168.1.0/24      md5
hostssl   all      all      0.0.0.0/0           md5
```

Getting the SSL key and certificate

For web servers, you must usually get your SSL certificate from a recognized **certificate authority (CA)**, as most browsers complain if the certificate is not issued by a known CA. They warn the user of the most common security risks and require confirmation before connecting to a server with a certificate issued by an unknown CA.

For your database server, it is usually sufficient to generate the certificate yourself, using OpenSSL. The following commands generate a self-signed certificate for your server:

```
openssl genrsa 2048 > server.key
openssl req -new -x509 -key server.key -out server.crt
```

 Read more on X.509 keys and certificates in OpenSSL's *HOWTO's* pages at https://github.com/openssl/openssl/tree/master/doc/HOWTO.

Setting up a client to use SSL

The behavior of the client application regarding SSL is controlled by an environment variable, PGSSLMODE. This can have the following values, as defined in the official PostgreSQL documentation:

SSL mode	Eavesdropping protection	MITM protection	Statement
disabled	No	No	I don't care about security, and I don't want to pay the overhead of encryption.
allow	Maybe	No	I don't care about security, but I will pay the overhead of encryption if the server insists on it.
prefer	Maybe	No	I don't care about encryption, but I wish to pay the overhead of encryption if the server supports it.
require	Yes	No	I want my data to be encrypted, and I accept the overhead. I trust that the network will ensure that I always connect to the server I want.

| verify-ca | Yes | Depends on the CA policy | I want my data encrypted, and I accept the overhead. I want to be sure that I connect to a server that I trust. |
| verify-full | Yes | Yes | I want my data encrypted, and I accept the overhead. I want to be sure that I connect to a server I trust, and that the server is the one I specify. |

MITM in the preceding table means **man-in-the-middle** attack; that is, someone posing as your server-perhaps by manipulating DNS records or IP routing tables-but who actually just observes and forwards the traffic.

For this to be possible with an SSL connection, this someone needs to have obtained a certificate that your client considers valid.

Checking server authenticity

The last two SSL modes allow you to be reasonably sure that you are actually talking to your server by checking the SSL certificate presented by the server.

In order to enable this useful security feature, the following files must be available on the client side. On Unix systems, they are located in the client home directory, in a subdirectory named `~/.postgresql`. On Windows, they are in `%APPDATA%\postgresql\`.

File	Contents	Effect
`root.crt`	Certificates of one or more trusted CAs	PostgreSQL verifies that the server certificate is signed by a trusted CA
`root.crl`	Certificates revoked by CAs	The server certificate must not be on this list

Only the `root.crt` file is required for the client to authenticate the server certificate. It can contain multiple root certificates against which the server certificate is compared.

Using SSL certificates to authenticate

This recipe shows you how to set up your PostgreSQL system so that it *requires* clients to present a valid X.509 certificate before allowing them to connect.

This can be used as an additional security layer to use double authentication, where the client must both have a valid certificate to set up the SSL connection and also know the database user's password. It can also be used as the sole authentication method, where the PostgreSQL server will first verify the client connection using the certificate presented by the client, and then retrieve the username from the same certificate.

Getting ready

Get, or generate, a root certificate and a client certificate to be used by the connecting client.

How to do it...

For testing purposes, or for just setting up a single trusted user, you can use a self-signed certificate:

```
openssl  genrsa  2048  >  client.key
openssl  req  -new  -x509  -key  server.key  -out  client.crt
```

On the server, set up a line in pg_hba.conf file with the hostssl method and the clientcert option set to 1:

```
hostssl  all    all    0.0.0.0/0          md5  clientcert=1
```

Put the client root certificate in the root.crt file in the server data directory ($PGDATA/root.crt). This file may contain multiple trusted root certificates.

If you are using a central certificate authority, you probably also have a certificate revocation list, which should be put in a root.crl file and regularly updated.

On the **client**, put the client's private key and certificate in ~/.postgresql/postgresql.key and ~/.postgresql/postgresql.crt. Make sure that the private key file is not world-readable or group-readable by running the following command:

```
chmod 0600 ~/.postgresql/postgresql.key
```

On the Windows client, the corresponding files are %APPDATA%\postgresql\postgresql.key and %APPDATA%\postgresql\postgresql.crt. No permission check is done, as the location is considered secure.

If the client certificate is not signed by the root CA but by an intermediate CA, then all the intermediate CA certificates up to the root certificate must be placed in the postgresql.crt file as well.

How it works...

If the clientcert=1 option is set for a hostssl row in pg_hba.conf, then PostgreSQL accepts only connection requests accompanied by a valid certificate.

The validity of the certificate is checked against certificates present in the root.crt file in the server data directory.

If there is a root.crl file, then the presented certificate is looked for in this file and, if found, is rejected.

After the client certificate is validated and the SSL connection is established, the server proceeds to validate the actual connecting user using whatever authentication method is specified in the corresponding hostssl line.

In the following example, clients from a special address can connect as any user when using an SSL certificate, and they must specify a SCRAM-SHA-256 password for non-SSL connections. Clients from all the other addresses must present a certificate and use md5 password authentication:

```
host      all    all    10.10.10.10/32    md5
hostssl   all    all    10.10.10.10/32    trust            clientcert=1
hostssl   all    all    all               scram-sha-256    clientcert=1
```

There's more...

In this section, we provide some additional content, describing an important optimization for an SSL-only database server, plus two extensions of the basic SSL configuration.

Avoiding duplicate SSL connection attempts

In the *Setting up a client to use SSL* section of the previous recipe, *Connecting using SSL*, we saw how the client's SSL behavior is affected by environment variables. Depending on how the SSLMODE environment variable is set on the client (either via compile-time settings, the PGSSLMODE environment variable, or the sslmode connection parameter), the client may attempt to connect without SSL first, and then attempt an SSL connection only after the server rejects the non-SSL connection.

This duplicates a connection attempt every time a client accesses an SSL-only server.

To make sure that the client tries to establish an SSL connection on the first attempt, SSLMODE must be set to prefer or higher.

Using multiple client certificates

You may sometimes need different certificates to connect to different PostgreSQL servers.

The location of the certificate and key files in postgresql.crt and postgresql.key in the table from the *Checking server authenticity* section is just the default, and can be overridden by specifying alternative file paths using the sslcert and sslkey connection parameters or the PGSSLCERT and PGSSLKEY environment variables.

Using the client certificate to select the database user

It is possible to use the client certificate for two purposes at once: proving that the connecting client is a valid one, and selecting the database user to be used for the connection.

For this, you set the authentication method to cert in the hostssl line:

```
hostssl    all    all    0.0.0.0/0           cert
```

As you can see, the clientcert=1 option used with hostssl to require client certificates is no longer required, being implied by the cert method itself.

When using the cert authentication method, a valid client certificate is required, and the cn (short for, common name) attribute of the certificate will be compared to the requested database username. The login will be allowed only if they match.

It is possible to use a User Name Map to map the common names in the certificates to database usernames by specifying the `map` option:

```
hostssl    all    all    0.0.0.0/0              cert    map=x509cnmap
```

Here, `x509cnmap` is the name that we have arbitrarily chosen for our mapping. More details on User Name Maps are provided in the next recipe, *Mapping external usernames to database roles*.

See also

To understand more about SSL in general, and the *OpenSSL library* used by PostgreSQL in particular, visit `http://www.openssl.org`, or get a good book about SSL.

To get started with the generation of simple SSL keys and certificates, see `https://github.com/openssl/openssl/blob/master/doc/HOWTO/certificates.txt`.

There is also a nice presentation named *Encrypted PostgreSQL* explaining these issues at PGCon 2009. The slides are available at `http://www.pgcon.org/2009/schedule/events/120.en.html`.

Mapping external usernames to database roles

In some cases, the authentication username is different from the PostgreSQL username. For instance, this can happen when using an external system for authentication, such as certificate authentication, as described in the previous recipe, or any other external or single sign-on system authentication method from `http://www.postgresql.org/docs/current/static/auth-methods.html` (GSSAPI, SSPI, Kerberos, Radius, or PAM). Or you may just need to enable an externally authenticated user to connect as multiple database users.

In such cases, you can specify rules to map the external username to the appropriate database role.

Getting ready

Prepare a list of usernames from the external authentication system and decide which database users they are allowed to connect as-that is, which external users map to which database users.

How to do it...

Create a `pg_ident.conf` file in the usual place (`PGDATA`), with lines in the following format:

```
map-name system-username database-username
```

Here, `map-name` is the value of the `map` option from the corresponding line in `pg_hba.conf`, `system-username` is the username that the external system authenticated the connection as, and `database-username` is the database user this system user is allowed to connect as. The same system user may be allowed to connect as multiple database users, so this is not a 1:1 mapping, but rather a list of allowed database users for each system user.

If `system-username` starts with a slash (`/`), then the rest of it is treated as a regular expression rather than a directly matching string, and it is possible to use the `\1` string in `database-username` to refer to the part captured by the parentheses in the regular expression. For example, consider the following lines:

```
salesmap    /^(.*)@sales\.comp\.com$       \1
salesmap    /^(.*)@sales\.comp\.com$     sales
salesmap    manager@sales.comp.com      auditor
```

These will allow any user authenticated with a `@sales.comp.com` e-mail address to connect both as a database user equal to the name before the `@` sign in their e-mail address, and as the `sales` user. They will additionally allow `manager@sales.comp.com` to connect as the auditor user. Then edit the `pg_hba.conf` line to specify the `map=salesmap` option

How it works...

After authenticating the connection using an external authentication system, PostgreSQL will usually proceed to check that the externally authenticated username matches the database username that the user wishes to connect as, and rejects the connection if these two do not match.

If there is a map= parameter specified for the current line in `pg_hba.conf`, then the system will scan the map line by line, and will let the client proceed with connecting if a match is found.

There's more...

By default, the map file is called `pg_ident.conf` (because it was first used for the `ident` authentication method).

Nowadays, it is possible to change the name of this file via the `ident_file` configuration parameter in `postgresql.conf`. It can also be located outside the `PGDATA` directory by setting `ident_file` to a full path.

A relative path can also be used, but since it is relative to where the `postgres` process is started, this is usually not a good idea.

Encrypting sensitive data

This recipe shows you how to encrypt data using the `pgcrypto` contrib package.

Getting ready

Make sure you (and/or your database server) are in a country where encryption is not illegal-it still is in some countries.

In order to create and manage PGP keys, you also need the well-known `GnuPG` command-line utility, which is available on practically all distributions.

`pgcrypto` is part of the contrib collection. Starting from version 10, on Debian and Ubuntu is part of the main `postgresql-10` server package, while in previous versions there was a separate package, for example, `postgresql-contrib-9.6`.

Install it on the database in which you want to use it, following the *Adding an external module to PostgreSQL* recipe from `Chapter 3`, *Configuration*.

You also need to have PGP keys set up:

```
pguser@laptop:~$ gpg --gen-key
```

Answer some questions here (the defaults are OK, unless you are an expert), select the key type as `DSA and Elgamal`, and enter an empty password.

Now, export the keys:

```
pguser@laptop:~$ gpg -a --export "PostgreSQL User (test key for PG Cookbook)
<pguser@somewhere.net>" > public.key
pguser@laptop:~$ gpg -a --export-secret-keys "PostgreSQL User (test key for
PG Cookbook) <pguser@somewhere.net>" > secret.key
```

Make sure only you and the `postgres` database user have access to the secret key:

```
pguser@laptop:~$ sudo chgrp postgres secret.key
pguser@laptop:~$ chmod 440 secret.key
pguser@laptop:~$ ls -l *.key
-rw-r--r-- 1 pguser pguser    1718 2016-03-26 13:53 public.key
-r--r----- 1 pguser postgres 1818 2016-03-26 13:54 secret.key
```

Last, but not least, make a copy of the public and the secret key; if you lose them, you'll lose the ability to encrypt/decrypt.

How to do it...

To ensure that the secret keys are never visible in database logs, write a wrapper function to get the keys from the file. You need to do it in an untrusted embedded language, such as PL/PythonU, as only untrusted languages can access the filesystem. You need to be a PostgreSQL superuser in order to create functions in untrusted languages. It's not difficult to write a PostgreSQL function that reads a text file. For convenience, here is an example that requires PL/PythonU:

```
create or replace function get_my_public_key() returns text as $$
return open('/home/pguser/public.key').read()
$$
language plpythonu;
revoke all on function get_my_public_key() from public;
create or replace function get_my_secret_key() returns text as $$
return open('/home/pguser/secret.key').read()
$$
language plpythonu;
revoke all on function get_my_secret_key() from public;
```

This can also be fully implemented in PL/pgSQL using the built-in PostgreSQL system function, pg_read_file (filename), and you don't have to bother with PL/PythonU at all. However, to use this function, you must place the files in the data directory as required by that function for additional security, so the database superuser is not allowed to access the rest of the filesystem directly.

If you don't want other database users to be able to see the keys, you also need to write wrapper functions for encryption and decryption, and then give access to these wrapper functions to end users.

The encryption function can be like this:

```
create or replace function encrypt_using_my_public_key(
    cleartext text,
    ciphertext out bytea
)
AS $$
DECLARE
    pubkey_bin bytea;
BEGIN
    -- text version of public key needs to be passed through function
dearmor() to get to raw key
    pubkey_bin := dearmor(get_my_public_key());

    ciphertext := pgp_pub_encrypt(cleartext, pubkey_bin);
END;
$$ language plpgsql security definer;
revoke all on function encrypt_using_my_public_key(text) from public;
grant execute on function encrypt_using_my_public_key(text) to bob;
```

The decryption function can be as follows:

```
create or replace function decrypt_using_my_secret_key(
    ciphertext bytea,
    cleartext out text
)
AS $$
DECLARE
    secret_key_bin bytea;
BEGIN
    -- text version of secret key needs to be passed through function
dearmor() to get to raw binary key
    secret_key_bin := dearmor(get_my_secret_key());
```

```
        cleartext := pgp_pub_decrypt(ciphertext, secret_key_bin);
END;
$$ language plpgsql security definer;
revoke all on function decrypt_using_my_secret_key(bytea) from public;
grant execute on function decrypt_using_my_secret_key(bytea) to bob;
```

Finally, we test the encryption:

```
test2=# select encrypt_using_my_public_key('X marks the spot!');
```

This function returns a `bytea` (that is, raw binary) result that looks something like the following:

```
encrypt_using_my_public_key |
\301\301N\003\223o\215\2125\203\252;\020\007\376-z\233\211H...
```

To see that it actually works, you must go both ways:

```
test2=# select decrypt_using_my_secret_key(encrypt_using_my_public_key('X
marks the spot!'));
 decrypt_using_my_secret_key
-------------------------------
 X marks the spot!
(1 row)
```

Yes, we got back our initial string!

How it works...

What we have done here is the following:

- Hidden the keys from non-superuser database users
- Provided wrappers for authorized users to use encryption and decryption functionalities

To ensure that your sensitive data is not stolen while in transit between the client and the database server, make sure you connect to PostgreSQL either using an SSL-encrypted connection or from localhost.

You also have to trust your server administrators and all the other users with superuser privileges to be sure that your encrypted data is safe. And, of course, you must trust the safety of the entire environment; PostgreSQL can decrypt the data, so any other user or software that has access to the same files can do the same.

There's more...

A higher level of security is possible, with more complex procedures and architecture, as shown in the next sections. We also mention a limited `pgcrypto` version that does not use OpenSSL.

For really sensitive data

For some data, you wouldn't want to risk keeping the decryption password on the same machine as the encrypted data.

In those cases, you can use **public-key cryptography**, also known as **asymmetric cryptography**, and carry out only the encryption part on the database server. This also means that you only have the encryption key on the database host, and not the key needed for decryption. Alternatively, you can deploy a separate, extra-secure encryption server in your server infrastructure that provides just the encrypting and decrypting functionality as a remote call.

This solution is secure because, in asymmetric cryptography, the private (that is, decryption) key cannot be derived from the corresponding public (that is, encryption) key, hence the names `public` and `private`, which denote the appropriate dissemination policies.

If you wish to prove the identity of the author of a file, the correct method is to use a digital signature, which is an entirely different application of cryptography. Note that this is not currently supported by `pgcrypto`, so you must implement your own methods as C functions or in a procedural language capable of using cryptographic libraries.

For really, really, really sensitive data!

For even more sensitive data, you may never want the data to leave the client computer unencrypted. Therefore, you need to encrypt the data before sending it to the database. In that case, PostgreSQL receives already encrypted data, and never sees the unencrypted version. This also means that the only useful indexes you can have are for use in `WHERE encrypted_column = encrypted_data` and for ensuring uniqueness.

Even these forms can be used only if the encryption algorithm always produces the same ciphertext (output) for the same plaintext (input), which is true only for weaker encryption algorithms. For example, it would be easy to determine the age or sex of a person if the same value is always encrypted into the same ciphertext. To avoid this vulnerability, strong encryption algorithms are able to produce a different ciphertext for the same value.

The versions of pgcrypto are usually compiled to use the *OpenSSL library* (http://www.openssl.org). If, for some reason, you don't have OpenSSL, or just don't want to use it, it is possible to compile pgcrypto without it, with a smaller number of supported encryption algorithms and a slightly reduced performance.

See also

- The page on pgcrypto in the PostgreSQL online documentation is available at http://www.postgresql.org/docs/current/static/pgcrypto.html
- The OpenSSL web page can be accessed at http://www.openssl.org/
- The *GNU Privacy Handbook* can be read at http://www.gnupg.org/gph/en/manual.html

7
Database Administration

In this chapter, we will cover the following recipes:

- Writing a script that either succeeds entirely or fails entirely
- Writing a psql script that exits on the first error
- Using psql variables
- Placing query output into psql variables
- Writing a conditional psql script
- Investigating a psql error
- Performing actions on many tables
- Adding/removing columns on a table
- Changing the data type of a column
- Changing the definition of a data type
- Adding/removing schemas
- Moving objects between schemas
- Adding/removing tablespaces
- Moving objects between tablespaces
- Accessing objects in other PostgreSQL databases
- Accessing objects in other foreign databases
- Updatable views
- Using materialized views

Introduction

In Chapter 5, *Tables and Data*, we looked at the contents of tables and various complexities.
Now we'll turn our attention to larger administration tasks that we need to perform from
time to time, such as creating things, moving things around, storing things neatly, and
removing them when they're no longer required.

The most sensible way to perform major administrative tasks is to write a script to do what you think is required. If you're unsure, you can always run the script on a system test server, and then run it again on the production server once you're happy. Manically typing commands against production database servers isn't wise. Worse, using an admin tool can lead to serious issues if that tool doesn't show you the SQL you're about to execute. If you haven't dropped your first live table yet, don't worry; you will. Perhaps you might want to read Chapter 11, *Backup and Recovery*, first, eh? Back it up using scripts.

Scripts are great because you can automate common tasks, and there's no need to sit there with a mouse, working your way through a hundred changes.

If you're drawn to the discussion about the command line versus GUI, then my thoughts and reasons are completely orthogonal to that. I want to encourage you to avoid errors and save time by repetitive and automatic execution of small administration programs or scripts. If it were safe or easy to do the equivalent of mouse movements in a script, then that would be an option; but it's definitely not. The only viable way to write a repeatable script is by writing text SQL commands.

Which scripting tool to use is a more interesting debate. We consider psql here because if you've got PostgreSQL, then you've certainly got it, without needing to install additional software. So we're on solid ground to provide examples that way.

On to the recipes! First, we'll start by looking at some scripting techniques that are valuable in PostgreSQL. This will make you more accurate and repeatable and free up time for other cool things.

Writing a script that either succeeds entirely or fails entirely

Database administration often involves applying a coordinated set of changes to the database. One of PostgreSQL's great strengths is the transaction system, wherein almost all actions can be executed inside a transaction. This allows us to build a script with many actions that will either all succeed or all fail. This means that if any of these actions fail, then all the other actions in the script are rolled back and never become visible to any other user, which can be critically important on a production system. This property is referred to as *atomicity* in the sense that the script is intended as a single unit that cannot be split, and this is the meaning of the *A* in the *ACID* properties of database transactions.

Transactions definitely apply to **Data Definition Language** (**DDL**), which refers to the set of SQL commands used to define, modify, and delete database objects. The term DDL goes back many years, but it persists because that subset is a useful short name for the commands that most administrators need to execute: CREATE, ALTER, DROP, and so on.

 Although most commands in PostgreSQL are transactional, there are a few that cannot be. The most common example is of commands that use sequences. They cannot be transactional because when a new sequence number is allocated, the effect of having *consumed* that number must become visible immediately, without waiting for that transaction to be committed. Otherwise, the same number will be given to another transaction, which is contrary to what sequences are supposed to do.

How to do it...

The basic way to ensure that we get all commands successful or none at all is to literally wrap our script into a transaction, as follows:

```
BEGIN; command 1; command 2; command 3; COMMIT;
```

Writing a transaction control command involves editing the script, which you may not want to do or even have access to do. There are, however, other ways as well.

From psql, you can do this by simply using the -1 or --single-transaction command-line options, as follows:

```
bash $ psql -1 -f myscript.sql
bash $ psql --single-transaction -f myscript.sql
```

The -1 option is short, but I recommend using --single-transaction, as it's much clearer which option is being selected.

How it works...

The entire script will fail if, at any point, one of the commands gives an error (or higher) message. Almost all of the SQL used to define objects (DDL) allows a way to avoid throwing errors. More precisely, commands that begin with the DROP keyword have an IF EXISTS option. This allows you to execute the DROP keyword, whether or not the object already exists.

Thus, by the end of the command, that object will not exist:

```
DROP VIEW IF EXISTS cust_view;
```

Similarly, most commands that begin with the CREATE keyword have the optional OR REPLACE suffix. This allows the CREATE statement to overwrite the definition if one already exists, or add the new object if it didn't exist yet, like this:

```
CREATE OR REPLACE VIEW cust_view AS SELECT * FROM cust;
```

In the cases where both the DROP IF EXISTS and CREATE OR REPLACE options exist, you might think that CREATE OR REPLACE is usually sufficient. However, if you change the output definition of a function or a view, then using OR REPLACE is not sufficient. In that case, you must use DROP and recreate it, as shown in the following example:

```
postgres=# CREATE OR REPLACE VIEW cust_view AS
SELECT col as title1 FROM cust;
CREATE VIEW
postgres=# CREATE OR REPLACE VIEW cust_view
AS SELECT col as title2 FROM cust;
ERROR:  cannot change name of view column "title1" to "title2"
```

Note also that CREATE INDEX does not have an OR REPLACE option. If you run it twice, you'll get two indexes on your table, unless you specifically name the index. There is a DROP INDEX IF EXISTS option, but it may take a long time to drop and recreate an index. An index exists just for the purpose of optimization, and it does not change the actual result of any query, so this different behavior is actually very convenient. This is also reflected in the fact that the SQL standard doesn't mention indexes at all, even though they exist in practically all database systems, because they do not affect the logical layer.

PostgreSQL does not support nested transaction control commands, which can lead to unexpected behavior. For instance, consider the following code, written in a *nested transaction* style:

```
postgres=# BEGIN;
BEGIN
postgres=# CREATE TABLE a(x int);
CREATE TABLE
postgres=# BEGIN;
WARNING:  there is already a transaction in progress
BEGIN
postgres=# CREATE TABLE b(x int);
CREATE TABLE
postgres=# COMMIT;
COMMIT
```

```
postgres=# ROLLBACK;
NOTICE:  there is no transaction in progress
ROLLBACK
```

A hypothetical author of such code probably meant to create table a first, and then create table b. Then, they changed their mind and rolled back both the *inner* transaction and the *outer* transaction. However, what PostgreSQL does is discard the second BEGIN statement so that the COMMIT statement is matched with the first BEGIN statement and the *inner* transaction becomes a top-level transaction. Hence, right after the COMMIT statement, we are outside a transaction block, so the next statement is assigned its own transaction. When ROLLBACK is issued as the next statement, PostgreSQL notices that the transaction is actually empty.

The danger in this particular example is that the user inadvertently committed a transaction, thus waving the right to roll it back, although we should say that a careful user would have noticed the warning and paused to think before going ahead.

From this example, you learn a valuable lesson: if you have used transaction control commands in your script, then wrapping them again in a higher-level script or command can cause problems of the worst kind, such as committing stuff that you wanted to roll back. This is important enough to deserve a boxed warning.

 PostgreSQL accepts nested transactional control commands, but does not act on them. After the first commit, the commands will be assumed to be transactions in their own right and will persist should the script fail. Be careful!

There's more...

The following commands cannot be included in a script that uses transactions in the way we just described:

- CREATE DATABASE/DROP DATABASE
- CREATE TABLESPACE/DROP TABLESPACE
- CREATE INDEX CONCURRENTLY
- VACUUM
- REINDEX DATABASE/REINDEX SYSTEM
- CLUSTER

None of these actions need to be run manually on a regular basis within complex programs, so this shouldn't be a problem for you.

Note also that these commands do not substantially alter the *logical* content of a database; that is, they don't create new user tables or alter any rows, so there's less need to use them inside complex transactions.

While PostgreSQL does not support nested transaction commands, it supports the notion of SAVEPOINT, which can be used to achieve the same behavior. Suppose we wanted to implement the following pseudocode:

```
(begin transaction T1)
  (statement 1)
  (begin transaction T2)
    (statement 2)
  (commit transaction T2)
  (statement 3)
(commit transaction t1)
```

The effect we seek has the following properties:

- If statements 1 and 3 succeed, and statement 2 fails, then statements 1 and 3 will be committed
- If all three statements succeed, then they will all be committed
- Otherwise, no statement will be committed

These properties also hold with the following PostgreSQL commands:

```
BEGIN;
  - (statement 1)
  SAVEPOINT T2;
  - (statement 2)
  RELEASE SAVEPOINT T2; /* we assume that statement 2 does not fail */
  - (statement 3)
COMMIT;
```

This form, as noted in the code, applies only if statement 2 does not fail. If it fails, we must replace RELEASE SAVEPOINT with ROLLBACK TO SAVEPOINT, or we will get an error. This is a slight difference with top-level transaction commands; a COMMIT statement is silently converted in a ROLLBACK when the transaction is in a failed state.

Writing a psql script that exits on the first error

The default mode for the psql script tool is to continue processing when it finds an error. This sounds dumb, but it exists for historical compatibility only. There are some easy and mostly permanent ways to avoid this, so let's look at them.

Getting ready

Let's start with a simple script, with a command we know will fail:

```
$ $EDITOR test.sql
mistake1;
mistake2;
mistake3;
```

Execute the following script using psql to see what the results look like:

```
$ psql -f test.sql
psql:test.sql:1: ERROR:  syntax error at or near "mistake1"
LINE 1: mistake1;
        ^
psql:test.sql:2: ERROR:  syntax error at or near "mistake2"
LINE 1: mistake2;
        ^
psql:test.sql:3: ERROR:  syntax error at or near "mistake3"
LINE 1: mistake3;
        ^
```

How to do it...

1. To exit the script on the first error, we can write the following command:

```
$ psql -f test.sql -v ON_ERROR_STOP=on
psql:test.sql:1: ERROR:  syntax error at or near "mistake1"
LINE 1: mistake1;
        ^
```

2. Alternatively, we can edit the `test.sql` file with the initial line shown here:

```
$ $EDITOR test.sql
\set ON_ERROR_STOP on
mistake1;
mistake2;
mistake3;
```

3. Note that the following command will *not* work because we have missed the crucial ON value:

```
$ psql -f test.sql -v ON_ERROR_STOP
```

How it works...

The ON_ERROR_STOP variable is a psql special variable that controls the behavior of psql as it executes in script mode. When this variable is set, a SQL error will generate an OS return code 3, whereas other OS-related errors will return code 1.

There's more...

You can place some psql commands in a profile that will get executed when you run psql. Adding ON_ERROR_STOP to your profile will ensure that this setting is applied to all psql sessions:

```
$ $EDITOR ~/.psqlrc
\set ON_ERROR_STOP
```

You can forcibly override this, and request psql to execute without a profile using -X. This is probably the safest thing to do for batch execution of scripts, so they always work in the same way, irrespective of the local settings.

ON_ERROR_STOP is one of some special variables that affect the way psql behaves. The full list is available at the following URL:

```
https://www.postgresql.org/docs/10/static/app-psql.html#APP-PSQL-VARIABLES
```

Using psql variables

In the previous recipe, we have seen how to use the ON_ERROR_STOP variable. Here we show how to work with any variable, including user-defined ones.

Getting ready

As an example, we create a script that does some work on a given table. We will keep it simple, because we just want to show how variables work.

For instance, we might want to add a text column to a table, and then set it to a given value. So we write the following lines into a file called vartest.sql:

```
ALTER TABLE mytable ADD COLUMN mycol text;
UPDATE mytable SET mycol = 'myval';
```

The script can be run as follows:

```
psql -f vartest.sql
```

How to do it...

We change vartest.sql as follows:

```
\set tabname mytable
\set colname mycol
\set colval 'myval'
ALTER TABLE :tabname ADD COLUMN :colname text;
UPDATE :tabname SET :colname = :'colval';
```

How it works...

What do these changes mean? We have defined three variables, setting them respectively to the table name, column name and column value. Then we have replaced the mentions of those specific values with the name of the variable preceded by a colon, which in psql means "replace with the value of this variable". In the case of colval, we have also surrounded the variable name by single quotes, meaning "treat the value as a string".

If we want `vartest.sql` to add a different column, we just have to make one change to the top of the script, where all variables are conveniently set. Then the new column name will be used.

There's more...

This was just one way to define variables. Another is to indicate them in the command line, when running the script:

```
psql -v tabname=mytab2 -f vartest.sql
```

Variables can also be set interactively. The following line will prompt the user, and then set the variable to whatever is typed before hitting *Enter*:

```
\prompt 'Insert the table name: ' tabname
```

In the next recipe, we will see how to set variables using an SQL query.

Placing query output into psql variables

It is also possible to store some values produced by a query into variables, for instance to reuse them later in other queries.

In this recipe we demonstrate this approach with a concrete example.

Getting ready

In recipe *Controlling automatic database maintenance* of Chapter 9, *Regular Maintenance*, we describe VACUUM, showing that it runs regularly on each table based on the number of rows that might need vacuuming ("dead rows"). VACUUM will run if that number exceeds a given threshold, which by default is just above 20% of the row count.

In this recipe we create a script that picks the table with the largest number of dead rows, and runs VACUUM on it.

How to do it...

The script is as follows:

```
SELECT schemaname
, relname
, n_dead_tup
, n_live_tup
FROM pg_stat_user_tables
ORDER BY n_dead_tup DESC
LIMIT 1
\gset
\qecho Running VACUUM on table :"relname" in schema :"schemaname"
\qecho Rows before: :n_dead_tup dead, :n_live_tup live
VACUUM ANALYZE :schemaname.:relname;
\qecho Waiting 1 second...
SELECT pg_sleep(1);
SELECT n_dead_tup AS n_dead_tup_now
,       n_live_tup AS n_live_tup_now
FROM pg_stat_user_tables
WHERE schemaname = :'schemaname'
AND relname = :'relname'
\gset
\qecho Rows after: :n_dead_tup_now dead, :n_live_tup_now live
```

How it works...

You might have noticed that the first query is not ended by a semicolon, as usual. This is because we end it with \gset instead, which means "run the query, and assign each returned value to a variable having the same name of the output column".

This command expects the query to return exactly one row, as you might expect too, and if not it does not set any variable.

The script waits one second before reading the updated number of dead and live rows. The reason for the wait is that such statistics are updated after the end of the transaction that makes the changes, which sends a signal to the statistics collector which then does the update.

There's more...

See the next recipe on how to improve the script with iterations so that it vacuums more than one table.

Writing a conditional psql script

psql supports conditional meta-commands \if, \elif, \else and \endif. In this recipe we demonstrate some of them.

Getting ready

We want to improve the vartest.sql script so that it runs VACUUM only if there actually are dead rows in that table.

How to do it...

We add conditional commands to vartest.sql resulting in the following script:

```
SELECT schemaname
, relname
, n_dead_tup
, n_live_tup
, n_dead_tup > 0 AS needs_vacuum
FROM pg_stat_user_tables
ORDER BY n_dead_tup DESC
LIMIT 1
\gset
\if :needs_vacuum
\qecho Running VACUUM on table :"relname" in schema :"schemaname"
\qecho Rows before: :n_dead_tup dead, :n_live_tup live
VACUUM ANALYZE :schemaname.:relname;
\qecho Waiting 1 second...
SELECT pg_sleep(1);
```

```
SELECT n_dead_tup AS n_dead_tup_now
,       n_live_tup AS n_live_tup_now
FROM pg_stat_user_tables
WHERE schemaname = :'schemaname' AND relname = :'relname'
\gset
\qecho Rows after: :n_dead_tup_now dead, :n_live_tup_now live
\else
\qecho Skipping VACUUM on table :"relname" in schema :"schemaname"
\endif
```

How it works...

We have added an extra column `needs_vacuum` to the first query, resulting in one more variable that we can use to make the VACUUM part conditional.

There's more...

Conditional statements are usually part of flow control statements, which include also iterations.

While iterating is not directly supported by psql, a similar effect can be achieved in other ways. For instance:

- A script, called for instance file.sql, can be iterated by adding some lines at the end, as in the following fragment:

```
SELECT /* add a termination condition as appropriate */ AS
do_loop
\gset
\if do_loop
\ir file.sql
\endif
```

- Instead of iterating, you can follow the approach described later in this chapter in the recipe *Performing actions on many tables*.

Investigating a psql error

Error messages can sometimes be cryptic, and you may be left wondering *why did this error happen at all?*

For this purpose, `psql` recognizes two variables, VERBOSITY and CONTEXT; valid values are terse, default, or verbose for the former, and never, errors, or always for the latter. A more verbose error message will hopefully specify extra detail, and the context information will be included. Here is an example to show the difference:

```
postgres=# \set VERBOSITY terse
postgres=# \set CONTEXT never
postgres=# select * from missingtable;
ERROR:  relation "missingtable" does not exist at character 15
```

This is quite a simple error, so we don't actually need the extra detail, but it is nevertheless useful for illustrating the extra detail you get when raising verbosity and enabling context information:

```
postgres=# \set VERBOSITY verbose
postgres=# \set CONTEXT errors
postgres=# select * from missingtable;
ERROR:  42P01: relation "missingtable" does not exist
LINE 1: select * from missingtable;
                      ^
LOCATION:  parserOpenTable, parse_relation.c:1159
```

Now you get the SQL error code 42P01, which you can look up in the PostgreSQL manual, and even a reference to the file and the line in the PostgreSQL source code where this error is raised, so you can investigate it (the beauty of open source!).

However, there is a problem with having to enable verbosity in advance: you need to do it before running the command. If all errors were reproducible, this would not be a huge inconvenience. But in certain cases you may hit a transient error, such as a *serialization failure*, which is difficult to detect itself; and it could sometimes happen that you struggle to reproduce the error, let alone analyze it.

The `\errverbose` metacommand in `psql` was introduced precisely to avoid these problems.

Getting ready

In fact, there isn't much to do, as the point of the `\errverbose` meta-command is precisely to capture information on the error without requiring any prior activity.

How to do it...

1. Suppose you hit an error as in the following query, and `verbose` reporting was not enabled:

```
postgres=# create table wrongname();
ERROR:   relation "wrongname" already exists
```

2. The extra detail that is not displayed is nevertheless remembered by `psql`, so you can view it as follows:

```
postgres=# \errverbose
ERROR:   42P07: relation "wrongname" already exists
LOCATION:   heap_create_with_catalog, heap.c:1067
```

There's more...

- The list of PostgreSQL error codes is available in the manual at the following URL
  https://www.postgresql.org/docs/current/static/errcodes-appendix.html
- The PostgreSQL source code can be downloaded or inspected from this URL
  https://git.postgresql.org/

Performing actions on many tables

As a database administrator, you will often need to apply multiple commands as part of the same overall task. That task could be one of the following:

- Many different actions on multiple tables
- The same action on multiple tables
- The same action on multiple tables in parallel
- Different actions-one on each table-in parallel

The first is a general case where you need to make a set of coordinated changes. The solution is *write a script*, as we've already discussed. We can also call this static scripting because you write the script manually and then execute it.

The second type of task can be achieved very simply with dynamic scripts, where we write a script that writes another script. This technique is the main topic of this recipe.

Performing actions in parallel sounds really cool, and it would be useful if it were easy. In some ways it is, but trying to run multiple tasks concurrently and trap and understand all the errors is much harder. And if you're thinking it won't matter if you don't check for errors, think again. If you run tasks in parallel, then you cannot run them inside the same transaction; so you definitely need error checking.

Don't worry! Running in parallel is usually not as bad as it may seem after reading the previous paragraph, and we'll explain it after a few basic examples.

Getting ready

Let's just create a basic schema to run some examples:

```
postgres=# create schema test;
CREATE SCHEMA
postgres=# create table test.a (col1 INTEGER);
CREATE TABLE
postgres=# create table test.b (col1 INTEGER);
CREATE TABLE
postgres=# create table test.c (col1 INTEGER);
CREATE TABLE
```

How to do it...

Our task is to run an SQL statement using this form, with X as the table name, against each of our three test tables:

```
ALTER TABLE X
ADD COLUMN last_update_timestamp TIMESTAMP WITH TIME ZONE;
```

The steps are as follows:

1. Our starting point is a script that lists the tables that we want to perform tasks against—something like the following:

```
postgres=# SELECT relname
        FROM pg_class c
        JOIN pg_namespace n
        ON c.relnamespace = n.oid
        WHERE n.nspname = 'test';
```

2. This displays the list of tables that we will act upon (so that you can check it):

```
relname
---------
a
b
c
(3 rows)
```

3. We then use the preceding SQL to generate the text for a SQL script, substituting the schema name and table name in the SQL text. We then output to a script file named multi.sql, as follows:

```
postgres=# \t on
postgres=# \o multi.sql
postgres=# SELECT 'ALTER TABLE '|| n.nspname
        || '.' || c.relname ||
' ADD COLUMN last_update_timestamp TIMESTAMP WITH TIME ZONE; '
FROM pg_class c
JOIN pg_namespace n
ON c.relnamespace = n.oid
WHERE n.nspname = 'test';
\o
```

4. Once we've generated the script, we can check whether all of it looks correct:

```
postgres=# \! cat multi.sql
 ALTER TABLE test.a ADD COLUMN
 last_update_timestamp TIMESTAMP WITH TIME ZONE;
 ALTER TABLE test.b ADD COLUMN
 last_update_timestamp TIMESTAMP WITH TIME ZONE;
 ALTER TABLE test.c ADD COLUMN
 last_update_timestamp TIMESTAMP WITH TIME ZONE;
```

5. Finally, we run the script and watch the results (success!):

```
postgres=# \i multi.sql
ALTER TABLE
ALTER TABLE
ALTER TABLE
```

How it works...

Overall, this is just an example of dynamic scripting, and it has been used by DBAs for many decades, even before PostgreSQL was born.

This method can go wrong in various ways, especially if you generate SQL text with syntax errors. Just fix that and carry on.

The \t command means *tuples only*, so keeping \t to on will ensure that there are no headers, command tags, or row counts following the results.

The \o FILENAME command redirects the output to a file until the subsequent \o command reverts to no redirection.

The \! command runs operating system commands, so \! cat will show the file contents on *nix systems.

The \i command redirects the input from a file, or in simpler terms, executes the named file. Running the script in this way may ignore earlier recipes, so I still recommend following those earlier guidelines.

The \ir command does the same as \i; the difference is that \ir is relative to the directory where the current script is, while \i is relative to the *current* directory. This directory is the one where the psql command line was started, and is changed by the \cd command.

Dynamic scripting can also be called a "quick and dirty" approach. The previous scripts didn't filter out views and other objects in the test schema, so you'll need to add that yourself, or not, as required.

There is another way of doing this as well:

```
DO $$
DECLARE t record;
BEGIN
    FOR t IN SELECT c.*, n.nspname
            FROM pg_class c JOIN pg_namespace n
            ON c.relnamespace = n.oid
            WHERE n.nspname = 'test' /* ; not needed */
    LOOP
            EXECUTE 'ALTER TABLE '|| quote_ident(t.nspname) ||
            '.' || quote_ident(t.relname) ||
             ' ADD COLUMN last_update_timestamp ' ||
            'TIMESTAMP WITH TIME ZONE';
    END LOOP;
END $$;
```

I don't prefer using this method because it executes the SQL directly and doesn't allow you to keep the script afterwards.

The preceding syntax with DO is called an **anonymous code block** because it's like a function without a name.

There's more...

Earlier, I said I'll explain how to run multiple tasks in parallel. Some practical approaches to this are possible, with a bit of discussion.

Making tasks run in parallel can be thought of as subdividing the main task so that we run x2, x4, x8, and other subscripts, rather than one large script.

First, you should note that error checking gets worse when you spawn more parallel tasks, whereas performance improves most for the first few subdivisions. Also, we're often constrained by CPU, RAM, or I/O resources for intensive tasks. This means that splitting a main task into two to four parallel subtasks isn't practical without some kind of tool to help us manage them.

There are two approaches here, depending on the two types of tasks:

- A task consists of many smaller tasks, all roughly of the same size
- A task consists of many smaller tasks, and the execution times vary according to the size and complexity of the database object

If we have lots of smaller tasks, then we can simply run our scripts multiple times using a simple round-robin split of tasks so that each subscript runs a part of all subtasks. Here is how to do it: each row in pg_class has a hidden column called oid, whose value is a 32-bit number allocated from an internal counter on table creation. Therefore, about half of the tables will have even values of oid, and we can achieve an even split by adding the following clauses:

- **Script 1**: Add WHERE c.oid % 2 = 0
- **Script 2**: Add WHERE c.oid % 2 = 1

The task we were performing as an example was to add a column to many tables. In the previous example, we were adding the column with no specified default; so the new column will have a NULL value, and as a result, it will run very quickly with ALTER TABLE, even on large tables. If we change the ALTER TABLE statement so as to specify a default, then PostgreSQL will need to rewrite the entire table. So the runtime will vary according to the table size (approximately, and also according to the number and type of indexes).

Now that our subtasks vary in runtime according to size, we need to be more careful when splitting the subtasks so that we can end up with multiple scripts that will run for about the same time.

If we already know that we have just a few big tables, it's easy to split those manually into their own scripts.

If the database has many large tables, then we can sort SQL statements by table size and then distribute them using round-robin distribution into multiple subscripts that will have approximately the same runtime. The following SQL script, which should be saved in a `make-script.sql` file, is an example of this technique:

```
\t on
\o script-:i.sql
SELECT sql FROM (
SELECT 'ALTER TABLE '|| n.nspname || '.' || c.relname ||
' ADD COLUMN last_update_timestamp TIMESTAMP WITH TIME ZONE   DEFAULT
now();' as sql
,row_number() OVER (ORDER BY pg_relation_size(c.oid))
FROM pg_class c
 JOIN pg_namespace n
 ON c.relnamespace = n.oid
WHERE n.nspname = 'test'
ORDER BY 2 DESC) as s
WHERE row_number % 2 = :i;
\o
```

Then, we generate the two scripts, as follows:

```
$ psql -v i=0 -f make-script.sql
$ psql -v i=1 -f make-script.sql
```

Finally, we execute the two jobs in parallel, like this:

```
$ psql -f script-0.sql &
$ psql -f script-1.sql &
```

Note how we used `psql` parameters—via the `-v` command line option—to select different rows using the same script.

Also, note how we used the `row_number()` window function to sort the data by size. Then, we split the data into pieces using the following line:

```
WHERE row_number % N = i;
```

Here, N is the total number of scripts we're producing, and i ranges between 0 and N minus 1 (we are using modular arithmetic to distribute the subtasks).

Adding/removing columns on a table

As designs change, we may want to add or remove columns from our data tables. These are common operations in development, though they need more careful planning on a running production database server, as they take full locks and may run for long periods.

How to do it...

You can add a new column to a table using this command:

```
ALTER TABLE mytable
ADD COLUMN last_update_timestamp TIMESTAMP WITHOUT TIME ZONE;
```

You can drop the same column using the following command:

```
ALTER TABLE mytable
DROP COLUMN last_update_timestamp;
```

You can combine multiple operations when using ALTER TABLE, which then applies the changes in a sequence. This allows you to do a useful trick, which is to add a column unconditionally, using IF EXISTS, as follows:

```
ALTER TABLE mytable
DROP COLUMN IF EXISTS last_update_timestamp,ADD COLUMN
last_update_timestamp TIMESTAMP WITHOUT TIME ZONE;
```

Note that this will have almost the same effect as the following command:

```
UPDATE mytable SET last_update_timestamp = NULL;
```

However, ALTER TABLE runs much faster. That's very cool if you want to perform an update, but not much fun if you want to keep the data in the existing column.

How it works...

The `ALTER TABLE` statement, which is used to add or drop a column, takes a full table lock (at the `AccessExclusiveLock` lock level) so that it can prevent all other actions on the table. So we want it to be as fast as possible.

The `DROP COLUMN` command doesn't actually remove the column from each row of the table; it just marks the column as dropped. This makes `DROP COLUMN` a very fast operation.

The `ADD COLUMN` command is also very fast if we are adding a nullable column with a null default value. If we use a `NOT NULL` constraint or specify an explicit default value, then we'll need to rewrite every row of the table, which can be quite slow.

The `ALTER TABLE` command allows us to execute many column operations at once, as shown in the main recipe. The `ALTER TABLE` command is optimized so that we are able to include all column operations in a single pass of the table, greatly improving the speed for complex sets of changes:

```
ALTER TABLE mytable
ADD COLUMN last_update_userid INTEGER DEFAULT 0,ADD COLUMN
last_update_comment TEXT;
```

If we rewrite the table, then the dropped columns are removed. If not, they may stay there for some time. Subsequent `INSERT` and `UPDATE` operations will insert a null value for the dropped column (s). Updates will reduce the size of the stored rows if they were not null already. So, in theory, you just have to wait, and the database will eventually reclaim the space. In practice, this works only if all the rows in the table are updated within a given period of time. Many tables contain historical data, so space may not be reclaimed at all without additional actions.

The PostgreSQL manual recommends changing the data type of a column to the same type-which forces rewriting of every row as a technique to reclaim the space taken by the dropped columns. I don't recommend this because it will completely lock the table for a long period, at least on larger databases. My recommendation is not to drop the column at all, if you can avoid it, when you're in production. Just keep track of the changes you would make if you get time, if ever. If you're looking at alternatives, then `VACUUM` will not rewrite the table, though a `VACUUM FULL` or a `CLUSTER` statement will. Be careful in those cases as well, because they also hold a full table lock.

There's more...

Indexes that depend on a dropped column are automatically dropped as well. All other objects that depend on the column(s), such as foreign keys from other tables, will cause the ALTER TABLE statement to be rejected. You can override this and drop everything in sight using the CASCADE option, as follows:

```
ALTER TABLE x
DROP COLUMN  last_update_timestamp
CASCADE;
```

Adding a column with a non-null default value can be done with ALTER TABLE ... ADD COLUMN ... DEFAULT ..., as shown above, which however holds an AccessExclusive lock for the whole duration of the command, which is not short as 100% of the rows must be rewritten.

The script introduced in the recipe *"Using psql variables"* in this chapter is an example of how to do the same without holding an AccessExclusive lock for a long time. This lighter solution has only another tiny difference: it doesn't use a single transaction, which would be pointless since it would hold the lock until the end.

If any row is inserted by another session between the ALTER TABLE and the UPDATE, and that row has a NULL value for the new column, then that value will be updated together with all the rows that existed before the ALTER TABLE, which is OK in most cases, but not in all, depending on the data model of the application.

A proper solution would involve using two sessions, to ensure that no such writes can happen in between, with a procedure that can be sketched as follows:

1. Open two sessions, and note their PIDs
2. In session 1, BEGIN a transaction, then take an ACCESS EXCLUSIVE lock on the table, which will be granted
3. Immediately after, but in session 2, BEGIN a transaction, then take a SHARE lock on the table, which will hang waiting for session 1
4. In a third session, display the ordered wait queue for locks on session 1 as follows:

   ```
   SELECT *
   FROM pg_stat_activity
   WHERE pg_blocking_pids(pid) @> array[pid1]
   ORDER BY state_change;
   ```

(here `pid1` is the PID of session 1) and check that PID2 is the second one in the list; if not, it means that step *3* was not fast enough, so ROLLBACK both sessions and repeat from step *1*.

5. In session 1, perform ALTER TABLE and then COMMIT
6. In session 2 (which will be unblocked by the previous step, and will therefore acquire the SHARE lock straight away), perform the UPDATE and then the COMMIT

Changing the data type of a column

Thankfully, changing column data types is not an everyday task, but when we need to do it, we must know all the details so that we can perform the conversion on a production system without any errors.

Getting ready

Let's start with a simple example of a table, as follows:

```
postgres=# select * from birthday;
```

This gives the following output:

```
 name  |   dob
-------+--------
 simon | 690926
(1 row)
```

The preceding table was created using this command:

```
CREATE TABLE birthday
( name        TEXT, dob        INTEGER);
```

How to do it...

Let's say we want to change the `dob` column to another data type. Let's try with a simple example first, as follows:

```
postgres=# ALTER TABLE birthday
postgres-# ALTER COLUMN dob SET DATA TYPE text;
ALTER TABLE
```

This works fine. Let's just change that back to the `integer` type so that we can try something more complex, such as a `date` data type:

```
postgres=# ALTER TABLE birthday
postgres-# ALTER COLUMN dob SET DATA TYPE integer;
ERROR:  column "dob" cannot be cast to type integer
```

Oh! What went wrong? Let's try using an explicit conversion with the `USING` clause, as follows:

```
postgres=# ALTER TABLE birthday
              ALTER COLUMN dob SET DATA TYPE integer
              USING dob::integer;
ALTER TABLE
```

This works as expected. Now let's try moving to a `date` type:

```
postgres=# ALTER TABLE birthday
ALTER COLUMN dob SET DATA TYPE date
USING date(to_date(dob::text, 'YYMMDD') -
      (CASE WHEN dob/10000 BETWEEN 16 AND 69 THEN interval '100
        years'
      ELSE interval '0' END));
```

Now it gives what we were hoping to see:

```
postgres=# select * from birthday;
 name  |    dob
-------+------------
 simon | 26/09/1969
(1 row)
```

With PostgreSQL, you can also set or drop default expressions, irrespective of whether or not the NOT NULL constraints are applied:

```
ALTER TABLE foo
ALTER COLUMN col DROP DEFAULT;
ALTER TABLE foo
ALTER COLUMN col SET DEFAULT 'expression';
ALTER TABLE foo
ALTER COLUMN col SET NOT NULL;
ALTER TABLE foo
ALTER COLUMN col DROP NOT NULL;
```

How it works...

Moving from the integer to the date type uses a complex USING expression. Let's break that down step by step so that we can see why, as follows:

```
postgres=# ALTER TABLE birthday
ALTER COLUMN dob SET DATA TYPE date
USING date(to_date(dob::text, 'YYMMDD') -
      (CASE WHEN dob/10000 BETWEEN 16 AND 69
      THEN interval '100 years'
      ELSE interval '0' END));
```

First, we can't move directly from integer to date. We need to convert it to text and then to date. The dob::text statement means *cast to text*.

Once we have text, we use the to_date() function to move to a date type.

This is not enough; our starting data was 690926, which we presume is a date in the YYMMDD format. When PostgreSQL converts this data to a date, it assumes that the two-digit year, 69, is in the current century because it chooses the year nearest to 2020. So it outputs 2069 rather than 1969. This is why a case statement is added to reduce any year between 16 and 69 to be a date in the previous century by explicitly subtracting an interval of 100 years. We do not need to take away one century for years after 69 because they are already placed in the 20th century.

It is very strongly recommended that you test this conversion by performing a SELECT first. Converting data types, especially to/from dates, always causes some problems, so don't try to do this quickly. Always take a backup of the data first.

There's more...

The USING clause can also be used to handle complex expressions involving other columns. This could be used for data transformations, which might be useful for DBAs in some circumstances, such as migrating to a new database design on a production database server. Let's put everything together in a full, working example. We will start with this table that has to be transformed:

```
postgres=# select * from cust;
 customerid | firstname | lastname | age
------------+-----------+----------+-----
          1 | Philip    | Marlowe  |  38
          2 | Richard   | Hannay   |  42
          3 | Holly     | Martins  |  25
          4 | Harry     | Palmer   |  36
(4 rows)
```

We want to transform it into a table design like the following:

```
postgres=# select * from cust;
 customerid |    custname    | age
------------+----------------+-----
          1 | Philip Marlowe |  38
          2 | Richard Hannay |  42
          3 | Holly Martins  |  25
          4 | Harry Palmer   |  36
(4 rows)
```

We can decide to do it using these simple steps:

```
ALTER TABLE cust ADD COLUMN custname text NOT NULL DEFAULT '';
UPDATE cust SET custname = firstname || ' ' || lastname;
ALTER TABLE cust DROP COLUMN firstname;
ALTER TABLE cust DROP COLUMN lastname;
```

We can also use the SQL commands directly or make them use a tool such as **OmniDB**. Following those steps may cause problems, as the changes aren't within a transaction, meaning that other users can see the changes when they are only half finished. Hence, it would be better to do this in a single transaction, using BEGIN and COMMIT. Also, those four changes require us to make two passes over the table.

However, we can perform the entire transformation in one pass using multiple clauses on the `ALTER TABLE` command. So instead, we do the following:

```
BEGIN;
ALTER TABLE cust
  ALTER COLUMN firstname SET DATA TYPE text
        USING firstname || ' ' || lastname,
  ALTER COLUMN firstname SET NOT NULL,
  ALTER COLUMN firstname SET DEFAULT '',
  DROP COLUMN lastname;
ALTER TABLE cust RENAME firstname TO custname;
COMMIT;
```

This is a great example of why I personally prefer using scripts to make such changes to large production databases rather than directly making the changes using a GUI.

Some type changes can be performed without actually rewriting rows, for example, if you are casting data from `varchar` to `text`, or from `NUMERIC(10,2)` to `NUMERIC(18,2)`, or simply to `NUMERIC`. Moreover, foreign key constraints will recognize type changes of this kind on the source table, and will therefore skip the constraint check whenever it is safe.

Changing the definition of a data type

PostgreSQL comes with several data types, but users can create custom types to most faithfully represent any value. Data type management is mostly, but not exclusively, a developer's job, and data type design goes beyond the scope of this book. This is a quick recipe that covers only the simpler problem of the need to apply a specific change to an existing data type.

Getting ready

Enumerative data types are defined like this:

```
CREATE TYPE satellites_urani AS ENUM ('titania','oberon');
```

The other popular case is composite data types, which are created as follows:

```
CREATE TYPE node AS
( node_name text,
  connstr text,
  standbys text[]);
```

How to do it...

If you made a mistake in the spelling of some enumerative values, and you realize it too late, you can fix it like in the following example:

```
ALTER TYPE satellites_urani RENAME VALUE 'titania' TO 'Titania';
ALTER TYPE satellites_urani RENAME VALUE 'oberon' TO 'Oberon';
```

This is very useful if the application expects—and uses—the right names.

A more complicate case is when you are upgrading your database to a new version, say because you want to consider some facts that were not available during the initial design, and you need extra values for the enumerative type that we defined in the preceding code. You want to put the new values in a certain position to preserve the correct ordering. For that, you can use an ALTER TYPE syntax, as follows:

```
ALTER TYPE satellites_urani ADD VALUE 'Ariel' BEFORE 'Titania';
ALTER TYPE satellites_urani ADD VALUE 'Umbriel' AFTER 'Ariel';
```

Composite data types can be changed with similar commands. Attributes can be renamed like in this example:

```
ALTER TYPE node
RENAME ATTRIBUTE slaves TO standbys;
```

And new attributes can be added as follows:

```
ALTER TYPE node
DROP ATTRIBUTE standbys,
ADD ATTRIBUTE async_standbys text[],
ADD ATTRIBUTE sync_standbys text[];
```

This form supports a list of changes, perhaps because composite types are more complex than a list of enumerative values, and can therefore, require complicated modifications.

How it works...

Each time you create a table, a composite type is automatically created with the same attribute names, types, and positions. Each ALTER TABLE command that changes table column definitions will silently issue a corresponding ALTER TYPE statement to keep the type in agreement with *its* table definition.

There's more...

When an attribute is removed from a composite data type, the corresponding values will instantly disappear from all the values of that same type stored in any database table. What actually happens is that these values are still inside the tables, but they have become invisible because their attribute is now marked as deleted, and the space they occupy will be reclaimed only when the contents of the composite type are parsed again. This can be forced with a query like the following:

```
UPDATE mytable SET mynode = mynode :: text :: node;
```

Here, `mytable` is a table that has a `mynode` column of the `node` type. This query converts the values to the `text` type, displaying only current attribute values, and then back to `node`. You may have noticed that this behavior is very similar to the example of the dropped column in the previous recipe.

Adding/removing schemas

Separating groups of objects is a good way of improving administration efficiency. You need to know how to create new schemas and remove schemas that are no longer required.

How to do it...

To add a new schema, issue this command:

```
CREATE SCHEMA sharedschema;
```

If you want that schema to be owned by a particular user, then you can add the following option:

```
CREATE SCHEMA sharedschema AUTHORIZATION scarlett;
```

If you want to create a new schema that has the same name as an existing user, so that the user becomes the owner, then try this:

```
CREATE SCHEMA AUTHORIZATION scarlett;
```

In many database systems, the schema name is the same as that of the owning user. PostgreSQL allows schemas owned by one user to have objects owned by another user within them. This can be especially confusing when you have a schema of the same name as that of the owning user. To avoid this, you should have two types of schema: schemas that are named the same as the owning user should be limited to only objects owned by that user. Other general schemas can have shared ownership.

To remove a schema named `str`, we can issue the following command:

```
DROP SCHEMA str;
```

If you want to ensure that the schema exists in all cases, you can issue the following command:

```
CREATE SCHEMA IF NOT EXISTS str;
```

This command has been added to version 9.3. Clearly, you need to be careful because the outcome of the command depends on the previous state of the database. As an example, try issuing the following:

```
CREATE TABLE str.tb (x int);
```

This can generate an error if the `str` schema contained that table before CREATE SCHEMA IF NOT EXISTS was run. Otherwise, there's no namespace error.

Irrespective of your PostgreSQL version, there isn't a CREATE OR REPLACE SCHEMA command, so when you want to create a schema, regardless of whether or not it already exists, you can do the following:

```
DROP SCHEMA IF EXISTS newschema;
CREATE SCHEMA newschema;
```

The DROP SCHEMA command won't work unless the schema is empty or unless you use the nuclear option:

```
DROP SCHEMA IF EXISTS newschema CASCADE;
```

The nuclear option kills all known germs and all your database objects (*even the good objects*).

There's more...

In the SQL standard, you can also create a schema and the objects it contains in one SQL statement. PostgreSQL accepts this syntax if you need it:

```
CREATE SCHEMA foo
      CREATE TABLE account
      (id          INTEGER NOT NULL PRIMARY KEY
      ,balance     NUMERIC(50,2))
      CREATE VIEW accountsample AS
      SELECT *
      FROM account
      WHERE random() < 0.1;
```

Mostly, I find this limiting. This syntax exists to allow us to create two or more objects at the same time. That can be achieved more easily using PostgreSQL's ability to allow transactional DDL, which was discussed in the *Writing a script that either succeeds entirely or fails entirely* recipe.

Using schema-level privileges

Privileges can be granted for objects in a schema using the GRANT command, as follows:

```
GRANT SELECT ON ALL TABLES IN SCHEMA sharedschema TO PUBLIC;
```

However, this will only affect tables that already exist. Tables created in the future will inherit privileges defined by the ALTER DEFAULT PRIVILEGES command, as follows:

```
ALTER DEFAULT PRIVILEGES IN SCHEMA sharedschema
GRANT SELECT ON TABLES TO PUBLIC;
```

Moving objects between schemas

Once you've created schemas for administration purposes, you'll want to move existing objects to keep things tidy.

How to do it...

To move one table from its current schema to a new schema, use the following:

```
ALTER TABLE cust
SET SCHEMA anotherschema;
```

If you want to move all objects, you can consider renaming the schema itself, using the following query:

```
ALTER SCHEMA existingschema RENAME TO anotherschema;
```

This only works if another schema with that name does not exist. Otherwise, you'll need to run `ALTER TABLE` for each table you want to move. You can use the earlier recipe *Performing actions on many tables* to achieve that.

Views, sequences, functions, aggregates, and domains can also be moved by `ALTER` commands with `SET SCHEMA` options.

How it works...

When you move tables to a new schema, all the indexes, triggers, and rules defined on those tables will also be moved to the new schema. If you've used a `SERIAL` data type and an implicit sequence has been created, then that also moves to the new schema. Schemas are purely an administrative concept and they do not affect the location of the table's data files. Tablespaces don't work this way, as we will see in later recipes.

Databases, users/roles, languages, and conversions don't exist in a schema. Schemas exist in a particular database. Schemas don't exist within schemas; they are not arranged in a tree or hierarchy. More details can be found in the *Using multiple schemas* recipe in `Chapter 4, Server Control`.

There's more...

Casts don't exist in a schema, though the data types and functions they reference do exist. These things are not typically something we want to move around anyway. This is just a note if you're wondering how things work.

Adding/removing tablespaces

Tablespaces allow us to store PostgreSQL data across different devices. We might want to do that for performance or administrative ease, or our database might just have run out of disk space.

Getting ready

Before we can create a useful tablespace, we need the underlying devices in a production-ready form.

Think carefully about the speed, volume, and robustness of the disks you are about to use. Make sure that they are configured correctly. Those decisions will affect your life for the next few months and years!

Disk performance is a subtle issue that most people think can be decided in a few seconds. We recommend reading Chapter 10, *Performance and Concurrency*, from this book, as well as additional books on the same topic.

Once you've done all of that, then you can create a directory for your tablespace. The directory must be:

- Empty
- Owned by the PostgreSQL owning user ID
- Specified with an absolute pathname

On Linux and Unix systems, you shouldn't use a mount point directly. Create a subdirectory and use that instead. That simplifies ownership and avoids some filesystem-specific issues, such as getting lost+found directories.

The directory also needs to follow sensible naming conventions so that we can clearly identify which tablespace goes with which server. Do not be tempted to use something simple, such as data, because it will make later administration more difficult. Be especially careful that test or development servers do not and cannot get confused with production systems.

How to do it...

Once you've created your directory, adding the tablespace is simple:

```
CREATE TABLESPACE new_tablespace
LOCATION '/usr/local/pgsql/new_tablespace';
```

The command to remove the tablespace is also simple and is as follows:

```
DROP TABLESPACE new_tablespace;
```

Every tablespace has a location assigned to it, with the exception of the pg_global and pg_default default tablespaces, for shared system catalogs and all other objects, respectively. They don't have a location because they live in a subdirectory of the data directory.

A tablespace can be dropped only when it is empty, so how do you know when a tablespace is empty?

Tablespaces can contain both permanent and temporary objects. Permanent data objects are tables, indexes, and TOAST objects. We don't need to worry too much about TOAST objects because they are created and always live in the same tablespace as their main table, and you cannot manipulate their privileges or ownership.

Indexes can exist in separate tablespaces as a performance option, though that requires explicit specification in the CREATE INDEX statement. The default is to create indexes in the same tablespace as the table to which they belong.

Temporary objects may also exist in a tablespace. These exist when users have explicitly created temporary tables or there may be implicitly created data files when large queries overflow their work_mem settings. These files are created according to the setting of the temp_tablespaces parameter. That might cause an issue because you can't tell for certain what the setting of temp_tablespaces is for each user. Users can change their setting of temp_tablespaces from the default value specified in the postgresql.conf file to something else.

We can identify the tablespace of each user object using the following query:

```
SELECT spcname
     , relname
     , CASE WHEN relpersistence = 't' THEN 'temp '
            WHEN relpersistence = 'u' THEN 'unlogged '
       ELSE '' END ||
       CASE
       WHEN relkind = 'r' THEN 'table'
```

```
         WHEN relkind = 'p' THEN 'partitioned table'
         WHEN relkind = 'f' THEN 'foreign table'
         WHEN relkind = 't' THEN 'TOAST table'
         WHEN relkind = 'v' THEN 'view'
         WHEN relkind = 'm' THEN 'materialized view'
         WHEN relkind = 'S' THEN 'sequence'
         WHEN relkind = 'c' THEN 'type'
         ELSE 'index' END as objtype
FROM pg_class c join pg_tablespace ts
ON (CASE WHEN c.reltablespace = 0 THEN
         (SELECT dattablespace FROM pg_database
          WHERE datname = current_database())
     ELSE c.reltablespace END) = ts.oid
WHERE relname NOT LIKE 'pg_toast%'
AND relnamespace NOT IN
     (SELECT oid FROM pg_namespace
      WHERE nspname IN ('pg_catalog', 'information_schema'))
;
```

This displays an output like the following:

```
    spcname         |   relname   |   objtype
--------------------+-------------+------------
 new_tablespace     | x           | table
 new_tablespace     | y           | table
 new_tablespace     | z           | temp table
 new_tablespace     | y_val_idx   | index
```

You may also want to look at the `spcowner`, `relowner`, `relacl`, and `spcacl` columns to determine who owns what and what they're allowed to do. The `relacl` and `spcacl` columns refer to the **access control list** (**ACL**) that details the privileges available on those objects. The `spcowner` and `relowner` columns record the owners of the tablespace and tables/indexes, respectively.

How it works...

A tablespace is just a directory where we store PostgreSQL data files. We use symbolic links from the `data` directory to the tablespace.

We exclude TOAST tables because they are always in the same tablespace as their parent tables, but remember that TOAST tables are always in a separate schema. You can exclude TOAST tables using the `relkind` column, but that would still include the indexes on the TOAST tables. TOAST tables and TOAST indexes both start with `pg_toast`, so we can exclude those easily from our queries.

The preceding query needs to be complex because `pg_class` entry for an object will show `reltablespace = 0` when an object is created in the database's default tablespace. So if you directly join `pg_class` and `pg_tablespace`, you end up losing rows.

Note that we can see that a temporary object exists, and we can see the tablespace in which it is created, even though we cannot refer to a temporary object in another user's session.

There's more...

Some more notes on best practices follow.

A tablespace can contain objects from multiple databases, so it's possible to be in a position where there are no objects visible in the current database. The tablespace just refuses to go away, giving the following error:

```
ERROR:  tablespace "old_tablespace" is not empty
```

You are strongly advised to make a separate tablespace for each database to avoid confusion. This can be especially confusing if you have the same schema names and table names in the separate databases.

How to avoid this? If you just created a new tablespace directory, you might want to create subdirectories within that for each database that needs space, and then change the subdirectories to tablespaces instead.

You may also wish to consider giving each tablespace a specific owner, using the following query:

```
ALTER TABLESPACE new_tablespace OWNER TO eliza;
```

This may help smooth administration.

You may also wish to set default tablespaces for a user so that tables are automatically created there by issuing the following query:

```
ALTER USER eliza SET default_tablespace = 'new_tablespace';
```

Putting pg_wal on a separate device

You may seek advice about placing the `pg_wal` directory on a separate device for performance reasons. This sounds very similar to tablespaces, though there is no explicit command to do this once you have a running database, and files in `pg_wal` are frequently written. So you must perform the steps outlined in the following example:

1. Stop the database server:

   ```
   [postgres@myhost ~]$ pg_ctl stop
   ```

2. Move `pg_wal` to a location supported by a different disk device:

   ```
   [postgres@myhost ~]$ mv $PGDATA/pg_wal   /mnt/newdisk/
   ```

3. Create a symbolic link from the old location to the new location:

   ```
   [postgres@myhost ~]$ ln -s /mnt/newdisk/pg_wal    $PGDATA/pg_wal
   ```

4. Restart the database server:

   ```
   [postgres@myhost ~]$ pg_ctl start
   ```

5. Verify that everything is working by committing any transaction (preferably, a transaction that does not damage the existing workload):

   ```
   [postgres@myhost ~]$ psql -c 'CREATE TABLE pg_wal (x int)'
   ```

Tablespace-level tuning

As each tablespace has different I/O characteristics, we may wish to alter the planner cost parameters for each tablespace. These can be set with the following command:

```
ALTER TABLESPACE new_tablespace SET
(seq_page_cost = 0.05, random_page_cost = 0.1);
```

In this example, settings are roughly appropriate for an SSD drive, and it assumes that the drive is 40 times faster than an HDD for random reads, and 20 times faster for sequential reads.

The values given need more discussion than we have time for here.

Moving objects between tablespaces

Moving data between tablespaces may sometimes be required.

Getting ready

First, create your tablespaces. Once the old and new tablespaces exist, we can issue the commands to move them.

How to do it...

Tablespaces can contain both permanent and temporary objects.

Permanent data objects are tables, indexes, and TOAST objects. We don't need to worry too much about TOAST objects because they are created in and always live in the same tablespace as their main table. So, if you alter the tablespace of a table, its TOAST objects will also move:

```
ALTER TABLE mytable SET TABLESPACE new_tablespace;
```

Indexes can exist in separate tablespaces, and moving a table leaves the indexes where they are. Don't forget to run ALTER INDEX commands as well, one for each index, as follows:

```
ALTER INDEX mytable_val_idx SET TABLESPACE new_tablespace;
```

Temporary objects cannot be explicitly moved to a new tablespace, so we take that to mean you want to *ensure they are created somewhere else in the future*. To do that you need to do the following:

1. Edit the temp_tablespaces parameter, as shown in the *Updating the parameter file* recipe in Chapter 3, *Configuration*.
2. Reload the server to allow new configuration settings to take effect.

There is no single command to do this that will work for all users.

How it works...

If you want to move a table and its indexes all in one pass, you can issue all the commands in a single transaction, as follows:

```
BEGIN;
ALTER TABLE mytable SET TABLESPACE new_tablespace;
ALTER INDEX mytable_val1_idx SET TABLESPACE new_tablespace;
ALTER INDEX mytable_val2_idx SET TABLESPACE new_tablespace;
COMMIT;
```

Moving tablespaces means bulk copying of data. Copying happens sequentially, block by block. That works well, but there's no way to avoid the fact that the bigger the table, the longer it will take.

Performance will be optimized if archiving or streaming replication is not active, as no WAL will be written in that case.

You should be aware that the table is fully locked (the AccessExclusiveLock lock) while the copy is taking place, so this can cause an effective outage for your application. Be very careful!

If you want to ensure that objects are created in the right place next time you create them, then you can use this query:

```
SET default_tablespace = 'new_tablespace';
```

You can run this automatically for all users that connect to a database using the following query:

```
ALTER DATABASE mydb SET default_tablespace = 'new_tablespace';
```

Take care that you do not run the following command by mistake, however:

```
ALTER DATABASE mydb SET TABLESPACE new_tablespace;
```

This literally moves all objects that do not have an explicitly defined tablespace into new_tablespace. For a large database, this will take a very long time, and your database will be completely locked while it runs; not cool, if you do it by accident!

There's more...

If you just discovered that indexes don't get moved when you move a table, then you may want to check whether any indexes are in tablespaces different from their parent tables. Run the following to check:

```
SELECT i.relname as index_name
     , tsi.spcname as index_tbsp
     , t.relname as table_name
     , tst.spcname as table_tbsp
  FROM ( pg_class t /* tables */
          JOIN pg_tablespace tst
            ON t.reltablespace = tst.oid
            OR ( t.reltablespace = 0
                 AND tst.spcname = 'pg_default' )
       )
  JOIN pg_index pgi
    ON pgi.indrelid = t.oid
  JOIN ( pg_class i /* indexes */
          JOIN pg_tablespace tsi
            ON i.reltablespace = tsi.oid
            OR ( i.reltablespace = 0
                 AND tsi.spcname = 'pg_default' )
       )
    ON pgi.indexrelid = i.oid
 WHERE i.relname NOT LIKE 'pg_toast%'
   AND i.reltablespace != t.reltablespace
;
```

If we have one table with an index in a separate tablespace, we might see this as a `psql` definition:

```
postgres=# \d y
      Table "public.y"
 Column | Type | Modifiers
--------+------+-----------
 val    | text |
Indexes:
    "y_val_idx" btree (val), tablespace "new_tablespace"
Tablespace: "new_tablespace2"
```

Running the previously presented query gives the following results:

```
   relname   |     spcname      | relname |     spcname
-------------+------------------+---------+----------------
 y_val_idx   | new_tablespace   | y       | new_tablespace2
(1 row)
```

Accessing objects in other PostgreSQL databases

Sometimes, you may want to access data in other PostgreSQL databases. The reasons may be as follows:

- You have more than one database server, and you need to extract data (such as reference) from one server and load it into the other.
- You want to access data that is in a different database on the same database server, which was split for administrative purposes.
- You want to perform some changes that you do not wish to rollback in the event of an error or transaction abort. These are known as **function side-effects** or **autonomous transactions**.

You might also be considering this because you are exploring the scale out, sharding, or load balancing approaches. If so, read the last part of this recipe, the *See also* section, and then skip to Chapter 12, *Replication and Upgrades*.

 PostgreSQL includes two separate mechanisms for accessing external PostgreSQL databases: dblink and the PostgreSQL Foreign Data Wrapper. The latter is more efficient and implements a part of the SQL standard, but does not fully replace dblink, therefore we provide two variants of this recipe.

Getting ready

First of all, let's make a distinction to prevent confusion:

- The **Foreign Data Wrapper** infrastructure, a mechanism to manage the definition of remote connections, servers, and users, is available in all supported PostgreSQL versions
- The **PostgreSQL Foreign Data Wrapper** is a specific contrib extension that uses the Foreign Data Wrapper infrastructure to connect to remote PostgreSQL servers.

In particular, the Foreign Data Wrapper infrastructure will be used to manage definitions in both cases, that is, when using the PostgreSQL Foreign Data Wrapper and when using the dblink module.

Foreign Data Wrapper extensions for other database systems will be discussed in the next recipe, *Accessing objects in other foreign databases*.

How to do it...

We will first describe the variant that uses `dblink`, which applies to all supported PostgreSQL versions:

1. First, we need to install the `dblink` contrib module. The general procedure is explained in the *Adding an external module to PostgreSQL* recipe of `Chapter 3, Configuration`.

2. Then, we create some access definitions. The preferred way is to use the following commands, which are SQL standard (SQL/MED):

   ```
   postgres=# CREATE FOREIGN DATA WRAPPER postgresql
    VALIDATOR postgresql_fdw_validator;
   CREATE FOREIGN DATA WRAPPER

   postgres=# CREATE SERVER otherdb
    FOREIGN DATA WRAPPER postgresql
    OPTIONS (host 'foo', dbname 'otherdb', port '5432');
   CREATE SERVER

   postgres=# CREATE USER MAPPING FOR PUBLIC
   SERVER otherdb;
   CREATE USER MAPPING
   ```

3. You must create `FOREIGN DATA WRAPPER` only once, though you need one `SERVER` for each PostgreSQL destination database to which you may wish to connect. This is just the connection definition, not the connection itself.

4. Creating a public user mapping with no options seems strange, though it will mean that we use the `libpq` default behavior. It will also mean that we will connect the remote database using the value of `PGUSER`, or if it is not set, use the operating system user. Clearly, if we want to use different credentials, then we must specify them with suitable options, either while creating the mapping or afterwards (`ALTER USER MAPPING`).

The VALIDATOR clause specifies a function whose purpose is to validate the parameters. That function is a part of the Foreign Data Wrapper and should have been provided by the author, so you need to create it only if you are developing a new type of Foreign Data Wrapper yourself.

5. Now connect using an unnamed connection, as follows:

```
SELECT dblink_connect('otherdb');
```

6. This produces the following output:

```
dblink_connect
----------------
 OK
(1 row)
```

7. We limit ourselves to unnamed connections for simplicity. It is also possible to create a named connection, that is, a connection that is assigned a string so that it can be referred to directly later. This is obviously useful if we want to manage several connections, but it comes at the price of actually having to manage their life cycle (connection and disconnection).

8. Suppose you want to execute the following command:

```
postgres=#  INSERT  INTO  audit_log  VALUES  (current_user,
now());
```

9. To do so, run it on the unnamed remote connection like this:

```
postgres=#  SELECT  dblink_exec('INSERT  INTO  audit_log
VALUES'  ||
        '  (current_user,  now())',  true);
```

10. This will give the following output:

```
dblink_exec
---------------
 INSERT 0 1
(1 row)
```

11. Notice that the remote command returns the command tag and number of rows processed as the return value of the function. The second option means "fail on error". If you look closely, there's also a subtle error-when the INSERT command is executed locally, we use this server's value of current_user. But when we execute remotely, we use the remote server's value of current_user, which might differ, depending on the user mapping defined previously.

12. Similarly, suppose you want to execute the following query on the unnamed remote connection:

```
SELECT generate_series(1,3)
```

13. We start by typing this:

```
SELECT *
FROM dblink('SELECT generate_series(1,3)')
```

14. This will result in the following error:

```
ERROR:     a  column  definition  list  is  required  for
functions   returning
"record"
LINE  2:  FROM  dblink('SELECT  generate_series(1,3)');
          ^
```

15. This error message is telling us that we need to specify the list of output columns and output types that we expect from the dblink() function, because PostgreSQL is unable to determine them automatically at parsing time (that is, without running the query).

16. We can add the missing information by providing an alias in the FROM clause, as in the following example:

```
SELECT *
FROM dblink('SELECT generate_series(1,3)')
  AS link(col1 integer);
```

17. This will succeed, and result in the following output:

```
col1
------
    1
    2
    3
(3 rows)
```

18. To disconnect from the unnamed connection, you can issue the following:

    ```
    SELECT dblink_disconnect();
    ```

19. You get the following output:

    ```
    dblink_connect
    ----------------
    OK
    (1 row)
    ```

Now we will describe the second variant of this recipe, which uses the PostgreSQL Foreign Data Wrapper instead of dblink.

1. The first step is to install the postgres_fdw contrib module, which is as simple as this:

    ```
    postgres=# CREATE EXTENSION postgres_fdw;
    ```

2. The result is as follows:

    ```
    CREATE EXTENSION
    ```

3. This extension automatically creates the corresponding Foreign Data Wrapper, as you can check with psql's \dew meta-command:

    ```
    postgres=# \dew
                            List of foreign-data wrappers
             Name    | Owner  |        Handler         |      Validator
    ---------------+--------+----------------------+------------------
    ---------
      postgres_fdw | gianni | postgres_fdw_handler |
    postgres_fdw_validator
    (1 row)
    ```

4. We can now define a server:

    ```
    postgres=# CREATE SERVER otherdb
    FOREIGN DATA WRAPPER postgres_fdw
    OPTIONS (host 'foo', dbname 'otherdb', port '5432');
    ```

5. This produces the following output:

    ```
    CREATE SERVER
    ```

6. Then, we can define the user mapping:

```
postgres=# CREATE USER MAPPING FOR PUBLIC SERVER otherdb;
```

7. The output is as follows:

```
CREATE USER MAPPING
```

As an example, we will access a portion of a remote table containing (integer, text) pairs:

```
postgres=# CREATE FOREIGN TABLE ft (
   num int ,
   word text )
SERVER otherdb
OPTIONS (
   schema_name 'public' ,
   table_name 't' );
```

The result is quite laconic:

```
CREATE FOREIGN TABLE
```

This table can now be operated almost like any other table. We check whether it is empty:

```
postgres=# select * from ft;
```

This is the output:

```
 num | word
-----+------
(0 rows)
```

8. We can insert rows as follows:

```
postgres=# insert into ft(num,word) values
(1,'One'), (2,'Two'),(3,'Three');
```

9. This query produces the following output:

```
INSERT 0 3
```

10. Then, we can verify that the aforementioned rows have been inserted:

```
postgres=# select * from ft;
```

11. This is confirmed by the output:

```
num | word
-----+-------
  1 | One
  2 | Two
  3 | Three
(3 rows)
```

Note that you don't have to manage connections or format text strings to assemble your queries. Most of the complexity is handled automatically by the Foreign Data Wrapper.

How it works...

The `dblink` module establishes a persistent connection with the other database. The `dblink` functions track the details of that connection, so you don't need to worry about doing so yourself. You should be aware that this is an external resource, and so the generic programming problem of *resource leaks* becomes possible. If you forget about your connection and forget to disconnect it, you may experience problems later. The remote connections will be terminated should your session disconnect.

Note that the remote connection persists even across transaction failures and other errors, so there is no need to reconnect.

The `postgres_fdw` extension can manage connections transparently and efficiently, so if your use case does not involve commands other than SELECT, INSERT, UPDATE, and DELETE then you should definitely go for it.

The `dblink()` module executes the remote query and will assemble the result set in the memory before the local reply begins to be sent. This means that very large queries might fail due to lack of memory, and everybody else will notice that. This isn't a problem; `dblink` is simply not designed to handle bulk data flows. Look at the *Loading data from flat files* recipe in Chapter 5, *Tables and Data*, if that's what you want to do.

Running slightly larger queries can be achieved using cursors. They allow us to bring the answer set back in smaller chunks. Conceptually, we need to open the cursor, loop while fetching rows until we are done, and then close the cursor. An example query for that is as follows:

```
postgres=# SELECT dblink_open('example',
       'SELECT generate_series(1,3)', true);
 dblink_open
---------------
 OK
(1 row)
postgres=# SELECT *
       FROM dblink_fetch('example', 10, true)
       AS link (col1 integer);
 col1
------
    1
    2
    3
(3 rows)
```

Notice that we didn't need to define the cursor when we opened it, though we do need to define the results from the cursor when we fetch from it, just as we did with a normal query. For instance, to fetch 10 rows at a time, we can do this:

```
postgres=# SELECT *
       FROM dblink_fetch('example', 10, true)
       AS link (col1 integer);
 col1
------
(0 rows)
postgres=# SELECT dblink_close('example');
 dblink_close
---------------
 OK(1 row)
```

The dblink module also allows you to use more than one connection. Using just one connection is generally not good for modular programming. For more complex situations, it's good practice to assume that the connection you want is not the same as the connection that another part of the program might need. The dblink module allows named connections, so you don't need to hope that the default connection is still the right connection. There is also a function named dblink_get_connections() that will allow you to see which connections you have active.

There's more...

Remote data sources look as if they can be treated as tables, and in fact, they are represented as such by Foreign Data Wrappers. Unfortunately, in practice, this doesn't work in all the ways you might hope and expect.

However, by writing your queries and code in the standard way, you give the database usable context information about what you are trying to achieve; future PostgreSQL versions might achieve better optimization on the same SQL code. This is a general advantage over custom solutions, which are usually opaque to the server and thus cannot be optimized further.

Ideally, we would like to use foreign tables interchangeably with local tables, with minimum possible performance penalty and maintenance cost, so it is important to know what already works and what is still on the wish list.

First, here's the good news: foreign tables can have statistics collected, just like ordinary tables, and they can be used as models to create local tables:

```
CREATE TABLE my_local_copy (LIKE my_foreign_table);
```

This is not supported by dblink, because it works on statements instead of managing tables. In general, there is no federated query optimizer. If we join a local table and a remote table with dblink, then data from the remote database is simply pulled through, even if it would have been quicker to send the data and then pull back matching rows. On the other hand, postgres_fdw can share information with the query planner, allowing some optimization, and more improvements are likely to come in following years, now that the infrastructure has been built.

As of version 10, postgres_fdw transparently pushes WHERE clauses to the remote server. Suppose you issue this:

```
SELECT * FROM ft WHERE num = 2;
```

Then, only the matching rows will be fetched, using any remote index if available. This is a massive advantage in working with selective queries on large tables.

The `dblink` module cannot automatically send a local WHERE clause to the remote database, so a query like the following would perform poorly:

```
SELECT *
 FROM dblink('otherdb',
      'SELECT * FROM bigtable') AS link ( ... )
 WHERE filtercolumn > 100;
```

We will need to explicitly add the WHERE clause to the remote query at the application level, like the following:

```
SELECT *
FROM dblink('otherdb',
      'SELECT * FROM bigtable' ||
      ' WHERE filtercolumn > 100') AS link ( ... );
```

This means that, in general, setting up views of remote data this way isn't very helpful, as it encourages users to think that the table location doesn't matter, whereas, from a performance perspective, it definitely does. This isn't really any different from other federated or remote access database products.

The version of `postgres_fdw` shipped with PostgreSQL 10 can delegate even more activities to the remote node. This includes—performing sorts or joins; computing aggregates carrying out entire UPDATE or DELETE statements, and evaluating operators or functions provided by suitable extensions.

There are also a few performance considerations that you may wish to consider. The first is that when the remote query executes, the current session waits for it to complete. You can also execute queries without waiting for them to return, using the following functions:

- `dblink_send_query()`
- `dblink_is_busy()`
- `dblink_get_result()`

If you are concerned about the overhead of connection time, then you may want to consider using a session pool. This will reserve a number of database connections, which will allow you to reduce apparent connection time. For more information, look at the *Setting up a connection pool recipe* in `Chapter 4`, *Server Control*.

There's more...

Another-and sometimes easier-way of accessing other databases is with a tool named **PL/Proxy**, available as a PostgreSQL extension. PL/Proxy allows you to create a local database function that is a proxy for a remote database function. PL/Proxy works only for functions, and some people regard this as a restriction, in a way similar to postgres_fdw, which operates only on rows in tables. That is why these solutions complement dblink, rather than replacing it.

Creating a local proxy function is simple:

```
CREATE FUNCTION my_task(VOID)
RETURNS SETOF text AS $$
    CONNECT 'dbname=myremoteserver';
    SELECT my_task();
$$ LANGUAGE plproxy;
```

You need a local function, but you don't need to call a remote function; you can use SQL statements directly. The following example shows a parameterized function:

```
CREATE FUNCTION get_cust_email(p_username text)
RETURNS SETOF text AS $$
    CONNECT 'dbname=myremoteserver';
    SELECT email FROM users WHERE username = p_username;
$$ LANGUAGE plproxy;
```

PL/Proxy is specifically designed to allow more complex architecture for sharding and load balancing. The RUN ON command allows us to dynamically specify the remote database on which we will run the SQL statement. So the preceding example becomes as follows:

```
CREATE FUNCTION get_cust_email(p_username text)
RETURNS SETOF text AS $$
    CLUSTER 'mycluster';
    RUN ON hashtext(p_username);
    SELECT email FROM users WHERE username = p_username;
$$ LANGUAGE plproxy;
```

You'll likely need to read Chapter 12, *Replication and Upgrades*, before you begin designing application architecture using these concepts.

Accessing objects in other foreign databases

In the previous recipe, you saw how to use objects from a different PostgreSQL database, either with `dblink` or by using the Foreign Data Wrapper infrastructure. Here we will explore another variant of the latter-using Foreign Data Wrappers to access databases other than PostgreSQL.

There are many Foreign Data Wrappers for other database systems, all of which are maintained as extensions independently from the PostgreSQL project. PGXN, the PostgreSQL Extension Network mentioned in Chapter 3, *Configuration*, is a good place where you can see which extensions are available.

Just note this so that you don't get confused: while you can find Foreign Data Wrappers to access several database systems, there are also other wrappers for different types of data sources, such as text files, web services, and so on.There is even `postgres_fdw`, a backport of the contrib module which we covered in the previous recipe, for users of older PostgreSQL versions that did not have it yet.

 When evaluating external extensions, I advise you to carefully examine the README file in each extension before making stable choices, as the code maturity varies a lot. Some extensions are still development experiments, while others are production-ready extensions, such as `oracle_fdw`.

Getting ready

For this example, we will use the Oracle Foreign Data Wrapper, `oracle_fdw`, whose version is 2.0.0.

You must have obtained and installed the required Oracle software as specified in the `oracle_fdw` documentation at `https://github.com/laurenz/oracle_fdw/blob/ORACLE_FDW_2_0_0/README.oracle_fdw#L497`.

The `oracle_fdw` wrapper is available in the PostgreSQL Extension Network, so you can follow the straightforward installation procedure described in the *Installing modules from PGXN* section of the *Adding an external module to PostgreSQL* recipe in Chapter 3, *Configuration*.

Obviously, you must have access to an Oracle database server.

How to do it...

Here, we provide stepwise instructions on how to connect to an Oracle server using `oracle_fdw`:

1. First, we ensure that the extension is loaded:

   ```
   CREATE EXTENSION IF NOT EXISTS oracle_fdw;
   ```

2. Then, we configure the server and the user mapping:

   ```
   CREATE SERVER myserv
   FOREIGN DATA WRAPPER oracle_fdw
   OPTIONS (dbserver '//myhost/MYDB');
   CREATE USER MAPPING FOR myuser
   SERVER myserv;
   ```

3. Then, we create a PostgreSQL foreign table with the same column names as the source table in Oracle, and with compatible column types:

   ```
   CREATE FOREIGN TABLE mytab(id bigint, descr text)
   SERVER myserv
   OPTIONS (user 'scott', password 'tiger');
   ```

4. Now, we can try to write to the table:

   ```
   INSERT INTO mytab VALUES (-1, 'Minus One');
   ```

5. Finally, we are able to read the values that we have inserted:

   ```
   SELECT * FROM mytab WHERE id = -1;
   ```

   This should result in the following output:

   ```
   id |   descr
   ----+-----------
   -1 | Minus One
   (1 row)
   ```

How it works...

Our query has a WHERE condition that filters the rows we select from the foreign table. As in the `postgres_fdw` example from the previous recipe, Foreign Data Wrappers do the clever thing: the WHERE condition is pushed to the remote server, and only the matching rows are retrieved.

This is good in two ways: firstly, we delegate some work to another system, and secondly, we reduce the overall network traffic by not transferring unnecessary data.

We also notice that the WHERE condition is expressed in the PostgreSQL syntax; the Foreign Data Wrapper is able to translate it into whatever form required by the remote system.

There's more...

PostgreSQL provides the infrastructure for collecting statistics on foreign tables, so the planner will be able to consider such information, provided that the feature is implemented in the specific Foreign Data Wrapper you are using. For example, statistics are supported by oracle_fdw.

The latest improvements for foreign tables include trigger support, IMPORT FOREIGN SCHEMA, and several improvements to the query planner.

Particularly useful for database administrators is the IMPORT FOREIGN SCHEMA syntax, which can be used to create, with a single statement, foreign tables for all tables and views in a given remote schema.

Among the query planner improvements, we wish to mention **Join Pushdown**. In a nutshell: a query that joins some foreign tables that belong to the same server is able to have the join performed transparently on the remote server. To avoid security issues, this can only happen if these tables are all accessed with the same role.

Another interesting extension is Multicorn (http://multicorn.org). It helps Python programmers create Foreign Data Wrappers by providing a dedicated interface. Multicorn reduces the creation of a basic Foreign Data Wrapper to the implementation of one Python method. Additional features, such as write access, are available through further optional methods.

Updatable views

PostgreSQL supports the SQL standard CREATE VIEW command, which supports automatic UPDATE, INSERT, and DELETE commands, provided they are simple enough.

Note that certain types of updates are forbidden just because it is either impossible or impractical to derive a corresponding list of modifications on the constituent tables. We'll discuss those issues here.

Getting ready

First, you need to consider that only simple views can be made to receive insertions, updates, and deletions easily. The SQL standard differentiates between views that are *simple* `updatable` and more complex views that cannot be expected to be updatable.

So, before we proceed, we need to understand what a simple updatable view is and what it is not. Let's start from the `cust` table:

```
postgres=# SELECT * FROM cust;
 customerid | firstname | lastname | age
------------+-----------+----------+-----
          1 | Philip    | Marlowe  |  38
          2 | Richard   | Hannay   |  42
          3 | Holly     | Martins  |  25
          4 | Harry     | Palmer   |  36
          4 | Mark      | Hall     |  47
(5 rows)
```

We create a very simple view on top of it, like the following:

```
CREATE VIEW cust_view AS
SELECT customerid
      ,firstname
      ,lastname
      ,age
FROM cust;
```

Each row in our view corresponds to one row in a single-source table, and each column is referred to directly without any further processing, except possibly for a column rename. Thus, we expect to be able to make INSERT, UPDATE, and DELETE commands pass through our view into the base table, which is what happens in PostgreSQL.

The following examples are three views where INSERT, UPDATE, and DELETE commands cannot be made to flow to the base table easily, for the reasons just described:

```
CREATE VIEW cust_avg AS
SELECT avg(age)
FROM cust;
CREATE VIEW cust_above_avg_age AS
SELECT customerid
          ,substr(firstname, 1, 20) as fname
          ,substr(lastname, 1, 20) as lname
          ,age -
          (SELECT avg(age)::integer
          FROM cust) as years_above_avg
```

```
FROM cust
WHERE age >
    (SELECT avg(age)
     FROM cust);

CREATE VIEW potential_spammers AS
SELECT customerid, spam_score(firstname,lastname)
FROM cust
ORDER BY spam_score(firstname,lastname) DESC
LIMIT 100;
```

The first view just shows a single row with the average of a numeric column. Changing an average directly doesn't make much sense. For instance, if we want to raise the average age by 1, should we increase all numbers by 1, resulting in an update of each row which is unusual? Or we should change some rows only, by a larger amount? A user who really wants to do this can update the cust table directly.

The second view shows a column called `years_above_avg`, which is the difference between the age of that customer and the average. Changing that column would be more complex than it seems at first glance: just consider that increasing the age by 10 would not result in increasing the `years_above_avg` by 10, because also the average will be affected.

The third view displays a computed column which can definitely not be updated directly - we can't change the value int the `spam_score` column without changing the algorithm implemented by the `spam_score()` function.

Now we can proceed to the steps to allow any or all of insertions, updates, or deletions to flow from views to base tables, having clarified whether this makes sense conceptually.

How to do it...

There is nothing to do for simple views—PostgreSQL will propagate modifications to the underlying table automatically.

Conversely, if the view is not simple enough, but you still have a clear idea of how you would like to propagate changes to the underlying table(s), then you can allow updatable views by telling PostgreSQL how to actually perform DML statements. (DML stands for Data Manipulation Language, which in PostgreSQL means INSERT, UPDATE, DELETE or TRUNCATE).

PostgreSQL supports two mechanisms to achieve updatable views, namely rewrite rules and INSTEAD OF triggers. The latter provide a mechanism to implement updatable views by creating trigger functions that execute arbitrary code every time a data-modification command is executed on the view.

The INSTEAD OF triggers are part of the SQL standard, and other database systems support them. Conversely, query rewrite rules are specific to PostgreSQL and cannot be found anywhere else in this exact form.

There is no clearly preferable method. On one hand, rules can be more efficient than triggers, but on the other hand, they can be more difficult to understand than triggers and could result in inefficient execution if the code is badly written (although the latter is not an exclusive property of rules, unfortunately).

To explain this point concretely, we will now provide an example using rules, and then we will re-implement the same example with triggers.

We start with a table of mountains and of their height in meters:

```
CREATE TABLE mountains_m
( name text primary key
, meters int not null
);
```

Then we create a view that adds a computed column expressing the height in feet, and that displays the data in descending height order:

```
CREATE VIEW mountains AS
SELECT *, ROUND(meters / 0.3048) AS feet
FROM mountains_m
ORDER BY meters DESC;
```

DML automatically flows to the base table when inserting only columns that are not computed:

```
INSERT INTO mountains(name, meters)
VALUES ('Everest', 8848);
TABLE mountains;
name    | meters | feet
--------+--------+--------
Everest|   8848 | 29029
(1 row)
```

However, when we try to insert data with the height specified in feet we get the following error:

```
INSERT INTO mountains(name, feet)
VALUES ('K2', 28251);
ERROR:  cannot insert into column "feet" of view "mountains"
DETAIL:  View columns that are not columns of their base relation are not
updatable.
```

So we create a rule that replaces the update with another query that works all the time:

```
CREATE RULE mountains_ins_rule AS
ON INSERT TO mountains DO INSTEAD
INSERT INTO mountains_m
VALUES (NEW.name, COALESCE (NEW.meters, NEW.feet * 0.3048));
```

Now we can insert in both `meters` and `feet`:

```
INSERT INTO mountains(name, feet)
VALUES ('K 2', 28251);
INSERT INTO mountains(name, meters)
VALUES ('Kangchenjunga', 8586);
TABLE mountains;
name             | meters | feet
-----------------+--------+-----
Everest          |   8848 | 29029
K 2              |   8611 | 28251
Kangchenjunga    |   8586 | 28169
(3 rows)
```

Updates are also propagated automatically, but only to non-computed columns:

```
UPDATE mountains SET name = 'K2' WHERE name = 'K 2';
TABLE mountains;
name             | meters | feet
-----------------+--------+--------
Everest          |   8848 | 29029
```

```
K2             |   8611 | 28251
Kangchenjunga |   8586 | 28169
(3 rows)
UPDATE mountains SET feet = 29064 WHERE name = 'K2';
ERROR:  cannot update column "feet" of view "mountains"
DETAIL:  View columns that are not columns of their base relation are not
updatable.
```

If we add another rule replacing updates with a query that covers all cases, then the last update will succeed and produce the desired effect:

```
CREATE RULE mountains_upd_rule AS
ON UPDATE TO mountains DO INSTEAD
UPDATE mountains_m
SET name = NEW.name, meters =
CASE
WHEN NEW.meters != OLD.meters
THEN NEW.meters
WHEN NEW.feet != OLD.feet
THEN NEW.feet * 0.3048
ELSE OLD.meters
END
WHERE name = OLD.name;
UPDATE mountains SET feet = 29064 WHERE name = 'K2';
TABLE mountains;
name           | meters | feet
---------------+--------+-------
K2             |   8859 | 29065
Everest        |   8848 | 29029
Kangchenjunga |   8586 | 28169
(3 rows)
```

The query used in this rule also covers the simpler case of a non-computed column:

```
UPDATE mountains SET meters = 8611 WHERE name = 'K2';
TABLE mountains;
name           | meters | feet
---------------+--------+-------
Everest        |   8848 | 29029
K2             |   8611 | 28251
Kangchenjunga |   8586 | 28169
(3 rows)
```

The same effect can be achieved by adding the following trigger, which replaces the two rules above:

```
CREATE FUNCTION mountains_tf()
RETURNS TRIGGER
LANGUAGE plpgsql
AS $$
BEGIN
IF TG_OP = 'INSERT' THEN
INSERT INTO mountains_m VALUES (NEW.name,
CASE
  WHEN NEW.meters IS NULL
  THEN NEW.feet * 0.3048
  ELSE NEW.meters
  END );
ELSIF TG_OP = 'UPDATE' THEN
UPDATE mountains_m
SET name = NEW.name, meters =
CASE
WHEN NEW.meters != OLD.meters
THEN NEW.meters
WHEN NEW.feet != OLD.feet
THEN NEW.feet * 0.3048
ELSE OLD.meters
END
WHERE name = OLD.name;
END IF;
RETURN NEW;
END;
$$;
CREATE TRIGGER mountains_tg
INSTEAD OF INSERT OR UPDATE ON mountains
FOR EACH ROW
EXECUTE PROCEDURE mountains_tf();
```

How it works...

In the rule-based example, we use the COALESCE function, which returns the first argument, if not null, or the second one otherwise. When the original INSERT statement does not specify a value in meters, then it uses the value in feet divided by 0.3048.

The second rule sets the value in meters to different expressions—if the value in meters was updated we use the new one; if the value in feet was updated, we use the new value in feet divided by 0.3048, and otherwise we use the old value in meters (that is, we don't change it).

The logic implemented in the trigger function is similar to the one above: note that we use the TG_OP automatic variable to handle INSERT and UPDATE separately.

We've just scratched the surface of what you can achieve with rules, though personally I find them too complex for widespread use.

You can do a lot of things with rules; you just need to be sure that everything you do makes sense and has a practical purpose. There are some other important points that I should mention about rules before you dive in and start using them everywhere.

Rules are applied by PostgreSQL after the SQL has been received by the server and parsed for syntax errors, but before the planner tries to optimize the SQL statement.

In the rules in the preceding recipe, we referenced the values of the old or the new row, just as we do within trigger functions, using the old and new keywords. Similarly, there are only new values in an INSERT command and only old values in a DELETE command.

One of the major downsides of using rules is that we cannot bulk load data into the table using the COPY command. Also, we cannot transform a stream of inserts into a single COPY command, nor can we do a COPY operation against the view. Bulk loading requires direct access to the table.

Suppose we have a view like the following:

```
CREATE VIEW cust_minor AS
SELECT customerid
  , firstname
, lastname
, age
FROM cust
WHERE age < 18;
```

Then, we have some more difficulties. If we wish to update this view, then you might read the manual and understand that we can use a conditional rule by adding a WHERE clause to match the WHERE clause in the view, as follows:

```
CREATE RULE cust_minor_update AS
ON   update TO cust_minor
WHERE new.age < 18
DO INSTEAD
UPDATE cust SET
  firstname = new.firstname
, lastname = new.lastname
, age = new.age
WHERE customerid = old.customerid;
```

This fails, however, as you can see if you try to update `cust_minor`. The fix is to add two rules, one as an unconditional rule that does nothing (literally) and needs to exist for internal reasons, and the other to do the work we want:

```
CREATE RULE cust_minor_update_dummy AS ON
update TO cust_minor
DO INSTEAD NOTHING;
CREATE RULE cust_minor_update_conditional AS
ON   update TO cust_minor
WHERE new.age < 18
DO INSTEAD
UPDATE cust SET firstname = new.firstname
, lastname = new.lastname
, age = new.age
WHERE customerid = old.customerid;
```

There's more...

There is yet another question posed by updatable views.

As an example, we shall use the `cust_minor` view we just defined, which does not allow performing insertions or updates such that the affected rows fall out of the view itself. For instance, consider this query:

```
UPDATE cust_minor SET age = 19 WHERE customerid = 123;
```

The preceding query will not affect any row because of the `WHERE age < 18` conditions in the rule definition.

The `CREATE VIEW` statement has a `WITH CHECK OPTION` clause; if specified, any update which excludes any row from the view will fail.

If a view includes some updatable columns together with other non-updatable columns (for example expressions, literals, and so on), then updates are allowed if they only change the updatable columns.

Finally, it should be noted that some, or perhaps many, DBAs have found rules to be a serious annoyance. Here's one more reason for that: let's try running our main example in a different way, mixing rules with triggers. We'd like to make that view updatable so that it behaves like the following view:

```
CREATE VIEW cust_view AS
SELECT customerid
       , firstname
       , lastname
       , age
FROM cust;
```

Before version 9.3, we couldn't create triggers on views, so let's try to create a table instead, as follows:

```
CREATE TABLE cust_view AS SELECT * FROM cust WHERE false;
```

We emulate the view by first creating a SELECT rule on the dummy table, and then try to create triggers on the table for the INSERT, UPDATE, and DELETE actions. The rule works only if it is named _RETURN and the table is completely empty:

```
postgres # CREATE RULE "_RETURN" AS
              ON SELECT TO cust_view
              DO INSTEAD
              SELECT * FROM cust;
CREATE RULE
postgres # CREATE TRIGGER cust_view_modify_after_trig
              AFTER INSERT OR UPDATE OR DELETE ON cust_view
              FOR EACH ROW
              EXECUTE PROCEDURE cust_view_modify_trig_proc();
ERROR:  "cust_view" is not a table
```

Huh? So what is it if it's not a table?

```
postgres # DROP TABLE cust_view;
ERROR:  "cust_view" is not a table
HINT:  Use DROP VIEW to remove a view
postgres # DROP VIEW cust_view;
DROP VIEW
```

Wow! That works! Yes, we created a table and then added a rule to it. This turned the table into a view. Now we realize that we can't put triggers on a view and we can't put a SELECT rule on a table without it becoming a view. Since triggers are not fired by SELECT, this route won't work at all. It is probably best to accept that if you want to load data into a table, then you have to refer to the table directly, rather than use a view.

Using materialized views

Every time we select rows from a view, we actually select from the result of the underlying query. If that query is slow and we need to use it more than once, then it makes sense to run the query once, save its output as a table, and then select the rows from the latter.

This procedure has been available for a long time, and version 9.3 saw the addition of the dedicated syntax, CREATE MATERIALIZED VIEW, which we will describe in this recipe.

Getting ready

Let's create two randomly populated tables, of which one is large:

```
CREATE TABLE dish
( dish_id SERIAL PRIMARY KEY
, dish_description text
);

CREATE TABLE eater
( eater_id SERIAL
, eating_date date
, dish_id int REFERENCES dish (dish_id)
);
INSERT INTO dish (dish_description)
VALUES ('Lentils'), ('Mango'), ('Plantain'), ('Rice'), ('Tea');

INSERT INTO eater(eating_date, dish_id)
SELECT floor(abs(sin(n)) * 365) :: int + date '2014-01-01'
, ceil(abs(sin(n :: float * n))*5) :: int
FROM generate_series(1,500000) AS rand(n);
```

Notice that the data is not truly random. It is generated by a deterministic procedure, so you get exactly the same result if you copy the preceding code.

How to do it...

Let's create the following view:

```
CREATE VIEW v_dish AS
SELECT dish_description, count(*)
FROM dish JOIN eater USING (dish_id)
GROUP BY dish_description
ORDER BY 1;
```

Then, we'll query it:

```
SELECT * FROM v_dish;
```

We obtain the following output:

```
dish_description   | count
-------------------+---------
 Lentils           |  64236
 Mango             |  66512
 Plantain          |  74058
 Rice              |  90222
 Tea               | 204972
(5 rows)
```

With a very similar syntax, we create a materialized view with the same underlying query:

```
CREATE MATERIALIZED VIEW m_dish AS
SELECT dish_description, count(*)
FROM dish JOIN eater USING (dish_id)
GROUP BY dish_description
ORDER BY 1;
```

The corresponding query yields the same output as before:

```
SELECT * FROM m_dish;
```

The materialized version is much faster than the non-materialized version. On my laptop, their execution times are 0.2 ms versus 300 ms.

How it works...

Creating a non-materialized view is exactly the same as creating an empty table with a SELECT rule, as we discovered from the previous recipe. No data is extracted until the view is actually used.

When creating a materialized view, the default is to run the query immediately and then store its results, like we do for table content.

In short, creating a materialized view is slow, but using it is fast. This is the opposite of standard views, which are created instantly and recomputed at every use.

There's more...

The output of a materialized view is physically stored like a regular table, and the analogy doesn't stop here. In both cases, it is possible to create indexes to speed up queries.

A materialized view will not automatically change when its constituent tables change. For that to happen, you must issue the following:

```
REFRESH MATERIALIZED VIEW m_dish;
```

This replaces all the contents of the view with newly computed ones.

It is possible to quickly create an empty materialized view and populate it later. Just add WITH NO DATA at the end of the CREATE MATERIALIZED VIEW statement. Obviously, the view cannot be used before being populated, which you can do with REFRESH MATERIALIZED VIEW, as you just saw.

A materialized view cannot be read while it is being refreshed. For that, you need to use the CONCURRENTLY clause at the expense of a somewhat slower refresh.

As you can understand from these paragraphs, currently there is only a partial advantage in using materialized views, compared to previous solutions such as this:

```
CREATE UNLOGGED TABLE m_dish AS SELECT * FROM v_dish;
```

However, when using a declarative language, such as SQL, the same syntax may automatically result in a more efficient algorithm in case of future improvements of PostgreSQL. For instance, one day PostgreSQL will be able to perform a faster refresh by simply replacing those rows that changed, instead of recomputing the entire content.

8
Monitoring and Diagnosis

In this chapter, you will find recipes for some common monitoring and diagnosis actions you will want to do inside your database. They are meant to answer specific questions that you often face when using PostgreSQL.

Databases are not isolated entities. They live on computer hardware using CPUs, RAM, and disk subsystems. Users access databases using networks. Depending on the setup, databases themselves may need network resources to function in any of the following ways: performing some authentication checks when users log in, using disks that are mounted over the network (not generally recommended), or making remote function calls to other databases.

This means that *monitoring only the database is not enough*. As a minimum, one should also monitor everything directly involved in using the database. This means knowing the following:

- Is the database host available? Does it accept connections?
- How much of the network bandwidth is in use? Have there been network interruptions and dropped connections?
- Is there enough RAM available for the most common tasks? How much of it is left?
- Is there enough disk space available? When will you run out of disk space?
- Is the disk subsystem keeping up? How much more load can it take?
- Can the CPU keep up with the load? How many spare idle cycles do the CPUs have?
- Are other network services the database access depends on (if any) available? For example, if you use Kerberos for authentication, you need to monitor it as well.
- How many context switches are happening when the database is running?
- For most of these things, you are interested in the history; that is, how have things evolved? Was everything mostly the same yesterday or last week?

- When did the disk usage start changing rapidly?
- For any larger installation, you probably have something already in place to monitor the health of your hosts and network.

The two aspects of monitoring are collecting historical data to see how things have evolved, and getting alerts when things go seriously wrong. Tools based on a **Round Robin Database Tool (RRDtool)** such as **Munin**, or time series databases such as Graphite's **Carbon**, and **Prometheus**, are quite popular for collecting the historical information on all aspects of the servers and presenting this information in an easy-to-follow graphical form, for which Grafana is a popular tool. Seeing several statistics on the same timescale can really help when trying to figure out why the system is behaving the way it is.

Another aspect of monitoring is getting alerts when something goes really wrong and needs (immediate) attention.

For alerting, one of the most widely used tools is **Icinga** (a fork of **Nagios**), an established solution. The aforementioned trending tools can integrate with it. check_postgres is a rather popular Icinga plugin for monitoring many standard aspects of a PostgreSQL database server.

Icinga is a stable and mature solution, based on the long-standing approach where each plugin decides whether a given measurement is cause of alarm, more complex to manage and maintain. A more recent tool is the aforementioned **Prometheus**, based on a design that separates data collection from the centralized alerting logic.

Should you need a solution for both the alerting and trending aspects of a monitoring tool, you might also want to look into **Zabbix**.

Furthermore, if you require integration with a system based on **Simple Network Management Protocol (SNMP)**, the pgsnmpd project offers some basic support. However, as it is not actively maintained, we recommend switching to one of the other monitoring approaches if at all possible.

In this chapter, we will cover the following recipes:

- Providing PostgreSQL information to monitoring tools
- Real-time viewing using pgAdmin or OmniDB
- Checking whether a user is connected
- Checking whether a computer is connected

- Repeatedly executing a query in psql
- Checking which queries are running
- Checking which queries are active or blocked
- Knowing who is blocking a query
- Killing a specific session
- Detecting an in-doubt prepared transaction
- Knowing whether anybody is using a specific table
- Knowing when a table was last used
- Usage of disk space by temporary data
- Understanding why queries slow down
- Investigating and reporting a bug
- Producing a daily summary of log file errors
- Analyzing the real-time performance of your queries

Providing PostgreSQL information to monitoring tools

It's best to use historical monitoring information when all of it is available from the same place and on the same timescale. Most monitoring systems are designed for generic purposes, while allowing application and system developers to integrate their specific checks with the monitoring infrastructure. This is possible through a plugin architecture. Adding new kinds of data inputs to them means installing a plugin. Sometimes, you may need to write or develop this plugin, but writing a plugin for something such as Cacti is easy. You just have to write a script that outputs monitored values in simple text format.

In most common scenarios, the monitoring system is centralized and data is collected directly (and remotely) by the system itself or through some distributed components that are responsible for sending the observed metrics back to the main node.

As far as PostgreSQL is concerned, some useful things to include in graphs are the number of connections, disk usage, number of queries, number of WAL files, most numbers from `pg_stat_user_tables` and `pg_stat_user_indexes`, and so on. One *Swiss Army knife* script, which can be used from both Cacti and Nagios/Icinga, is `check_postgres`. It is available at `http://bucardo.org/wiki/Check_postgres`. It has ready-made reporting actions for a large array of things worth monitoring in PostgreSQL.

For Munin, there are some PostgreSQL plugins available at the Munin plugin repository at `https://github.com/munin-monitoring/contrib/tree/master/plugins/postgresql`.

The following screenshot shows a Munin graph about PostgreSQL buffer cache hits for a specific database, where cache hits (the blue line) dominate reads from the disk (the green line):

Finding more information about generic monitoring tools

Setting up the tools themselves is a larger topic, and it is beyond the scope of this book. In fact, each of these tools has more than one book written about them. The basic setup information and the tools themselves can be found at the following URLs:

- RRDtool: http://www.mrtg.org/rrdtool/
- Cacti: http://www.cacti.net/
- Icinga: http://www.icinga.org
- Munin: http://munin-monitoring.org/
- Nagios: http://www.nagios.org/
- Zabbix: http://www.zabbix.org/

Real-time viewing using pgAdmin or OmniDB

You can also use a GUI tool such as pgAdmin or OmniDB, which we discussed first in Chapter 1, *First Steps* to get a quick view of what is going on in the database.

Getting ready

If you use pgAdmin, for better control you need to install the adminpack extension in the destination database by issuing this command:

```
CREATE EXTENSION adminpack;
```

This extension is a part of the additionally supplied modules of PostgreSQL (aka contrib). It provides several administration functions that pgAdmin (and other tools) can use in order to manage, control, and monitor a Postgres server from a remote location.

How to do it... (with pgAdmin)

The following section illustrates the pgAdmin tool.

Once you have installed `adminpack`, connect to the database server; this will open a window similar to that shown in the following screenshot, reporting a general view plus information on connections, locks, and running transactions:

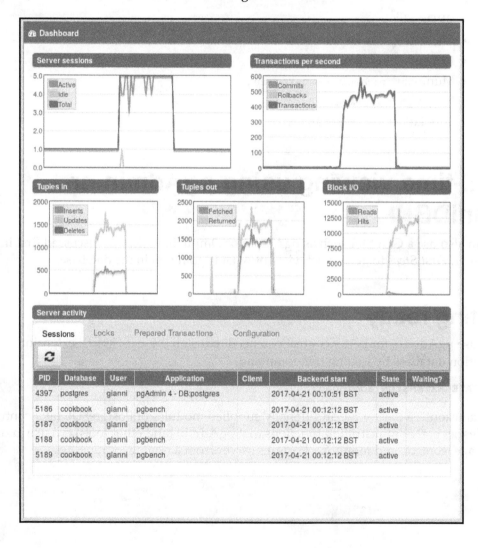

How to do it… (with OmniDB)

Here's another section that illustrates the OmniDB tool:

After starting OmniDB and opening a database, a tab called **Monitoring** is automatically displayed, as in the following screenshot:

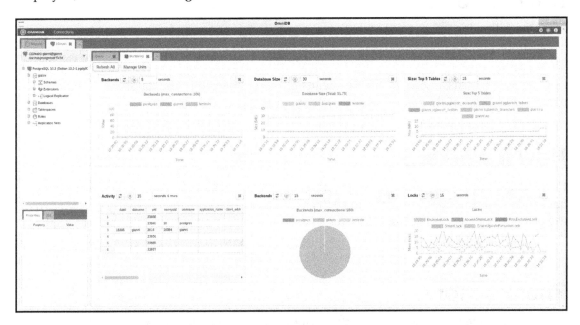

The **Monitoring** tab shows a series of charts and diagrams about sessions, locks, activity, database size, and table size.

The display can be customized by adding/removing charts from a list of predefined templates, or by creating a bespoke chart, by modifying the data script and/or the chart script.

The easiest way to add a new type of chart is to take an existing one, understanding first what information it displays, and then using it as a starting point for making a different one.

Checking whether a user is connected

Here, we will show you how to learn whether a certain database user is currently connected to the database.

Getting ready

If you are logged in as a superuser you will have full access to monitoring information.

How to do it...

Issue the following query to see whether the `bob` user is connected:

```
SELECT datname FROM pg_stat_activity WHERE usename = 'bob';
```

If this query returns any rows, then it means `bob` is connected to the database. The returned value is the name of the database to which the user is connected.

How it works...

PostgreSQL's `pg_stat_activity` system view keeps track of all running PostgreSQL backends. This includes information such as the query that is being currently executed, or the last query that was executed by each backend; who is connected; when the connection, the transaction, and/or the query were started; and so on.

There's more...

Please spend a few minutes reading the PostgreSQL documentation, which contains more detailed information about `pg_stat_activity`, available at `http://www.postgresql.org/docs/current/static/monitoring-stats.html#PG-STAT-ACTIVITY-VIEW`.

You can find answers to many administration-related questions by analyzing the `pg_stat_activity` view. One common example is outlined in the next recipe.

Checking whether a computer is connected

Often, several different processes may connect as the same database user. In that case, you may actually want to know whether there is a connection from a specific computer.

How to do it...

You can get this information from the `pg_stat_activity` view, as it includes the connected clients' IP address, port, and hostname (where applicable). The port is only needed if you have more than one connection from the same client computer and you need to do further digging to see which process there connects to which database. Run the following command:

```
SELECT datname, usename, client_addr, client_port,
       application_name FROM pg_stat_activity;
```

The `client_addr` and `client_port` parameters help you look up the exact computer and even the process on that computer that has connected to the specific database. You can also retrieve the hostname of the remote computer through the `client_hostname` option (this requires `log_hostname` to be set to `on`).

There's more...

I would always recommend including `application_name` in your reports. This field has become widely recognized and honored by third-party application developers (I advise you to do the same with your own applications).

For information on how to set the application name for your connections, refer to *Database Connection Control Functions* in the PostgreSQL documentation at `http://www.postgresql.org/docs/current/static/libpq-connect.html`.

Repeatedly executing a query in psql

Sometimes we want to execute a query more than once, repeated at regular intervals; in this recipe we see an interesting `psql` command that does exactly that.

How to do it...

The `\watch` meta-command allows psql users to automatically (and continuously) re-execute a query.

This behavior is similar to the `watch` utility of some Linux and Unix environments.

In the following example, we run a simple query on `pg_stat_activity` and ask psql to repeat it every 5 seconds. You can exit at any time by pressing *Ctrl + C*:

```
gabriele=> SELECT count(*) FROM pg_stat_activity;
 count
-------
     1
(1 row)

gabriele=> \watch 5
Watch every 5s        Tue Aug 27 21:47:24 2013

 count
-------
     1
(1 row)
<snip>
```

There's more...

For further information about the psql utility, refer to the PostgreSQL documentation at `http://www.postgresql.org/docs/current/static/app-psql.html`.

Checking which queries are running

Here we will show you how to check which query is currently running.

Getting ready

You have to make sure that you are logged in as a superuser or as the same database user you want to check. Also, ensure that the parameter `track_activities = on` is set (which it normally should be, being the default setting). If not, check the *Updating the parameter file* recipe in `Chapter 3`, *Configuration*.

How to do it...

To see which connected users are running at this moment, just run the following:

```
SELECT datname, usename, state, query
       FROM pg_stat_activity;
```

On systems with a lot of users, you may notice that the majority of backends have state set to idle. This denotes that no query is actually running, and PostgreSQL is waiting for new commands from the user. The query field shows the statement that was last executed by that particular backend.

If, on the other hand, you are interested in active queries only, limit your selection to those records that have state set to active:

```
SELECT datname, usename, state, query
       FROM pg_stat_activity WHERE state = 'active';
```

How it works...

When track_activities = on is set, PostgreSQL collects data about all running queries. Users with sufficient rights can then view this data using the pg_stat_activity system view.

The pg_stat_activity view uses a system function named pg_stat_get_activity (procpid int). You can use this function directly to watch for the activity of a specific backend by supplying the process ID as an argument. Giving NULL as an argument returns information for all backends.

There's more...

Sometimes, you don't care about getting all queries that are currently running. You may be only interested in seeing some of these, or you may not like to connect to the database just to see what is running.

Catching queries that only run for a few milliseconds

As most queries on modern **online transaction processing** (**OLTP**) systems take only a few milliseconds to run, it is often hard to catch the active ones when simply probing the pg_stat_activity table.

Most likely, you will be able to see only the last executed query for those backends that have `state` different from `active`. In some cases, this can be enough.

In general, if you need to perform a deeper analysis, I strongly recommend installing and configuring the `pg_stat_statements` module, which is described in the *Analyzing the real-time performance of your queries* recipe in this chapter. Another option is to run a post analysis of log files using pgBadger. Depending on the workload of your system, you may want to limit the production of highly granular log files (that is, log all queries) to a short period of time. For further information on pgBadger, refer to the *Producing a daily summary of log file errors* recipe of this chapter.

Watching the longest queries

Another thing of interest that you may want to look for is long-running queries. To get a list of running queries ordered by how long they have been executing, use the following:

```
SELECT
    current_timestamp - query_start AS runtime,
    datname, usename, query
FROM pg_stat_activity
WHERE state = 'active'
ORDER BY 1 DESC;
```

This will return currently running queries, with the longest running queries in the front.

On busy systems, you may want to limit the set of queries returned to only the first few queries (add `LIMIT 10` at the end) or only the queries that have been running over a certain period of time. For example, to get a list of queries that have been running for more than a minute, use this query:

```
SELECT
    current_timestamp - query_start AS runtime,
    datname, usename, query
FROM pg_stat_activity
WHERE state = 'active'
    AND current_timestamp - query_start > '1 min'
ORDER BY 1 DESC;
```

Watching queries from ps

If you want, you can also make queries being run show up in process titles by setting the following in the `postgresql.conf` file:

```
update_process_title = on
```

Although the `ps` and `top` output are not the best places for watching database queries, they may make sense in some circumstances.

See also

- The page in PostgreSQL's online documentation that covers the appropriate settings is available at `http://www.postgresql.org/docs/current/static/runtime-config-statistics.html`

Checking which queries are active or blocked

Here, we will show you how to know whether a query is actually running or waiting for another query.

Getting ready

If you are logged in as superuser you will have full access to monitoring information.

How to do it...

1. You can run the following query:

```
SELECT datname
, usename
, wait_event_type
, wait_event
, query
FROM pg_stat_activity
WHERE wait_event_type IS NOT NULL
AND wait_event_type NOT IN ('Activity', 'Client');
```

2. The output will look like the following:

```
-[ RECORD 1 ]---+-----------------
datname         | postgres
usename         | gianni
wait_event_type | Lock
wait_event      | relation
query           | select * from t;
```

How it works...

The `pg_stat_activity` system view includes the `wait_event_type` and `wait_event` columns, which are set respectively to the kind of wait and to the kind of object that is blocked.

The preceding query uses the `wait_event` field to filter out only those queries that are waiting.

There's more...

Further explanation about the preceding queries is appropriate here.

No need for the = true part

As the `waiting` column is already Boolean, you can safely omit the `= true` part from the query and simply write the following:

```
SELECT datname, usename, query
       FROM pg_stat_activity
WHERE waiting;
```

Do we catch all queries waiting on locks?

PostgreSQL provides a version of the `pg_stat_activity` view capable of capturing many kinds of waits; however, in older versions `pg_stat_activity` could only detect waits on locks such as those placed on SQL objects, via the `pg_stat_activity.waiting` field.

Although this is the main cause of waiting when using pure SQL, it is possible to write a query in any of PostgreSQL's embedded languages that can wait on other system resources, such as waiting for an HTTP response, for a file write to get completed, or just waiting on a timer.

As an example, you can make your backend sleep for a certain number of seconds using `pg_sleep(seconds)`. While you are monitoring `pg_stat_activity`, open a new terminal session with `psql` and run the following statement in it:

```
db=# SELECT pg_sleep(10);
<it "stops" for 10 seconds here>
pg_sleep
----------

(1 row)
```

It will show up as *not waiting* in the `pg_stat_activity` view, even though the query is, in fact, blocked in the timer.

Knowing who is blocking a query

Once you have found out that a query is blocked, you need to know who or what is blocking them.

Getting ready

If you are logged in as a superuser you will have full access to monitoring information.

How to do it...

1. You can write the following query:

```
SELECT datname
, usename
, wait_event_type
, wait_event
, pg_blocking_pids(pid) AS blocked_by
, query
FROM pg_stat_activity
WHERE wait_event_type IS NOT NULL
AND wait_event_type NOT IN ('Activity', 'Client');
```

2. You will get an output like the following:

```
-[ RECORD 1 ]---+-----------------
datname         | postgres
usename         | gianni
wait_event_type | Lock
wait_event      | relation
blocked_by      | {18142}
query           | select * from t;
```

This is in fact the query described in the previous recipe, with the addition of the column called `blocked_by`. Recall that the PID is the unique identifier assigned by the operating system to each session; for more details, see Chapter 4, *Server Control*. Here the PID is used by the `pg_blocking_pids(pid)` system function to identify blocking sessions.

Parallel queries allow powerful queries using multiple cores, but also increase the number of ways in which one query can be blocked by another; think how complicated it can be to extract dependencies and display them neatly if there are multiple PIDs for a single session.

How it works...

The query is relatively simple: we just introduced the `pg_blocking_pids()` function, which returns an array composed by the PIDs of all the sessions that are blocking the session with the given PID.

Killing a specific session

Sometimes, the only way to let the system continue as a whole is by *surgically* terminating some offending database sessions. Yes, you read it right: surgically. You might indeed be tempted to *reboot* the server, but you should think of that as a last resort in a business continuity scenario.

In this recipe, you will learn how to intervene, from gracefully canceling a query to brutally killing the actual process from the command line.

How to do it...

You can either run this function as a superuser or with the same user as that of the offending backend (look for the `usename` field in the `pg_stat_activity` view).

Once you have figured out the backend you need to kill, use the function named `pg_terminate_backend(pid)` to kill it.

How it works...

When a backend executes the `pg_terminate_backend(pid)` function, it sends a signal, `SIGTERM`, to the backend as an argument after verifying that the process identified by the argument `pid` is actually a PostgreSQL backend.

The backend receiving this signal stops whatever it is doing, and terminates it in a controlled way.

The client using that backend loses the connection to the database. Depending on how the client application is written, it may silently reconnect, or it may show an error to the user.

There's more...

Killing the session may not always be what you really want, so consider other options as well.

It might also be a good idea to look at the *Server Signaling Functions* section in the PostgreSQL documentation at http://www.postgresql.org/docs/current/static/functions-admin.html#FUNCTIONS-ADMIN-SIGNAL.

Try to cancel the query first

First, you may want to try pg_cancel_backend(pid), a milder version of pg_terminate_backend(pid).

The difference between these two is that pg_cancel_backend() just cancels the current query, whereas pg_terminate_backend() really kills the backend (therefore, this can be used for idle or idle in transaction backends).

What if the backend won't terminate?

If pg_terminate_backend(pid) fails to kill the backend and you really need to reset the database state to make it continue processing requests, then you have yet another option: sending SIGKILL to the offending backend.

This can be done only from the command line as the root or the postgres system user, and on the same host the database is running on, by executing the following code:

```
kill -9 <backend_pid>
```

This command kills that backend immediately, without giving it a chance to clean up. Consequently, the postmaster is forced to kill all the other backends as well and restart the whole cluster.

Therefore, it actually does not matter which of the PostgreSQL backends you kill.

You must be extremely careful if you have set the synchronous_commit parameter to off. You may end up losing some supposedly committed transactions if you use kill -9 on a backend.

Thus, kill -9 is the last resort, but only if nothing else helps, and not on a regular basis.

Using statement_timeout to clean up queries that take too long to run

Often, you know that you don't have any use for queries running longer than a given time. Maybe your web frontend just refuses to wait for more than 10 seconds for a query to complete and returns a default answer to users if it takes longer, abandoning the query.

In such a case, it might be a good idea to set `statement_timeout = 10 sec`, either in `postgresql.conf` or as a per-user or per-database setting. Once you do so, queries running too long won't consume precious resources and make others' queries fail.

The queries terminated by a statement timeout show up in the log, as follows:

```
hannu=# SET statement_timeout TO '3 s';
SET
hannu=# SELECT pg_sleep(10);
ERROR:  canceling statement due to statement timeout
```

For the older versions of PostgreSQL, they show up as a more confusing message: `query canceled due to user request`.

Killing idle in transaction queries

Sometimes, people start a transaction, run some queries, and then just leave, without ending the transaction. This can leave some system resources in a state where some housekeeping processes can't be run. They may even have done something more serious, such as locking a table, thereby causing immediate *denial of service* for other users who need that table.

You can use the following query to kill all backends that have an open transaction but have been doing nothing for the last 10 minutes:

```
SELECT pg_terminate_backend(pid)
  FROM pg_stat_activity
WHERE state = 'idle in transaction'
   AND current_timestamp - query_start > '10 min';
```

You can even schedule this to run every minute while you are trying to find the specific frontend application that ignores open transactions, or when you have a lazy administration that leaves a psql connection open, or when a flaky network drops clients without the server noticing it.

Killing the backend from the command line

Another possibility to terminate a backend is by using a Unix/Linux command named `kill N`. This command orders the `SIGTERM` signal to process `N` on the system where it is running. You have to be either the `root` user or the user running the database backends (usually `postgres`) to be able to send signals to processes.

You can cancel a backend (and simulate the `pg_cancel_backend(pid)` function) by sending a `SIGINT` signal:

```
kill -SIGINT <backend_pid>
```

For more detailed information and the exact syntax, type `man kill` from your favorite shell environment.

Detecting an in-doubt prepared transaction

While using **two-phase commit** (**2PC**), you may end up in a situation where you have something locked but cannot find a backend that holds the locks. This recipe describes how to detect such a case.

How to do it...

1. You need to look up the `pg_locks` table for those entries with an empty `pid` value. Run this query:

    ```
    SELECT t.schemaname || '.' || t.relname AS tablename,
           l.pid, l.granted
           FROM pg_locks l JOIN pg_stat_user_tables t
           ON l.relation = t.relid;
    ```

2. The output will be something similar to the following:

    ```
    tablename |  pid  | granted
    ----------+-------+---------
        db.x  |       |  t
        db.x  | 27289 |  f
    (2 rows)
    ```

The preceding example shows a lock on the db.x table, which has no process associated with it.

If you need to remove a particular prepared transaction, you can refer to the *Removing old prepared transactions* recipe in Chapter 9, *Regular Maintenance*.

Knowing whether anybody is using a specific table

This recipe helps you when you are in doubt whether some obscure table is used any more or it is left over from the past and just takes up space.

Getting ready

Make sure that you are a superuser, or at least have full rights to the table in question.

How to do it...

1. To see whether a table is currently in active use (that is, whether anyone is using it while you are watching it), run the following query on the database you plan to inspect:

```
CREATE TEMPORARY TABLE tmp_stat_user_tables AS
        SELECT * FROM pg_stat_user_tables;
```

2. Then wait a little, and see what has changed:

```
SELECT * FROM pg_stat_user_tables n
  JOIN tmp_stat_user_tables t
    ON n.relid=t.relid
    AND
(n.seq_scan,n.idx_scan,n.n_tup_ins,n.n_tup_upd,n.n_tup_del)
    <>
(t.seq_scan,t.idx_scan,t.n_tup_ins,t.n_tup_upd,t.n_tup_del);
```

How it works...

The `pg_stat_user_tables` view shows the current statistics for table usage.

To see whether a table is used, you check for changes in its usage counts.

The previous query selects all the tables where any of the usage counts for SELECT or data manipulation have changed.

There's more...

You can use one of the following approaches to detect usage changes.

The quick-and-dirty way

If you are sure that you have no use for the cumulative statistics gathered by PostgreSQL, you can just reset all table statistics by executing the following command:

```
SELECT pg_stat_reset();
```

This sets all statistics to zero, and you can detect table use by just looking for tables where any usage count is not zero.

Of course, you can make a backup copy of the statistics table first, as follows:

```
CREATE TABLE backup_stat_user_tables AS
        SELECT current_timestamp AS snaptime,
                *
    FROM pg_stat_user_tables;
```

Collecting daily usage statistics

It is often useful to have historical usage statistics for tables when trying to solve performance problems or understand usage patterns.

For this purpose, you can collect usage data in a regular manner, daily or even more often, using either a cron or a PostgreSQL-specific scheduler such as pg_agent. Advanced users can take advantage of background workers to schedule such an activity. For more information on background worker processes, go to http://www.postgresql.org/docs/current/static/bgworker.html.

The following query adds a snapshot of current usage statistics with a timestamp to the table created earlier:

```
INSERT INTO backup_stat_user_tables
        SELECT current_timestamp AS snaptime,
                *
    FROM pg_stat_user_tables;
```

Knowing when a table was last used

Once you know that a table is not currently used, the next question is *When was it last used?*

Getting ready

Using a user with appropriate privileges.

How to do it...

PostgreSQL does not have any built-in *last used* information about tables, so you have to use other means to figure it out.

If you have set up a cron job to collect usage statistics, as described in the previous chapter, then it is relatively easy to find out the last date of change using a SQL query.

Other than this, there are basically two possibilities, neither of which gives you absolutely reliable answers.

You can either look at the actual timestamps of the files in which the data is stored, or you can use the xmin and xmax system columns to find out the latest transaction ID that changed the table data.

In this recipe, we cover the first case and focus on the date information in the table's files.

The following PL/pgSQL function looks for the table's data files to get the value of their last access and modification times:

```
CREATE OR REPLACE FUNCTION table_file_access_info(
    IN schemaname text, IN tablename text,
    OUT last_access timestamp with time zone,
    OUT last_change timestamp with time zone
    ) LANGUAGE plpgsql AS $func$
DECLARE
    tabledir text;
    filenode text;
BEGIN
    SELECT regexp_replace(
        current_setting('data_directory') || '/' ||
pg_relation_filepath(c.oid),
        pg_relation_filenode(c.oid) || '$', ''),
        pg_relation_filenode(c.oid)
```

```
        INTO tabledir, filenode
        FROM pg_class c
        JOIN pg_namespace ns
          ON c.relnamespace = ns.oid
         AND c.relname = tablename
         AND ns.nspname = schemaname;
     RAISE NOTICE 'tabledir: % - filenode: %', tabledir, filenode;
     -- find latest access and modification times over all segments
     SELECT max((pg_stat_file(tabledir || filename)).access),
            max((pg_stat_file(tabledir || filename)).modification)
       INTO last_access, last_change
       FROM pg_ls_dir(tabledir) AS filename
       -- only use files matching <basefilename>[.segmentnumber]
      WHERE filename ~ ('^' || filenode || '([.]?[0-9]+)?$');
  END;
  $func$;
```

How it works..

The `table_file_access_info(schemaname, tablename)` function returns the last access and modification times for a given table using the filesystem as a source of information.

The last query uses this data to get the latest time any of these files were modified or read by PostgreSQL. Beware that this is not a very reliable way to get information about the latest use of any table, but it gives you a rough upper-limit estimate about when it was last modified or read (for example, consider the autovacuum process accessing a table).

You can definitely improve and personalize the preceding function. I advise you to look at the PostgreSQL documentation and read about two built-in functions, `pg_ls_dir(dirname text)` and `pg_stat_file(filename text)`.

Another good source of information is the *Database File Layout* page in the PostgreSQL documentation at
`http://www.postgresql.org/docs/current/static/storage-file-layout.html`.

There's more...

Recently, there have been discussions about adding last-used data to the information about tables that PostgreSQL keeps, so it is quite possible that answering the question *when did anybody last use this table?* will be much easier in the next version of PostgreSQL.

Usage of disk space by temporary data

In addition to ordinary persistent tables, you can also create temporary tables.

Also, PostgreSQL may use temporary files for query processing if it can't fit all the necessary data into the memory.

So, how do you find out how much data is used by temporary tables and files? You can do this using any untrusted embedded language, or directly on the database host.

Getting ready

You have to use an untrusted language, because trusted languages run in a sandbox, which prohibits them from directly accessing the host filesystem.

How to do it...

Perform the following steps:

1. First, check whether your database defines special tablespaces for temporary files, as follows:

   ```
   SELECT current_setting('temp_tablespaces');
   ```

2. As explained later on in this recipe, if the setting is empty, it means PostgreSQL is not using temporary tablespaces, and temporary objects will be located in the default tablespace for each database.

3. On the other hand, if `temp_tablespaces` has one or more tablespaces, then your task is easy because all temporary files, both those used for temporary tables and those used for query processing, are inside the directories of these tablespaces. The following query (which uses `WITH` queries and string and array functions) demonstrates how to check the space used by temporary tablespaces:

   ```
   WITH temporary_tablespaces AS (SELECT
    unnest(string_to_array(
     current_setting('temp_tablespaces'), ',')
    ) AS temp_tablespace
   )
   SELECT tt.temp_tablespace,
   pg_tablespace_location(t.oid) AS location,
   ```

```
      pg_tablespace_size(t.oid) AS size
FROM temporary_tablespaces tt
JOIN pg_tablespace t ON t.spcname = tt.temp_tablespace
ORDER BY 1;
```

The output shows very limited use of temporary space (I ran the preceding query while I had two open transactions that had just created small, temporary tables using random data through `generate_series()`):

```
temp_tablespace  |    location    |   size
-----------------+----------------+---------
 pgtemp1         | /srv/pgtemp1   | 3633152
 pgtemp2         | /srv/pgtemp2   |  376832
(2 rows)
```

Even though you can obtain similar results using different queries, or just by checking the disk usage from the filesystem through `du` (once you know the location of tablespaces), I would like to focus on two functions here:

- `pg_tablespace_location(oid)`: This provides the location of the tablespace with the given `oid`
- `pg_tablespace_size(oid)` or `pg_tablespace_size(name)`: This allows us to check the size used by a named tablespace directly within PostgreSQL

Because the amount of temporary disk space used can vary a lot in an active system, you may want to repeat the query several times to get a better picture of how the disk usage changes (with psql, use `\watch`, as explained in the *Checking whether a user is connected* recipe).

 Further information on these functions can be found at `http://www.postgresql.org/docs/current/static/functions-admin.html`.

On the other hand, if the `temp_tablespaces` setting is empty, then the temporary tables are stored in the same directory as ordinary tables, and the temporary files used for query processing are stored in the `pgsql_tmp` directory inside the main database directory.

Look up the cluster's home directory using this query:

```
SELECT current_setting('data_directory') || '/base/pgsql_tmp'
```

The size of this directory gives the total size of current temporary files for query processing.

The total size of temporary files used by a database can be found in the `pg_stat_database` system view, and specifically in the two fields `temp_files` and `temp_bytes`. The following query returns the cumulative number of temporary files and the space used by every database since the last reset (`stats_reset`):

```
SELECT datname, temp_files, temp_bytes, stats_reset
  FROM pg_stat_database;
```

The `pg_stat_database` view holds very important statistics. I recommend that you look at the official documentation at
`http://www.postgresql.org/docs/current/static/monitoring-stats.html#PG-STAT-DAT ABASE-VIEW` for detailed information and to get further ideas on how to improve your monitoring skills.

How it works...

Because all temporary tables and other temporary on-disk data are stored in files, you can use PostgreSQL's internal tables to find the locations of these files, and then determine the total size of these files.

There's more...

While the preceding information about temporary tables is correct, it is not the entire story.

Finding out whether a temporary file is in use any more

Because temporary files are not as carefully preserved as ordinary tables (this is actually one of the benefits of temporary tables, as less bookkeeping makes them faster), it may sometimes happen that a system crash leaves a few temporary files, which can (in the worst cases) take up a significant amount of disk space.

As a rule, you can clean up such files by shutting down the PostgreSQL server and then deleting all files from the `pgsql_tmp` directory.

Logging temporary file usage

If you set `log_temp_files = 0` or a larger value, then the creation of all temporary files that are larger than this value in kilobytes is logged to the standard PostgreSQL log.

If, while monitoring the log and the `pg_stat_database` view, you notice an increase in temporary file activity, you should consider increasing `work_mem`, either globally or (preferably) on a query/session basis.

Understanding why queries slow down

In production environments with large databases and high concurrent access, it might happen that queries that used to run in tens of milliseconds suddenly take several seconds.

Likewise, a summary query for a report that used to run in a few seconds might take half an hour to complete.

Here are some ways to find out what is slowing them down.

Getting ready

Any questions of the type *Why is this different today from what it was last week*? are much easier to answer if you have some kind of historical data collection setup.

Tools such as Cacti or Munin (for monitoring general server characteristics such as CPU and RAM usage, disk I/O, network traffic, and load average) are very useful to see what has changed recently, and to try to correlate these changes with the observed performance of some database operations.

Also, collecting historical statistics data from `pg_stat_*` tables, whether daily, hourly, or even every five minutes if you have enough disk space, is also very useful for detecting possible causes of sudden changes or a gradual degradation in performance.

If you are gathering both of these, then that's even better. If you have none, then the question is actually: *Why is this query slow?*

But don't despair! There are a few things you can do to try to restore performance.

How to do it...

First, analyze your database using this code:

```
db_01=# analyse;
ANALYZE
Time: 6231.313 ms
db_01=#
```

This is the first thing to try, as it is usually cheap and is meant to be done quite often anyway.

If this restores the query's performance or at least improves the current performance considerably, then it means that autovacuum is not doing its task well, and the next thing to do is to find out why.

You must ensure that the performance improvement is not due to caching of the pages required by the requested query. Make sure that you repeat your query several times before classifying it as slow. Looking at `pg_stat_statements` (which is covered later in this chapter) can help you analyze the impact of a particular query in terms of caching, by inspecting two fields: `shared_blks_hit` and `shared_blks_read`.

How it works...

The `ANALYZE` command updates statistics about data size and data distribution in all tables. If a table size has changed significantly without its statistics being updated, then PostgreSQL's statistics-based optimizer may choose a bad plan. Manually running the `ANALYZE` command updates the statistics for all tables.

There's more...

There are a few other common problems.

Do the queries return significantly more data than they did earlier?

If you've initially tested your queries on almost empty tables, it is entirely possible that you are querying much more data than you need.

As an example, if you select all users' items and then show the first 10 items, this query runs very fast when the user has 10 or even 50 items, but not so well when they have 50,000.

Ensure that you don't ask for more data than you need. Use the LIMIT clause to return less data to your application (and to give the optimizer at least a chance to select a plan that processes less data when selecting: it may also have a lower startup cost). In some cases, you can evaluate the use of cursors for your applications.

Do the queries also run slowly when they are run alone?

If you can, then try to run the same slow query when the database has no (or very few) other queries running concurrently. If it runs well in this situation, then it may be that the database host is just overloaded (CPU, memory, or disk I/O) or other applications are interfering with Postgres on the same server. Consequently, a plan that works well under a light load is not so good any more. It may even be that this is not a very good query plan with which to begin, and you were fooled by modern computers being really fast:

```
db=# select count(*) from t;
   count
---------
 1000000
(1 row)
Time: 329.743 ms
```

As you can see, scanning 1 million rows takes just 0.3 seconds on a laptop that is a few years old if these rows are already cached.

However, if you have a few such queries running in parallel, and also other queries competing for memory, this query is likely to slow down an order of magnitude or two.

See Chapter 10, *Performance and Concurrency*, for general advice on performance tuning.

Is the second run of the same query also slow?

This test is related to the previous test, and it checks whether the slowdown is caused by some of the necessary data not fitting into the memory or being pushed out of the memory by other queries.

If the second run of the query is fast, then you probably lack enough memory. Again, see Chapter 10, *Performance and Concurrency*, for details about this.

Table and index bloat

Table bloat is something that can develop over time if some maintenance processes can't be run properly. In other words, due to the way **Multiversion Concurrency Control** (**MVCC**) works, your table will contain a lot of older versions of rows, if these versions can't be removed in a timely manner.

There are several ways this can develop, but all involve lots of updates or deletes and inserts, while autovacuum is prevented from doing its job of getting rid of old tuples. It is possible that, even after the old versions are deleted, the table stays at its newly acquired and large size, thanks to visible rows being located at the end of the table and preventing PostgreSQL from shrinking the file. There have been cases where a one-row table has grown to several gigabytes in size.

If you suspect that some tables may contain bloat, then run the following query:

```
SELECT pg_relation_size(relid) AS tablesize,schemaname,relname,n_live_tup
FROM pg_stat_user_tables
WHERE relname = <tablename>;
```

Then, see whether the relation of `tablesize` to `n_live_tup` makes sense.

For example, if the table size is tens of megabytes, and there are only a small number of rows, then you have bloat, and proper `VACUUM` strategies are necessary (as explained in `Chapter 9`, *Regular Maintenance*).

It is important to check that the statistics are up-to-date. You might indeed need to run `ANALYSE` on the table and run the query again.

See also

- The *Collecting daily usage statistics* section shows one way to collect info on table changes
- `Chapter 9`, *Regular Maintenance*
- `Chapter 10`, *Performance and Concurrency*
- The *How many rows in a table?* recipe in `Chapter 2`, *Exploring the Database*, for an introduction to MVCC
- The `auto_explain` contrib module at http://www.postgresql.org/docs/current/static/auto-explain.html

Investigating and reporting a bug

When you find out that PostgreSQL is not doing what it should, then it's time to investigate.

Getting ready

It is a good idea to make a full copy of your PostgreSQL installation before you start investigating. This will help you restart several times and be sure that you are actually investigating the results of the bug, and not chasing your own tail by looking at changes introduced by your last investigation and debugging attempt.

Do not forget to include your tablespaces too in the full copy.

How to do it...

Try to make a minimal repeatable test scenario that exhibits this bug. Sometimes, the bug disappears while doing this, but mostly it is needed to make the process easy. It is almost impossible to fix a bug that you can't observe and repeat at will.

If it is about query processing, then you can usually provide a minimal dump file (the result of running `pg_dump`) of your database together with a SQL script that exhibits the error.

If you have corrupt data, then you may want to make a subset of the corrupted data files available for people who have the knowledge and time to look at it. Sometimes, you can find such people on the PostgreSQL hackers' list, and sometimes you have to hire someone or even fix it yourself. The more preparatory work you do yourself and the better you formulate your questions, the higher the chance you have of finding help quickly.

If you suspect a data corruption bug and feel adventurous, then you can read about data formats at `http://www.postgresql.org/docs/current/static/storage.html`, and investigate your data tables using the `pageinspect` package from contrib.

When reporting a bug, always include at least the PostgreSQL version you are using and the operating system on which you are using it.

More detailed information on this process is available at the PostgreSQL Wiki. By following the official recommendations at
`http://wiki.postgresql.org/wiki/Guide_to_reporting_problems` and
`http://wiki.postgresql.org/wiki/SlowQueryQuestions`, you will have a higher chance of getting your questions answered.

How it works...

If everything works really well, then it goes like the following:

- A user submits a well-researched bug report to the PostgreSQL hackers' list.
- Some discussions follow on the list, and the user may be asked to provide some additional information.
- Somebody finds out what is wrong and proposes a fix.
- The fix is discussed on the hackers' list.
- The bug is fixed. There is a patch for the current version, and the fix is sure to be included in the next version.
- Sometimes, the fix is backported to older versions.

Unfortunately, any step may go wrong due to various reasons, such as nobody feeling that this is their area of expertise, the right people not having time and hoping for someone else to deal with it, and these other people not reading the list at the right moment.

If this happens, follow up your question in a day or two to try to understand why there was no reaction.

Producing a daily summary of log file errors

PostgreSQL can generate gigabytes of logs per day. Lots of data is good if you want to investigate some specific event, but it is not what you will use for daily monitoring of database health.

In this recipe, we'll see how to perform a post analysis of our log files and get reports (and insights) about what has happened in a given period of time.

A different approach is to perform real-time analysis of queries through the `pg_stat_statements` extension, which will be covered in the next recipe.

Getting ready

Make sure that your PostgreSQL is set up to rotate log files, for example, daily. I personally prefer to integrate PostgreSQL with `rsyslog` and `logrotate` for log management on Linux or Unix systems, but you can use any method that is allowed by PostgreSQL (CSV or standard error, for example).

A typical default setup will divert log messages to `stderr`, and you can set up log rotation directly in PostgreSQL through the `log_rotation_age` configuration option.

Once you have your logs ready, it is time to feed them to a PostgreSQL log-processing program. Here, we describe how to do so using pgBadger, a multi-platform application written in Perl that has recently become more popular than its famous predecessor, **pgFouine**.

Some of the cool features of pgBadger include—multi-file processing, parallel processing, auto-detection of the input format, on-the-fly decompression, as well as very light HTML reports with Javascript-generated charts (that have zooming capabilities), as shown here:

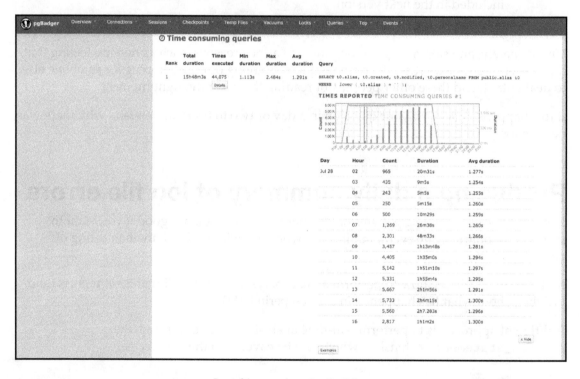

Report of time-consuming queries with pgBadger

For most Linux systems, you should be able to use your default package manager to install pgBadger. Otherwise, you can simply download its sources.

Configure your PostgreSQL server to produce log files in a format that `pgBadger` understands. Everything is thoroughly described in the online documentation for pgBadger at `http://dalibo.github.io/pgbadger/`.

Suppose you are using `syslog` and you want to exclude queries that take less than a second to be executed. You can have a logging configuration of your PostgreSQL server similar to this:

```
log_destination = syslog
syslog_facility = LOCAL0
syslog_ident = 'postgres'
log_line_prefix = 'user=%u,db=%d,client=%h '
log_temp_files = 0
log_statement = ddl
log_min_duration_statement = 1000
log_min_messages = info
log_checkpoints = on
log_lock_waits = on
```

The documentation for pgBadger is a great source of information regarding PostgreSQL configuration in terms of logging. You are advised to read that together with the *Error Reporting and Logging* section of the Postgres documentation available at `http://www.postgresql.org/docs/current/static/runtime-config-logging.html`.

How to do it...

Set up a cron job to run regularly (for example once every hour, day, or week) and let pgBadger analyze one or more log files. Here, you can find a very simple example that can be used to prepare daily reports every hour.

For the sake of simplicity, the script has been purged of any error check. Production usage requires the addition of some basic shell controls:

```
#!/bin/bash
outdir=/var/www/reports
begin=$(date +'%Y-%m-%d %H:00:00' -d '-1 day')
end=$(date +'%Y-%m-%d %H:00:00')
outfile="$outdir/daily-$(date +'%H').html"

pgbadger -q -b "$begin" -e "$end" -o "$outfile" \
    /var/log/postgres.log.1 /var/log/postgres.log
```

The preceding script informs pgbadger to analyze the current log file
(/var/log/postgresql.log) and the previously rotated file
(/var/log/postgres.log.1), to limit the reporting activity to the last 24 hours (see how
the date command was used to generate timestamps), and then write the output to the
$outfile HTML file.

Once again, this is just a very simple use case for pgBadger. I strongly advise you to look at
the documentation and investigate all the options and possibilities that pgBadger offers.

I want to end this recipe with a practical idea that you can explore with your system
administrators. You might have noticed that the output directory has been set as a common
default DocumentRoot for Apache servers (/var/www).

A very practical way to use pgBadger is to integrate it with a web server.

Production environments may benefit from SSL encryption, basic authentication, and the
mod_dir module, which allows you to make your reports automatically available through
the internet (or your intranet).

How it works...

The pgBadger tool condenses and ranks error messages for easy viewing, and produces a
nicely formatted report in HTML. From that report, you can find out the most frequent
errors.

As a rule, it is good practice not to tolerate errors in database logs if you can avoid them.
Once the errors start showing up in the log and report, you should find their cause and fix
them.

While it is tempting to leave the errors there and consider them as just a small nuisance
because *they do no harm*, simple errors are often an indication of other problems in the
application. These problems, if not found and understood, may lead to all kinds of larger
problems, such as security breaches or eventual data corruption at the logical level.

There's more...

If you have only a small number of errors in your log files, then it may be sufficient to run
each log file through grep to find errors:

```
user@dbhost: $ egrep "FATAL|ERROR" /var/log/postgres.log
```

Analyzing the real-time performance of your queries

The `pg_stat_statements` extension adds the capability to track execution statistics of queries that are run in a database, including the number of calls, total execution time, total number of returned rows, and internal information on memory and I/O access.

It is evident how this approach opens up new opportunities in PostgreSQL performance analysis, by allowing DBAs to get insights directly from the database through SQL and in real time.

Getting ready

The `pg_stat_statements` module is available as a contrib module of PostgreSQL. The extension must be installed as a superuser in the desired databases. It also requires administrators to add the library in the `postgresql.conf` file, as follows:

```
shared_preload_libraries = 'pg_stat_statements'
```

This change requires restarting the PostgreSQL server.

Finally, in order to use it, the extension must be installed in the desired database through the usual CREATE EXTENSION command (run as a superuser):

```
gabriele=# CREATE EXTENSION pg_stat_statements;
CREATE EXTENSION
```

How to do it...

Connect to a database where you have installed the `pg_stat_statements` extension, preferably as a superuser.

You can start by retrieving a list of the most frequent queries:

```
SELECT query FROM pg_stat_statements ORDER BY calls DESC;
```

Alternatively, you can retrieve the queries with the highest average execution time:

```
SELECT query, total_time/calls AS avg, calls
      FROM pg_stat_statements ORDER BY 2 DESC;
```

These are just examples. I strongly recommend that you look at the PostgreSQL documentation at
`http://www.postgresql.org/docs/current/static/pgstatstatements.html` for more detailed information on the structure of the `pg_stat_statements` view.

How it works...

Since the `pg_stat_statements` shared library has been loaded by the PostgreSQL server, Postgres starts collecting statistics for every database in the instance.

The extension simply installs the `pg_stat_statements` view and the `pg_stat_statements_reset()` function in the current database, allowing the DBA to inspect the available statistics.

By default, read access to the `pg_stat_statements` view is granted to every user who can access the database (even though standard users are allowed to see only the SQL statements of their queries).

The `pg_stat_statements_reset()` function can be used to discard the statistics collected by the server up to that moment, and set all the counters to 0. It requires a superuser in order to be run.

There's more...

A very important `pg_stat_statements` feature is the normalization of queries that can be planned (`SELECT`, `INSERT`, `DELETE`, and `UPDATE`). You might have indeed noticed some ? characters in the `query` field returned by the queries outlined in the previous section. The normalization process intercepts constants in SQL statements run by users and replaces them with a placeholder (identified by a question mark).

Consider the following queries:

```
SELECT * FROM bands WHERE name = 'AC/DC';
SELECT * FROM bands WHERE name = 'Lynyrd Skynyrd';
```

After the normalization process, these two queries appear as one in `pg_stat_statements`:

```
gabriele=# SELECT query, calls FROM pg_stat_statements;
                query                  | calls
---------------------------------------+-------
 SELECT * FROM bands WHERE name = ?;   |    2
 &mldr; <snip> &mldr;
```

This is the expected behavior, isn't it?

The extension comes with a few configuration options, such as the maximum number of queries to be tracked.

9
Regular Maintenance

PostgreSQL prefers regular maintenance, so please read the recipe that discusses maintenance planning (the one in this chapter).

We recognize that you're here for a reason and are looking for a quick solution to your needs. You're probably thinking—*Fix me first, and I'll plan later*. So off we go!

PostgreSQL provides a utility command named VACUUM, which is a jokey name for a garbage collector that sweeps up all the bad things and fixes them - or at least, most of them. That's the single most important thing you need to remember to do—I say single, because closely connected to that is the ANALYZE command, which collects optimizer statistics. It's possible to run VACUUM and ANALYZE as a single joint command, VACUUM ANALYZE, and those actions are automatically executed for you when appropriate by autovacuum, a special background process that runs as part of the PostgreSQL server.

VACUUM performs a range of cleanup activities, some of them too complex to describe without a whole sideline into their internals. VACUUM has been heavily optimized over a 20-year period to take the minimum required lock levels on tables and execute in the most efficient manner possible, skipping all the unnecessary work and using L2 cache CPU optimizations when work is required.

Many experienced PostgreSQL DBAs will prefer to execute their own VACUUM commands, though autovacuum now provides a fine degree of control, which—if enabled and controlled—can save much of your time. Using both manual and automatic vacuuming gives you control and a safety net.

In this chapter, we will cover the following recipes:

- Controlling automatic database maintenance
- Avoiding auto-freezing and page corruptions
- Removing issues that cause bloat
- Removing old prepared transactions
- Actions for heavy users of temporary tables
- Identifying and fixing bloated tables and indexes
- Monitoring and tuning vacuum
- Maintaining indexes
- Adding a constraint without checking existing rows
- Finding unused indexes
- Carefully removing unwanted indexes
- Planning maintenance

Controlling automatic database maintenance

Autovacuum is enabled by default in PostgreSQL, and mostly does a great job of maintaining your PostgreSQL database. We say mostly because it doesn't know everything you do about the database, such as the best time to perform maintenance actions.

Getting ready

Exercising control requires some thinking about what you actually want:

- What are the best times of day to do things? When are system resources more available?
- Which days are quiet, and which are not?
- Which tables are critical to the application, and which are not?

How to do it...

The first thing to do is make sure that `autovacuum` is switched on, which is the default. Check that you have the following parameters enabled in your `postgresql.conf` file:

```
autovacuum = on
track_counts = on
```

PostgreSQL controls `autovacuum` with more than 40 individually tunable parameters. That provides a wide range of options, though it can be a little daunting.

The following are the relevant parameters that can be set in `postgresql.conf` to tune the `VACUUM` command:

```
vacuum_cost_page_dirty
vacuum_cost_page_hit
vacuum_cost_page_miss
vacuum_cost_delay
vacuum_cost_limit
vacuum_freeze_min_age
vacuum_freeze_table_age
vacuum_multixact_freeze_min_age
vacuum_multixact_freeze_table_age
```

There are also parameters that apply specifically to the `autovacuum` process:

```
autovacuum
autovacuum_work_mem
autovacuum_max_workers
autovacuum_naptime
autovacuum_vacuum_scale_factor
autovacuum_vacuum_threshold
autovacuum_analyze_scale_factor
autovacuum_analyze_threshold
autovacuum_vacuum_cost_delay
autovacuum_vacuum_cost_limit
autovacuum_freeze_max_age
autovacuum_multixact_freeze_max_age
log_autovacuum_min_duration
```

The preceding parameters apply to all tables at once. Individual tables can be controlled by storage parameters, which are set using the following command:

```
ALTER TABLE mytable SET (storage_parameter = value);
```

The storage parameters that relate to maintenance are as follows:

```
autovacuum_enabled
autovacuum_vacuum_cost_delay
autovacuum_vacuum_cost_limit
autovacuum_vacuum_scale_factor
autovacuum_vacuum_threshold
autovacuum_freeze_min_age
autovacuum_freeze_max_age
autovacuum_freeze_table_age
autovacuum_multixact_freeze_min_age
autovacuum_multixact_freeze_max_age
autovacuum_multixact_freeze_table_age
autovacuum_analyze_scale_factor
autovacuum_analyze_threshold
log_autovacuum_min_duration
```

The `toast` tables can be controlled with the following parameters:

```
toast.autovacuum_enabled
toast.autovacuum_vacuum_cost_delay
toast.autovacuum_vacuum_cost_limit
toast.autovacuum_vacuum_scale_factor
toast.autovacuum_vacuum_threshold
toast.autovacuum_freeze_min_age
toast.autovacuum_freeze_max_age
toast.autovacuum_freeze_table_age
toast.autovacuum_multixact_freeze_min_age
toast.autovacuum_multixact_freeze_max_age
toast.autovacuum_multixact_freeze_table_age
toast.log_autovacuum_min_duration
```

How it works...

If `autovacuum` is set, then it will wake up every `autovacuum_naptime` seconds, and decide whether to run VACUUM, ANALYZE, or both (don't modify that).

There will never be more than `autovacuum_max_workers` maintenance processes running at any time. As these autovacuum workers perform I/O, they accumulate cost points until they hit the `autovacuum_vacuum_cost_limit` value, after which they sleep for an `autovacuum_vacuum_cost_delay` period of time. This is designed to throttle the resource utilization of autovacuum to prevent it from using all of the available disk performance, which it should never do. So increasing `autovacuum_vacuum_cost_delay` will slow down each VACUUM to reduce the impact on user activity. Autovacuum will run ANALYZE when there have been at least `autovacuum_analyze_threshold` changes and a fraction of the table defined by `autovacuum_analyze_scale_factor` has been inserted, updated, or deleted.

Autovacuum will run VACUUM when there have been at least `autovacuum_vacuum_threshold` changes, and a fraction of the table defined by `autovacuum_vacuum_scale_factor` has been updated or deleted.

The `autovacuum_*` parameters only change vacuums and analyze operations executed by autovacuum. User initiated VACUUM and ANALYZE commands are affected by `vacuum_vacuum_cost_delay` and other `vacuum_*` parameters.

If you set `log_autovacuum_min_duration`, then any autovacuum process that runs for longer than this value will be logged to the server log, like the following:

```
2010-04-29 01:33:55 BST (13130) LOG:   automatic vacuum of table
"postgres.public.pgbench_accounts": index scans: 1
      pages: 0 removed, 3279 remain
      tuples: 100000 removed, 100000 remain
      system usage: CPU 0.19s/0.36u sec elapsed 19.01 sec
2010-04-29 01:33:59 BST (13130) LOG:   automatic analyze of table
"postgres.public.pgbench_accounts"
      system usage: CPU 0.06s/0.18u sec elapsed 3.66 sec
```

Most of the preceding global parameters can also be set at the table level. For example, if you think that you don't want a table to be autovacuumed, then you can set this:

```
ALTER TABLE big_table SET (autovacuum_enabled = off);
```

It's also possible to set parameters for toast tables. A toast table is the location where oversize column values get placed, which the documents refer to as *supplementary storage tables*. If there are no oversize values, then the toast table will occupy little space. Tables with very wide values often have large toast tables. **TOAST** (short for **the oversize attribute storage technique**) is optimized for UPDATE. If you have a heavily updated table, the toast table is untouched, so it may make sense to turn off autovacuuming of the toast table, as follows:

```
ALTER TABLE pgbench_accounts
SET ( toast.autovacuum_enabled = off);
```

This will turn off autovacuuming of the toast table.

Note that autovacuuming of the toast table is performed completely separately from the main table, even though you can't ask for an explicit include or exclude of the toast table yourself when running VACUUM.

Use the following query to display the reloptions for tables and their toast tables:

```
postgres=#
SELECT n.nspname
, c.relname
, array_to_string(
    c.reloptions ||
ARRAY(
SELECT 'toast.' || x
FROM unnest(tc.reloptions) AS x
), ', ')
AS relopts
FROM pg_class c
LEFT JOIN pg_class tc    ON c.reltoastrelid = tc.oid
JOIN pg_namespace n ON c.relnamespace  = n.oid
WHERE c.relkind = 'r'
AND nspname NOT IN ('pg_catalog', 'information_schema');
```

This query gives the following output:

```
nspname |       relname     |     relopts
--------+-------------------+-------------------------------
 public | pgbench_accounts  | fillfactor=100,
                              autovacuum_enabled=on,
                              autovacuum_vacuum_cost_delay=20
 public | pgbench_tellers   | fillfactor=100
 public | pgbench_branches  | fillfactor=100
 public | pgbench_history   |
 public | text_archive      | toast.autovacuum_enabled=off
```

VACUUM allows insertions, updates, and deletions while it runs, but it prevents actions such as ALTER TABLE and CREATE INDEX. That's not a problem since you should be using CREATE INDEX CONCURRENTLY. Autovacuum can detect if a user has requested a conflicting lock on the table while it runs, and it will cancel itself if it is getting in the user's way. VACUUM doesn't cancel itself since we expect the DBA would not want it to be canceled.

Note that VACUUM does not shrink a table when it runs, unless there is a large run of space at the end of a table, and nobody is accessing the table when we try to shrink it. To shrink a table properly, you'll need VACUUM FULL, but it locks up the whole table for a long time, and should be avoided if possible. The VACUUM FULL command will literally rewrite every row of the table and completely rebuild all indexes. This process is faster than it used to be, though it still takes a long time for larger tables.

There's more...

The postgresql.conf file also allows include directives, which look like the following:

```
include 'autovacuum.conf'
```

These specify another file that will be read at that point, just as if those parameters had been included in the main file.

This can be used to maintain multiple sets of files for the autovacuum configuration. Let's say we have a website that is busy mainly during the daytime, with some occasional night-time use. We decide to have two profiles: one for daytime, when we want less aggressive autovacuuming, and another at night, where we can allow more aggressive vacuuming:

1. We add the following lines to `postgresql.conf`:

   ```
   autovacuum = on
   autovacuum_max_workers = 3
   include 'autovacuum.conf'
   ```

2. We remove all other `autovacuum` parameters

3. We then create a file named `autovacuum.conf.day`, containing the following parameters:

   ```
   autovacuum_analyze_scale_factor = 0.1
   autovacuum_analyze_threshold = 50
   autovacuum_vacuum_cost_delay = 30
   autovacuum_vacuum_cost_limit = -1
   autovacuum_vacuum_scale_factor = 0.2
   autovacuum_vacuum_threshold = 50
   ```

4. Then, we create another file, named `autovacuum.conf.night`, which contains the following parameters:

   ```
   autovacuum_analyze_scale_factor = 0.05
   autovacuum_analyze_threshold = 50
   autovacuum_vacuum_cost_delay = 10
   autovacuum_vacuum_cost_limit = -1
   autovacuum_vacuum_scale_factor = 0.1
   autovacuum_vacuum_threshold = 50
   ```

5. To swap profiles, we simply do this:

   ```
   $ ln -sf autovacuum.conf.night autovacuum.conf
   $ pg_ctl reload
   ```

The latter is the command to reload the server configuration, and it must be customized depending on your platform.

This then allows us to switch profiles twice per day without needing to edit the configuration files. You can also tell easily which is the active profile simply by looking at the full details of the linked file (using `ls -l`). The exact details of the schedule are up to you. Night and day was just an example, which is unlikely to suit everybody.

See also

- The `autovacuum_freeze_max_age` parameter is explained in the next recipe, *Avoiding auto-freezing and page corruptions*, as are the more complex table-level parameters

Avoiding auto-freezing and page corruptions

There are some aspects of VACUUM whose reason to exist is complex to explain, and occasionally they have negative behavior. Let's look more deeply at those, and find some solutions.

How to do it...

PostgreSQL uses internal transaction identifiers that are 4 bytes long, so we only have 2^{32} transaction IDs (about four billion). PostgreSQL starts again from the beginning when that wraps around, allocating new identifiers in a circular manner. The reason we do this is that moving to an 8-byte identifier has various other negative effects and costs that we would rather not pay, so we keep the 4-byte transaction identifier, which means we need to do regular sweeps to replace old transaction identifiers with a special value that is not interpreted in a circular way, and is called **Frozen Transaction ID**; that's why this procedure is known as *freezing*.

There are two routes that a row can take in PostgreSQL—a row version dies and needs to be removed by VACUUM, or a row version gets old enough and needs to be frozen, which is also performed by the VACUUM process.

Why do we care? Suppose that we load a table with 100 million rows, and everything is fine. When those rows have been there long enough to begin being frozen, the next VACUUM operation on that table will rewrite all of them to freeze their transaction identifiers. Put another way, autovacuum will wake up and start using lots of I/O to perform the freezing.

The most obvious way to forestall the problem is to explicitly vacuum a table after a major load. Of course, that doesn't remove the problem entirely, and you might not have time for that.

The knee-jerk reaction for many people is to turn off autovacuum, because it keeps waking up at the most inconvenient times. My way is described in the *Controlling automatic database maintenance* recipe.

Freezing takes place when a transaction identifier on a row becomes more than `vacuum_freeze_min_age` transactions older than the current next value. Normal VACUUM operations will perform a small amount of freezing as you go, and in most cases, you won't notice that at all. As explained in the earlier example, large transactions leave many rows with the same transaction identifiers, so those might cause problems at the freezing time.

The VACUUM command is normally optimized to only look at the chunks of a table that require cleaning, both for normal vacuum and freezing operations.

If you fiddle with those parameters to try to forestall heavy VACUUM operations, then you'll notice that the `autovacuum_freeze_max_age` parameter controls when the table will be scanned by a forced VACUUM command. To put that another way, you can't turn off the need to freeze rows, but you can get to choose when this happens. My advice is to control autovacuum as described in the previous recipe, or perform explicit VACUUM operations at a time of your choosing.

The VACUUM command is also an efficient way to confirm the absence of page corruptions, so it is worth scanning the whole database, block-by-block, from time to time. To do this, you can run the following command on each of your databases:

```
VACUUM (DISABLE_PAGE_SKIPPING);
```

You can do this table by table, as well. There's nothing special about whole database VACUUM operations anymore; in earlier versions of PostgreSQL this was important, so you may read in random places on the web that this is a good idea.

If you've never had a corrupt block, then you may only need to scan every two to three months. If you start to get corrupt blocks, then you may want to increase the scan rate to confirm everything is OK. Corrupt blocks are usually hardware induced, though they show up as database errors. It's possible but rare that the corruption was from a PostgreSQL bug instead.

There's no easy way to fix page corruptions at present. There are, however, ways to investigate and extract data from corrupt blocks, for example, using the `pageinspect` contrib utility that Simon wrote. You can also detect them automatically by creating the whole cluster using the following:

```
initdb --data-checksums
```

This command initializes the data directory and enables data block checksums. This means that, every time something changes in a block, PostgreSQL will compute the new checksum, and then store in that same block the resulting block checksums, so that a simple programme can detect it.

Removing issues that cause bloat

Bloat can be caused by long running queries or long running write transactions that execute alongside write-heavy workloads. Resolving that is mostly down to understanding the workloads running on the server.

Getting ready

Look at the age of the oldest snapshots that are running, like this:

```
postgres=# SELECT now() -
  CASE
  WHEN backend_xid IS NOT NULL
  THEN xact_start
  ELSE query_start END
  AS age
, pid
, backend_xid AS xid
, backend_xmin AS xmin
, state
FROM  pg_stat_activity
WHERE backend_type = 'client backend'
ORDER BY 1 DESC;
age              | pid   | xid      | xmin     |        state
-----------------+-------+----------+----------+--------------------
00:00:25.791098  | 27624 |          | 10671262 | active
00:00:08.018103  | 27591 |          |          | idle in transaction
00:00:00.002444  | 27630 | 10703641 | 10703639 | active
00:00:00.001506  | 27631 | 10703642 | 10703640 | active
00:00:00.000324  | 27632 | 10703643 | 10703641 | active
00:00:00         | 27379 |          | 10703641 | active
```

The preceding example shows an update workload of three sessions alongside one session that is waiting in *idle in transaction* state, plus two other sessions that are only reading data.

How to do it...

If you have sessions stuck in idle in transaction state, then you may want to consider setting the `idle_in_transaction_session_timeout` parameter, so that transactions in that mode will be canceled. The default for that is zero, meaning there will be no cancellation.

If not, try running shorter transactions or shorter queries.

If that is not an option, then consider setting `old_snapshot_threshold`. This parameter sets a time delay after which dead rows are at risk of being removed. If a query attempts to read data that has been removed then we cancel the query. All queries executing in less time than the `old_snapshot_threshold` parameter will be safe. This is a very similar concept to the way *Hot Standby* works (see `Chapter 12`, *Replication and Upgrades*).

How it works...

`VACUUM` cannot remove dead rows until they are invisible to all users. The earliest data visible to a session is defined by its oldest snapshot's `xmin` value, or if that is not set then by the backend's `xid` value if that is set.

There's more...

A session which is not running any query is in the *idle* state if outside of a transaction, or in the *idle in transaction* state if it is inside a transaction, that is, between a `BEGIN` and the corresponding `COMMIT`. Recall recipe *Writing a script that either succeeds entirely or fails entirely* in `Chapter 7`, *Database Administration*, for how `BEGIN` and `COMMIT` can be used to wrap several commands into one transaction.

The reason to distinguish between these two states is that locks are released at the end of a transaction. Hence an *idle in transaction* session is not currently doing anything, but it might be preventing other queries, including VACUUM, from accessing some tables.

Removing old prepared transactions

You may have been routed here from other recipes, so you might not even know what prepared transactions are, let alone what an old prepared transaction looks like.

The good news is that prepared transactions don't just happen; they happen in certain situations. If you don't know what I'm talking about, it's OK! You won't need to, and better still, you probably don't have any prepared transactions either.

Prepared transactions are part of the two-phase commit feature, also known as **2PC**. A transaction commits in two stages rather than one, allowing multiple databases to have synchronized commits. Its typical use is to combine multiple so-called resource managers using the **XA** protocol, usually provided by a **Transaction Manager** (**TM**), as used by the **Java Transaction API** (**JTA**) and others. If none of this meant anything to you, then you probably don't have any prepared transactions.

Getting ready

First, check the setting of `max_prepared_transactions`:

```
SHOW max_prepared_transactions;
```

If your setting is more than zero, then check whether you have any prepared transactions. As an example, you may find something like the following:

```
postgres=# SELECT * FROM pg_prepared_xacts;
-[ RECORD 1 ]-------------------------------
transaction | 459812
gid         | prep1
prepared    | 2017-04-11   13:21:51.912374+01
owner       | postgres
database    | postgres
```

Here, the `gid` (global identifier) will usually have been automatically generated.

How to do it...

Removing a prepared transaction is also referred to as *resolving in-doubt transactions*. The transaction is literally stuck between committing and aborting. The database or transaction manager may have crashed, leaving the transaction midway through the two-phase commit process.

If you have a connection pool of 100 active connections and something crashes, you'll probably find 1 to 20 transactions stuck in the prepared state, depending on how long your average transaction is.

To resolve the transaction, we need to decide whether we want that change or not. The best way is to check what happened externally to PostgreSQL. That should help you decide.

If you need further help, look at the *There's more...* section.

If you wish to commit the changes, then use this command:

```
COMMIT PREPARED 'prep1';
```

If you want to rollback the changes, then use the following command:

```
ROLLBACK PREPARED 'prep1';
```

How it works...

Prepared transactions are persistent across crashes, so you can't just do a fast restart to get rid of them. They have both an internal transaction identifier and an external global identifier. Either of these can be used to locate locked resources and decide how to resolve the transactions.

There's more...

If you're not sure what the prepared transaction actually did, you can go and look, though that is time-consuming. The `pg_locks` view shows locks that are held by prepared transactions. You can get a full report of what is being locked by using the following query:

```
postgres=# SELECT l.locktype, x.database, l.relation, l.page,
l.tuple,l.classid, l.objid, l.objsubid, l.mode, x.transaction, x.gid,
x.prepared, x.owner
FROM pg_locks l JOIN pg_prepared_xacts x ON l.virtualtransaction = '-1/' ||
x.transaction::text;
```

The documents mention that you can join `pg_locks` to `pg_prepared_xacts`, but they don't mention that if you join directly on the transaction ID, all it tells you is that there is a transaction lock, unless there are some row-level locks. The table locks are listed as being held by a virtual transaction. A simpler query is the following:

```
postgres=# SELECT DISTINCT x.database, l.relation FROM pg_locks l JOIN
pg_prepared_xacts x ON l.virtualtransaction = '-1/' || x.transaction::text
WHERE l.locktype != 'transactionid'; database | relation
---------+----------
postgres |   16390
postgres |   16401
 (2 rows)
```

This tells you which relations in which databases have been touched by the remaining prepared transactions. We can't tell the names because we'd need to connect to those databases to check.

Finally, we can inspect which rows have been changed by the transaction. We will use `xmin`, which is a hidden column in each table. For more details on that, refer to the *Identifying and fixing bloated tables and indexes* recipe in this chapter.

You can then fully scan each of those tables, looking for changes like the following:

```
SELECT * FROM table WHERE xmax = 121083;
```

This query will show you all the rows in that table that will be deleted or updated by transaction `121083`, taken from the transaction column of `pg_prepared_xacts`.

Not all rows touched by the transaction can be displayed, however. Newly inserted rows and new versions of updated rows will not be accessible in this way, for the very good reason that they must be invisible before the transaction is committed.

As you might expect, the PostgreSQL developers did their homework properly. Say that you have some prepared transactions and you change `max_prepared_transactions` to zero, which requires a restart to come into effect. No prepared transaction will sneak into your database unnoticed. When starting, PostgreSQL will try to recover every prepared transaction, and refuse to start unless `max_prepared_transactions` is large enough.

Actions for heavy users of temporary tables

If you are a heavy user of temporary tables in your applications, then there are some additional actions that you may need to perform.

How to do it...

There are four main things to check, which are as follows:

1. Make sure you run VACUUM on system tables, or enable `autovacuum` to do this for you.
2. Monitor running queries to see how many temporary files are active and how large they are.
3. Tune the memory parameters. Think about increasing the `temp_buffers` parameter, but be careful not to over-allocate memory by doing so.

4. Separate the temp table's I/O. In a query-intensive system, you may find that reads/writes to temporary files exceed reads/writes on permanent data tables and indexes. In this case, you should create new tablespace(s) on separate disks, and ensure that the `temp_tablespaces` parameter is configured to use the additional tablespace(s).

How it works...

When we create a temporary table, we insert entries into the `pg_class`, `pg_type`, and `pg_attribute` catalog tables. These catalog tables and their indexes begin to grow and bloat—an issue covered in later recipes. To control that growth, you can either vacuum those tables manually, or let `autovacuum` do its work. You cannot run `ALTER TABLE` against system tables, so it is not possible to set specific `autovacuum` settings for any of these tables.

If you vacuum the system catalog tables manually, make sure you get all of the system tables. You can get the full list of tables to vacuum and a list of their indexes using the following query:

```
postgres=# SELECT relname, pg_relation_size(oid) FROM pg_class
WHERE relkind in ('i','r') AND relnamespace = 'pg_catalog'::regnamespace
ORDER BY 2 DESC;
```

This results in the following output:

```
             relname               | pg_relation_size
-----------------------------------+------------------
 pg_proc                           |           450560
 pg_depend                         |           344064
 pg_attribute                      |           286720
 pg_depend_depender_index          |           204800
 pg_depend_reference_index         |           204800
 pg_proc_proname_args_nsp_index    |           180224
 pg_description                    |           172032
 pg_attribute_relid_attnam_index   |           114688
 pg_operator                       |           106496
 pg_statistic                      |           106496
 pg_description_o_c_o_index        |            98304
 pg_attribute_relid_attnum_index   |            81920
 pg_proc_oid_index                 |            73728
 pg_rewrite                        |            73728
 pg_class                          |            57344
```

```
pg_type                       |         57344
pg_class_relname_nsp_index    |         40960
...(partial listing)
```

The preceding values are for a newly created database. These tables can get very large if not properly maintained, with values of 11 GB for one index being witnessed in one unlucky installation.

Identifying and fixing bloated tables and indexes

PostgreSQL implements **Multiversion Concurrency Control** (**MVCC**), which allows users to read data at the same time as writers make changes. This is an important feature for concurrency in database applications, as it can allow the following:

- Better performance because of fewer locks
- Greatly reduced deadlocking
- Simplified application design and management

MVCC is a core part of PostgreSQL and cannot be turned off; nor would you really want it to be. The internals of MVCC have some implications for the DBA that need to be understood: each row represents a row version, and therefore it has two system columns, xmin and xmax, indicating the identifiers of the two transactions when the version was created and deleted, respectively. The value of xmax is NULL if that version has not been deleted yet.

The general idea is that, instead of actually removing row versions, we alter their visibility by changing their xmin and/or xmax values. Precisely, when a row is inserted, its xmin value is set to the number of the creating transaction, while xmax is emptied; when a row is deleted, xmax is set to the number of the deleting transaction, without actually removing the row. An UPDATE operation is treated exactly like a DELETE followed by an INSERT; the deleted row represents the older version, and the row inserted is the newer version. Finally, when rolling back a transaction, all of its changes are made invisible by marking that transaction ID as aborted.

In this way, we get faster DELETE, UPDATE, and ROLLBACK statements, but the price of these benefits is that the SQL UPDATE command can cause tables and indexes to grow in size, because they leave behind dead row versions. The DELETE and aborted INSERT statements take up space, which must be reclaimed by garbage collection. VACUUM is the mechanism by which we reclaim space, though there is another internal feature named **Heap-Only Tuples (HOT)**, which does much of this work for us automatically.

Knowing this, many people become worried by, and spend much time trying to rid themselves of, dead row versions. Many users will be familiar with tools used to perform tasks, such as defragmentation, shrinking, reorganization, and table optimization. These tasks are necessary, but you should not be unduly worried by the need for vacuuming in PostgreSQL. Many users execute VACUUM far too frequently, while at the same time complaining about the cost of doing so.

This recipe is all about understanding when you need to run VACUUM by estimating the amount of bloat in tables and indexes.

How to do it...

The best way to understand things is to look at things the same way that autovacuum does, using a view created with the following query:

```
CREATE OR REPLACE VIEW av_needed AS
SELECT N.nspname, C.relname
, pg_stat_get_tuples_inserted(C.oid) AS n_tup_ins
, pg_stat_get_tuples_updated(C.oid) AS n_tup_upd
, pg_stat_get_tuples_deleted(C.oid) AS n_tup_del
, CASE WHEN pg_stat_get_tuples_updated(C.oid) > 0
       THEN pg_stat_get_tuples_hot_updated(C.oid)::real
          / pg_stat_get_tuples_updated(C.oid)
       END
  AS HOT_update_ratio
, pg_stat_get_live_tuples(C.oid) AS n_live_tup
, pg_stat_get_dead_tuples(C.oid) AS n_dead_tup
, C.reltuples AS reltuples
, round( current_setting('autovacuum_vacuum_threshold')::integer
         + current_setting('autovacuum_vacuum_scale_factor')::numeric
         * C.reltuples)
  AS av_threshold
, date_trunc('minute',
    greatest(pg_stat_get_last_vacuum_time(C.oid),
             pg_stat_get_last_autovacuum_time(C.oid)))
  AS last_vacuum
```

```
  , date_trunc('minute',
      greatest(pg_stat_get_last_analyze_time(C.oid),
               pg_stat_get_last_analyze_time(C.oid)))
    AS last_analyze
  , pg_stat_get_dead_tuples(C.oid) >
    round( current_setting('autovacuum_vacuum_threshold')::integer
         + current_setting('autovacuum_vacuum_scale_factor')::numeric
         * C.reltuples)
    AS av_needed
  , CASE WHEN reltuples > 0
         THEN round(100.0 * pg_stat_get_dead_tuples(C.oid) / reltuples)
         ELSE 0 END
    AS pct_dead
  FROM pg_class C
  LEFT JOIN pg_namespace N ON (N.oid = C.relnamespace)
  WHERE C.relkind IN ('r', 't', 'm')
    AND N.nspname NOT IN ('pg_catalog', 'information_schema')
    AND N.nspname NOT LIKE 'pg_toast%'
  ORDER BY av_needed DESC, n_dead_tup DESC;
```

We can then use this to look at individual tables, as follows:

```
postgres=# \x
postgres=# SELECT * FROM av_needed WHERE nspname = 'public' AND relname =
'pgbench_accounts';
```

Thus, we get this output:

```
-[ RECORD 1 ]----+-------------------------
nspname          | public
relname          | pgbench_accounts
n_tup_ins        | 100001
n_tup_upd        | 117201
n_tup_del        | 1
hot_update_ratio | 0.123454578032611
n_live_tup       | 100000
n_dead_tup       | 0
reltuples        | 100000
av_threshold     | 20050
last_vacuum      | 2010-04-29 01:33:00+01
last_analyze     | 2010-04-28 15:21:00+01
av_needed        | f
pct_dead         | 0
```

How it works...

We can compare the number of dead row versions, shown as `n_dead_tup` against the required threshold, `av_threshold`.

The preceding query doesn't take into account table-specific autovacuum thresholds. It could do so if you really need it, but the main purpose of the query is to give us information to understand what is happening, and then set the parameters accordingly—not the other way around.

Notice that the table query shows insertions, updates, and deletions, so you can understand your workload better. There is also something named the `hot_update_ratio`. This shows the fraction of updates that take advantage of the HOT feature, which allows a table to self-vacuum as the table changes. If that ratio is high, then you may avoid VACUUM activities altogether or at least for long periods. If the ratio is low, then you will need to execute VACUUM commands or autovacuums more frequently. Note that the ratio never reaches 1.0, so if you have it above 0.95, then that is very good and you need not think about it further.

HOT updates take place when the UPDATE statement does not change any of the column values that are indexed by any index, and there is enough free space in the disk page where the updated row is located. If you change even one column that is indexed by just one index, then it will be a non-HOT update, and there will be a performance hit. So careful selection of indexes can improve update performance and reduce the need for maintenance. Also, if HOT updates do occur, though not often enough for your liking, you might want to try to decrease the `fillfactor` storage parameter for the table to make more space for them. Remember that this will be important only on your most active tables. Seldom touched tables don't need much tuning.

To recap, non-HOT updates cause indexes to bloat. The following query is useful in investigating the index size and how it changes over time. It runs fairly quickly, and can be used to monitor whether your indexes are changing in size over time:

```
SELECT
nspname,relname,
round(100 * pg_relation_size(indexrelid) /
                    pg_relation_size(indrelid)) / 100
                AS index_ratio,
   pg_size_pretty(pg_relation_size(indexrelid))
                AS index_size,
   pg_size_pretty(pg_relation_size(indrelid))
                AS table_size
FROM pg_index I
LEFT JOIN pg_class C ON (C.oid = I.indexrelid)
```

```
LEFT JOIN pg_namespace N ON (N.oid = C.relnamespace)
WHERE
  nspname NOT IN ('pg_catalog', 'information_schema', 'pg_toast') AND
  C.relkind='i' AND
  pg_relation_size(indrelid) > 0;
```

Another route is to use the `pgstattuple` contrib module which provides very detailed statistics. You can scan tables using `pgstattuple()`, as follows:

```
test=> SELECT * FROM pgstattuple('pg_catalog.pg_proc');
```

The output will look like the following:

```
-[ RECORD 1 ]------+-------
table_len          | 458752
tuple_count        | 1470
tuple_len          | 438896
tuple_percent      | 95.67
dead_tuple_count   | 11
dead_tuple_len     | 3157
dead_tuple_percent | 0.69
free_space         | 8932
free_percent       | 1.95
```

The downside of `pgstattuple` is that it derives exact statistics by scanning the whole table and literally counting everything. If you have time to scan the table, you may as well vacuum the whole table anyway. So a better idea is to use `pgstattuple_approx()`, which is much, much faster, and yet is still fairly accurate. It works by accessing the table's visibility map first and then only scanning the pages that need VACUUM, so I recommend you use it in all cases for checking tables (there is no equivalent for indexes):

```
Postgres=# select * from pgstattuple_approx('pgbench_accounts');
-[ RECORD 1 ]--------+-----------------
table_len            | 268591104
scanned_percent      | 0
approx_tuple_count   | 1001738
approx_tuple_len     | 137442656
approx_tuple_percent | 51.1717082037088
dead_tuple_count     | 0
dead_tuple_len       | 0
dead_tuple_percent   | 0
approx_free_space    | 131148448
approx_free_percent  | 48.8282917962912
```

You can also scan indexes using `pgstatindex()`, as follows:

```
postgres=> SELECT * FROM pgstatindex('pg_cast_oid_index');
-[ RECORD 1 ]------+------
version            | 2
tree_level         | 0
index_size         | 8192
root_block_no      | 1
internal_pages     | 0
leaf_pages         | 1
empty_pages        | 0
deleted_pages      | 0
avg_leaf_density   | 50.27
leaf_fragmentation | 0
```

There's more...

You may want this as a Nagios plugin.

Look at `check_postgres_bloat`, which is a part of the `check_postgres` plugins.

It provides some flexible options to assess bloat. Unfortunately, it's not that well documented, but if you've read this, it should make sense. You'll need to play with it to get the thresholding correct anyway, so that shouldn't be a problem.

Note also that the only way to know for certain the exact bloat of a table or index is to scan the whole relation. Anything else is just an estimate, and might lead to you running maintenance either too early or too late.

Monitoring and tuning vacuum

If you're currently waiting for a long running vacuum (or autovacuum) to finish, go straight to the *How to do it...* section.

If you've just had a long running vacuum then you may want to think about setting a few parameters.

Getting ready

`autovacuum_max_workers` should always be set to more than 2. Setting it too high may not be very useful, so be careful.

Setting `vacuum_cost_delay` too high is counterproductive. VACUUM is your friend, not your enemy, so delaying it until it doesn't happen at all just makes things worse.

`maintenance_work_mem` should be set to anything up to 1 GB, according to how much memory you can allocate to this task at this time.

Let's watch what happens when we run a large VACUUM. First, locate which process is running the VACUUM by using the `pg_stat_activity` view to identify the specific `pid`.

How to do it...

Repeatedly execute this query to see the progress of the VACUUM command:

```
postgres=# SELECT * FROM pg_stat_progress_vacuum WHERE pid = 34399;
```

How it works...

VACUUM works in three phases. The first main phase is *scanning heap*. The `heap_blks_scanned` columns will increase from 0 up to the value of `heap_blks_total`:

```
Pid                 | 34399
datid               | 12515
datname             | postgres
relid               | 16422
phase               | scanning heap
heap_blks_total     | 32787
heap_blks_scanned   | 25207
heap_blks_vacuumed  | 0
index_vacuum_count  | 0
max_dead_tuples     | 9541017
num_dead_tuples     | 537600
```

The number of blocks vacuumed is shown as `heap_blks_vacuumed` and the resulting rows to be removed are shown as `num_dead_tuples`. After this we switch to the second phase where we start vacuuming indexes:

```
Pid                 | 34399
datid               | 12515
datname             | postgres
relid               | 16422
phase               | vacuuming indexes
heap_blks_total     | 32787
heap_blks_scanned   | 32787
heap_blks_vacuumed  | 0
index_vacuum_count  | 0
max_dead_tuples     | 9541017
num_dead_tuples     | 999966
```

Though while this phase is happening the progress data doesn't change until it has vacuumed all of the indexes. This phase can take a long time; more indexes increase the time required. Once indexes are vacuumed, we move onto the third phase where we return to the *vacuuming heap*:

```
Pid                 | 34399
datid               | 12515
datname             | postgres
relid               | 16422
phase               | vacuuming heap
heap_blks_total     | 32787
heap_blks_scanned   | 32787
heap_blks_vacuumed  | 25051
index_vacuum_count  | 1
max_dead_tuples     | 9541017
num_dead_tuples     | 999966
```

The value of `max_dead_tuples` is defined by the setting of `maintenance_work_mem`: PostgreSQL makes space for the largest meaningful number of entries allowed by that setting. If the `num_dead_tuples` is higher than `max_dead_tuples` then we repeat phases two and three until complete, so it's a good idea to set `maintenance_work_mem` high enough to avoid that.

VACUUM moves through various other fairly short phases. If there are many empty blocks at the end of the table VACUUM will attempt to get an `AccessExclusiveLock` on the table, and once acquired, it will truncate the end of the table—showing a phase of truncating heap. Truncation does not occur every time, because PostgreSQL will attempt it only if the gain is significant and if there's no conflicting lock; if it does it can often last a long time.

All phases of VACUUM will be slowed down by vacuum_cost_delay, but there's nothing you can do there to speed it up.

If you need to change the settings to speed up a running process then autovacuum will pick up any new default settings when you reload the postgresql.conf file.

There's more...

VACUUM doesn't run in parallel on a single table.

If you want to run multiple VACUUMs at once you can do it like this, for example, running four vacuums at once to scan all databases:

```
$ vacuumdb --jobs=4 --all
```

If you run multiple VACUUMs at once you'll use more memory and I/O, so be careful. The exact calculation is complex, especially if you have tables with custom VACUUM settings, but the general idea is that I/O can be slowed down by raising vacuum_cost_delay or lowering vacuum_cost_limit.

Maintaining indexes

Indexes can become a problem in many database applications that involve a high proportion of INSERT/DELETE commands. Just as tables can become bloated, so can indexes.

In the previous recipe, you saw that non-HOT updates can cause bloated indexes. Non-primary-key indexes are also prone to some bloat from normal INSERT commands, as is common in most relational databases.

Autovacuum does not detect bloated indexes, nor does it do anything to rebuild indexes. So we need to look at other ways to maintain indexes.

Getting ready

PostgreSQL supports commands that will rebuild indexes for you. The client utility, `reindexdb`, allows you to execute the `REINDEX` command in a convenient way from the operating system:

```
$ reindexdb
```

This executes the SQL `REINDEX` command on every table in the default database. If you want to reindex all databases, then use the following:

```
$ reindexdb -a
```

That's what the manual says anyway. My experience is that most indexes don't need rebuilding, and even if they do, `REINDEX` puts a full-table lock (`AccessExclusiveLock`) on the table while it runs. That locks your database for possibly hours, and I advise that you think about not doing that.

Try these steps instead:

1. First, let's create a test table with two indexes—a primary key and an additional index as follows:

   ```
   DROP  TABLE  IF  EXISTS  test; CREATE  TABLE  test
   (id  INTEGER  PRIMARY  KEY
   ,category  TEXT
   ,  value  TEXT);
   CREATE  INDEX  ON  test  (category);
   ```

2. Now let's look at the internal identifier of the tables, `oid`, and the current file number (`relfilenodes`), as follows:

   ```
   SELECT oid, relname, relfilenode
   FROM pg_class
   WHERE oid in (SELECT indexrelid
                 FROM pg_index
                 WHERE indrelid = 'test'::regclass);
     oid  |      relname      | relfilenode
   -------+-------------------+-------------
    16639 | test_pkey         |       16639
    16641 | test_category_idx |       16641
   (2 rows)
   ```

How to do it...

PostgreSQL supports a command known as CREATE INDEX CONCURRENTLY, which builds an index without taking a full table lock. PostgreSQL also supports the ability to have two indexes, with different names, that have exactly the same definition. So, the trick is to build another index identical to the one you wish to rebuild, drop the old index, and then rename the new index to the same name as the old index. Et voilà, fresh index, and no locking! Let's see that in slow motion:

```
CREATE INDEX CONCURRENTLY new_index
  ON test (category);
BEGIN;
DROP INDEX test_category_idx;
ALTER INDEX new_index RENAME TO test_category_idx;
COMMIT;
```

When we check our internal identifiers again, we get the following:

```
SELECT oid, relname, relfilenode
FROM pg_class
WHERE oid in (SELECT indexrelid
                FROM pg_index
                WHERE indrelid = 'test'::regclass);
  oid  |        relname       | relfilenode
-------+----------------------+-------------
 16639 | test_pkey            |       16639
 16642 | test_category_idx    |       16642
(2 rows)
```

So we can see that test_category_idx is now a completely new index.

That seems pretty good, and it works on primary keys too, but in a slightly complex way—you need to create a new index using UNIQUE and CONCURRENTLY, and then issue this to make it a primary key:

```
ALTER TABLE ... ADD PRIMARY KEY USING INDEX ...
```

This is not optimal yet, because a primary key could be the target of one or more foreign keys. In that case, we need to drop and recreate the foreign keys, which unfortunately has no CONCURRENTLY variant. The next recipe, *Adding a constraint without checking existing rows*, is a recommended reading.

How it works...

The `CREATE INDEX CONCURRENTLY` statement allows `INSERT`, `UPDATE`, and `DELETE` commands while the index is being created. It cannot be executed inside another transaction, and only one index per table can be created concurrently at any time.

Swapping the indexes is easy and doesn't use any trickery.

There's more...

If you are fairly new to database systems, you might think rebuilding indexes for performance is something that only PostgreSQL needs to do. Other DBMSs require this as well, they just maybe don't say so.

Indexes are designed for performance, and in all databases, deleting index entries causes contention and loss of performance. PostgreSQL does not remove index entries for a row when that row is deleted, so an index can be filled with dead entries. PostgreSQL does attempt to remove dead entries when a block becomes full, but that doesn't stop a small numbers of dead entries from accumulating in many data blocks.

No `REINDEX CONCURRENTLY` command has been added yet to PostgreSQL.

Adding a constraint without checking existing rows

A table constraint is a guarantee that must be satisfied by all the rows in the table. Therefore, adding a constraint to a table is a two-phase procedure—first, the constraint is created, and then all the existing rows are checked. Both happen in the same transaction, and the table cannot be accessed in the meantime. The constraint becomes visible after the check, yielding perfect consistency, which is usually the desired behavior—at the expense of availability, which is not that great.

This recipe demonstrates another case—how to enforce a constraint on future transactions *only*, without checking existing rows. This may be desirable in some specific cases, such as the following two:

- Enabling the constraint on newer rows of a large table that cannot remain unavailable for a long time
- Enforcing the constraint on newer rows, while keeping older rows that are known to violate the constraint

The constraint is marked as NOT VALID to make it clear that it does not exclude violations, unlike ordinary constraints.

As seen following, it is possible to validate the constraint at a later time, for example, when allowed by the workload or business continuity requirements. All existing rows will be checked, and then the NOT VALID mark will be removed from the constraint. Conversely, in the other example, the constraint will never be validated, and its only purpose will be to prevent further violations by rejecting incompatible transactions.

Getting ready

We'll start this recipe by creating two tables with a few test rows:

```
postgres=# CREATE TABLE ft(fk int PRIMARY KEY, fs text);
CREATE TABLE
postgres=# CREATE TABLE pt(pk int, ps text);
CREATE TABLE
postgres=# INSERT INTO ft(fk,fs) VALUES (1,'one'), (2,'two');
INSERT 0 2
postgres=# INSERT INTO pt(pk,ps) VALUES (1,'I'), (2,'II'), (3,'III');
INSERT 0 3
```

How to do it...

We have inserted inconsistent data on purpose so that any attempt to check existing rows will be revealed by an error message.

If we attempt to create an ordinary foreign key, we get an error, since the number 3 does not appear in the ft table:

```
postgres=# ALTER TABLE pt ADD CONSTRAINT pc FOREIGN KEY (pk) REFERENCES
ft(fk);
ERROR: insert or update on table "pt" violates foreign key constraint
pc"
DETAIL: Key (pk)=(3) is not present in table "ft".
```

However, the same constraint can be successfully created as NOT VALID:

```
postgres=# ALTER TABLE pt ADD CONSTRAINT pc FOREIGN KEY (pk) REFERENCES
ft(fk) NOT VALID;
ALTER TABLE
```

 Note that the invalid state of the foreign key is mentioned by psql.

```
postgres=# \d pt
        Table "public.pt"
 Column |  Type   | Modifiers
--------+---------+-----------
 pk     | integer |
 ps     | text    |
Foreign-key constraints:
    "pc" FOREIGN KEY (pk) REFERENCES ft(fk) NOT VALID
```

The violation is detected when we try to transform the NOT VALID constraint into a valid one:

```
postgres=# ALTER TABLE pt VALIDATE CONSTRAINT pc;
ERROR: insert or update on table "pt" violates foreign key constraint
pc"
DETAIL: Key (pk)=(3) is not present in table "ft".
```

Validation becomes possible after removing the inconsistency, and the foreign key is upgraded to an ordinary one:

```
postgres=# DELETE FROM pt WHERE pk = 3;
DELETE 1
postgres=# ALTER TABLE pt VALIDATE CONSTRAINT pc;
ALTER TABLE
postgres=# \d pt
        Table "public.pt"
 Column |  Type   | Modifiers
```

```
--------+---------+-----------
 pk      | integer |
 ps      | text    |
Foreign-key constraints:
    "pc" FOREIGN KEY (pk) REFERENCES ft(fk)
```

How it works...

ALTER TABLE ... ADD CONSTRAINT.. NOT VALID uses the ShareRowExclusiveLock that blocks writes and VACUUM, yet allows reads on the table to continue. The command ALTER TABLE ... VALIDATE CONSTRAINT executes using a ShareUpdateExclusiveLock that allows both reads and writes on the table yet blocks DDL and VACUUM while it scans the table.

PostgreSQL takes SQL locks according to the ISO standard, that is, locks are taken during the transaction and then released at its end. This means that algorithms like this one, where there is a short activity requiring stronger locks, followed by a longer activity that needs only lighter locks, cannot be implemented as a single command.

Finding unused indexes

Selecting the correct set of indexes for a workload is known to be a hard problem. It usually involves trial and error by developers and DBAs to get a good mix of indexes.

Tools for identifying slow queries exist, and many SELECT statements can be improved by the addition of an index.

What many people forget is to check whether the mix of indexes remains valuable over time, which is something for the DBA to investigate and optimize.

How to do it...

PostgreSQL keeps track of each access against an index. We can view that information and use it to see whether an index is unused, as follows:

```
postgres=# SELECT schemaname, relname, indexrelname, idx_scan FROM
pg_stat_user_indexes ORDER BY idx_scan;
 schemaname |          indexrelname        | idx_scan
------------+------------------------------+----------
 public     | pgbench_accounts_bid_idx     |        0
 public     | pgbench_branches_pkey        |    14575
 public     | pgbench_tellers_pkey         |    15350
 public     | pgbench_accounts_pkey        |   114400
(4 rows)
```

As we can see in the preceding code, there is one index that is totally unused, alongside others that have some usage. You now need to decide whether unused means you should remove the index. That is a more complex question, and we first need to explain how it works.

How it works...

The PostgreSQL statistics accumulate various pieces of useful information. These statistics can be reset to zero using an administrator function. Also, as the data accumulates over time, we usually find that objects that have been there for longer periods of time have higher apparent usage. So if we see a low number for idx_scan, then it might be that the index was newly created (as was the case in my preceding demonstration), or that the index is only used by a part of the application that runs only at certain times of a day, week, month, and so on.

Another important consideration is that the index may be a unique constraint index that exists specifically to safeguard against duplicate INSERT commands. An INSERT operation does not show up as an idx_scan, even if the index was actually used while checking the uniqueness of the newly inserted values, whereas an UPDATE or DELETE might show up, because they have to locate the row first. So a table that only has INSERT commands against it will appear to have unused indexes.

Also, some indexes that show usage might be showing usage that was historical, and there is no further usage. Or it might be the case that some queries use an index where they could just as easily and almost as cheaply use an alternative index. Those things are for you to explore and understand before you take action. A very common approach is to regularly monitor such numbers in order to gain knowledge by examining their evolution over time on both the master database and on any replicated hot standby nodes.

In the end, you may decide from this that you want to remove an index. If only there was a way to try removing an index and then put it back again quickly, in case you cause problems! Rebuilding an index might take hours on a big table, so these decisions can be a little scary. No worries! Just follow the next recipe, *Carefully removing unwanted indexes*.

Carefully removing unwanted indexes

Carefully removing? You mean press *Enter* gently after typing DROP INDEX? Err, no!

The thinking is that it takes a long time to build an index, and a short time to drop it.

What we want is a way of removing an index such that if we discover that removing it was a mistake, we can put the index back again quickly.

Getting ready

The following query will list all invalid indexes, if any:

```
SELECT ir.relname AS indexname
, it.relname AS tablename
, n.nspname AS schemaname
FROM pg_index i
JOIN pg_class ir ON ir.oid = i.indexrelid
JOIN pg_class it ON it.oid = i.indrelid
JOIN pg_namespace n ON n.oid = it.relnamespace
WHERE NOT i.indisvalid;
```

Take note of these indexes, so that later you can tell whether a given index is invalid because we marked it as invalid during this recipe, in which case it can safely be marked as valid, or because it was already invalid for other reasons.

How to do it...

We will describe a procedure that allows us to deactivate an index without actually dropping it, so that we can appreciate what its contribution was and possibly reactivate it:

1. First, create the following function:

```
CREATE OR REPLACE FUNCTION trial_drop_index(iname TEXT)
RETURNS VOID
LANGUAGE SQL AS $$ UPDATE pg_index
SET indisvalid = false
WHERE indexrelid = $1::regclass;
$$;
```

2. Then, run it to do a trial of dropping the index.
3. If you experience performance issues after dropping the index, then use this function to undrop the index:

```
CREATE OR REPLACE FUNCTION trial_undrop_index(iname TEXT)
RETURNS VOID
LANGUAGE SQL AS
$$ UPDATE pg_index
SET indisvalid = true
WHERE indexrelid = $1::regclass;
$$;
```

Be careful to avoid undropping any index that was detected by the query in the *Getting Ready* section; if it wasn't marked as invalid when applying this recipe, then it may be unusable because it really is not valid.

How it works...

This recipe also uses some inside knowledge. When we create an index using CREATE INDEX CONCURRENTLY, it is a two-stage process. The first phase builds the index and then marks it invalid. INSERT, UPDATE, and DELETE statements now begin maintaining the index, but we perform a further pass over the table to see if we missed anything, before declaring the index valid. User queries don't use the index until it says that it is valid.

Once the index is built and the valid flag is set, then if we set the flag to invalid, the index will still be maintained. It's just that it will not be used by queries. This allows us to turn the index off quickly, though with the option to turn it on again if we realize that we actually do need the index after all. This makes it practical to test whether dropping the index will alter the performance of any of your most important queries.

Planning maintenance

In these busy times, many people believe, *if it ain't broken, don't fix it*. I believe that too, but it isn't an excuse for not taking action to maintain your database servers and be sure that nothing will break.

Database maintenance is about making your database run smoothly.

Monitoring systems are not a substitute for good planning. They alert you to unplanned situations that need attention. The more unplanned things you respond to, the greater the chance that you will need to respond to multiple emergencies at once. And when that happens, something will break. Ultimately, that is your fault. If you wish to take your responsibilities seriously, you should plan ahead.

How to do it...

This recipe is about planning, so we'll provide discussion points rather than portions of code. We'll cover the main points that should be addressed, and also provide a list of points as food for thought, around which the actual implementation should be built:

- **Let's break a rule**: If you don't have a backup, take one now. I mean now, go on, off you go! Then, let's talk some more about planning maintenance. If you already do, well done! It's hard to keep your job as a DBA if you lose data because of missing backups, especially today, when everybody's grandmother knows to keep her photos backed up.
- **First, plan your time**: Decide a regular date on which to perform certain actions. Don't allow yourself to be a puppet of your monitoring system, running up and down every time the lights change. If you keep getting dragged off on other assignments, then you must understand that you need to get a good handle on the database maintenance to make sure that it doesn't bite you.

- **Don't be scared**: It's easy to worry about what you don't know, and either overreact or underreact. Your database probably doesn't need to be inspected daily, but never is definitely a bad practice.

How it works...

Build a regular cycle of activity around the following tasks:

- **Capacity planning**: Observe long-term trends in system performance and keep track of the growth of database volumes. Plan to schedule any new data feeds and new projects that increase the rates of change. This is best done monthly so that you monitor what has happened and what will happen.
- **Backups, recovery testing, and emergency planning**: Organize regular reviews of written plans and test scripts. Check the tape rotation, confirm that you still have the password to the off-site backups, and so on. Some sysadmins run a test recovery every night so that they always know that a successful recovery is possible.
- **Vacuum and index maintenance**: To reduce bloat, as well as collecting optimizer statistics through ANALYZE. Also, regularly check index usage and drop unused indexes

    Consider VACUUM again, with the need to manage the less frequent **freezing** process. This is listed as a separate task so that you don't ignore this and let it bite you later!

- **Server log file analysis**: How many times has the server restarted? Are you sure you know about each incident?
- **Security and intrusion detection**: Has your database already been hacked? What did they do?
- **Understanding usage patterns**: If you don't know much about what your database is used for, then I'll wager it is not very well tuned or maintained.
- **Long-term performance analysis**: It's a common occurrence for me to get asked to come and tune a system that is slow. Often what happens is that a database server gets slower over a very long period. Nobody ever noticed any particular day when it got slow—it just got slower over time. Keeping records of response times over time can help confirm whether everything is as good now as it was months or years earlier. This activity is where you might reconsider current index choices.

Many of these activities are mentioned in this chapter or throughout the rest of the cookbook. Some are not because they aren't so much technical tasks, but more about planning and understanding of your environment.

You might also find time to consider the following:

- **Data quality**: Are the contents of the database accurate and meaningful? Could the data be enhanced?
- **Business intelligence**: Is the data being used for everything that can bring value to the organization?

Performance and Concurrency

10

In this chapter, we will cover the following recipes:

- Finding slow SQL statements
- Collecting regular statistics from pg_stat* views
- Finding out what makes SQL slow
- Reducing the number of rows returned
- Simplifying complex SQL queries
- Speeding up queries without rewriting them
- Discovering why a query is not using an index
- Forcing a query to use an index
- Using parallel query
- Using Optimistic locking
- Reporting performance problems

Introduction

Performance and concurrency are two problems that are often tightly coupled -- when concurrency problems are encountered, performance usually degrades, in some cases a lot. If you take care of concurrency problems, you will achieve better performance.

In this chapter, we will show you how to find slow queries and also how to find queries that make other queries slow.

Performance tuning, unfortunately, is still not an exact science, so you may also encounter a performance problem not covered by any of the given methods.

We will also show you how to get help in the final recipe, *Reporting performance problems*, in case none of the other recipes covered here work.

Finding slow SQL statements

There are two main kinds of slowness that can manifest themselves in a database.

The first kind is a single query that can be too slow to be really usable, such as a customer information query in a CRM running for minutes, a password check query running in tens of seconds, or a daily data aggregation query running for more than a day. These can be found by logging queries that take over a certain amount of time, either at the client end or in the database.

The second kind is a query that is run frequently (say a few thousand times a second) and used to run in single-digit milliseconds, but is now running in several tens or even hundreds of milliseconds, thus slowing down the system. This kind of slowness is much harder to find.

Here, we will show you several ways to find the statements that are either slow or cause the database as a whole to slow down (although they are not slow by themselves).

Getting ready

Connect to the database as the user whose statements you want to investigate, or as a superuser to investigate all users' queries.

Check that you have the `pg_stat_statements` extension installed:

```
postgres=# \x
postgres=# \dx pg_stat_statements
```

List of installed extensions:

```
-[ RECORD 1 ]---------------------------------------------------------
Name        | pg_stat_statements
Version     | 1.4
Schema      | public
Description | track execution statistics of all SQL statements executed
```

If not, then issue the following command:

```
postgres=# CREATE EXTENSION pg_stat_statements;
postgres=# ALTER SYSTEM
           SET shared_preload_libraries = 'pg_stat_statements';
```

Then restart the server, or refer to the Using an installed module and Managing installed extensions recipes from Chapter 3, Configuration, for more details.

How to do it...

Run this query to look at the top 10 highest workloads on your server side:

```
postgres=# SELECT calls, total_time, query FROM pg_stat_statements
           ORDER BY total_time DESC LIMIT 10;
```

The output is ordered by total_time, so it doesn't matter whether it was a single query or thousands of smaller queries.

There are many additional columns useful in tracking down further information about particular entries:

```
postgres=# \d pg_stat_statements
            View "public.pg_stat_statements"
        Column         |       Type        | Modifiers
-----------------------+-------------------+-----------
 userid                | oid               |
 dbid                  | oid               |
 queryid               | bigint            |
 query                 | text              |
 calls                 | bigint            |
 total_time            | double precision  |
 min_time              | double precision  |
 max_time              | double precision  |
 mean_time             | double precision  |
 stddev_time           | double precision  |
 rows                  | bigint            |
 shared_blks_hit       | bigint            |
 shared_blks_read      | bigint            |
 shared_blks_dirtied   | bigint            |
 shared_blks_written   | bigint            |
 local_blks_hit        | bigint            |
 local_blks_read       | bigint            |
 local_blks_dirtied    | bigint            |
 local_blks_written    | bigint            |
```

```
temp_blks_read       | bigint           |
temp_blks_written    | bigint           |
blk_read_time        | double precision |
blk_write_time       | double precision |
```

How it works...

`pg_stat_statements` collects data on all running queries by accumulating data in memory, producing minimal overheads.

Similar SQL statements are normalized so that the constants and parameters used for execution are removed. This allows you to see all similar SQL statements in one line of the report, rather than seeing thousands of lines, which would be fairly useless. While useful, it can sometimes mean that it's hard to work out which parameter values are actually causing the problem.

There's more...

Another way to find slow queries is to set up PostgreSQL to log them all. So if you decide to monitor a query taking over 10 seconds, then set up logging queries over 10 seconds by executing the following:

```
postgres=# ALTER SYSTEM
            SET log_min_duration_statement = 10000;
```

Remember that the duration is in milliseconds. After doing this, reload PostgreSQL. All queries that are slow enough to exceed the threshold will be logged.

The PostgreSQL log files are usually located together with other log files; for example, on Debian/Ubuntu Linux, they are in the `/var/log/postgresql/` directory.

You can also log every query, though that can often swamp the log files and cause performance problems itself and so is hardly ever recommend.

Query logging will show the parameters used for the slow query, even when `pg_stat_statements` does not.

Collect regular statistics from pg_stat* views

This recipe describes how to collect the statistics needed to understand what is going on in the database system on a regular basis so that they can be used to further optimize the queries that are slow or are becoming slow as the database changes.

We have included an example extension, called `pgstatslog`. It can be used to track these changes. The extension works on PostgreSQL 9.1+.

Look at the *Using an installed module* and *managing installed extensions* recipes from `Chapter 3`, *Configuration*, for an overview of the extensions infrastructure in PostgreSQL.

Getting ready

Find the `pgstatslog` directory in the set of files distributed along with this book.

Find out the directory to place shared files using `pg_config --sharedir` and then copy the files to the `extension` subdirectory of that directory.

Now that the extension has been installed in your PostgreSQL server, it is time to install it in each database that you want to monitor:

```
postgres=# CREATE EXTENSION pgstatslog;
CREATE EXTENSION
```

You can verify that the extension is installed by typing `\dx` in `psql`.

How to do it...

You can collect information by executing the following query for each database that you intend to monitor:

```
SELECT collect_deltas();
```

This will collect the changes in the `pg_stat_user_*` and `pg_statio_user_*` tables that have occurred since the last invocation.

You should probably set up a cron job to run on a regular basis so that you have good coverage of what happens at what time of the day and week. Running it at an interval of 5 – 15 minutes should usually give you enough temporal resolution to understand what is going on with your tables.

For example, you can add this (or a similar variation) to the `postgres` user's cron table:

```
*/5 * * * * /usr/bin/psql -c 'SELECT collect_deltas()' mydbname
```

How it works...

The `collect_deltas()` function makes static copies of the `pg_stat_user_tables`, `pg_statio_user_tables`, `pg_stat_user_indexes`, and `pg_statio_user_indexes` tables at each run. It then compares the current copies with the copies saved at the last run, and saves the timestamped deltas in the `stat_user_tables_delta_log` and `stat_user_indexes_delta_log` log tables. These tables can then be analyzed later to get an insight into access and I/O patterns.

The latest set of deltas is also kept in the `stat_user_tables_delta` and `stat_user_indexes_delta` tables, which can be used for external monitoring systems, such as Cacti, to get a graphical representation of it.

There's more...

The `collect_deltas()` function simply appends data to the same tables. This should not cause performance problems, as the large log tables are without indexes. Thus, insertions in them are fast, but if you are low on disk space and have many tables, you may want to introduce a rotation scheme for these tables that throws away older data.

In case you experience performance issues with the proposed approach, you might want to either purge the old data from the `*_delta_log` tables (and keep a window of the last four weeks) or use horizontal partitioning.

In the first approach, you can set a weekly cron job that deletes all records that are older than four weeks from the tables. For this purpose, we have created the `rotate_deltas()` function in the `pgstatslog` extension.

Take some time and investigate the content of the extension, in particular the `pgstatslog-1.0.sql` file. It contains definitions for tables, views, and functions, as well as usage instructions.

In the second approach, you can keep longer series of data, by creating weekly partitions, for example, and let PostgreSQL manage partitioning. PostgreSQL 10's partitioning scheme should be effective for the use case of time series data logging, as shown at `http://www.postgresql.org/docs/current/static/ddl-partitioning.html` and `http://www.postgresql.org/docs/current/static/tutorial-inheritance.html`.

Another statistics collection package

If you are interested in a more powerful way of tracking database statistics over time, I suggest you look at `pg_statsinfo`, an open source package available at `http://pgstatsinfo.sourceforge.net/` and developed by our friends from NTT.

Finding out what makes SQL slow

An SQL statement can be slow for a lot of reasons. Here, we will give a short list of these, with at least one way of recognizing each reason.

Getting ready

If the SQL statement is still running, look at `Chapter 8`, *Monitoring and Diagnosis*.

How to do it...

The core issues are likely to be one of these:

- You're asking it to do too much work
- Something is stopping it from doing the work

This might not sound that helpful at first, but it's good to know that there's nothing really magical going on that you can't understand if you look.

In more detail, the main reasons are:

- Returning too much data
- Processing too much data index needed
- Wrong plan for other reasons
- Cache or I/O problems
- Locking problems

The first reason can be handled as described in the Reducing the number of rows returned recipe. Reasons 2-4 can be investigated from two perspectives: The SQL itself and the objects that the SQL touches. Let's start by looking at the SQL itself by running the query with EXPLAIN ANALYZE. We're going to use the optional form as follows:

```
postgres=# EXPLAIN (ANALYZE, BUFFERS) ...SQL...
```

The EXPLAIN command provides output to describe the execution plan of the SQL, showing access paths and costs (in abstract units). The ANALYZE option causes the statement to be executed (be careful), with instrumentation to show the number of rows accessed and the timings for that part of the plan. The BUFFERS option provides information about the number of database buffers read and the number of buffers that were hit in the cache. Taken together, we have everything we need to diagnose whether the SQL performance is slow from reasons 2-4:

```
postgres=# EXPLAIN (ANALYZE, BUFFERS) SELECT count(*) FROM t;
                          QUERY PLAN
-----------------------------------------------------------------
  Aggregate  (cost=4427.27..4427.28 rows=1 width=0) \
             (actual time=32.953..32.954 rows=1 loops=1)
    Buffers: shared hit=X read=Y
   ->  Seq Scan on t  (cost=0.00..4425.01 rows=901 width=0) \
              (actual time=30.350..31.646 rows=901 loops=1)
          Buffers: shared hit=X read=Y
 Planning time: 0.045 ms
  Execution time: 33.128 ms
 (6 rows)
```

Let's use the technique to look at an SQL statement that would benefit from an index.

For example, if you want to get the three latest rows in a one million row table, run this query:

```
SELECT * FROM events ORDER BY id DESC LIMIT 3;
```

You can either read through just three rows using an index on the id SERIAL column, or you can perform a sequential scan of all rows followed by a sort, as shown in the following snippet. Your choice depends on whether you have an usable index on the field from which you want to get the top three rows:

```
postgres=# CREATE TABLE events(id SERIAL);
CREATE TABLE
postgres=# INSERT INTO events SELECT generate_series(1,1000000);
INSERT 0 1000000
postgres=# EXPLAIN (ANALYZE)
            SELECT * FROM events ORDER BY id DESC LIMIT 3;
                            QUERY PLAN
-------------------------------------------------------------------
 Limit  (cost=25500.67..25500.68 rows=3 width=4) \
         (actual time=3143.493..3143.502 rows=3 loops=1)
    ->  Sort  (cost=25500.67..27853.87 rows=941280 width=4)
            (actual time=3143.488..3143.490 rows=3 loops=1)
         Sort Key: id DESC
         Sort Method:  top-N heapsort  Memory: 25kB
    ->  Seq Scan on events
            (cost=0.00..13334.80 rows=941280 width=4)
            (actual time=0.105..1534.418 rows=1000000 loops=1)
 Planning time: 0.331 ms
  Execution time: 3143.584 ms
(10 rows)
postgres=# CREATE INDEX events_id_ndx ON events(id);
CREATE INDEX
postgres=# EXPLAIN (ANALYZE)
            SELECT * FROM events ORDER BY id DESC LIMIT 3;
                            QUERY PLAN
-------------------------------------------------------------------
 Limit  (cost=0.00..0.08 rows=3 width=4) (actual
   time=0.295..0.311 rows=3 loops=1)
    ->  Index Scan Backward using events_id_ndx on events
           (cost=0.00..27717.34 rows=1000000 width=4) (actual
           time=0.289..0.295 rows=3 loops=1)
 Total runtime: 0.364 ms
(3 rows)
```

This produces a huge difference in query runtime, even when all of the data is in the cache.

If you run the same analysis using EXPLAIN (ANALYZE, BUFFERS) on your production system you'll be able to see the cache effects as well. Remember that each new index you add increases the pressure on the cache so it is possible to have too many indexes.

As we mentioned earlier, you can also look at the statistics for the objects touched by queries. In `pg_stat_user_tables`, fast growth of `seq_tup_read` means that there are lots of sequential scans occurring. The ratio of `seq_tup_read` to `seq_scan` shows how many tuples each `seqscan` reads. Similarly, the `idx_scan` and `idx_tup_fetch` columns show whether indexes are being used, and how effective they are.

There's more...

If not enough of the data fits in shared buffers, lots of rereading of the same data happens, causing performance issues. In `pg_statio_user_tables`, watch the `heap_blks_hit` and `heap_blks_read` fields, or the equivalent ones for index and toast relations. They give you a fairly good idea of how much of your data is found in PostgreSQL's shared buffers (`heap_blks_hit`) and how much had to be fetched from the disk (`heap_blks_read`). If you see large numbers of blocks being read from the disk continuously, you may want to tune those queries; or if you determine that the disk reads were justified, you can make the configured `shared_buffers` value bigger.

If your `shared_buffers` parameter is tuned properly and you can't rewrite the query to perform less block I/O, you might need a beefier computer.

You can find a lot of resources on the Web that explain how shared buffers work and how to set them based on your available hardware and your expected data access patterns. Our professional advice is to always test your database servers and perform benchmarks before you deploy them in production. Information on the `shared_buffers` configuration parameter can be found at

`http://www.postgresql.org/docs/current/static/runtime-config-resource.html`.

Not enough CPU power or disk I/O capacity for the current load

These issues are usually caused by suboptimal query plans, but sometimes, your computer is just not powerful enough.

In this case, `top` is your friend. For quick checks, run this from the command line:

```
user@host:~$ top
```

First, watch the percentage of idle CPU from `top`. If this is in low single digits for most of the time, you probably have problems with the CPU's power.

If you have a high load average with a lot of CPU idle left, you are probably out of disk bandwidth. In this case, you should also have lots of postgres processes in the `D` status, meaning that the process is in an uninterruptible state (usually waiting for I/O).

Locking problems

Thanks to its MVCC design, PostgreSQL does not suffer from most locking problems, such as writers locking out readers or readers locking out writers, but it still has to take locks when more than one process wants to update the same row. Also, it has to hold the write lock until the current writer's transaction finishes.

So, if you have a database design where many queries update the same record, you can have a locking problem.

Refer to the *Knowing who is blocking a query* recipe of `Chapter 8`, *Monitoring and Diagnosis*, for more detailed information.

To diagnose locking problems retrospectively, use the `log_lock_waits` parameter to generate log output for locks held for a long time.

EXPLAIN options

Use the `FORMAT` option, to retrieve the output of `EXPLAIN` in a different format, such as `JSON`, `XML`, and `YAML`. This could allow us to write programs to manipulate the outputs.

The following command is an example of this:

```
EXPLAIN (ANALYZE, BUFFERS, FORMAT JSON) SELECT count(*) FROM t;
```

See also

- For further information on the syntax of the `EXPLAIN` SQL command, refer to the PostgreSQL documentation at
  `http://www.postgresql.org/docs/current/static/sql-explain.html`.

Reducing the number of rows returned

Although often the problem is producing many rows in the first place, it is made worse by returning all of the unnecessary rows to the client. This is especially true if the client and server are not on the same host.

Here are some ways to reduce the traffic between the client and server.

How to do it...

Consider the following scenario: a full-text search returns 10,000 documents, but only the first 20 are displayed to users. In this case, order the documents by ranking on the server, and return only the top 20 that actually need to be displayed:

```
SELECT title, ts_rank_cd(body_tsv, query, 20) AS text_rank
FROM articles, plainto_tsquery('spicy potatoes') AS query
WHERE body_tsv @@ query
ORDER BY rank DESC
LIMIT 20
;
```

If you need the next 20 documents, don't just query with a limit of 40 and throw away the first 20. Instead, use OFFSET 20 LIMIT 20 to return the next 20 documents.

To gain some stability so that documents with the same rank still come out in the same order when using OFFSET 20, add a unique field (like the id column of the articles table) to ORDER BY in both queries:

```
SELECT title, ts_rank_cd(body_tsv, query, 20) AS text_rank
FROM articles, plainto_tsquery('spicy potatoes') AS query
WHERE body_tsv @@ query
ORDER BY rank DESC, articles.id
OFFSET 20 LIMIT 20;
```

Another use case is an application that requests all products of a branch office, to run a complex calculation over them. In such a case, try to do as much data analysis as possible inside the database.

There is no need to run the following:

```
SELECT * FROM accounts WHERE branch_id = 7;
```

Also, instead of counting and summing the rows on the client side, you can run this:

```
SELECT count(*), sum(balance) FROM accounts WHERE branch_id = 7;
```

With some research on the SQL language, which is supported by PostgreSQL, you can carry out an amazingly large portion of your computation using plain SQL (for example, do not underestimate the power of window functions).

If SQL is not enough, you can use PL/pgSQL, or any other embedded procedural languages supported by PostgreSQL for even more flexibility.

There's more...

Consider one more scenario: an application runs a huge number of small lookup queries. This can easily happen with modern **Object Relational Mappers (ORMs)** and other toolkits that do a lot of work for the programmer, but at the same time, hide a lot of what is happening.

For example, if you define an HTML report over a query in a templating language, and then define a lookup function to resolve an ID inside the template, you may end up with a form that performs a separate, small lookup for each row displayed, even when most of the values looked up are the same. This doesn't usually pose a big problem for the database, as queries of the SELECT name FROM departments WHERE id = 7 form are really fast when the row for id = 7 is in shared buffers. However, repeating this query thousands of times still takes seconds, due to network latency, process scheduling for each request, and other factors.

The two proposed solutions are as follows:

- Make sure that the value is cached by your ORM
- Perform the lookup inside the query that gets the main data so that it can be displayed directly

Exactly how to carry out these solutions depends on the toolkit, but they are both worth investigating, as they really can make a difference in speed and resource usage.

See also

- PostgreSQL 9.5 introduced the TABLESAMPLE clause into SQL. This allows you to run commands much faster by using a sample of a table's rows, giving an approximate answer. In certain cases, this can be just as useful as the most accurate answer:

```
postgres=# SELECT avg(id) FROM events;
        avg
--------------------
 500000.500
(1 row)
postgres=# SELECT  avg(id)  FROM events TABLESAMPLE system(1);
        avg
--------------------
 507434.635
(1 row)
postgres=# EXPLAIN (ANALYZE, BUFFERS) SELECT avg(id) FROM
events;
                                                        QUERY
PLAN
----------------------------------------------------------------
----------------------------------------------------------
 Aggregate  (cost=16925.00..16925.01 rows=1 width=32) (actual
time=204.841..204.841 rows=1 loops=1)
   Buffers: shared hit=96 read=4329
   -> Seq Scan on events  (cost=0.00..14425.00 rows=1000000
width=4) (actual time=1.272..105.452 rows=1000000 loops=1)
         Buffers: shared hit=96 read=4329
 Planning time: 0.059 ms
 Execution time: 204.912 ms
(6 rows)
postgres=# EXPLAIN (ANALYZE, BUFFERS)
         SELECT avg(id) FROM events TABLESAMPLE system(1);
                                                   QUERY PLAN
----------------------------------------------------------------
--------------------------------------------------------
 Aggregate  (cost=301.00..301.01 rows=1 width=32) (actual
time=4.627..4.627 rows=1 loops=1)
   Buffers: shared hit=1 read=46
   -> Sample Scan on events  (cost=0.00..276.00 rows=10000
width=4) (actual time=0.074..2.833 rows=10622 loops=1)
         Sampling: system ('1'::real)
         Buffers: shared hit=1 read=46
```

```
Planning time: 0.066 ms
Execution time: 4.702 ms
(7 rows)
```

Simplifying complex SQL queries

There are two types of complexity that you can encounter in SQL queries.

First, the complexity can be directly visible in the query, if it has hundreds or even thousands of rows of SQL code in a single query. This can cause both maintenance headaches and slow execution.

The complexity can also be hidden in subviews, so the SQL code of the query may seem simple, but it uses other views and/or functions to do part of the work, which can, in turn, use others. This is much better for maintenance, but it can still cause performance problems.

Both types of queries can either be written manually by programmers or data analysts, or emerge as a result of a query generator.

Getting ready

First, verify that you really have a complex query.

A query that simply returns lots of database fields is not complex by itself. In order to be complex, the query has to join lots of tables in complex ways.

The easiest way to find out whether the query is complex is to look at the output of EXPLAIN. If it has lots of rows, the query is complex, and it's not just that there is a lot of text.

All examples in this recipe have been written with a very typical use case in mind: sales.

What follows is a description of the fictitious model used in this recipe. The most important fact is the sale event, stored in the sale table (I specifically used the word fact, as this is the right term to use in a *data warehousing* context). Every sale takes place at a point of sale (the salespoint table), at a specific time, and involves an item. That item is stored in a warehouse (see the item and warehouse tables, as well as the item_in_wh link table).

Both the warehouse and the salespoint are located in a geographical area (the location table). This is important, for example, to study the provenance of a transaction.

Here is a simplified entity-relationship model, useful for understanding all the joins that occur in the following queries:

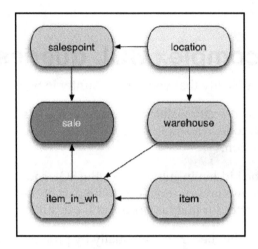

How to do it...

Simplifying a query usually means restructuring it so that parts of it can be defined separately, and then used by other parts.

We'll illustrate the possibilities by rewriting the following query in several ways.

The complex query in our example case is a so-called **pivot** or **cross-tab** query. This query retrieves the quarterly profit for non-local sales from all shops, as shown in the following:

```
SELECT shop.sp_name AS shop_name,
       q1_nloc_profit.profit AS q1_profit,
       q2_nloc_profit.profit AS q2_profit,
       q3_nloc_profit.profit AS q3_profit,
       q4_nloc_profit.profit AS q4_profit,
       year_nloc_profit.profit AS year_profit
  FROM (SELECT * FROM salespoint ORDER BY sp_name) AS shop
  LEFT JOIN (
       SELECT
           spoint_id,
           sum(sale_price) - sum(cost) AS profit,
           count(*) AS nr_of_sales
       FROM sale s
       JOIN item_in_wh iw ON s.item_in_wh_id=iw.id
       JOIN item i ON iw.item_id = i.id
```

```
        JOIN salespoint sp ON s.spoint_id = sp.id
        JOIN location sploc ON sp.loc_id = sploc.id
        JOIN warehouse wh ON iw.whouse_id = wh.id
        JOIN location whloc ON wh.loc_id = whloc.id
       WHERE sale_time >= '2013-01-01'
         AND sale_time <  '2013-04-01'
         AND sploc.id != whloc.id
       GROUP BY 1
      ) AS q1_nloc_profit
      ON shop.id = Q1_NLOC_PROFIT.spoint_id
   LEFT JOIN (
  < similar subquery for 2nd quarter >
      ) AS q2_nloc_profit
      ON shop.id = q2_nloc_profit.spoint_id
   LEFT JOIN (
  < similar subquery for 3rd quarter >
      ) AS q3_nloc_profit
      ON shop.id = q3_nloc_profit.spoint_id
   LEFT JOIN (
  < similar subquery for 4th  quarter >
      ) AS q4_nloc_profit
      ON shop.id = q4_nloc_profit.spoint_id
   LEFT JOIN (
  < similar subquery for full year >
      ) AS year_nloc_profit
      ON shop.id = year_nloc_profit.spoint_id
 ORDER BY 1
 ;
```

As the preceding query has an almost identical repeating part for finding the sales for a period (the four quarters of 2013, in this case), it makes sense to move it to a separate view (for the whole year), and then use that view in the main reporting query, as follows:

```
CREATE VIEW non_local_quarterly_profit_2013 AS
     SELECT
        spoint_id,
        extract('quarter' from sale_time) as sale_quarter,
        sum(sale_price) - sum(cost) AS profit,
        count(*) AS nr_of_sales
     FROM sale s
     JOIN item_in_wh iw ON s.item_in_wh_id=iw.id
     JOIN item i ON iw.item_id = i.id
     JOIN salespoint sp ON s.spoint_id = sp.id
     JOIN location sploc ON sp.loc_id = sploc.id
     JOIN warehouse wh ON iw.whouse_id = wh.id
     JOIN location whloc ON wh.loc_id = whloc.id
    WHERE sale_time >= '2013-01-01'
```

```
            AND sale_time <  '2014-01-01'
            AND sploc.id != whloc.id
         GROUP BY 1,2;
    SELECT shop.sp_name AS shop_name,
           q1_nloc_profit.profit as q1_profit,
           q2_nloc_profit.profit as q2_profit,
           q3_nloc_profit.profit as q3_profit,
           q4_nloc_profit.profit as q4_profit,
           year_nloc_profit.profit as year_profit
      FROM (SELECT * FROM salespoint ORDER BY sp_name) AS shop
      LEFT JOIN non_local_quarterly_profit_2013 AS q1_nloc_profit
         ON shop.id = Q1_NLOC_PROFIT.spoint_id
       AND q1_nloc_profit.sale_quarter = 1
      LEFT JOIN non_local_quarterly_profit_2013 AS q2_nloc_profit
         ON shop.id = Q2_NLOC_PROFIT.spoint_id
      AND q2_nloc_profit.sale_quarter = 2
      LEFT JOIN non_local_quarterly_profit_2013 AS q3_nloc_profit
         ON shop.id = Q3_NLOC_PROFIT.spoint_id
      AND q3_nloc_profit.sale_quarter = 3
      LEFT JOIN non_local_quarterly_profit_2013 AS q4_nloc_profit
         ON shop.id = Q4_NLOC_PROFIT.spoint_id
      AND q4_nloc_profit.sale_quarter = 4
      LEFT JOIN (
          SELECT spoint_id, sum(profit) AS profit
            FROM non_local_quarterly_profit_2013 GROUP BY 1
      ) AS year_nloc_profit
         ON shop.id = year_nloc_profit.spoint_id
    ORDER BY 1;
```

Moving the subquery to a view has not only made the query shorter, but also easier to understand and maintain.

You might want to consider **materialized views**. Even though their support does not yet allow differential updates, you can still benefit from on-demand refreshing of the view results and, most importantly, indexes. Materialized views are described later in this recipe.

Before that, we will be using common table expressions (also known as WITH queries) instead of a separate view. Starting with PostgreSQL version 8.4 indeed, you can use the WITH statement to define the view in line, as follows:

```
WITH nlqp AS (
    SELECT
        spoint_id,
        extract('quarter' from sale_time) as sale_quarter,
        sum(sale_price) - sum(cost) AS profit,
        count(*) AS nr_of_sales
      FROM sale s
```

```
                JOIN item_in_wh iw ON s.item_in_wh_id=iw.id
                JOIN item i ON iw.item_id = i.id
                JOIN salespoint sp ON s.spoint_id = sp.id
                JOIN location sploc ON sp.loc_id = sploc.id
                JOIN warehouse wh ON iw.whouse_id = wh.id
                JOIN location whloc ON wh.loc_id = whloc.id
            WHERE sale_time >= '2013-01-01'
             AND sale_time <  '2014-01-01'
             AND sploc.id != whloc.id
            GROUP BY 1,2
    )
    SELECT shop.sp_name AS shop_name,
            q1_nloc_profit.profit as q1_profit,
            q2_nloc_profit.profit as q2_profit,
            q3_nloc_profit.profit as q3_profit,
            q4_nloc_profit.profit as q4_profit,
            year_nloc_profit.profit as year_profit
       FROM (SELECT * FROM salespoint ORDER BY sp_name) AS shop
       LEFT JOIN nlqp AS q1_nloc_profit
            ON shop.id = Q1_NLOC_PROFIT.spoint_id
         AND q1_nloc_profit.sale_quarter = 1
       LEFT JOIN nlqp AS q2_nloc_profit
            ON shop.id = Q2_NLOC_PROFIT.spoint_id
         AND q2_nloc_profit.sale_quarter = 2
       LEFT JOIN nlqp AS q3_nloc_profit
            ON shop.id = Q3_NLOC_PROFIT.spoint_id
         AND q3_nloc_profit.sale_quarter = 3
       LEFT JOIN nlqp AS q4_nloc_profit
            ON shop.id = Q4_NLOC_PROFIT.spoint_id
         AND q4_nloc_profit.sale_quarter = 4
       LEFT JOIN (
               SELECT spoint_id, sum(profit) AS profit
                 FROM nlqp GROUP BY 1
             ) AS year_nloc_profit
            ON shop.id = year_nloc_profit.spoint_id
      ORDER BY 1;
```

For more information on WITH queries (also known as **Common Table Expressions (CTEs)**), read the official documentation at
http://www.postgresql.org/docs/current/static/queries-with.html.

There's more...

Another ace in the hole is represented by temporary tables used for parts of the query. By default, a temporary table is dropped at the end of a Postgres session, but the behavior can be changed at the time of creation.

PostgreSQL itself can choose to materialize parts of the query during the query optimization phase, but sometimes, it fails to make the best choice for the query plan, either due to insufficient statistics, or because-as it can happen for large query plans, where **genetic query optimization (GEQO)** is used-it may have just overlooked some possible query plans.

If you think that materializing (separately preparing) some parts of the query is a good idea, you can do it using a temporary table, simply by running `CREATE TEMPORARY TABLE my_temptable01 AS <the part of the query you want to materialize>` and then using `my_temptable01` in the main query, instead of the materialized part.

You can even create indexes on the temporary table for PostgreSQL to use in the main query:

```
BEGIN;
CREATE TEMPORARY TABLE nlqp_temp ON COMMIT DROP
  AS
       SELECT
            spoint_id,
            extract('quarter' from sale_time) as sale_quarter,
            sum(sale_price) - sum(cost) AS profit,
            count(*) AS nr_of_sales
         FROM sale s
         JOIN item_in_wh iw ON s.item_in_wh_id=iw.id
         JOIN item i ON iw.item_id = i.id
         JOIN salespoint sp ON s.spoint_id = sp.id
         JOIN location sploc ON sp.loc_id = sploc.id
         JOIN warehouse wh ON iw.whouse_id = wh.id
         JOIN location whloc ON wh.loc_id = whloc.id
        WHERE sale_time >= '2013-01-01'
          AND sale_time <  '2014-01-01'
          AND sploc.id != whloc.id
        GROUP BY 1,2
  ;
```

You can create indexes on the table and analyze the temporary table here:

```
SELECT shop.sp_name AS shop_name,
       q1_NLP.profit as q1_profit,
```

```
        q2_NLP.profit as q2_profit,
        q3_NLP.profit as q3_profit,
        q4_NLP.profit as q4_profit,
        year_NLP.profit as year_profit
    FROM (SELECT * FROM salespoint ORDER BY sp_name) AS shop
    LEFT JOIN nlqp_temp AS q1_NLP
        ON shop.id = Q1_NLP.spoint_id AND q1_NLP.sale_quarter = 1
    LEFT JOIN nlqp_temp AS q2_NLP
        ON shop.id = Q2_NLP.spoint_id AND q2_NLP.sale_quarter = 2
    LEFT JOIN nlqp_temp AS q3_NLP
        ON shop.id = Q3_NLP.spoint_id AND q3_NLP.sale_quarter = 3
    LEFT JOIN nlqp_temp AS q4_NLP
        ON shop.id = Q4_NLP.spoint_id AND q4_NLP.sale_quarter = 4
    LEFT JOIN (
            select spoint_id, sum(profit) AS profit FROM nlqp_temp GROUP BY 1
        ) AS year_NLP
        ON shop.id = year_NLP.spoint_id
    ORDER BY 1
    ;
    COMMIT; -- here the temp table goes away
```

Using materialized views (long-living, temporary tables)

If the part you put in the temporary table is large, does not change very often, and/or is hard to compute, then you may be able to do it less often for each query by using a technique named **materialized views**.

Materialized views are views that are prepared before they are used (similar to a cached table). They are either fully regenerated as underlying data changes or in some cases, can update only those rows that depend on the changed data.

PostgreSQL natively supports materialized views through the CREATE MATERIALIZED VIEW, ALTER MATERIALIZED VIEW, REFRESH MATERIALIZED VIEW, and DROP MATERIALIZED VIEW commands. At the time of writing, PostgreSQL supports full regeneration only of the cached tables, using concurrent REFRESH of the MATERIALIZED VIEW.

A fundamental aspect of materialized views is that they can have their own indexes, like any other table. See http://www.postgresql.org/docs/current/static/sql-creatematerializedview.html for more information on creating materialized views.

For instance, you can rewrite the example of the previous recipe using a `materialized view` instead of a temporary table:

```
CREATE MATERIALIZED VIEW nlqp_temp AS
        SELECT spoint_id,
            extract('quarter' from sale_time) as sale_quarter,
            sum(sale_price) - sum(cost) AS profit,
            count(*) AS nr_of_sales
        FROM sale s
        JOIN item_in_wh iw ON s.item_in_wh_id=iw.id
        JOIN item i ON iw.item_id = i.id
        JOIN salespoint sp ON s.spoint_id = sp.id
        JOIN location sploc ON sp.loc_id = sploc.id
        JOIN warehouse wh ON iw.whouse_id = wh.id
        JOIN location whloc ON wh.loc_id = whloc.id
            WHERE sale_time >= '2013-01-01'
            AND sale_time <  '2014-01-01'
            AND sploc.id != whloc.id
            GROUP BY 1,2
```

Using set-returning functions for some parts of queries

Another possibility for achieving similar results to temporary tables and/or materialized views is by using a **set-returning function** for some parts of the query.

It is easy to have a materialized view freshness check inside a function. However, a detailed analysis and an overview of these techniques go beyond the goals of this book, as they require a deep understanding of the PL/pgSQL procedural language.

Speeding up queries without rewriting them

Often, you either can't or don't want to rewrite the query. However, you can still try and speed it up through any of the techniques discussed here.

How to do it...

By now, we assume that you've looked at various problems already, so the following are more advanced ideas for you to try.

Increasing work_mem

For queries involving large sorts or for join queries it may be useful to increase the amount of working memory that can be used for query execution. Try setting:

```
SET work_mem = '1TB';
```

Then, run `EXPLAIN` (not `EXPLAIN ANALYZE`). If the `EXPLAIN` changes for the query, then it may benefit from more memory. I'm guessing that you don't have access to 1 terabyte of RAM; the previous setting was only used to prove that the query plan is dependent upon available memory. So now, issue the following:

```
RESET work_mem;
```

And choose a more appropriate value for production use, such as:

```
SET work_mem = '128MB';
```

Remember to increase `maintenace_work_mem` when creating indexes or adding foreign keys, rather than `work_mem`.

More ideas with indexes

Try and add a multicolumn index that is specifically tuned for that query.

If you have a query that, for example, selects rows from the `t1` table on the `a` column and sorts on the `b` column, then creating the following index enables PostgreSQL to do it all in one index scan:

```
CREATE INDEX t1_a_b_ndx ON t1(a, b);
```

PostgreSQL 9.2 introduced a new plan type: **index-only scans**. This allows you to utilize a technique known as **covering indexes.** If all the columns requested by the `SELECT` list of a query are available in an index, that particular index is a covering index for that query. This technique allows PostgreSQL to fetch valid rows directly from the index, without accessing the table (**heap**), so performance improves significantly.

Another often underestimated (or unknown) feature of PostgreSQL is **partial indexes**. If you use `SELECT` on a condition, especially if this condition only selects a small number of rows, you can use a conditional index on that expression, like this:

```
CREATE INDEX t1_proc_ndx ON t1(i1)
WHERE needs_processing = TRUE;
```

The index will be used by queries that have a WHERE clause that includes the index clause, like the following

```
SELECT id, ... WHERE needs_processing AND i1 = 5;
```

There are many types of indexes in Postgres, so you may find that there are multiple types of indexes that can be used for a particular task, and many options to choose from:

- Identifier data: BTREE, HASH
- Text data: GIST, GIN
- JSONB or XML data:GIN
- Time-range data: BRIN
- Geographical data: BRIN, GIST, and SP-GIST

Performance gains in Postgres can also be obtained with another technique: **clustering tables on specific indexes**. However, index access may still not be very efficient if the values accessed by the index are distributed randomly all over the table. If you know that some fields are likely to be accessed together, then cluster the table on an index defined on those fields. For a multicolumn index, you can use the following command:

```
CLUSTER t1_a_b_ndx ON t1;
```

Clustering a table on an index rewrites the whole table in index order. This can lock the table for a long time, so don't do it on a busy system. Also, CLUSTER is a one-time command. New rows do not get inserted in cluster order, and to keep the performance gains, you may need to cluster the table every now and then.

Once a table is clustered on an index, you don't need to specify the index name in following cluster commands. It is enough to type this:

```
CLUSTER t1;
```

It still takes time to rewrite the entire table, though it is probably a little faster once most of the table is in index order.

There's more...

We complete this recipe by listing four examples of query performance issues that can be addressed with a specific solution.

Time Series Partitioning

If you have a huge table and a query to select only a subset of that table, then you may wish to use a **BRIN index** (**block range index**). These give performance improvements when the data is naturally ordered as it is added to the table, such as logtime columns or a naturally ascending `OrderId` column. Adding a BRIN index is fast and very easy and works well for the use case of time series data logging, though less well under intensive updates.
An INSERTs into BRIN indexes are specifically designed to **not** slow down as the table gets bigger, so they perform much better than btree indexes.

You may also think that you need to manually partition a table. This can involve significant effort to set up an effective partitioning scheme so it doesn't really count as a technique without rewriting anything, so try BRIN first.

```
CREATE TABLE measurement (
logtime        TIMESTAMP NOT NULL,
measures       JSONB NOT NULL);
CREATE INDEX ON measurement USING BRIN (logtime);
```

Partitioning syntax was introduced in PostgreSQL 10. In this release, it is effective for INSERTs and large/slow `SELECT` queries, which makes it suitable for time series logging and business intelligence. It is not yet fully optimized for fast OLTP `SELECT`, `UPDATE`, or `DELETE` commands unless you explicitly request those commands against the specific partition you wish to target. Those restrictions are substantially lifted in the forthcoming PostgreSQL 11 release, allowing partitioning to be effective for more use cases.

For example, to create a table for time series data, you may want something like this:

```
CREATE TABLE measurement (
logtime        TIMESTAMP NOT NULL,
    measures     JSONB NOT NULL
 ) PARTITION BY RANGE (logtime);
CREATE TABLE measurement_week1 PARTITION OF measurement
 FOR VALUES FROM ('2018-04-01') TO ('2018-05-01');
CREATE INDEX ON measurement_week1 USING BRIN (logtime);
CREATE TABLE measurement_week2 PARTITION OF measurement
 FOR VALUES FROM ('2018-05-01') TO ('2018-06-01');
CREATE INDEX ON measurement_week2 USING BRIN (logtime);
etc
```

Notice that you can use both BRIN indexes and partitioning at the same time, so there is less need to have huge numbers of partitions. Typical partition size should allow the whole current partition to sit within shared buffers. `http://www.postgresql.org/docs/current/static/ddl-partitioning.html`.

Using a TABLESAMPLE view

Where some queries access a table, replace that with a view that retrieves fewer rows using a `TABLESAMPLE` clause. In this example, we use a sampling method that produces a sample of the table using a scan lasting no longer than 5 secs; if the table is small enough the answer is exact - otherwise progressive sampling is used to ensure that we meet out time objective:

```
CREATE EXTENSION tsm_system_time;
CREATE SCHEMA fast_access_schema;
CREATE VIEW tablename AS
 SELECT * FROM data_schema TABLESAMPLE system_time(5000); --5 secs
SET search_path = 'fast_access_schema, data_schema';
```

So, the application can use the new table without changing the SQL. Be careful, as some answers can change when you're accessing fewer rows (for example, `sum()`), making this particular idea somewhat restricted; the overall idea of using views is still useful.

In case of many updates, set fillfactor on the table

If you often update only some tables and can arrange your query/queries so that you don't change any indexed fields, then setting `fillfactor` to a lower value than the default of `100` for those tables enables PostgreSQL to use **Heap-Only Tuples** (**HOT**) updates, which can be an order of magnitude faster than ordinary updates. HOT updates not only avoid creating new index entries, but can also perform a fast mini-vacuum inside the page to make room for new rows:

```
ALTER TABLE t1 SET (fillfactor = 70);
```

This tells PostgreSQL to fill only `70` percent of each page in table `t1` when performing insertions, so that 30 percent is left for use by in-page (HOT) updates.

Rewriting the schema – a more radical approach

In some cases, it may make sense to rewrite the database schema and provide an old view for unchanged queries using views, triggers, rules, and functions.

One such case occurs when refactoring the database, and you would want old queries to keep running while changes are made.

Another case is an external application that is unusable with the provided schema, but can be made to perform OK with a different distribution of data between tables.

Discovering why a query is not using an index

This recipe explains what to do if you think your query should use an index, yet it does not.

There could be several reasons for this, but most often, the reason is that the optimizer believes that, based on the available distribution statistics, it is cheaper and faster to use a query plan that does not use that specific index.

Getting ready

First, check that your index exists, and ensure that the table has been analyzed. If there is any doubt, rerun it to be sure:

```
postgres=# ANALYZE;
ANALYZE
```

How to do it...

Force index usage and compare plan costs with an index and without, as follows:

```
postgres=# EXPLAIN ANALYZE SELECT count(*) FROM itable WHERE id > 500;
                          QUERY PLAN
-----------------------------------------------------------------
  Aggregate   (cost=188.75..188.76 rows=1 width=0)
              (actual time=37.958..37.959 rows=1 loops=1)
     ->  Seq Scan on itable   (cost=0.00..165.00 rows=9500 width=0)
              (actual time=0.290..18.792 rows=9500 loops=1)
          Filter: (id > 500)
 Total runtime: 38.027 ms
 (4 rows)
postgres=# SET enable_seqscan TO false;
SET
postgres=# EXPLAIN ANALYZE SELECT count(*) FROM itable WHERE id > 500;
```

```
                         QUERY PLAN
-----------------------------------------------------------------
   Aggregate   (cost=323.25..323.26 rows=1 width=0)
              (actual time=44.467..44.469 rows=1 loops=1)
    ->   Index Scan using itable_pkey on itable
              (cost=0.00..299.50 rows=9500 width=0)
              (actual time=0.100..23.240 rows=9500 loops=1)
           Index Cond: (id > 500)
  Total runtime: 44.556 ms
  (4 rows)
```

Note that you must use EXPLAIN ANALYZE, rather than just EXPLAIN. EXPLAIN ANALYZE shows you how much data is being requested and measures the actual execution time, while EXPLAIN only shows what the optimizer thinks will happen. EXPLAIN ANALYZE is slower, but it gives an accurate picture of what is happening.

How it works...

Setting the enable_seqscan parameter to off, we greatly increase the cost of sequential scans for the query. This setting is never recommended for production use, only for testing.

This allows us to generate two different plans, one with a SeqScan and one without. The optimizer works by selecting the lowest cost option available. In this case, the cost of the SeqScan is 188.75 and the cost of the IndexScan is 323.25, so for this specific case, the IndexScan will not be used.

Remember that each case is different, and always relates to the exact data distribution.

There's more...

Be sure that the WHERE clause you are using can be used with the type of index you have. For example, the WHERE clause abs(val) < 2 won't use an index, because you're performing a function on the column, while val BETWEEN -2 AND 2 could use the index. With more advanced operators and data types, it's easy to get confused as to the type of clause that will work, so check the docs for the data type carefully.

In PostgreSQL 10, join statistics are also improved by the use of foreign keys, since they can be used in some queries to prove that joins on those keys return exactly one row.

Forcing a query to use an index

Often, we think we know better than the database optimizer. Most of the time your expectation is wrong and if you look carefully you'll see that. So recheck everything and come back later.

It is a classic error to try to get the database optimizer to use indexes when the database has very little data in it. Put some genuine data in the database first, then worry about it. Better yet, load some data on a test server first, rather than doing this in production.

Sometimes the optimizer gets it wrong. You feel elated, and possibly angry, that the database optimizer doesn't see what you see. Please bear in mind that the data distributions within your database change over time, and this causes the optimizer to change its plans over time, also. If you have found a case where the optimizer is wrong, it might have been correct last week, and will be correct again next week: it correctly calculated that a change of plan was required, but it made that change slightly ahead of time, or slightly too late. Again, trying to force the optimizer to do the right thing *now* might prevent it from doing the right thing *later*, when the plan changes again.

Some optimizer estimation errors can be corrected using CREATE STATISTICS, a new command in PostgreSQL 10, described in this recipe's *There's more...* section.

In the long run, it is not recommended to try to force the use of a particular index.

Getting ready

Still here? Oh well.

In fact, it is not possible to tell PostgreSQL to use an index by submitting an access path hint, like other DBMS products do. However, you can trick it into using an index by telling the optimizer that all other options are prohibitively expensive.

First, you have to make sure that it is worth it to use the index. This is best done on a development or testing system, but if you are careful, it can also be done on the production server. Sometimes, it is very hard to generate a load similar to a live system in a test environment, and then your best option may be to carefully test it on the production server.

As the PostgreSQL optimizer does not take into account the parallel load caused by other backends, it may make sense to lie to PostgreSQL about some statistics in order to make it use indexes.

How to do it...

The most common problem is selecting too much data.

A typical point of confusion comes from data that has a few very common values among a larger group. Requesting data for the very common values costs more because we need to bring back more rows. As we bring back more rows the cost of using the index increases. So it is possible that we won't use the index for the very common values, whereas we would use the index for the less common values. To use an index effectively, make sure you're reducing the number of rows returned.

Another technique for making indexes more usable is **partial indexes**. Instead of indexing all values in a column, you might choose to index only the set of rows that are frequently accessed; for example, by excluding NULL or other unwanted data. By making the index smaller, it will be cheaper to access and fit within the cache better, avoiding pointless work by targeting the index at only the important data. Data statistics are kept for such indexes, so it can also improve the accuracy of query planning. For example:

```
CREATE INDEX ON customer(id)
  WHERE blocked = false AND subscription_status = 'paid';
```

Another nudge towards using indexes is to set random_page_cost to a lower value—maybe even equal to seq_page_cost. This makes PostgreSQL prefer index scans on more occasions, but it still does not produce entirely unreasonable plans, at least for cases where data is mostly cached in shared buffers, or system disk caches or underlying disks are solid-state drives.

The default values for these parameters are as follows:

```
random_page_cost = 4;
seq_page_cost = 1;
```

Try setting this:

```
set random_page_cost = 2;
```

See if it helps; if not, you can try setting it to 1.

Changing random_page_cost allows you to react to whether data is on disk or in memory. Letting the optimizer know that more of an index is in the cache will help it to understand that using the index is actually cheaper.

Index scan performance for larger scans can also be improved by allowing multiple asynchronous I/O operations by increasing the `effective_io_concurrency`. Both `random_page_cost` and `effective_io_concurrency` can be set for specific tablespaces, or for individual queries.

Rather than trying to force the use of an index, you might want to consider using a parallel query to speed up scans, so refer to the *Using parallel query* recipe.

There's more...

If you have multi-column indexes (or joins), the optimizer will assume that the column values are independent of each other, which can lead to mis-estimation in cases where there is a correlation between the values.

If you have two dependent columns, such as `state` and `area_code`, then you can define additional statistics that will be collected when you next `ANALYZE` the table:

```
CREATE STATISTICS cust_s1 (ndistinct, dependencies) ON state, area_code
FROM cust;
```

Execution time of `ANALYZE` will increase to collect the additional stats information, plus there is a small increase in query planning time so use this sparingly when you can confirm this will make a difference. You don't need to have both ndistinct and dependencies in all cases, only when it matters.

Include the table name in the statistics you create since the name cannot be repeated on different tables. In future releases we will also add cross-table statistics.

Unfortunately you cannot yet collect statistics on individual fields within JSON documents, nor collect dependency information between them; this command applies to whole column values only at this time.

There's even more

If you absolutely, positively have to use the index, then you'll want to know about an extension called `pg_hint_plan`. It is available for PostgreSQL 9.1 and later versions. For more information and to download it, go to `http://pghintplan.sourceforge.jp/`.

It works, but as I said before, try to avoid fixing things now and causing yourself pain later.

Using parallel query

PostgreSQL 10 now has an increasingly effective parallel query feature.

Response times from long running queries can be improved by the use of parallel processing. The concept is that we divide a large task up into multiple smaller pieces. We get the answer faster, but we use more resources to do that.

Very short queries won't get faster by using parallel query, so if you have lots of those you'll gain more by thinking about better indexing strategies. Parallel Query is aimed at making very large tasks faster, so it is useful for reporting and business intelligence queries.

How to do it...

Take a query that needs to do a big chunk of work, such as this:

```
\timing
SELECT count(*) FROM accounts;
count
---------
1000000
(1 row)
Time: 261.652 ms
SET max_parallel_workers_per_gather = 8;
SELECT count(*) FROM accounts;
count
---------
1000000
(1 row)
Time: 180.513 ms
```

By setting the `max_parallel_workers_per_gather` parameter, we've improved performance using parallel query. Note that we didn't need to change the query at all.

In PostgreSQL 9.6 and 10, parallel query only works for read-only queries, so only `SELECT` statements that do not contain the `FOR` clause (for example, `SELECT ... FOR UPDATE`). In addition, a parallel query can only use functions or aggregates that are marked as `PARALLEL SAFE`. No user-defined functions are marked `PARALLEL SAFE` by default, so read the docs carefully to see if your functions can be enabled for parallelism for the current release.

How it works...

By default a query will use only one process. Parallel query is enabled by setting `max_parallel_workers_per_gather` to a value higher than zero. This parameter specifies the maximum number of **additional** processes that are available, if needed. So a setting of 1 will mean you have the leader process plus one additional worker process, so two processes in total.

The query optimizer will decide if parallel query is a useful plan based upon cost, just like other aspects of the optimizer. Importantly, it will decide how many parallel workers to use in its plan, up to the maximum you specify.

Across the whole server the maximum number of worker processes available is specified by the `max_worker_processes` parameter, set at server start only. PostgreSQL 10 introduces the `max_parallel_workers` parameter to further control the number of worker processes available.

At execution time, the query will use its planned number of worker processes if that many are available. The plan for our earlier example of parallel query looks like this:

```
postgres=# EXPLAIN ANALYZE
  SELECT count(*) FROM demo;
                QUERY PLAN
----------------------------------------------------------------
Finalize Aggregate  (cost=78117.63..78117.64 rows=1 width=8) (actual
time=203.426..203.426 rows=1 loops=1)
   -> Gather  (cost=78117.21..78117.62 rows=4 width=8) (actual
time=203.286..203.421 rows=5 loops=1)
        Workers Planned: 4
        Workers Launched: 4
        -> Partial Aggregate  (cost=77117.21..77117.22 rows=1 width=8)
(actual time=194.315..194.315 rows=1 loops=5)
            -> Parallel Seq Scan on demo  (cost=0.00..76863.57
rows=101457 width=0) (actual time=115.632..164.688 rows=200200 loops=5)
 Planning time: 0.076 ms
 Execution time: 206.197 ms
(8 rows)
```

If worker processes aren't available, the query will run with fewer worker processes. As a result, it pays to not be too greedy, since if all concurrent users specify more workers than are available, you'll end up with variable performance as the number of concurrent parallel queries changes.

Also note that the performance increase from adding more workers isn't linear for anything other than simple plans, so there are diminishing returns from using too many workers, anyway. The biggest gains are from adding the first few extra processes.

As a result of those factors, I recommend a setting of just 1-3 extra worker processes for general use—meaning two processes will be used for queries, when needed. For specific long running queries, there may be as many as 8-16 workers, though that will vary considerably, depending on the kind of servers you're running on.

There's more...

PostgreSQL 9.6 includes the basic parallel query feature. In this release, it works with Seq Scans, aggregation, and to a certain extent with joins. For many cases this is a very useful addition. PostgreSQL 10 adds plan improvements that allows parallel query to work with btree index scans, bitmap heap scans, merge joins and non-correlated subqueries. Also, in PostgreSQL 10 you can now get parallel query plans from SQL inside procedural language functions.

If you have an immediate requirement for higher levels of scalability or very large databases then you'll want to look at the Postgres-XL project. Postgres-XL is an open source project using The PostgreSQL License that has modified PostgreSQL to provide multi-node parallel query, or massively parallel processing (MPP) as it's commonly known. MPP parallel queries are much faster than single node parallel queries. The project has been running for many years now and provides a full function version of Postgres aimed at larger and/or more scalable workloads. Almost all operations are fully parallelized, including many types of queries as well as maintenance commands and DDL operations. Postgres-XL features are expected to be integrated into PostgreSQL core within the next two-three years.

Using optimistic locking

If you perform work in one long transaction the database will lock rows for long periods of time. Long lock times often result in application performance issues because of long lock waits:

```
BEGIN;
SELECT * FROM accounts WHERE holder_name ='BOB' FOR UPDATE;
<do some calculations here>
UPDATE accounts SET balance = 42.00 WHERE holder_name ='BOB';
COMMIT;
```

If that is happening, then you may gain some performance by moving from explicit locking (SELECT ... FOR UPDATE) to optimistic locking.

Optimistic locking assumes that others don't update the same record, and checks this at update time, instead of locking the record for the time it takes to process the information on the client side.

How to do it...

Rewrite your application so that the SQL is transformed into two separate transactions, with a double-check to ensure that the rows haven't changed (pay attention to the placeholders):

```
SELECT A.*, (A.*::text) AS old_acc_info
FROM accounts a WHERE holder_name ='BOB';
<do some calculations here>
UPDATE accounts SET balance = 42.00
WHERE holder_name ='BOB'
AND (A.*::text) = <old_acc_info from select above>;
```

Then, check whether the UPDATE operation really did update one row in your application code. If it did not, then the account for BOB was modified between SELECT and UPDATE, and you probably need to rerun your entire operation (both transactions).

How it works...

Instead of locking Bob's row for the time the data from the first SELECT command is processed in the client, PostgreSQL queries the old state of Bob's account record in the old_acc_info variable, and then uses this value to check that the record has not changed when we eventually update.

You can also save all fields individually, and then check them all in the UPDATE query; or, if you have an automatic last_change field, then you can use it. Alternatively, if you actually care about only a few fields changing, such as balance, and can ignore others, such as email, then you only need to check the relevant fields in the UPDATE statement.

There's more...

You can also use the serializable transaction isolation level when you need to be absolutely sure that the data you are looking at is not affected by other user changes.

The default transaction isolation level in PostgreSQL is read committed, but you can choose from two more levels, repeatable read and serializable, if you require stricter control over visibility of data within a transaction;
see `http://www.postgresql.org/docs/current/static/transaction-iso.html`.

Another design pattern available in some cases is to use a single statement for the UPDATE and return data to the user via the RETURNING clause; for example:

```
UPDATE accounts
  SET balance = balance - i_amount
WHERE username = i_username
AND balance - i_amount > - max_credit
RETURNING balance;
```

In some cases, moving the entire computation to the database function is a very good idea. If you can pass all of the necessary information to the database for processing as a database function, it will run even faster, as you save several round-trips to the database. If you use a PL/pgSQL function, you also benefit from automatically saving query plans on the first call in a session and using saved plans in subsequent calls.

Therefore, the preceding transaction is replaced by a function in the database like the following:

```
CREATE OR REPLACE FUNCTION consume_balance
( i_username text
, i_amount numeric(10,2)
, max_credit numeric(10,2)
, OUT success boolean
, OUT remaining_balance numeric(10,2)
) AS
$$
BEGIN
  UPDATE accounts SET balance = balance - i_amount
  WHERE username = i_username
  AND balance - i_amount > - max_credit
  RETURNING balance
  INTO remaining_balance;
  IF NOT FOUND THEN
    success := FALSE;
    SELECT balance
    FROM accounts
```

```
    WHERE username = i_username
    INTO remaining_balance;
  ELSE
    success := TRUE;
  END IF;
END;
$$ LANGUAGE plpgsql;
```

You can call it by simply running this line from your client:

```
SELECT * FROM consume_balance ('bob', 7, 0);
```

The output will return the success variable. It tells you whether there was a sufficient balance in Bob's account. The output will also return a number telling the balance bob has left after this operation.

Reporting performance problems

Sometimes you face performance issues and feel lost, but you should never feel alone when working with one of the most successful open source projects ever.

How to do it...

If you need to get some advice on your performance problems, then the right place to do so is the performance mailing list at `http://archives.postgresql.org/pgsql-performance/`.

You may want to first ensure that it is not a well-known problem by searching the mailing list archives.

A very good description of what to include in your performance problem report is available at `http://wiki.postgresql.org/wiki/Guide_to_reporting_problems`.

There's more...

More performance-related information can be found at `http://wiki.postgresql.org/wiki/Performance_Optimization`.

11
Backup and Recovery

In this chapter, we will cover the following recipes:

- Understanding and controlling crash recovery
- Planning backups
- Hot logical backup of one database
- Hot logical backup of all databases
- Backup of database object definitions
- Standalone hot physical database backup
- Hot physical backup and continuous archiving
- Recovery of all databases
- Recovery to a point in time
- Recovery of a dropped/damaged table
- Recovery of a dropped/damaged database
- Improving performance of backup/recovery
- Incremental/differential backup and restore
- Hot physical backups with Barman
- Recovery with Barman

Introduction

Most people admit that backups are essential, though they also devote a very small amount of time to thinking about the topic.

The first recipe is about understanding and controlling crash recovery. You need to understand what happens if the database server crashes so that you can understand when you might need to perform a recovery operation.

The next recipe is all about planning. That's really the best place to start before you perform backups.

The physical backup mechanisms here were initially written by Simon Riggs (one of the authors of this book) for PostgreSQL 8.0 in 2004, and have been supported by him ever since, now with increasing help from the community as its popularity grows. 2ndQuadrant has also been providing database recovery services since 2004, and regrettably, many people have needed them as a result of missing or damaged backups.

It is important to note that, in the last few years, the native streaming replication protocol has become more and more relevant in PostgreSQL. It can be used for backup purposes too; not only to take a base backup with `pg_basebackup`, but also to stream WAL files using `pg_receivewal`.

As authors, we had a dilemma when planning this book. Should we introduce streaming replication before backups or leave it to the replication section? For now we decided to leave it out of this chapter and postpone it until the next. We would like your feedback on this subject for future editions of the book.

As a final note, all of the examples regarding physical backup and recovery in this chapter are thoroughly explained so that you understand what is happening behind the scenes. However, unless you have a specific task that you have to do, we highly recommend that, when in production, you use Barman (our open source backup and recovery tool), or a similar product that is specialized in this area. The last two recipes in this chapter will introduce Barman.

Understanding and controlling crash recovery

Crash recovery is the PostgreSQL subsystem that saves us, should the server crash or fail as part of a system crash.

It's good to understand a little about it and to do what we can to control it in our favor.

How to do it...

If PostgreSQL crashes, there will be a message in the server log with the severity level set to PANIC. PostgreSQL will immediately restart and attempt to recover using the transaction log or **Write-Ahead Log (WAL)**.

The WAL consists of a series of files written to the pg_wal subdirectory of the PostgreSQL data directory. Each change made to the database is recorded first in WAL, hence the name *write-ahead* log, as a synonym of *transaction log*. When a transaction commits, the default (and safe) behavior is to force the WAL records to disk. Should PostgreSQL crash, the WAL will be replayed, which returns the database to the point of the last committed transaction, and thus ensures the durability of any database changes.

Database changes themselves aren't written to disk at transaction commit. Those changes are written to disk some time later by the background writer on a well-tuned server.

Crash recovery replays the WAL, but from what point does it start to recover? Recovery starts from points in the WAL known as **checkpoints**. The duration of a crash recovery depends on the number of changes in the transaction log since the last checkpoint. A checkpoint is a known safe starting point for recovery, since it guarantees that all the previous changes to the database have already been written to disk.

A checkpoint can become a performance bottleneck on busy database servers because of the number of writes required. We will see a number of ways to fine-tune that, but you must also understand the effect that those tuning options may have on crash recovery.

A checkpoint can be either immediate or scheduled. Immediate checkpoints are triggered by some action of a superuser, such as the CHECKPOINT command. Scheduled checkpoints are decided automatically by PostgreSQL.

Two parameters control the occurrence of scheduled checkpoints. The first is checkpoint_timeout, which is the number of seconds until the next checkpoint. While this parameter is time-based, the second parameter, max_wal_size, influences the amount of WAL data that will be written before a checkpoint is triggered; the actual limit is computed from that parameter, taking into account the fact that WAL files can be deleted after two checkpoints. A checkpoint is called whenever either of these two limits is reached.

It's tempting to banish checkpoints as much as possible by setting the following parameters:

```
max_wal_size = 20GB
checkpoint_timeout = 3600
```

However, if you do this, you should give some thought to how long crash recovery will take if you do, and whether you want that; you must consider as well how many changes will accumulate before the next checkpoint—and more importantly how much I/O those changes will generate.

Also, you should make sure that the `pg_wal` directory is mounted on disks with enough disk space. By default, `max_wal_size` is set to 1 GB. The amount of disk space required by `pg_wal` might also be influenced by:

- Unexpected spikes in workload
- Failures in continuous archiving (see `archive_command` in the *Hot physical backup and continuous archiving* section)
- The `wal_keep_segments` setting (you will need *16 MB x wal_keep_segments of space*)

In contrast with `max_wal_size`, with `min_wal_size` you can control the minimum size allotted to WAL storage, and allow PostgreSQL to recycle existing WAL files instead of removing them.

How it works...

Recovery continues until the end of the transaction log. WAL data is being written continually, so there is no defined end point; it is literally the last correct record. Each WAL record is individually CRC-checked so that we know whether a record is complete and valid before trying to process it. Each record contains a pointer to the previous record, so we can tell that the record forms a valid link in the chain of actions recorded in the WAL. As a result of that, recovery always ends with some kind of error in reading the next WAL record. That is normal and means *the next record does not exist (yet)*.

Recovery performance can be very fast, though its speed does depend on the actions being recovered. The best way to test recovery performance is to set up a standby replication server, described in `Chapter 12`, *Replication and Upgrades*, because it is actually implemented as a variant of crash recovery.

There's more...

It's possible for a problem to be caused by replaying the transaction log, so that the database server will fail to start.

Some people's response to this is to use a utility named `pg_resetwal`, which removes the current transaction log files and tidies up after that operation has taken place.

The `pg_resetwal` utility destroys data changes, and that means data loss. If you do decide to run that utility, make sure you take a backup of the `pg_wal` directory first. Our advice is to seek immediate assistance rather than do this. You don't know for certain that doing this will fix a problem, though once you've done it, you will have difficulty going back.

Planning backups

This recipe is all about thinking ahead and planning. If you're reading this recipe before you take a backup, well done!

The key thing to understand is that you should plan your recovery, not your backup. The type of backup you take influences the type of recovery that is possible, so you must give some thought to what you are trying to achieve beforehand.

If you want to plan your recovery, then you need to consider the different types of failure that can occur. What type of recovery do you wish to perform?

You need to consider the following main aspects:

- Full or partial database?
- Everything or just object definitions?
- **Point-in-time recovery (PITR)**
- Restore performance

We need to look at the characteristics of the utilities to understand what our backup and recovery options are. It's often beneficial to have multiple types of backup to cover the different types of failure possible.

Your main backup options are the following:

- Logical backup, using `pg_dump`
- Physical backup, which is a filesystem backup

The `pg_dump` utility comes in two main flavors—`pg_dump` and `pg_dumpall`.
The `pg_dump` utility has a `-F` option for producing backups in various file formats. The file format is very important when it comes to restoring from backup, so you need to pay close attention to it.

As far as physical backup is concerned, in this chapter we focus on file system backup using `pg_start_backup()` and `pg_stop_backup()`. However, it is important to note that PostgreSQL has its own built-in application for physical base backups, `pg_basebackup`, which relies on the native streaming replication protocol. As authors, in order to distribute the content more evenly, we have decided to cover `pg_basebackup` and streaming replication in the next chapter, that is, `Chapter 12`, *Replication and Upgrades*.

How to do it...

The following table shows the features available, depending on the backup technique selected. The details of these techniques are covered in the remaining recipes in this chapter:

	SQL dump to an archive file: `pg_dump -F c`	**SQL dump to a script file:** `pg_dump -F p` **or** `pg_dumpall`	**Filesystem backup using:** `pg_start_backup`
Backup type	Logical	Logical	Physical
Recover to point in time	No	No	Yes
Zero data loss	No	No	Yes (see note 6)
Back up all databases	One at a time	Yes (`pg_dumpall`)	Yes
All databases backed up at the same time	No	No	Yes
Selective backup	Yes	Yes	No (see note 2)
Incremental backup	No	No	Possible (see note 3)
Selective restore	Yes	Possible (see note 1)	No (see note 4)
`DROP TABLE` recovery	Yes	Yes	Possible (see note 4)

Compressed backup files	Yes	Yes	Yes
Backup in multiple files	No	No	Yes
	SQL dump to an archive file: pg_dump -F c	**SQL dump to a script file:** pg_dump -F p or pg_dumpall	**Filesystem backup using:** pg_start_backup
Parallel backup possible	No	No	Yes
Parallel restore possible	Yes	No	Yes
Restore to later release	Yes	Yes	No
Standalone backup	Yes	Yes	Yes (see note 6)
Allows DDL during backup	No	No	Yes

The following notes were referenced in the preceding table:

1. If you've generated a script with pg_dump or pg_dumpall and need to restore just a single object, then you will need to go deeper. You will need to write a Perl script (or similar) to read the file and extract the parts you want. This is messy and time-consuming, but probably faster than restoring the whole thing to a second server and then extracting just the parts you need with another pg_dump.
2. Selective backup with a physical backup is possible, but will cause problems later when you try to restore.
3. See the *Incremental/differential backup and restore* recipe.
4. Selective restore with a physical backup isn't possible with the currently supplied utilities. See the *Recovery of a dropped/damaged table* recipe for partial recovery.
5. See the *Standalone hot physical database backup* recipe.
6. See the *Hot physical backups with Barman* recipe. Barman 2 fully supports synchronous WAL streaming, allowing you to achieve **recovery point objective (RPO)** equal to 0, meaning *zero data loss*.

Hot logical backups of one database

Logical backup makes a copy of the data in the database by dumping the content of each table as well as object definitions for that same database (such as schemas, tables, indexes, views, privileges, triggers, constraints, and so on).

How to do it...

The command to do this is simple. The following is an example using a database called pgbench:

```
pg_dump -F c pgbench > dumpfile
```

Or, you can use the following command:

```
pg_dump -F c -f dumpfile pgbench
```

You can also do this through **pgAdmin 4**, as shown in the following screenshot:

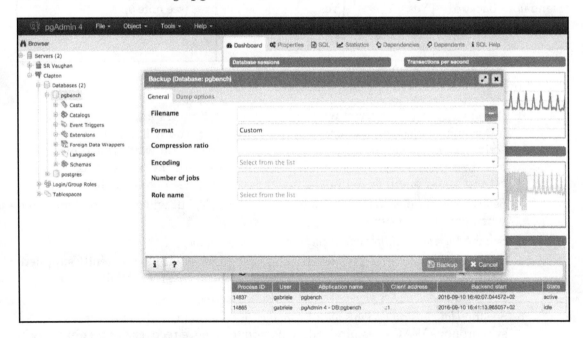

How it works...

The `pg_dump` utility produces a single output file. This output file can use the `split` command to separate the file into multiple pieces, if required.

The `pg_dump` archive file, also known as the **custom format**, is lightly compressed by default. Compression can be removed or made more aggressive.

Even though, by default, `pg_dump` writes an SQL script directly to standard output, it is recommended to use the archive file instead, by enabling the custom format through the "`-F c`" option. As covered later in the chapter, backing up in the form of archive files gives you more flexibility and versatility when restoring. Archive files must be used with a tool called `pg_restore`.

The `pg_dump` utility runs by executing SQL statements against the database to unload data. When PostgreSQL runs an SQL statement, we take a *snapshot* of transactions that are currently running, which freezes our viewpoint of the database. The `pg_dump` utility can take a parallel dump of a single database using the **snapshot export** feature.

We can't (yet) share that snapshot across sessions connected to more than one database, so we cannot run an exactly consistent `pg_dump` in parallel across multiple databases.

The time of the snapshot is the only moment we can recover to—we can't recover to a time either before or after. Note that the snapshot time is the start of the backup, not the end.

When `pg_dump` runs, it holds the very lowest kind of lock on the tables being dumped. Those are designed to prevent DDL from running against the tables while the dump takes place. If a dump is run at the point at which other DDLs are already running, then the dump will sit and wait. If you want to limit the waiting time, you can do so by setting the `--lock-wait-timeout` option.

Since `pg_dump` runs SQL queries to extract data, it will have some performance impact. This must be taken into account when executing on a live server.

The `pg_dump` utility allows you to take a selective backup of tables. The `-t` option also allows you to specify views and sequences. There's no way to dump other object types individually using `pg_dump`. You can use some supplied functions to extract individual snippets of information from the catalog.

More details on these functions are available
at https://www.postgresql.org/docs/current/static/functions-info.
html#FUNCTIONS-INFO-CATALOG-TABLE

The pg_dump utility works against earlier releases of PostgreSQL, so it can be used to migrate data between releases.

When migrating your database from an earlier version, it is generally recommended to use pg_dump of the same version of the target PostgreSQL. For example, if you are migrating a PostgreSQL 9.3 database to PostgreSQL 10, you should use pg_dump v10 to remotely connect to the 9.3 server and back up the database.

As far as extensions are concerned, pg_dump is aware of any objects (namely tables and functions) that have been installed as part of an additional package, such as PostGIS or Slony. Thanks to that, they can be recreated by issuing appropriate CREATE EXTENSION commands instead of dumping and restoring them together with the other database objects. Extension support removes such difficulties when restoring from a logical backup, maintaining the list of additional tables that have been created as part of the software installation process. Look at the *Managing installed extensions* recipe in Chapter 3, *Configuration,* for more details.

There's more...

What time was the pg_dump taken? The snapshot for a pg_dump is taken at the beginning of a backup. The file modification time will tell you when the dump finished. The dump is consistent at the time of the snapshot, so you may need to know that time.

If you are making a script dump, you can do a verbose dump, as follows:

```
pg_dump -v
```

This then adds the time to the top of the script. Custom dumps store the start time as well, and that can be accessed using the following:

```
pg_restore --schema-only -v dumpfile 2>/dev/null | head | grep Started
-- Started on 2017-06-03 09:05:46 BST
```

See also

Note that pg_dump does not dump roles (such as users and groups) and tablespaces. Those two are only dumped by pg_dumpall; see the following recipes for more detailed descriptions.

Hot logical backups of all databases

If you have more than one database in your PostgreSQL server, you may want to take a logical backup of all the databases at the same time.

How to do it...

Our recommendation is that you do exactly what you did for one database to each database in your cluster.

You can run individual dumps in parallel if you want to speed things up.

Once this is complete, dump the global information also using the following:

```
pg_dumpall -g
```

How it works...

To back up all databases, you may be told you need to use the pg_dumpall utility. The following are four good reasons why you shouldn't do that:

- If you use pg_dumpall the only output produced will be in a script file. Script files can't benefit from all the features of archive files, such as parallel and selective restore of pg_restore. By making your backup in this way, you will immediately deprive yourself of flexibility and versatility at restore time.
- The pg_dumpall utility produces dumps of each database one after another. This means that pg_dumpall is slower than running multiple pg_dump tasks in parallel, one against each database.

- The dumps of individual databases are not consistent to a particular point in time. As we pointed out in a previous recipe, if you start the dump at 04:00 and it ends at 07:00, then you cannot be sure exactly what time the dump relates to; it could be anytime between 04:00 and 07:00.
- Options for `pg_dumpall` and `pg_dump` are similar in many ways. `pg_dump` has more options and therefore gives you more flexibility.

See also

If you are taking a logical backup of all your databases for disaster recovery purposes, you should look at *hot physical backup* options instead.

Backups of database object definitions

Sometimes, it's useful to get a dump of the object definitions that make up a database. This is useful for comparing what's in the database against the definitions in a data-or object-modeling tool. It's also useful to make sure you can recreate objects in the correct schema, tablespace, and database with the correct ownership and permissions.

How to do it...

The basic command to dump the definitions only for every database of your PostgreSQL instance is the following:

```
pg_dumpall --schema-only > myscriptdump.sql
```

This includes all objects, including roles, tablespaces, databases, schemas, tables, indexes, triggers, constraints, views, functions, ownerships, and privileges.

If you want to dump PostgreSQL role definitions, use this command:

```
pg_dumpall --roles-only > myroles.sql
```

If you want to dump PostgreSQL tablespace definitions, use the following:

```
pg_dumpall --tablespaces-only > mytablespaces.sql
```

If you want to dump both roles and tablespaces, use this command:

```
pg_dumpall --globals-only > myglobals.sql
```

The output is a human-readable script file that can be re-executed to recreate each of the databases.

 The short form for the `--globals-only` option is `-g`, which we have already seen in a previous recipe, *Hot logical backups of all databases*. Similar abbreviations exist for `--schema-only` (`-s`), `--tablespaces-only` (`-t`), and `--roles-only` (`-r`).

There's more...

In PostgreSQL, the word *schema* is also used to organize a set of related objects of a database in a logical container, similar to a directory. It is also known as a *namespace*. Be careful that you don't confuse what is happening here. The `--schema-only` option makes a backup of the *database schema*, that is, the definitions of all objects in the database (and in all namespaces). To make a backup of the data and definitions in just one namespace and one database, use `pg_dump` with the `-n` option. To make a backup of only the definitions, in just one namespace and one database, use `pg_dump` with both `-n` and `--schema-only` together.

You can also take advantage of a previously generated archive file (see *Hot logical backups of one database*) and generate a script file using `pg_restore`, as follows:

```
pg_restore --schema-only mydumpfile > myscriptdump.sql
```

Standalone hot physical database backup

Hot physical backup is an important capability for databases.

Physical backup allows us to get a completely consistent view of the changes to all databases at once. Physical backup also allows us to back up even while DDL changes are being executed on the database. Apart from resource constraints, there is no additional overhead or locking with this approach.

Physical backup procedures used to be slightly more complex than logical backup procedures, but in version 10 some defaults have been changed, making them easier; after these changes, making a backup with `pg_basebackup` has become very easy, even with default settings.

As specified in the introduction to this chapter, taking a backup with `pg_basebackup` is covered in `Chapter 12`, *Replication and Upgrades*, and in this chapter we will focus on the variant of the filesystem backup that uses `pg_start_backup()` and `pg_stop_backup()`, which is the only way to overcome some of the limitations of `pg_basebackup`, for instance if you want an incremental backup, or a parallel backup. For similar reasons, this method is also supported by many advanced backup solutions, such as Barman.

So, let's start with a simple procedure to produce a standalone backup.

Getting ready

The following steps assume that a number of environment variables have been set, which are as follows:

- `$PGDATA` is the path to the PostgreSQL data directory, ending with /
- All required PostgreSQL connection parameters have been set

These assumptions are not strictly required, but they make the whole procedure simpler and more readable, because we can avoid adding lots of command line options to specify the data directory or any connection detail every time we connect to the database.

The initial procedure is step 1 onwards. If you are running subsequent backups, start from step 3.

How to do it...

The steps are as follows:

1. Create a new backup directory as a sibling of `$PGDATA`, if it is not already present, as follows:

   ```
   cd $PGDATA
   mkdir ../standalone
   ```

2. Create the `archive` directory as follows:

   ```
   mkdir ../standalone/archive
   ```

3. Start archiving with the following command:

```
pg_receivewal -D ../standalone/archive/
```

This command will not return, because `pg_receivewal` will run until interrupted. So you must open a new terminal session to perform the next steps, starting with step 4.

We describe first how to configure streaming archiving (steps 2 and 3); for file-based archiving follow the alternate steps *2a* and *3a* instead.

- 2a: Set an `archive_command`. In `postgresql.conf` you will need to add the following lines and restart the server, or just confirm that they are present:

  ```
  archive_mode  =  on
  archive_command = 'test ! -f
  ../standalone/archiving_active ||
  cp -i %p ../standalone/archive/%f'
  ```

  The last setting is only split into two lines for typesetting reasons; in `postgresql.conf`, you must keep it in a single line.

  You must also check that `wal_level` is set to either `replica` or `logical`, which is normally true as `replica` is the default setting.

- 3a: Start archiving, as follows:

  ```
  cd $PGDATA
  mkdir ../standalone/archive
  touch ../standalone/archiving_active
  ```

Irrespective of whether you have chosen streaming archiving, or file-based archiving, you can now proceed with step 4:

4. Define the name of the backup file. The following example includes time information in the file name:

```
BACKUP_FILENAME=$(date '+%Y%m%d%H%M').tar
```

5. Start the backup, as follows:

```
psql -c "select pg_start_backup('standalone')"
```

This step could take a while, because PostgreSQL performs a checkpoint before returning, to ensure that the data files copied in the next step include all the latest data changes. See the recipe *Understanding and controlling crash recovery* earlier in this chapter for more details about checkpoints.

6. Take a base backup-copy the data files (excluding the content of the pg_wal directory), using this command:

```
tar -cv --exclude="pg_wal/*" \
-f ../standalone/$BACKUP_FILENAME *
```

7. Stop the backup, as follows:

```
psql -c "select pg_stop_backup(), current_timestamp"
```

8. If you have followed preceding steps 2 and 3 (for example, if you are using streaming archiving), stop archiving by hitting *CTRL + C* in the terminal session where pg_receivewal is running:

- 8a: Alternatively, if you have chosen steps *2a* and *3a* above instead (for example, file-based archiving), enter the standalone directory and stop archiving, as follows:

```
rm ../standalone/archiving_active
```

9. Add the archived files to the standalone backup, as follows:

```
cd ../standalone
tar -rf $BACKUP_FILENAME archive
```

10. Write a recovery.conf file with which to recover:

```
echo "restore_command = 'cp archive/%f %p'" > recovery.conf
echo "recovery_end_command = 'rm -R archive' " >> recovery.conf
```

11. Add the recovery.conf to the tar archive, as follows:

```
tar -rf $BACKUP_FILENAME recovery.conf
```

12. Clean up:

```
rm -rf archive recovery.conf
```

13. Store $BACKUP_FILENAME somewhere safe. A safe place is definitely not on the same server.

This procedure ends with a file named $BACKUP_FILENAME in the standalone directory. It is imperative to remember to copy it somewhere safe. This file contains everything that you need to recover, including a recovery parameter file.

How it works...

The backup produced by the preceding procedure only allows you to restore to a single point in time. That point is the time of the pg_stop_backup() function.

A physical backup takes a copy of all files in the database (step 6—the *base backup*). That alone is not sufficient as a backup and you need the other steps as well. A simple copy of the database produces a time-inconsistent copy of the database files. To make the backup time consistent, we need to add all the changes that took place from the start to the end of the backup. That's why we have steps 5 and 7 to bracket our backup step.

In technical terms, steps 5 and 7 take advantage of the API that controls exclusive backups, meaning that there can only be one physical backup at a time and it has to be performed on a master server.

PostgreSQL supports non-exclusive backups as well, allowing users to perform pg_start_backup() and pg_stop_backup() functions on a read-only standby server. To make a backup non-exclusive, just add the parameter exclusive := false to those functions. However, programming backup scripts for the non-exclusive backup method is more complex and it is not covered in this recipe.

The changes made are put in the standalone/archive directory as a set of archived transaction log or WAL files. Steps 2 and 3 start streaming archiving, while the alternate steps, 2a and 3a, set the parameters that copy the files to the archive and start file-based archiving. Note that changing archive_mode requires us to restart the database server, so we use a well-known trick to avoid restarting while switching archiving on and off—archive_command is conditional upon the existence of a file named archiving_active, whose presence enables or disables the archiving process.

Note that these are just two of the possible ways to configure archiving, so PostgreSQL doesn't always need to work this way. Steps 3 and 8 enable and disable archiving respectively, so we only store copies of the WAL files created during the period of the backup. Thus, steps 1 and 2 are setup and steps 3 to 9 are where the backup happens. Step 10 onwards is gift wrapping, so that the backup script ends with everything in one neat file and proper cleanup operations take place.

Step 9 appends the WAL files to the backup file so that it is just one file.

Steps 10 and 11 add a `recovery.conf` file with its parameters set up so that there are no manual steps when we recover from this backup. This is explained in detail in the *Recovery of all databases* recipe.

In case your `PGDATA` does not contain configuration files, such as `postgresql.conf` and `pg_hba.conf`, you might have to manually copy them before performing a recovery. Remember that standard Debian and Ubuntu installations keep configuration files outside `PGDATA`, specifically under `/etc/postgresql`.

The important thing to understand in this recipe is that we need both the base backup and the appropriate archived WAL files to allow us to recover. Without both of these, we have nothing. Most of the steps are designed to ensure that we really will have the appropriate WAL files in all cases.

There's more...

One advantage of file-based WAL archiving is that it works in a *push* mode, without requiring inbound access to the database server. On the other hand, streaming WAL archiving has the advantage of transferring WAL as soon as it is produced, without waiting that the 16 MB WAL segment is completed, which usually results in little or no data loss even in the event of a disaster.

Summing up, neither choice is superior to the other one, so we opted for documenting both. PostgreSQL ships a command-line utility called `pg_basebackup`, which uses the streaming replication infrastructure to carry out steps 4 to 6, as reported previously.

As an alternative, it is simpler than using `rsync` and issuing `pg_start_backup()` and `pg_stop_backup()` manually, but it's not a complete replacement because it has some limitations and restrictions.

If you want to make your life easier, you can rely on software that is specialized in backup and recovery. In this book we will cover a software that we at 2ndQuadrant have written and that has become very popular among PostgreSQL users: Barman. This open source tool is covered in two recipes—*Hot physical backups with Barman* and *Recovery with Barman*.

See also

It's common to use continuous archiving when using the physical backup technique because this allows you to recover to any point in time, should you need that.

Hot physical backup and continuous archiving

This recipe describes how to set up a hot physical backup with a continuous archiving mechanism. The purpose of continuous archiving is to allow us to recover to any point in time after the completion of the backup.

Manually performing each step of this procedure is a great way to gain a clear understanding of PostgreSQL's backup and restore infrastructure. However, to reduce the chances of human errors, it is best practice to avoid reliance on complex activities that must be performed by a human operator.

Procedures such as taking a hot physical backup or restoring it up to a given point in time can be performed using specialized third-party tools such as:

- **Barman**: http://www.pgbarman.org/
- **OmniPITR**: https://github.com/omniti-labs/omnipitr
- **PgBackRest**: http://www.pgbackrest.org/
- **PgHoard**: https://github.com/ohmu/pghoard
- **WAL-E**: https://github.com/wal-e/wal-e

Being the creators and developers of Barman, our preference goes with this tool. However, we strongly advise that you to look at each of the aforementioned tools and make your own decision based on your needs. If you are interested in Barman, you can read two recipes later in this chapter—*Hot physical backups with Barman,* and *Recovery with Barman.*

Getting ready

This recipe builds upon the previous recipe, *Standalone hot physical database backup*. You should read that before following this recipe.

Before starting, you need to decide a few things:

- Where will you store the WAL files (known as the archive)?
- How will you send WAL files to the archive?
- Where will you store your base backups?
- How will you take base backups?
- How many backups (also known as retention policies) will you keep?
- What is your policy for maintaining the archive?

These are hard questions to answer immediately. So, we will give a practical example as a way of explaining how this works, and then let you decide how you would like it to operate.

How to do it...

The rest of this recipe assumes the following answers to the key questions:

- The archive is a directory, such as `/backups/archive`, on a remote server for disaster recovery named $DRNODE
- We send WAL files to the archive using `rsync`; however, WAL streaming can also be used, by changing the recipe in a way similar to the previous one
- Base backups are also stored on $DRNODE, in the `/backups/base` directory
- Base backups are made using `rsync`

The following steps assume that a number of environment variables have been set, which are as follows:

- `$PGDATA` is the path to the PostgreSQL data directory, ending with /
- `$DRNODE` is the name of the remote server
- `$BACKUP_NAME` is an identifier for the backup
- All the required PostgreSQL connection parameters have been set

We also assume that the Postgres user can connect via SSH to the backup server from the server where PostgreSQL is running, without having to type a passphrase. This standard procedure is described in detail in several places, including Barman's documentation at `http://docs.pgbarman.org/`.

The procedure is as follows:

1. Create the archive and backup directories on a backup server.
2. Set an `archive_command`. In `postgresql.conf`, you will need to add the following lines and restart the server, or just confirm that they are present:

   ```
   archive_mode = on
   archive_command = 'rsync -a %p $DRNODE:/archive/%f'
   ```

3. Define the name of the backup, like this example:

   ```
   BACKUP_NAME=$(date '+%Y%m%d%H%M')
   ```

4. Start the backup, as follows:

   ```
   psql -c "select pg_start_backup('$BACKUP_NAME')"
   ```

5. Copy the data files (excluding the content of the `pg_wal` directory), like this:

   ```
   rsync -cva --inplace -exclude='pg_wal/*' \
   ${PGDATA}/      $DRNODE:/backups/base/$BACKUP_NAME/
   ```

6. Stop the backup, as follows:

   ```
   psql -c "select pg_stop_backup(), current_timestamp"
   ```

It's also good practice to put a `README.backup` file in the data directory prior to the backup so that it forms part of the set of files that make up the base backup. This should say something intelligent about the location of the archive, including any identification numbers, names, and so on.

Notice that we didn't put a `recovery.conf` in the backup this time. That's because we're assuming we want flexibility at the time of recovery, rather than a gift-wrapped solution. The reason for that is that we don't know when, where, or how we will be recovering, nor do we need to make that decision yet.

How it works...

The key point here is that we must have both the base backup and the archive in order to recover. Where you put them is entirely up to you. You can use any filesystem backup technology and/or filesystem backup management system to do this.

Many backup management systems have claimed that they have a PostgreSQL interface or plugin, but most of the time they only support logical backups. However, there's no need for them to officially support PostgreSQL; there is no any *Runs on PostgreSQL* badge or certification required. If you can copy files, then you can run the preceding processes to keep your database safe.

In the event the network or backup server goes down, then the command will begin to fail. When the `archive_command` fails, it will repeatedly retry until it succeeds.

You can monitor the status of the `archive_command` and get current statistics through the `pg_stat_archiver` view in the catalog.

PostgreSQL does not remove WAL files from `pg_wal` directory until they have been successfully archived, so the end result is that your `pg_wal` directory fills up. It's a good idea to have an `archive_command` that reacts better to that condition, though this is left as an improvement for the sysadmin. A typical action is to make it an emergency call-out so that we can resolve the problem manually. Automatic resolution is difficult to get right, as this condition is one for which it is hard to test.

While continuously archiving, we will generate a considerable number of WAL files. If `archive_timeout` is set to 30 seconds, we will generate a minimum of $2*60*24 = 2,880$ files per day, with each being 16 MB in size. This amounts to a total volume of 46 GB per day (minimum).

With a reasonable transaction rate, a database server might generate 100 GB of archive data per day. Use this as a rough figure for calculations until you get actual measurements. Of course, the rate could be much higher, with rates of 1 TB per day or higher being possible.

Clearly, we would only want to store WAL files that are useful for backup, so when we decide that we no longer wish to keep a backup, we will also want to remove files from the archive. In each base backup, you will find a file called `backup_label`. The earliest WAL file required by a physical backup is the filename mentioned in the first line of the `backup_label` file. We can use a `contrib` module called `pg_archive_cleanup` to remove any WAL files created earlier than the earliest file.

Recovery of all databases

Recovery of a complete database server, including all of its databases, is an important feature. This recipe covers how to execute a recovery in the simplest way possible.

Some complexities are discussed here, though most are covered in later recipes.

Getting ready

Find a suitable server on which to perform the restore.

Before you recover onto a live server, always take another backup. Whatever problem you thought you had could get worse if you aren't prepared.

How to do it...

Here, we'll provide four distinct examples, depending on what type of backup was taken.

Logical – from custom dump taken with pg_dump -F c

The procedure is as follows:

1. Restore of all databases means simply restoring each individual database from each dump you took. Confirm that you have the correct backup before you restore:

```
pg_restore --schema-only -v dumpfile | head | grep Started
```

2. Reload global objects from the script file, as follows:

```
psql -f myglobals.sql
```

3. Reload all databases. Create the databases using parallel tasks to speed things up. This can be executed remotely without the need to transfer a dumpfile between systems. Note that there is a separate dumpfile for each database:

```
pg_restore -C -d postgres -j 4 dumpfile
```

Logical – from the script dump created by pg_dump -F p

As in the previous method, this can be executed remotely without needing to transfer the dumpfile between systems:

1. Confirm that you have the correct backup before you restore. If the following command returns nothing, then it means the file is not timestamped, and you'll have to identify it in a different way:

   ```
   head myscriptdump.sql | grep Started
   ```

2. Reload globals from the script file, as follows:

   ```
   psql -f myglobals.sql
   ```

3. Reload all scripts as follows:

   ```
   psql -f myscriptdump.sql
   ```

Logical – from the script dump created by pg_dumpall

In order to recover a full backup generated by `pg_dumpall`, you need to execute the following steps on a PostgreSQL server that has just been initialized:

1. Confirm that you have the correct backup before you restore. If the following command returns nothing, then it means the file is not timestamped, and you'll have to identify it in a different way:

   ```
   head myscriptdump.sql | grep Started
   ```

2. Reload the script in full:

   ```
   psql -f myscriptdump.sql
   ```

Physical

The steps are as follows:

1. If you've used the Standalone hot physical database backup recipe, then recovery is very easy. Restore the backup file in the target server.
2. Extract the backup file to the new data directory.

3. Confirm that you have the correct backup before you restore:

```
$ cat backup_label
START WAL LOCATION: 0/12000020 (file 000000010000000000000012)
CHECKPOINT LOCATION: 0/12000058
START TIME: 2017-06-03 19:53:23 BST
LABEL: standalone
```

4. Verify that all file permissions and ownerships are correct and links are valid. This should already be the case if you are using the Postgres user ID everywhere, which is recommended.
5. Start the server.

This procedure is so simple because in the *Standalone hot physical database backup* recipe we gift-wrapped everything for you. That also helped you understand that you need both a base backup and the appropriate WAL files.

If you've used other techniques, then you need to step through the tasks to make sure you cover everything required, as follows:

1. Shut down any server running in the data directory.
2. Restore the backup so that any files in the data directory that have matching names are replaced with the version from the backup. (The manual says, *delete all files and then restore the backup*. You could speed up the recovery operation reusing the existing data directory, but unless you are familiar with `rsync` we recommend going by the book. You can look at the source code of Barman for an example, or otherwise simply use it.) Remember that this step can be performed in parallel to speed things up, though it is up to you to script that.
3. Ensure that all file permissions and ownerships are correct and links are valid. This should already be the case if you are using the Postgres user ID everywhere, which is recommended.
4. Remove any files that are in `pg_wal/`. If you've been following our recipes, you'll be able to skip this step because they were never backed up in the first place.
5. Add a `recovery.conf` file and set its file permissions correctly.
6. Start the server.

The only part that requires some thought and checking is selecting which parameters to use for the `recovery.conf` file. There's only one that matters here, and that is the `restore_command`.

The `restore_command` tells us how to restore archived WAL files. It needs to be the command that will be executed to bring back WAL files from the archive.

If you are thinking ahead, there'll be a `README.backup` file for you to read to find out how to set the `restore_command`. If it is not there, then presumably you've got the location of the WAL files you've been saving written down somewhere. Say, for example, that your files are being saved to a directory named `/backups/pg/servername/archive`, owned by the Postgres user.

On a remote server named `backup1`, we would then write all this on one line of the `recovery.conf` file, as follows:

```
restore_command = 'scp backup1:/backups/pg/servername/archive/%f
    %p'
```

How it works...

PostgreSQL is designed to require very minimal information to perform a recovery. We'll try hard to wrap all the details up for you:

- **Logical recovery**: Recreates database objects by executing SQL statements. If performance is an issue, look at the *Improving performance of backup/recovery* recipe.
- **Physical recovery**: Reapplies data changes at the block level, and so tends to be much faster than logical recovery. It requires both a base backup and a set of archived WAL files.

There is a file named `backup_label` in the data directory of the base backup. If you want to know the start and stop WAL locations of the base backup, look for a `.backup` file in the archive.

Recovery then starts to apply changes from the starting WAL location and it must proceed as far as the stop address for the backup to be valid.

After the recovery is complete, the `recovery.conf` file is renamed to `recovery.done` to prevent the server from re-entering recovery.

The server log records each WAL file restored from the archive, so you can check the progress and rate of recovery. You can query the archive to find the name of the latest restored WAL file to allow you to calculate how many files are left to recover.

The `restore_command` should return 0 if a file has been restored and non-zero for cases of failure. Recovery will proceed until there are no more WAL files remaining, so eventually there will be an error recorded in the logs.

If you have lost some of the WAL files, or they are damaged, then recovery will stop at that point. No further changes after that will be applied, and you will likely lose those changes. This would be the time to call your support vendor.

There's more...

You can start and stop the server once recovery has started without any problems. It will not interfere with the recovery.

You can connect to the database server while it is recovering and run queries, if that is useful. This is known as **hot standby** mode, and is discussed in `Chapter 12`, *Replication and Upgrades*.

See also

- Once the recovery reaches the stop address, you can stop it at any point, as discussed in the *Recovery to a point in time* recipe
- The procedure described in this recipe is covered by the command-line utility, Barman, mentioned in the *Hot physical backup and continuous archiving* recipe

Recovery to a point in time

If your database suffers a problem at 3:22 p.m. and your backup was taken at 4:00 a.m. you're probably hoping there is a way to recover the changes made between those two times. What you need is known as **Point-in-Time Recovery (PITR)**.

Regrettably, if you've made a backup with the `pg_dump` utility at 4:00 a.m., then you won't be able to recover to any other time. As a result, the term PITR has become synonymous with the physical backup and restore technique in PostgreSQL.

Getting ready

If you have a backup made with `pg_dump` utility, then give up all hope of using that as a starting point for a PITR. It's a frequently asked question, but the answer is still *no*. The reason it gets asked is exactly why we are pleading with you to plan your backups ahead of time.

First, you need to decide from what point in time you would like to recover. If the answer is *as late as possible*, then you don't need to do a PITR at all, just recover until the end of the logs.

How to do it...

How do you decide to what point to recover? The point where we stop recovery is known as the recovery target. The most straightforward way is to do this based on a timestamp.

In `recovery.conf` file, you can add (or uncomment) a line that says the following, or something similar: `recovery_target_time = '2017-06-01 16:59:14.27452+01'`

Note that you need to be careful to specify the time zone of the target so that it matches the time zone of the server that wrote the log. That might differ from the time zone of the current server, so be sure to double-check them.

After that, you can check the progress during a recovery by running queries in hot standby mode. By default, when hot standby is enabled, the recovered server is paused once the target is reached. You can change this behavior with the `recovery_target_action` option in `recovery.conf` file, as discussed in the *Delaying, pausing, and synchronizing replication* recipe in `Chapter 12`, *Replication and Upgrades*.

How it works...

Recovery works by applying individual WAL records. These correspond to individual block changes, so there are many WAL records for each transaction. The final part of any successful transaction is a commit WAL record, though there are abort records as well. Each transaction completion record has a timestamp that allows us to decide whether or not to stop at that point.

You can also define a recovery target using a transaction ID (xid), though finding out which xid to use is somewhat difficult, and you may need to refer to external records, if they exist.

Another practical way, which rarely applies after an unexpected disaster, is to define a recovery target with a label, formally known as a named restore point. A restore point is created with the `pg_create_restore_point()` function, requiring superuser privileges. For example: you have to perform a critical update of part of the data in your database. As a precaution, before you start the update, you can execute the following query as a superuser:

```
SELECT pg_create_restore_point('before_critical_update');
```

Then use the label `before_critical_update` in the `recovery_target_name` option.

The recovery target is specified in the `recovery.conf` file and cannot change while the server is running. If you want to change the recovery target, you can shut down the server, edit `recovery.conf`, and then restart the server. Be careful, however; if you change the recovery target and recovery is already past the new point, it can lead to errors. If you define a `recovery_target_timestamp` that has already been passed, then the recovery will stop almost immediately, though this will be after the correct stopping point. If you define a `recovery_target_xid` or `recovery_target_name` that has already been passed, then the recovery will just continue until the end of the logs. Restarting a recovery from the beginning using a fresh restore of the base backup is always the safest option.

Once a server completes the recovery, it will assign a new timeline. Once a server is fully available, we can write new changes to the database. Those changes might differ from the changes we made in a previous future history of the database. So, we differentiate between alternate futures using different timelines. If we need to go back and run the recovery again, we can create a new server history using the original or subsequent timelines. The best way to think about this is that it is exactly like a *Sci-fi* novel—you can't change the past, but you can return to an earlier time and take a different action instead. However, you'll need to be careful not to get confused.

There's more...

The pg_dump utility cannot be used as a base backup for a PITR. The reason is that a log replay contains the physical changes to data blocks, not the logical changes based on primary keys. If you reload the pg_dump utility, the data will likely go back into different data blocks, so the changes won't correctly reference the data.

WAL files don't contain enough information to fully reconstruct all the SQL that produced those changes. Later feature additions to PostgreSQL may add the required information to WAL files. It will be very interesting and exciting to follow how logical replication evolves in the future.

See also

PostgreSQL can pause, resume, and stop recovery while the server is up dynamically. This allows you to use the hot standby facility to locate the correct stopping point more easily. You can trick hot standby into stopping recovery, which may help. See the *Delaying, pausing, and synchronizing replication* recipe in Chapter 12, *Replication and Upgrades*, on managing hot standby. This procedure is also covered by the command-line utility Barman, mentioned in the *Hot physical backup and continuous archiving* recipe.

You can use the pg_waldump utility to print the content of WAL files in a human-readable way. This can be very valuable to locate the exact transaction ID, or timestamp, or when a certain change was committed, for instance if we want to stop recovery exactly before that. pg_waldump is part of PostgreSQL and is described here: https://www.postgresql.org/docs/10/static/pgwaldump.html

Recovery of a dropped/damaged table

You may drop or even damage a table in some way. Tables could be damaged for physical reasons, such as disk corruption, or they could also be damaged by running poorly specified UPDATE or DELETE commands, which update too many rows or overwrite critical data.

Recovering from this backup situation is a common request.

How to do it...

The methods differ, depending on the type of backup you have available. If you have multiple types of backup, you have a choice.

Logical - from custom dump taken with pg_dump -F c

If you've taken a logical backup using the `pg_dump` utility in a custom file, then you can simply extract the table you want from the `dumpfile`, like the following:

```
pg_restore -t mydroppedtable dumpfile | psql
```

Alternatively, you can directly connect to the database using `-d`.

The preceding command tries to recreate the table and then load data into it. Note that the `pg_restore -t` option does not dump any of the indexes on the selected table. This means we need a slightly more complex procedure than would first appear, and the procedure needs to vary depending on whether we are repairing a damaged table or putting back a dropped table.

To repair a damaged table, we want to replace the data in the table in a single transaction. There isn't a specific option to do this, so we need to do the following:

1. Dump the data of the table (the `-a` option) to a script file, as follows:

    ```
    pg_restore -a -t mydamagedtable dumpfile >
    mydamagedtable.sql
    ```

2. Edit a script named `repair_mydamagedtable.sql` with the following code:

    ```
    BEGIN;
    TRUNCATE mydamagedtable;
    \i mydamagedtable.sql
    COMMIT;
    ```

3. Then, run it using the following command:

    ```
    psql -f repair_mydamagedtable.sql
    ```

If you've dropped a table then you need to perform these steps:

1. Create a new database in which to work, and name it `restorework`, as follows:

   CREATE DATABASE restorework;

2. Restore the complete schema (`-s` option) to the new database, like this:

   pg_restore -s -d restorework dumpfile

3. Now, dump only the definitions of the dropped table in a new file. It will contain `CREATE TABLE`, indexes, and other constraints and grants. Note that this database has no data in it, so specifying `-s` is optional, as follows:

   pg_dump -t mydroppedtable -s restorework > mydroppedtable.sql

4. Now, recreate the table on the main database:

   psql -f mydroppedtable.sql

5. Now, reload only the data into the `maindb` database:

   pg_restore -t mydroppedtable -a -d maindb dumpfile

If you've got a very large table, then the fourth step can be a problem because it builds indexes as well. If you want, you can manually edit the script in two pieces, one before the load (*preload*) and one after the load (*postload*). There are some ideas for that at the end of this recipe.

Logical – from the script dump

Once you have located the PostgreSQL server on which you will prepare and verify the data to restore (the staging server), you can proceed like this:

1. Reload the script in full on the staging server, as follows:

   psql -f myscriptdump.sql

2. From the recovered database server, dump the table, its data, and all the definitions of the dropped table into a new file:

   pg_dump -t mydroppedtable -F c mydatabase > dumpfile

3. Now, recreate the table in the original server and database, using parallel tasks to speed things up:

```
pg_restore -d mydatabase -j 2 dumpfile
```

 The last step can be executed remotely without having to transfer the dumpfile between systems. Just add connection parameters to pg_restore, as in the following example:

pg_restore -h remotehost -U remoteuser ....

The only way to extract a single table from a script dump without doing all the preceding steps is to write a custom script to read and extract only those parts of the file that you want. This can be complicated because you may need certain SET commands at the top of the file, the table, and data in the middle of the file, and the indexes and constraints on the table are near the end of the file. Writing a custom script can be very complex. The safer route is to follow the recipe we just described.

Physical

To recover a single table from a physical backup, you first need to recreate a PostgreSQL server from scratch, usually in a confined environment. Typically, this server is called the **recovery server**, if dedicated to recovery drills and procedures, or the **staging server**, if used for a broader set of cases including testing. Then you need to proceed as follows:

1. Recover the database server in full, as described in previous recipes on physical recovery, including all databases and all tables. You may wish to stop at a useful point in time, in which case you can look at the *Recovery to a point in time* recipe later in the chapter.
2. From the recovered database server, dump the table, its data, and all the definitions of the dropped table into a new file, as follows:

```
pg_dump -t mydroppedtable -F c mydatabase > dumpfile
```

3. Now, recreate the table in the original server and database using parallel tasks to speed things up. This can be executed remotely without needing to transfer the dumpfile between systems:

```
pg_restore -d mydatabase -j 2 dumpfile
```

How it works...

Restoring a single table from a logical backup is relatively easy, as each logical object is backed up separately from the others, and its data and metadata can be filtered out.

However, a physical backup is composed by a set of binary data files, in a complex storage format that can be interpreted by a PostgreSQL engine.

This means that the only way to extract individual objects from it, at present, is to restore the backup on a new instance, and then make a logical dump as explained in the previous recipe: there's no way to restore a single table from a physical backup in just a single step.

See also

The `pg_dump` and `pg_restore` utilities are able to split the dump into three parts—pre-data, data, and post-data. Both commands support a section option used to specify which section(s) should be dumped or reloaded.

Recovery of a dropped/damaged database

Recovering a complete database is also required sometimes. It's actually a lot easier than recovering a single table. Many users choose to place all their tables in a single database; in that case, this recipe isn't relevant.

How to do it...

The methods differ, depending on the type of backup you have available. If you have multiple types of backup, you have a choice.

Logical – from the custom dump -F c

Recreate the database in the original server using parallel tasks to speed things along. This can be executed remotely without needing to transfer the `dumpfile` between systems, as shown in the following example, where we use the `-j` option to specify four parallel processes:

```
pg_restore -h myhost -d postgres --create -j 4 dumpfile
```

Logical – from the script dump created by pg_dump

Recreate the database in the original server. This can be executed remotely without needing to transfer the dumpfile between systems, as shown here, where we must create the empty database first:

```
createdb -h myhost myfreshdb
psql -h myhost -f myscriptdump.sql myfreshdb
```

Logical – from the script dump created by pg_dumpall

There's no easy way to extract the required tables from a script dump. You need to operate on a separate PostgreSQL server, for recovery or staging purposes, and then:

1. Reload the script in full, as follows:

   ```
   psql -f myscriptdump.sql
   ```

2. Once the restore is complete, you can dump the tables in the database by following the *Hot logical backups of one database* recipe.

3. Now, recreate the database on the original server as described for logical dumps earlier in this recipe.

Physical

To recover a single database from a physical backup, you need to work on a separate PostgreSQL server (for recovery or staging purposes) and then you must:

1. Recover the database server in full, as described in the previous recipes on physical recovery, including all databases and all tables. You may wish to stop at a useful point in time, in which case you can look at the *Recovery to a point in time* recipe, earlier in the chapter.

2. Once the restore is complete, you can dump the tables in the database by following the *Hot logical backups of one database* recipe.

3. Now, recreate the database on the original server as described for logical dumps earlier in this recipe.

Improving performance of backup/recovery

Performance is often a concern in any medium-sized or large database.

Backup performance is often a delicate issue, because resource usage may need to be limited to remain within certain boundaries. There may also be a restriction on the maximum runtime for the backup, for example, a backup that runs every Sunday.

Again, restore performance may be more important than backup performance, even if backup is the more obvious concern.

Getting ready

If performance is a concern or is likely to be, then you should read the *Planning backups* recipe first.

How to do it...

Backup and restore performance can be improved in different ways, depending on the backup type:

- **Physical backup**: Improving the performance of a physical backup can be done by performing the backup in parallel and copying the files using more than one task. The more tasks you use, the more it will impact the current system. When backing up, you can skip certain files. You won't need the following:
  - Any files placed in the data directory by DBA that shouldn't actually be there
  - Any files in `pg_wal`
  - Any old server log files in `pg_log` (even the current one)

  Remember, it's safer not to try to exclude files at all because, if you miss something critical, you may end up with data loss. Also remember that your backup speed may be bottlenecked by your disks or your network. Some larger systems have dedicated networks in place, solely for backups.

- **Logical backup**: As explained in a previous recipe, if you want to back up all databases in a database server, then you should use multiple `pg_dump` tasks running in parallel. You may want to increase the dump speed of a `pg_dump` task, but there really isn't an easy way of doing that right now. If you're using compression, look at the *There's more...* at the end of this recipe.
- **Physical restore**: Just as with physical backup, it's possible for us to put everything back quicker if we use parallel copy, which is able to speed things up by automatically reusing existing files.
- **Logical restore**: Whether you use `psql` or `pg_restore`, you can speed up the program by assigning `maintenance_work_mem = 128MB` or more, either in `postgresql.conf` or on the user that will run the restore. If neither of those ways is easily possible, you can specify the option using the `PGOPTIONS` environment variable, as follows:

```
export PGOPTIONS ="-c work_mem = 128000"
```

This will then be used to set that option value for subsequent connections.

If you are running archiving or streaming replication, then transaction log writes may become a problem. This can be mitigated by increasing the size of the WAL buffer and making checkpoints less frequent for the duration of the recovery operation. Set `wal_buffers` between 16 MB and 64 MB, and set `max_wal_size` to a large value such as 20 GB so that it has room to breathe.

If you aren't running archiving or streaming replication, or you've turned it off during the restore, then you'll be able to minimize the amount of transaction log writes. In that case, you may wish to use the single-transaction option, as that will also help improve performance.

If a `pg_dump` was made using -F c (custom format), then we can restore in parallel, as follows:

```
pg_restore -j NumJobs
```

You'll have to be careful about how you select the degree of parallelism to use. A good starting point is the number of CPUs of the server. Be very careful that you don't overflow the available memory when using parallel restore. Each job will use memory up to the value of `maintenance_work_mem`, so the whole restore could begin swapping when it hits larger indexes later in the restore. Plan the size of `shared_buffers` and `maintenance_work_mem` according to the number of jobs specified.

Whatever you do, make sure you run ANALYZE afterwards on every object that was created. This will happen automatically if autovacuum is enabled. It often helps to disable autovacuum completely while running a large restore, so double-check that you have it switched on again after the restore. The consequence of skipping this step will be extremely poor performance when you start your application again, which can easily make everybody panic.

How it works...

A physical backup and restore is completely up to you. Copy those files as fast as you like, and in any way you like. Put them back in the same way or a different way.

Logical backup and restore involves moving data out of and into the database. That's typically going to be slower than physical backup and restore. Particularly with a restore, rebuilding indexes and constraints takes time, even when run in parallel. Plan ahead and measure the performance of your backup and restore techniques so that you have a chance when you need your database back in a hurry.

There's more...

Compressing backups is often considered as a way to reduce the size of the backup for storage. Even mild compression can use large amounts of CPU. In some cases, this might offset network transfer costs, so there isn't any hard rule as to whether compression is always good.

Compression for WAL files from physical backups is a common practice. Physical backups can be compressed in various ways, depending on the exact backup mechanism used. By default, the custom dump format for logical backups will be compressed. Even when compressed, the objects can be accessed individually if required.

Using --compress with script dumps will result in a compressed text file, just as if you had dumped the file and then compressed it. Access to individual tables is not possible.

Using multiple processes is known as pipeline parallelism. If you're using physical backup, then you can copy the data in multiple streams, which also allows you to take advantage of parallel compression/decompression.

See also

If taking a backup is an expensive operation, then a way around that is to take the backup from a replica instead, which offloads the cost of the backup operation away from the master. Look at the recipes in `Chapter 12`, *Replication and Upgrades*, to see how to set up a replica.

Incremental/differential backup and restore

If you have performance problems with a backup of a large PostgreSQL database, then you may consider incremental or differential backups.

An incremental backup is a backup of all files that have changed since the last backup, either incremental or full. In order to restore a given incremental backup, you must restore the full backup and then all the incremental backups in between.

A differential backup is a backup of all individual changes since the last full backup. In order to restore a differential backup you need only that backup and the full backup it refers to.

How to do it...

To perform a differential physical backup, you can use `rsync` to compare the existing files against the previous full backup, and then overwrite only the changed data blocks. It's a bad plan to overwrite your last backup because, if the new backup fails, you are left without backups. Therefore, keep two or more copies. An example backup schedule can be as follows:

Day of the week	Backup set 1	Backup set 2
Sunday	New full backup to set 1	New full backup to set 2
Monday	Differential to set 1	Differential to set 2
Tuesday	Differential to set 1	Differential to set 2

Wednesday	Differential to set 1	Differential to set 2
Thursday	Differential to set 1	Differential to set 2
Friday	Differential to set 1	Differential to set 2
Saturday	Differential to set 1	Differential to set 2

You should keep at least two full backup sets.

Many large databases have tables that are insert-only. In that case, it's easy to store parts of those tables. If the tables are partitioned by insertion date, creation date, or a similar field, it makes our task much simpler. Either way, you're still going to need a good way of recording which data is where in your backup.

In general, there's no easy way to run a differential backup using pg_dump.

How it works...

PostgreSQL doesn't explicitly keep track of the last changed date or similar information for a file or table. PostgreSQL tables are held as files, so you should be able to rely on the modification time (mtime) of the files on the filesystem.

Another problem with this approach is that filesystem timestamps might not have a resolution that is sufficiently granular to separate all changes. This means that some additional verification, such as computing a checksum, is required to confirm that two files with the same mtime are indeed identical. If, for this or some other reason, you don't trust mtime, or it has been disabled, then incremental and differential backups are not for you.

The pg_dump utility doesn't allow WHERE clauses to be specified, so even if you add your own columns to track last_changed_date, you'll still need to manually perform that somehow.

There's more...

The article at http://en.wikipedia.org/wiki/Backup_rotation_scheme gives further useful information.

When thinking about incremental backups, you should note that replication techniques work by continually applying changes to a full backup. This could be considered a technique for an incremental updated backup, also known as an *incremental forever* backup strategy. The changes are applied ahead of time so that you can restore easily and quickly. You should still take a backup, but you can take it from the replication standby instead.

It's possible to write a utility that takes a differential backup of data blocks. You can read each data block and check the block's **Log Sequence Number** (**LSN**) to see whether it has changed in comparison to a previous copy. This is similar to the approach followed by pgBackRest.

In the *Hot physical backup and continuous archiving* recipe, we discussed using third-party backup and recovery software. All the tools we mentioned support compression of WAL files by invoking popular general-purpose compression utilities such as bzip2, gzip and lzh directly on WAL files. This is safe and does not increase the actual risk of data loss. Such utilities have been extensively used for many years, and all serious bugs have been ironed out.

The pg_rman and pgBackRest utilities can also read changed data pages and interpret their contents, for instance to compress them using detailed knowledge of the internals of PostgreSQL's data page format, or for deciding whether to include the page in an incremental/differential backup. Any bugs that exist there could cause data loss in your backups, and issues with third-party tools aren't resolved by the main PostgreSQL project. This is why we personally advise against using third party software that operates on individual data pages without a formal support contract. Various companies support this; ask them.

In order to avoid taking those risks, the Barman utility follows the opposite approach of not handling directly the contents of each PostgreSQL data page, choosing instead to delegate the file transfer logic to other well-known tools such as rsync or pg_basebackup.

Hot physical backups with Barman

The main reason we came up with the idea of starting a new open source project for disaster recovery of PostgreSQL databases was the lack (back in 2011) of a simple and standard procedure for managing backups and, most importantly, recovery. Disasters and failures in ICT will happen.

As a database administrator, your duty is to plan for backups and recovery of PostgreSQL databases and perform regular tests in order to sweep away stress and fear, which typically follow those unexpected events. Barman, which stands for Backup and Recovery Manager, is definitely a tool that you can use for these purposes.

Before you dive into this recipe and the next one, which will introduce you to Barman, I recommend that you read the following recipes from earlier in this chapter—*Understanding and controlling crash recovery, Planning backups, Hot physical backup and continuous archiving,* and *Recovery to a point in time.* Although Barman hides the complexity of the underlying concepts, it is important that you be aware of them, as it will make you more resilient to installation, configuration, and recovery issues with Barman.

Barman is currently available only for Linux systems and is written in Python. It supports PostgreSQL versions from 8.3 onwards. Among its main features worth citing are remote backup, remote recovery, multiple server management, backup catalogs, incremental backups, retention policies, WAL streaming, compression of WAL files, and backup from a standby server.

For the sake of simplicity, in this recipe we will assume the following architecture:

- One Linux server named `angus`, running your PostgreSQL production database server
- One Linux server named `malcolm`, running Barman for disaster recovery of your PostgreSQL database server
- Both the servers are in the same LAN and, for better business continuity objectives, the only resource they share is the network

Later on, we will see how easy it is with Barman to add more Postgres servers (such as `bon`) to our disaster recovery solution on malcolm.

Getting ready

Although Barman can be installed via sources or through pip—Python's main package manager, the easiest way to install Barman is by using the software package manager of your Linux distribution.

Currently, 2ndQuadrant maintains packages for RHEL, CentOS 6/7, Debian, and Ubuntu systems. If you are using a different distribution or another Unix system, you can follow the instructions written in the official documentation of Barman, available at `http://docs.pgbarman.org/`.

In this book, we will cover the installation of Barman 2.3 (currently the latest stable release) on CentOS 7 and Ubuntu 16.04 LTS Linux servers.

If you are using RHEL or CentOS 7 on the malcolm server, you need to install the following repositories:

- Fedora **Extra Packages Enterprise Linux (EPEL)**, available at `http://fedoraproject.org/wiki/EPEL`
- PostgreSQL Global Development Group RPM repository, available at `http://yum.postgresql.org/`

Then, as root, type this:

```
yum install barman
```

If you are using Ubuntu on `malcolm`, you need to install the APT PostgreSQL repository, following the instructions available at `http://apt.postgresql.org/`. Then, as root, type this:

```
apt-get install barman
```

From now on, we will assume the following:

- A freshly installed PostgreSQL is running on `angus` as the `postgres` system user and listening to the default port (`5432`). Its configuration allows the `barman` system user on `malcolm` to connect as the `postgres` database user without having to type a password.
- Barman is installed on `malcolm` and runs as the `barman` system user.
- TCP connections for SSH and PostgreSQL are allowed between the two servers (check your firewall settings).
- Two-way automated communication via SSH is properly set up between these users.
- You have created a superuser called Barman in your PostgreSQL server on `angus` and it can only connect from the `malcolm` server. See Chapter 1, *First Steps*, the *Enabling access for network/remote users* recipe and Chapter 6, *Security*, the *PostgreSQL Superuser* recipe.

The last operation requires exchanging a public SSH key without passphrase between the `postgres` user on `angus` and the `barman` user on `malcolm`. If you are not familiar with this topic, which goes beyond the scope of this book, you are advised to follow Barman's documentation or surf the net for more information.

Alternatively, if your system administrator complains about opening SSH access to your PostgreSQL server, you can always take your backups via streaming replication. Indeed, Barman transparently integrates with `pg_basebackup`, meaning that base backups can be taken through the `5432` port and permissions can be granted at PostgreSQL level.

However, in this book we will concentrate on the copy method, which uses `rsync` via SSH. If you are interested in setting up backups via streaming replication, look at Barman's documentation, in particular the `backup_method` and `streaming_conninfo` options, as well as *Setting up streaming replication* recipe in `Chapter 12`, *Replication and Upgrades*.

How to do it...

We will start by looking at Barman's main configuration file:

1. As root on `malcolm`, open the `/etc/barman.conf` file for editing. This file contains global options for Barman. Once you are familiar with the main configuration options, I recommend that you set the default compression method by uncommenting the following line:

   ```
   compression = gzip
   ```

2. Add the configuration file for the `angus` server. Drop the `angus.conf` file, containing the following lines, into the `/etc/barman.d` directory:

   ```
   [angus]
   description =  "PostgreSQL Database on angus"
   active = off
   archiver = on
   backup_method = rsync
   ssh_command = ssh postgres@angus
   conninfo = host=angus user=barman dbname=postgres
   ```

3. You have just added the `angus` server to the list of Postgres servers managed by Barman. The server is temporarily inactive until configuration is completed. You can verify this by typing `barman list-server`, as follows:

   ```
   [root@malcolm]# barman list-server
   angus - PostgreSQL Database on angus (inactive)
   ```

4. In this recipe, you will be executing commands as root user. Be aware, however, that every command will be executed by the `barman` system user (or, more generally, as specified in the configuration file by the `barman_user` option).

Anyway, it is now time to set up continuous archiving of WAL files between Postgres and Barman. Execute the `barman show-server angus` command and write down the directory for incoming WALs (`incoming_wals_directory`):

```
[root@malcolm]# barman show-server angus

Server angus (inactive):
active: False
archive_command: None
archive_mode: None
        incoming_wals_directory:
        /var/lib/barman/angus/incoming
```

5. The next task is to initialize the directory layout for the `angus` server, through the `check` command. You are advised to add this command to your monitoring infrastructure as, among other things, it ensures that the connection to the Postgres server via `SSH` and `libpq` is working properly, as well as continuous archiving. It returns `0` if everything is fine:

```
[root@malcolm]#

barman check angus
Server angus (inactive):
  WAL archive: FAILED (please make sure WAL    shipping is
setup)
  PostgreSQL: OK
  superuser: OK
  wal_level: FAILED (please set it to a higher level than
'minimal')
  directories: OK
  retention policy settings: OK
  backup maximum age: OK (no last_backup_maximum_age provided)
  compression settings: OK
  failed backups: OK (there are 0 failed backups)
  minimum redundancy requirements: OK (have 0 backups, expected
at least 0)
  ssh: OK (PostgreSQL server)
  not in recovery: OK
  archive_mode: FAILED (please set it to 'on' or 'always')
  archive_command: FAILED (please set it accordingly to
documentation)
  archiver errors: OK

[root@malcolm]# echo $?
1
```

6. As you can see, the returned value is 1, meaning that the angus server is not yet ready for backup. The output suggests that archive_mode and archive_command in Postgres are not set for continuous archiving. Connect to angus and modify the postgresql.conf file by adding this:

```
archive_mode = on
archive_command = 'rsync -a %p
barman@malcolm:/var/lib/barman/angus/incoming/%f'

wal_level = replica
```

7. Restart the PostgreSQL server.
8. Activate the server in Barman, by removing the line that starts with active.
9. Run the check command on malcolm (suppressing the output with -q) again, and compare the results with what you got earlier:

```
[root@malcolm]# barman -q check angus
[root@malcolm]# echo $?
0
```

It returned 0. Everything is all good! PostgreSQL on angus should now be regularly shipping WAL files to Barman on malcolm, depending on the write workload of your database.

Do not worry if the check command complains with the following error:

```
WAL archive: FAILED (please make sure WAL shipping is setup)
```

It is a precautionary measure we had to take in order to prevent users from going live without a working archiving process. That means that your server (like angus in this case) has a very low workload and no WAL files have yet been produced, shipped, and archived. If you want to speed up the installation, you can execute the following commands:

```
[root@malcolm]# barman switch-wal --force --archive angus
[root@malcolm]# barman archive-wal angus
```

I recommend that you check both the PostgreSQL and Barman log files and verify that WALs are correctly shipped. Continuous archiving is indeed the main requirement for physical backups in Postgres.

10. Once you have set up continuous archiving, in order to add the disaster recovery capability to your Postgres server, you need to have at least one full base backup. Taking a full base backup in Barman is as easy as typing one single command. It should not be hard for you to guess that the command to execute is `barman backup angus`.

Barman initiates the physical backup procedure and waits for the checkpoint to happen, before copying the data files from `angus` to `malcom` using `rsync`:

```
[root@malcolm]# barman backup angus
Starting backup using rsync-exclusive method for server angus
in /var/lib/barman/angus/base/20171003T194717
Backup start at xlog location: 0/3000028
(000000010000000000000003, 00000028)
This is the first backup for server angus
WAL segments preceding the current backup have been found:
    000000010000000000000001 from server angus has been removed
Copying files.
Copy done.
This is the first backup for server angus
Asking PostgreSQL server to finalize the backup.
Backup size: 21.1 MiB
Backup end at xlog location: 0/3000130
(000000010000000000000003, 00000130)
Backup completed
Processing xlog segments from file archival for angus
    000000010000000000000002
    000000010000000000000003
    000000010000000000000003.00000028.backup
```

It is worth noting that, during the backup procedure, your PostgreSQL server is available for both read and write operations. This is because PostgreSQL natively implements hot backup, a feature that other DBMS vendors might make you pay for.

From now on, your `angus` PostgreSQL server is continuously backed up on `malcolm`. You can now schedule weekly backups (using the `barman` user's cron) and manage retention policies so that you can build a catalog of backups covering you for weeks, months, or years of data, and allowing you to perform recovery operations at any point in time between the first available backup and the last successfully archived WAL file.

How it works...

Barman is a Python application that wraps PostgreSQL core technology for continuous backup and PITR. It also adds some practical functionality focused on helping the database administrator manage disaster recovery of one or more PostgreSQL servers.

When devising Barman, we decided to keep the design simple and not to use any daemon or client/server architecture. Maintenance operations are simply delegated to the `barman cron` command, which is mainly responsible for archiving WAL files (moving them from the incoming directory to the WAL file and compressing them) and managing retention policies.

If you have installed Barman through RPM or APT packages, you will notice that maintenance is run every minute through cron:

```
[root@malcolm ~]# cat /etc/cron.d/barman
# m h  dom mon dow   user      command
  * *   *   *   *    barman    [ -x /usr/bin/barman ] && /usr/bin/barman -q
cron
```

Barman follows the *convention over configuration* paradigm and uses an INI format configuration file with options operating at two different levels:

- **Global options**: These are options specified in the [barman] section, used by any Barman command and for every server. Several global options can be overridden at the server level.
- **Server options**: These are options specified in the [SERVER_ID] section, used by server commands. These options can be customized at the server level (including overriding general settings).

The SERVER_ID placeholder (such as angus) is fundamental, as it identifies the server in the catalog (therefore, it must be unique).

Similarly, commands in Barman are of two types:

- **Global commands**: These are general commands, not tied with any server in particular, such as a list of the servers managed by the Barman installation (list-server) and maintenance (cron)

- **Server commands**: These are commands executed on a specific server, such as diagnostics (`check` and `status`), backup control (`backup`, `list-backup`, `delete` and `show-backup`), and recovery control (recover, which is discussed in the next recipe, *Recovery with Barman*)

The previous sections of this recipe showed you how to add a server (`angus`) to a Barman installation on the `malcolm` server. You can easily add a second server (`bon`) to the Barman server on malcolm. All you have to do is create the `bon.conf` file in the `/etc/barman.d` directory and repeat the steps outlined in the *How it works...* section, as you have done for `angus`.

There's more...

Every time you execute the `barman backup` command for a given server, you take a full base backup (a more generic term for this is periodical full backup). Once completed, this backup can be used as a base for any recovery operation from the start time of the backup to the last available WAL file for that server (provided there is continuity among all the WAL segments).

As mentioned earlier, by scheduling daily or weekly automated backups, you end up having several periodic backups for a server. In Barman's jargon, this is known as the backup catalog and it is one of our favorite features of this tool.

At any time, you can get a list of available backups for a given server through the `list-backup` command:

```
[root@malcolm ~]# barman list-backup angus
7angus 20171003T194717 - Mon Oct  3 19:47:20 2017 - Size: 21.1 MiB - WAL
Size: 26.6 KiB
```

The last informative command you might want to get familiar with is `show-backup`, which gives you detailed information on a specific backup regarding the server, base backup time, WAL archive, and context within the catalog (for example, the last available backup):

```
[root@malcolm ~]# barman show-backup angus 20171003T194717
```

Rather than the full backup ID (`20171003T194717`), you can use a few synonyms, such as these:

- **Last or latest**: This refers to the latest available backup (the last in the catalog)
- **First or oldest**: This refers to the oldest available backup (the first in the catalog)

For the `show-backup` command, however, we will use a real and concrete example, taken directly from one of our customer's installations of Barman on a 16.4 TB Postgres 9.4 database:

```
Backup 20170930T130002:
    Server Name            : skynyrd
    Status                 : DONE
    PostgreSQL Version     : 90409
    PGDATA directory       : /srv/pgdata

    Base backup information:
        Disk usage         : 16.4 TiB (16.4 TiB with WALs)
        Incremental size   : 5.7 TiB (-65.08%)
        Timeline           : 1
        Begin WAL          : 0000000100000358800000063
        End WAL            : 00000001000035A0000000A2
        WAL number         : 6208
        WAL compression ratio: 79.15%
        Begin time         : 2017-09-30   13:00:04.245110+00:00

        End time           : 2017-10-01   13:24:47.322288+00:00
        Begin Offset       : 24272
        End Offset         : 11100576
        Begin XLOG         : 3588/63005ED0
        End XLOG           : 35A0/A2A961A0

    WAL information:
        No of files        : 3240
        Disk usage         : 11.9 GiB
        WAL rate           : 104.33/hour
        Compression ratio  : 76.43%
        Last available     : 00000001000035AD0000004A

    Catalog information:
        Retention Policy   : not enforced
        Previous Backup    : 20170923T130001
        Next Backup        : - (this is the latest base backup)
```

As you can see, Barman is a production-ready tool that can be used in large, business-critical contexts, as well as in basic Postgres installations. It provides good **Recovery Point Objective (RPO)** outcomes, allowing you to limit potential data loss to a single WAL file.

Finally, Barman also supports WAL streaming, which dramatically reduces the amount of data you can lose. With synchronous replication and replication slot support, you can achieve *zero data loss* backups. For further information, please refer to Barman's documentation, in particular: `streaming_archiver`, `streaming_archiver_name`, `streaming_conninfo`, and `slot_name`.

Barman is distributed under GNU GPL 3 terms and is available for download at `http://www.pgbarman.org/`.

There is also a module for Puppet available at `https://github.com/2ndquadrant-it/puppet-barman`.

For further and more detailed information, refer to the following:

- The `man barman` command, which gives the man page for the Barman application
- The `man 5 barman` command, which gives the man page for the configuration file
- The `barman help` command, which gives a list of the available commands
- The official documentation for Barman, publicly available at `http://docs.pgbarman.org/`
- The mailing list for community support at `http://www.pgbarman.org/support/`

Recovery with Barman

This recipe assumes that you have read the previous recipe, *Hot physical backups with Barman*, and successfully installed Barman on the `malcolm` server, backing up the Postgres databases running on `angus` and `bon`. We will use the same nomenclature in the examples in this recipe.

A recovery procedure is a reaction to a failure. In database terms, this could be related to an unintentional human error (for example, a DROP operation on a table), an attack (think of Little Bobby Tables), a hardware failure (for example, a broken hard drive), or (less likely) a natural disaster.

Even though you might be tempted to think that you are immune to disasters or failures (we wish you were), you are advised to perform regular tests and simulations of recovery procedures. If you have a team of engineers, we suggest that you schedule a simulation every six months (at least) and regularly test your backups through the safest way of checking their content—performing a recovery.

You don't want to take backups for years and, in the moment of need, suddenly discover that they have not been working for the last three months.

Barman allows you to perform two types of recovery:

- **Local recovery**: This involves restoring a PostgreSQL instance on the same server where Barman resides
- **Remote recovery**: This involves restoring a PostgreSQL instance directly from the Barman server to another server, through the network

It is important to note that the terms *local* and *remote* are defined from Barman's standpoint, as every recovery command is executed where Barman is installed.

In this recipe, we will cover a single use case—total failure of one of the servers where PostgreSQL is running (fortunately, it is backed up by Barman) and a full remote recovery on a third server.

Getting ready

Even though Barman can centrally manage backups of several servers that have different versions of PostgreSQL, when it comes to recovery, the same requirements for PostgreSQL's PITR technology apply. In particular, the following:

- You must recover on a server with the same hardware architecture and PostgreSQL version
- Recovery is full, meaning the entire Postgres cluster will be restored (and not a single database)

The use case of this recipe is the following:

- The bon server has been lost forever, due to a permanent hardware failure
- The brian server, having similar characteristics to bon, has been selected for recovery
- The same Linux distribution and PostgreSQL packages have been installed on brian

- Barman will be used to perform remote recovery of the latest backup available for bon on the brian server

In order to proceed, you need to add the public SSH key of the barman user on malcolm in the ~/.ssh/authorized_keys file of the Postgres user on brian. If you are not familiar with the process of exchanging a public SSH key, which goes beyond the scope of this book, you are advised to follow Barman's documentation or surf the net for more information.

The first step is to make sure that the PGDATA directory, as specified in the bon backup, exists on brian and can be written by the postgres user.

Ask barman for the location of PGDATA by querying the latest available backup metadata:

```
barman show-backup bon last
```

Write down the content of the PGDATA directory entry:

```
PGDATA directory   : /var/lib/pgsql/10/data
```

You might have noticed that we are using the default PGDATA directory for a RHEL/CentOS cluster based on packages maintained by the PostgreSQL community. On Ubuntu, you will probably have /var/lib/postgresql/10/main.

As the second step, also make sure that PostgreSQL is not running on Brian, using either the service or pg_ctl command.

Executing a recovery operation on a target directory used by a running PostgreSQL instance will permanently damage that instance. Be extremely careful when you perform such an operation.

How to do it...

Connect as the barman user on malcolm and type the following:

```
barman recover --remote-ssh-command 'ssh postgres@brian' bon last
/var/lib/pgsql/9.6/data
```

The preceding command will use the latest available backup for the `bon` server and prepare everything you need to restore your server in the PostgreSQL destination directory (`/var/lib/pgsql/10/data`), as shown in the output:

```
Starting remote restore for server bon using backup 20171003T194717
Destination directory: /var/lib/pgsql/10/data
Copying the base backup.
Copying required WAL segments.
Generating archive status files
Identify dangerous settings in destination directory.

IMPORTANT
These settings have been modified to prevent data losses

postgresql.conf line 645: archive_command = false

Your PostgreSQL server has been successfully prepared for recovery!
```

Once again, Ubuntu users will have to use a different destination directory, such as `/var/lib/postgresql/10/main`.

Before you start the server, you are advised to connect to `Brian` as Postgres and inspect the content of the Postgres destination directory. You should notice that its content should be very similar to what was in the `bon` server before the crash.

You are also strongly encouraged to review the content of the `postgresql.conf` file before starting the server, even though Barman takes care of disabling or removing some potentially dangerous options. The most critical option is `archive_command`, which is preemptively set to `false`, forcing you to deliberately analyze and consider new continuous archiving strategies (for example, you might want to add the new `Brian` server to Barman by repeating the steps outlined in the previous recipe).

When you are ready, you can start Postgres as a standard service. On CentOS 7, for example, you can execute as root, as follows:

```
systemctl start postgresql-10
```

On Ubuntu, use this command:

```
systemctl start postgresql
```

Look at the logs to verify that you do not have any problems, and then at `ps -axf`.

Your PostgreSQL databases that were hosted on `bon` have been successfully restored on `brian`, using all the WAL files shipped to the backup server.

How it works...

When executed with the `--remote-ssh-command` option, the `recover` command will activate remote recovery and will use those credentials to connect to the remote server (similar to what the `ssh-command` configuration option does in the backup phase but in reverse—see the *Hot physical backups with Barman* recipe). Internally, Barman relies on `rsync` for this operation.

When performing a full recovery (up to the latest available archived WAL file), Barman recreates the structure of the `PGDATA` according to the backup. It will then deposit all the needed WAL files in the `pg_wal` directory.

A careful analysis of the content of the restored `PGDATA directory` shows that no `recovery.conf` file is generated by Barman in the case of a full recovery.

It will just simulate a standard crash recovery of PostgreSQL and start replaying the WAL files from the REDO point, contrary to the *Recovery of all databases* recipe, where `recovery.conf` was used.

We decided to adopt this strategy in Barman so that we could maintain the same timeline (as a `recovery.conf` file would start a new era in the cluster's existence), and avoid setting `restore_command`.

There's more...

If you are using tablespaces, you may be wondering if and how Barman manages them. Barman fully supports tablespaces, including their relocation at recovery time, through the `--tablespace runtime` option. For information on the syntax of the relocation rules, type any of the following commands:

- `barman help recover`
- `man barman`

In this recipe, we have seen only one use case, which covers remote recovery. As mentioned before, however, Barman also allows DBAs to recover instances of PostgreSQL on the same server as Barman.

This is called local recovery. For local recovery, you will need to have installed the binaries and libraries of the same version of PostgreSQL on the Barman server as the backup file you want to restore.

You can dedicate a directory in Barman for local recovery, to be used as the destination directory for your recover commands.

A typical use case for local recovery is to restore the situation of a PostgreSQL server at a specific point in time, usually before an unintentional action such as the DROP of a table.

Barman supports PITR, as explained in the *Recovery to a point in time* recipe, through three options that define the recovery target:

- `--target-time TARGET_TIME`: The target is a timestamp
- `--target-xid TARGET_XID`: The target is a transaction ID
- `--target-name TARGET_NAME`: The target is a named restore point, previously created with the `pg_create_restore_point(name)` function

When executed with one of these options, Barman will generate the `recovery.conf` file for you. Advanced users might want to activate the hot standby facility and take advantage of the `recovery_target_action` option (by default set to `pause`, and effective only if `hot_standby` is enabled in the `postgresql.conf` file).

This will allow you to check whether the database is in the desired state or not. If not, you can stop the server, change the recovery target time, and start it again. Repeat this operation until you reach your goal, keeping in mind that PostgreSQL can only roll forward WAL files (they are called REDO operations for a reason).

You can then follow the instructions outlined in the *Recovery of a dropped/damaged table* recipe to restore the objects in the primary database.

At the end of any recovery operation, remember to stop the running of local servers and remove recovered instances (even though this is not mandatory, as Barman uses `rsync` and will be able to perform an incremental copy of the files where applicable).

Another interesting feature of Barman is the `get-wal` command, which transforms Barman in an infinite basin of WAL files. Instead of copying WAL files before the actual start of the server, you can let PostgreSQL pull the required WAL files on demand at recovery time, via `restore_command`. For further information, look at the `barman-cli` package, specifically the `barman-wal-restore` script at `https://github.com/2ndquadrant-it/barman-cli`

As a final note for this recipe, another important use case for Barman is to regularly create copies of the server to be used for business intelligence purposes or even staging/development. These environments do not normally require a strict up-to-date situation and are very often happy to work on a snapshot of the previous day. A typical workflow for this use case can be like this:

1. Stop the PostgreSQL server on the BI/staging server.
2. Issue a full remote recovery operation of the desired backup from Barman to the BI server (`rsync` will use the existing data directory for incremental copy).
3. Start the PostgreSQL server on the BI/staging server.

This recipe has covered only a few aspects of the recovery process in Barman. For further and more detailed information, refer to:

- The official documentation for Barman, publicly available at `http://docs.pgbarman.org/`
- The mailing list for community support at `http://www.pgbarman.org/support/`
- The Barman section of our blog at `https://blog.2ndquadrant.com/tag/barman`.

12
Replication and Upgrades

Replication isn't magic, though it can be pretty cool! It's even cooler when it works, and that's what this chapter is all about.

Replication requires understanding, effort, and patience. There are a significant number of points to get right. My emphasis here is on providing simple approaches to get you started, and some clear best practices on operational robustness.

PostgreSQL has included some form of native or in-core replication since version 8.2, though that support has steadily improved over time. External projects and tools have always been a significant part of the PostgreSQL landscape, with most of them being written and supported by very skilled PostgreSQL technical developers. Some people with a negative viewpoint have observed that this weakens PostgreSQL or emphasizes shortcomings. My view would be that PostgreSQL has been lucky enough to be supported by a huge range of replication tools, together offering a wide set of supported use cases from which to build practical solutions. This view extends throughout this chapter on replication, with many recipes using tools that are not part of the core PostgreSQL project yet.

All the tools mentioned in this chapter are actively enhanced by current core PostgreSQL developers. The pace of change in this area is high, and it is likely that some of the restrictions mentioned here could well be removed by the time you read this book. Double-check the documentation for each tool or project.

Which technique is the best? is a question that gets asked many times. The answer varies depending on the exact circumstances. In many cases, people use one technique on one server and a different technique on other servers. Even the developers of particular tools use other tools when it is appropriate. Use the right tools for the job. All the tools and techniques listed in this chapter have been recommended by me at some time, in relevant circumstances. If something isn't mentioned here by me, that does probably imply that it is less favorable for various reasons, and there are some tools and techniques that I would personally avoid altogether in their present form or level of maturity.

I (*Simon Riggs*) must also confess to being the developer or designer of many parts of the basic technology presented here. That gives me some advantages and disadvantages over other authors. It means I understand some things better than others, which hopefully translates into better descriptions and comparisons. It may also hamper me by providing too narrow a focus, though the world is big and this book is already long enough!

This book, and especially this chapter, cover technology in depth. As a result, we face the risk of minor errors. We've gone to a lot of trouble to test all of our recommendations, but just as with software, I learn that books can be buggy too. I hope our efforts to present actual commands rather than just words will be appreciated by you.

In this chapter, we will cover the following recipes:

- Replication best practices
- Setting up file-based replication – deprecated
- Setting up streaming replication
- Setting up streaming replication security
- Hot Standby and read scalability
- Managing streaming replication
- Using repmgr
- Using replication slots
- Monitoring replication
- Performance and synchronous replication
- Delaying, pausing, and synchronizing replication
- Logical replication
- Bi-Directional Replication
- Archiving transaction log data
- Upgrading – minor releases
- Major upgrades in-place
- Major upgrades online

Replication concepts

Replication technology can be confusing. You might be forgiven for thinking that people have a reason to keep it that way. My observation is that there are many techniques, each with their own advocates, and the strengths and weaknesses are often hotly debated.

There are some simple underlying concepts that can help you understand the various options available. The terms used here are designed to avoid favoring any particular technique, and we've used standard industry terms whenever available.

Topics

Database replication is the term we use to describe the technology used to maintain a copy of a set of data on a remote system.

There are usually two main reasons for you wanting to do this, and those reasons are often combined:

- **High Availability**: Reducing the chances of data unavailability by having multiple systems, each holding a full copy of the data.
- **Data Movement**: Allowing data to be used by additional applications or workload on additional hardware. Examples of this are **Reference Data Management** (**RDM**), where a single central server might provide information to many other applications, and **Business Intelligence/Reporting Systems**.

Of course, both of those topics are complex areas, and there are many architectures and possibilities for implementing each of them.

What we will talk about here is High Availability, where there is *no transformation* of the data. We simply copy the data from one PostgreSQL database server to another. So we are specifically avoiding all discussion on ETL tools, EAI tools, inter-database migration, data warehousing strategies, and so on. Those are valid topics in IT architecture; it's just that we don't cover them in this book.

Basic concepts

Let's look at the basic architecture. Typically, individual database servers are referred to as nodes. The whole group of database servers involved in replication is known as a cluster. That is the common usage of the term, but be careful; the term **cluster** is also used for two other quite separate meanings elsewhere in PostgreSQL. Firstly, cluster is sometimes used to refer to the database instance, though I prefer the term **database server**. Secondly, there is a command named `cluster`. It is designed to sort data in a specific order within a table.

A database server that allows a user to make changes is known as a **master** or **primary**, or may be described as a source of changes.

A database server that only allows read-only access is known as a **Hot Standby**, or sometimes, a slave server or read replica.

The key aspect of replication is that data changes are captured on a master, and then transferred to other nodes. In some cases, a node may send data changes to other nodes, which is a process known as **cascading** or **relay**. Thus, the master is a sending node, but a sending node does not need to be a master.

Replication is often categorized by whether more than one master node is allowed, in which case it will be known as multimaster replication. There is a significant difference between how single-master and multimaster systems work, so we'll discuss that aspect in more detail later. Each has its advantages and disadvantages.

History and scope

PostgreSQL didn't always have in-core replication. For many years, PostgreSQL users needed to use one of many external packages to provide this important feature.

Slony was the first package to provide useful replication features. Londiste was a variant system that was somewhat easier to use. Both of those systems provided single-master replication based around triggers. Another variant of this idea was the **Bucardo** package, which offered multimaster replication using triggers.

Trigger-based replication has now been superseded by transaction-log-based replication, which provides considerable performance improvements. There is some discussion on exactly how much difference that makes, but log-based replication is approximately twice as fast, though many users have reported much higher gains. Trigger-based systems also have considerably higher replication lag. Lastly, triggers need to be added to each table involved in replication, making these systems more time-consuming to manage and sensitive to production problems. These factors taken together mean that trigger-based systems will likely be avoided for new developments, and I'm taking the decision not to cover them at all in the latest edition of this book.

Outside the world of PostgreSQL, there are many competing concepts and much recent research. This is a practical book, so we've mostly avoided comments on research or topics on computer science.

The focus of this chapter is replication technologies that are part of the core software of PostgreSQL, or will be so in the reasonably near future. The first of these is known as **streaming replication**, introduced in PostgreSQL 9.0, but based on earlier file-based mechanisms for physical transaction log replication. In this book, we refer to this as **Physical Streaming Replication (PSR)** because we take the transaction log (often known as the **Write-Ahead Log (WAL)**) and ship that data to the remote node. The WAL contains an exact physical copy of the changes made to a data block, so the remote node is an exact copy of the master. Therefore, the remote node cannot execute transactions that write to the database; this type of node is known as a standby.

Starting in PostgreSQL 9.4, we introduced an efficient mechanism for reading the transaction log (WAL) and transforming it into a stream of changes, a process known as **logical decoding**. This is then the basis for the later, even more useful mechanism, known as **Logical Streaming Replication (LSR)**. This allows a receiver to replicate data without needing to keep an exact copy of the data blocks, as we do with PSR. This has significant advantages, which we will discuss later.

PSR requires us to have only a single master node, though it allows multiple standbys. LSR can be used for all the same purposes as PSR. It just has fewer restrictions and allows a great range of additional use cases. Crucially, LSR can be used as the basis of multimaster clusters.

PSR and LSR are sometimes known as **Physical Log Streaming Replication (PLSR)** and **Logical Log Streaming Replication (LLSR)**. Those terms are sometimes used to explain differences between transaction-log-based and trigger-based replication.

Practical aspects

Since we refer to the transfer of replicated data as streaming, it becomes natural to talk about the flow of data between nodes as if it were a river or stream. Cascaded data can flow through a series of nodes to create complex architectures. From the perspective of any node, it may have downstream nodes that receive replicated data from it and/or upstream nodes that send data to it. Practical limits need to be understood to allow us to understand and design replication architectures.

After a transaction commits on the master, the time taken to transfer data changes to a remote node is usually referred to as the **latency**, or **replication delay**. Once the remote node has received the data, changes must then be applied to the remote node, which takes an amount of time known as the **apply delay**. The total time a record takes from the master to a downstream node is the replication delay plus the apply delay. Be careful to note that some authors describe those terms differently, and sometimes confuse the two, which is easy to do. Also, note that these delays will be different for any two nodes.

Replication delay is best expressed as an interval (in seconds), but that is much harder to measure than it first appears. In PostgreSQL 10, the delays of particular phases of replication are given with the lag columns on `pg_stat_replication`. These are derived from sampling the message stream and interpolating the current delay from recent samples.

All forms of replication are initialized in roughly the same way. First, you enable change capture, and then make a full replica of the dataset on the remote node, which we refer to as the **base backup**. After that, we begin applying the changes, starting from the point immediately before the base backup started and continuing with any changes that occurred while the base backup was taking place. As a result, the replication delay immediately following the initial copy task will be equal to the duration of the initial copy task. The remote node will then begin to catch up with the master, and the replication delay will begin to reduce. The time taken to get the lowest replication delay possible is known as the catch-up interval. If the master is busy generating new changes, which can increase the time it takes for the new node to catch up, you should try to generate new nodes during quieter periods, if any exist. Note that in some cases, the catch-up period will be too long to be acceptable. Be sure to include this understanding in your planning and monitoring. The faster and more efficient your replication system, the easier it will be to operate in the real world. *Performance matters!*

Either replication will copy all tables, or in some cases, we can copy a subset of tables, in which case we call it **selective replication**. If you choose selective replication, you should note that the management overhead increases roughly as the number of objects managed increases. Replicated objects are often manipulated in groups known as **replication sets** to help minimize the administrative overhead.

Data loss

By default, PostgreSQL provides **asynchronous replication**, where data is streamed out whenever convenient for the server. If replicated data is acknowledged back to the user prior to commit, we refer to that as **synchronous replication**.

With synchronous replication, the replication delay *directly* affects the elapsed time of transactions on the master. With asynchronous replication, the master may continue at full speed, though this opens up a possible risk that the standby may not be able to keep pace with the master. All replication must be monitored to ensure that a significant lag does not develop, which is why we must be careful to monitor the replication delay.

Synchronous replication guarantees that data is written to at least two nodes before the user or application is told that a transaction has committed. You can specify the number of nodes and other details that you wish to use in your configuration.

Single-master replication

In single-master replication, if the master dies, one of the standbys must take its place. Otherwise, we will not be able to accept new write transactions. Thus, the designations master and standby are just roles that any node can take at some point. To move the master role to another node, we perform a procedure named **switchover**. If the master dies and does not recover, then the more severe role change is known as a **failover**. In many ways, these can be similar, but it helps to use different terms for each event.

We use the term clusterware for software that manages the cluster. Clusterware may provide features such as automatic failover, and in some cases, load balancing.

The complexity of failover makes single-master replication harder to configure correctly than many people would like it to be. The good news is that from an application perspective it is safe and easy to retrofit this style of replication to an existing system. Or put another way, since application developers frequently don't worry about High Availability and replication until the very end of the project, single-master replication is frequently the best solution, be it PSR or LSR.

Multinode architectures

Multinode architectures allow users to write data to multiple nodes concurrently. There are two main categories: tightly coupled and loosely coupled:

- **Tightly coupled database clusters**: These allow a single image of the database, so there is less perception that you're even connected to a cluster at all. This consistency comes at a price—the nodes of the cluster cannot be geographically separated, which means if you need to protect against site disasters, then you'll need additional technology to allow disaster recovery. Clustering requires replication as well.

- **Loosely coupled database clusters**: These have greater independence for each node, allowing us to spread out nodes across wide areas, such as across multiple continents. You can connect to each node individually. There are two benefits of this. The first is that all data access can be performed quickly against local copies of the data. The second benefit is that we don't need to work out how to route read-only transactions to (a) standby node (s) and read/write transactions to the master node.

Clustered or massively parallel databases

An example of a tightly coupled system is the open source Postgres-XL. This supersedes the earlier Postgres-XC clustering software. These systems introduced the concept of a **Global Transaction Manager** (**GTM**), which allows nodes in a tightly coupled system to work together while guaranteeing consistency across reads and writes.

Postgres-XL spreads data across multiple nodes. Larger tables can be distributed evenly, using a hash-based distribution scheme. This feature allows Postgres-XL to scale well for both high-transaction-rate (OLTP) and business intelligence (OLAP) systems.

On Postgres-XL, smaller tables can be duplicated on all nodes. Changes to smaller tables are coordinated, so there is no possibility of the multiple copies diverging from one another. The synchronization cost is high, and XL is not suitable for geographically distributed databases, though it does support High Availability.

Postgres-XL is not covered in more detail in this book, simply because of lack of time and space. Postgres-XL is released with *The PostgreSQL licence*.

Multimaster replication

An example of a loosely coupled system would be **Bi-Directional Replication** (**BDR**). Postgres-BDR does not utilize a GTM, so the nodes contain data that is eventually consistent between nodes. This is a performance optimization since tests showed that trying to use tightly coupled approaches catastrophically limits performance when servers are geographically separated.

In its simplest multimaster configuration, each node has a copy of similar data. You can update data on any node and the changes will flow to other nodes. This makes it ideal for databases that have users in many different locations, which is probably the case with most websites. Each location can have its own copy of the application code and database, giving fast response times for all your users, wherever they are located.

It is *possible* to make changes to the same data at the same time on different nodes, causing update conflicts. These could become a problem, but the reality is that it is also *easily possible* to design applications that do not generate conflicts in normal running, especially if each user is modifying their own data (for example, in social media, retail, and so on).

We need to understand where conflicts might arise so that we can resolve them. On a single node, any application that allows concurrent updates to the same data will experience poor performance because of contention. The negative effect of contention will get much worse on multimaster clusters. In addition, multiple nodes require us to allow for the possibility that the updated data differs, so we must implement conflict-handling logic to resolve data differences between nodes. With some thought and planning, we can use multimaster technologies very effectively in the real world.

Visit `http://en.wikipedia.org/wiki/Replication_(computer_science)` for more information on this.

Scalability tools

Many PostgreSQL users have designed applications that scale naturally by routing database requests based on the client number or a similar natural sharding key. This is what we call manual sharding at the application level.

For PostgreSQL 10 and earlier versions, PostgreSQL does not directly support features for automatic write scalability, such as sharding. This is an active area of work, and much will change in this area, though it may take some time.

Postgres-XL provides automatic hash sharding and is currently the most complete open source implementation that allows automatic write scalability at the database level.

PL/Proxy provides a mature mechanism for database scalability. It was originally designed for Skype, but it is also in use at a number of high-volume sites. It provides most of the things that you'll need to create a scalable cluster. PL/Proxy requires that you define your main database accesses as functions, which requires early decisions about your application architecture.

Other approaches to replication

This book covers in-database replication only. Replication is also possible in the application layer (that is, above the database) or in the **Operating System (OS)** layers (that is, below the database):

- **Application-level replication**: For example, HA-JDBC and rubyrep
- **OS-level replication**: For example, DRBD

None of these approaches are very satisfying, since core database features cannot easily integrate with them in ways that truly work. From a sysadmin's perspective, they work, but not very well from the perspective of a database architect.

Replication best practices

Some general best practices for running replication systems are described in this recipe.

Getting ready

Reading the list of best practices should be the very first thing you do when designing your database architecture. So the best way to get ready for it is to avoid doing anything and start with the next section *How to do it*.

How to do it...

- Use the latest release of PostgreSQL. Replication features are changing fast, with each new release improving on the previous in major ways based on our real-world experience. The idea that earlier releases are somehow more stable, and thus more easily usable, is definitely not the case for replication.
- Use similar hardware and OS on all systems. Replication allows nodes to switch roles. If we switchover or failover to different hardware, we may get performance issues and it will be hard to maintain a smoothly running application.
- Configure all systems identically as far as possible. Use the same mount points, directory names, and users; keep everything possible the same. Don't be tempted to make one system more important than others in some way. It's just a single point of failure and gets confusing.

- Give systems/servers good names to reduce confusion. Never, ever call one of your systems master and the other slave. When you do a switchover, you will get very confused! Try to pick system names that have nothing to do whatsoever with their role. Replication roles will inevitably change; system names should not. If one system fails, and you add a new system, never reuse the name of the old system: pick another name, or it will be too confusing. Don't pick names that relate to something in the business. Colors are also a bad choice, because if you have two servers named yellow and red, you then end up saying things like *there is a red alert on server yellow*, which can easily be confusing. Don't pick place names either. Otherwise, you'll be confused trying to remember that London is in Edinburgh and Paris is in Rome. Make sure you use names, rather than IP addresses.

- Set the `application_name` parameter to be the server name in the replication connection string. Set the `cluster_name` parameter to be the server name in the `postgresql.conf`.

- Make sure all tables are marked as LOGGED (the default). UNLOGGED and TEMPORARY tables will not be replicated by either **PSR** or **LSR**.

- Keep the system clocks synchronized. This helps you keep sane when looking at log files produced by multiple servers. You should automate this, rather than do it manually, but however you do it, make sure it works.

- Use a single, unambiguous time zone. Use **Coordinated Universal Time** (UTC) or something similar. Don't pick a time zone that has **Daylight Saving Time** (**DST**), especially in regions that have complex DST rules. This just leads to (human) confusion with replication, as servers are often in different countries and time zone differences vary throughout the year. Do this even if you start with all servers in one country, because over the lifetime of the application, you may need to add new servers in different locations. Think ahead.

- Monitor each of the database servers. If you want High Availability, then you'll need to regularly check that your servers are operational. I speak to many people who would like to regard replication as a one-shot deal. Think of it more as a marriage, and plan for it to be a happy one!

- Monitor the replication delay between servers. All forms of replication are only useful if the data is flowing correctly between the servers. Monitoring the time it takes for the data to go from one server to another is essential to understanding whether replication is working for you or not. Replication can be bursty, so you'll need to watch to make sure it stays within sensible limits. You may be able to set tuning parameters to keep things low, or you may need to look at other factors.

The important point is that your replication delay is directly related to the amount of data you're likely to lose when running asynchronous replication. Be careful here because it is the replication delay, not the apply delay, that affects data loss. A long apply delay may be more acceptable as a result.

As described previously, your initial replication delay will be high, and it should reduce to a lower and more stable value over a period of time. For large databases, this could take days, so be careful to monitor during the catch-up period.

There's more...

The preceding list doesn't actually say this explicitly, but you should use the same major version of PostgreSQL for all systems. With PSR, you are required to do that, so it doesn't even need to be said.

I've heard people argue that it's OK to have dissimilar systems and even that it's a good idea because if you get a bug, it only affects one node. I'd say that the massive increase in complexity is much more likely to cause problems.

Setting up file-based replication – deprecated

This technique is mostly superseded by streaming replication (PSR), so if you are a novice, you probably do not want this recipe yet. Nonetheless, this is relevant and useful as part of a comprehensive backup strategy. It is also worth understanding how this works, as this technique can also be used as the starting phase for a large streaming replication setup. Look at the following recipes for some further details on that.

Log shipping is a replication technique used by many database management systems. The master records database changes in its transaction log, and then the log files are shipped from the master to the standby, where the log is replayed.

File-based log shipping has been available for PostgreSQL for many years now. It is simple, has very low overhead, and is a trustworthy form of replication.

Getting ready

If you haven't read the *Replication concepts* section and the *Replication best practices* recipe at the start of this chapter, go and read them now. Replication is complex, and even if you think *no problem, I know that*, it's worth just checking out the basic concepts and names that I'll be using here. Note that log-shipping replication refers to the master node as the primary node, and these two terms are used interchangeably.

How to do it...

Follow these steps for initial configuration of file-based log shipping:

1. Identify your archive location and ensure that it has sufficient space. This recipe assumes that the archive is a directory on the standby node, identified by the `$PGARCHIVE` environment variable. This is set on both the master and standby nodes, as the master must write to the archive and the standby must read from it. The standby node is identified on the master using `$STANDBYNODE`.

2. Configure replication security. Perform a key exchange to allow the master and the standby to run the `rsync` command in either direction.

3. Adjust the master's parameters in `postgresql.conf`, as follows:

```
wal_level = 'archive'
archive_mode = on
archive_command = 'scp %p $STANDBYNODE:$PGARCHIVE/%f'
archive_timeout = 30
```

4. Adjust Hot Standby parameters if required (see the *Hot Standby and read scalability* recipe).

5. Take a base backup, very similar to the process for taking a physical backup described in `Chapter 11`, *Backup and Recovery*.

6. Start the backup by running the following command:

```
psql -c "select pg_start_backup('base backup for log
shipping')"
```

7. Copy the data files (excluding the `pg_wal` directory). Note that this requires some security configuration to ensure that `rsync` can be executed without needing to provide a password when it executes. If you skipped step 2, do this now, as follows:

```
rsync -cva --inplace --exclude=*pg_wal* \
${PGDATA}/ $STANDBYNODE:$PGDATA
```

8. Stop the backup by running the following command:

```
psql -c "select pg_stop_backup(), current_timestamp"
```

9. Set the `recovery.conf` parameters in the `data` directory on the `standby` server, as follows:

```
standby_mode  =  'on'
restore_command  =  'cp  $PGARCHIVE/%f  %p'
archive_cleanup_command  =  'pg_archivecleanup  $PGARCHIVE  %r'
trigger_file  =  '/tmp/postgresql.trigger.5432'
```

10. Start the `standby` server.
11. Carefully monitor the replication delay until the catch-up period is over. During the initial catch-up period, the replication delay will be much higher than we would normally expect it to be. You are advised to set `hot_standby` to `off` for the initial period only.

Use a script; don't do this by hand, even when testing or just exploring the capabilities. If you make a mistake, you'd want to rerun things from the start again, and doing things manually is both laborious and an extra source of error.

How it works...

Transaction log (WAL) files will be written on the master. Setting `wal_level` to `archive` ensures that we collect all of the changed data, and that WAL is never optimized away. WAL is sent from the master to the archive using `archive_command`, and from there, the standby reads WAL files using `restore_command`. Then, it replays the changes.

The `archive_command` is executed when a file becomes full, or an `archive_timeout` number of seconds have passed since any user inserted change data into the transaction log. If the server does not write any new transaction log data for an extended period, then files will switch every `checkpoint_timeout` seconds. This is normal, and not a problem.

The preceding configuration assumes that the archive is on the standby, so the `restore_command` shown is a simple copy command (`cp`). If the archive were on a third system, then we would need to either mount the filesystem remotely or use a network copy command.

The `archive_cleanup_command` ensures that the archive only holds the files that the standby needs for restarting, in case it stops for any reason. Files older than the last file required are deleted regularly to ensure that the archive does not overflow. Note that if the standby is down for an extended period, then the number of files in the archive will continue to accumulate, and eventually they will overflow. The number of files in the archive should also be monitored.

In the configuration shown in this recipe, a command named `pg_archivecleanup` is used to remove files from the archive. (This used to be a contrib module but is now part of the main server). The `pg_archivecleanup` module is designed to work with one standby node at a time. Note that `pg_archivecleanup` requires two parameters: the `archive` directory and `%r`, with a space between them. PostgreSQL transforms `%r` into the cut-off filename.

If you wish to have multiple standby nodes, then a shared archive would be a single point of failure and should be avoided, so each standby should maintain its own archive. We must modify the `archive_command` to be a script, rather than execute the command directly.

This allows us to handle archiving to multiple destinations:

```
archive_command = 'myarchivescript %p %f'
```

Then, we can write `myarchivescript` so that it looks something like the following, though you'll need to add suitable error checking for your environment:

```
scp $1 $STANDBYNODE1:$PGARCHIVE/$2
scp $1 $STANDBYNODE2:$PGARCHIVE/$2
scp $1 $STANDBYNODE3:$PGARCHIVE/$2
```

The initial copy, or base backup, is performed using the `rsync` utility, which may require you to have direct security authorization, for example, using SSH and key exchange. You may also choose to perform the base backup a different way. If so, feel free to substitute your preferred method.

There's more...

Monitoring file-based log shipping can be performed in a number of ways. You can look at the current files on both the `master` and `standby`, as follows:

```
ps -ef | grep archiver        on master
postgres: archiver process    last was   00000001000000000000040
ps -ef | grep startup         on standby
postgres: startup process     waiting for  00000001000000000000041
```

This allows you to see the replication delay in terms of the number of WAL files by which the `standby` is behind the `master`. Prior to PostgreSQL 9.0, it was difficult to measure the replication delay as a time interval with any accuracy, and some hackish methods were needed. Those aren't presented here. The latest ways of monitoring replication are covered in more detail in the *Monitoring replication* recipe.

See also

- If you have configuration instructions written for versions ranging from PostgreSQL 8.2 to 8.4, then they will work almost exactly the same from PostgreSQL 9.0 onwards. The only difference is that you will also need to specify `wal_level`, as just shown.
- Note that the procedures covered here are not the default configuration, and they do differ from earlier releases. In PostgreSQL 9.0, the `pg_standby` utility is no longer required, as many of its features are now performed directly by the server.
- If you prefer to continue using `pg_standby` with PostgreSQL 9.0, then you do not need to use the `archive_cleanup_command`, `standby_mode`, or `trigger_file` parameters at all.

Setting up streaming replication

Log shipping is a replication technique used by many database management systems. The master records change in its transaction log (WAL), and then the log data is shipped from the master to the standby, where the log is replayed.

In PostgreSQL, PSR transfers WAL data directly from the master to the standby, giving us integrated security and reduced replication delay.

There are two main ways to set up streaming replication: with or without an additional archive. Setting it up without an external archive is presented here, as it is the more simple and efficient way. However, there is one downside that suggests that the simple approach may not be appropriate for larger databases, which is explained later in the recipe.

Getting ready

If you haven't read the *Replication concepts* section and the *Replication best practices* recipes at the start of this chapter, go and read them now. Note that streaming replication refers to the master node as the primary node, and the two terms can be used interchangeably.

How to do it...

You can use the following procedure for base backups:

1. Identify your master and standby nodes, and ensure that they have been configured according to the *Replication best practices* recipe.
2. Configure replication security. Create or confirm the existence of the replication user on the master node:

   ```
   CREATE USER repuser
     REPLICATION
     LOGIN
     CONNECTION LIMIT 2
     ENCRYPTED PASSWORD 'changeme';
   ```

3. Allow the replication user to authenticate. The following example allows access from any IP address using MD5-encrypted password authentication; you may wish to consider other options. Add the following line to pg_hba.conf:

   ```
   host    replication    repuser    0.0.0.1/0    md5
   ```

4. Set the logging options in postgresql.conf on both the master and the standby so that you can get more information regarding replication connection attempts and associated failures:

   ```
   log_connections = on
   ```

5. Set `max_wal_senders` on the master in `postgresql.conf`, or increase it if the value is already nonzero:

```
max_wal_senders = 2
wal_level = 'archive'
archive_mode = on
archive_command = 'cd .'
```

6. Adjust the Hot Standby parameters if required (see later recipe).
7. Create replication slot, if needed (see later recipe).
8. Take a base backup:

```
pg_basebackup -d 'connection string' -D /path/to_data_dir
```

9. You are advised to use the following additional option on the `pg_basebackup` command line. This option allows the required WAL files to be streamed alongside the base backup on a second session, greatly improving the startup time on larger databases, without the need to fuss over large settings of `wal_keep_segments` (as seen in step *6*):

```
--wal-method=stream
```

10. If the backup uses too many server resources (CPU, memory, disk, or bandwidth), you can throttle down the speed for the backup using the following additional option on the `pg_basebackup` command line. The RATE value is specified in kb/s by default:

```
--max-rate=RATE
```

11. If you are using replication slots, specify the slot name:

```
--slot=myslotname
```

12. Set the `recovery.conf` parameters on the standby. Note that `primary_conninfo` must not specify a database name, though it can contain any other PostgreSQL connection option. Note also that all options in `recovery.conf` are enclosed in quotes, whereas the `postgresql.conf` parameters need not be. For PostgreSQL 9.4 and later versions, you can skip this step if you wish by specifying the `--write-recovery-conf` option on pg_basebackup:

```
standby_mode = 'on'
primary_conninfo = 'host=192.168.0.1 user=repuser'
# trigger_file = ''   # no need for trigger file 9.1+
```

13. Start the standby server.

14. Carefully monitor the replication delay until the catch-up period is over. During the initial catch-up period, the replication delay will be much higher than we would normally expect it to be.

> The `pg_basebackup` utility also allows you to produce a compressed TAR file,
> using this command:

```
pg_basebackup -F -z
```

An alternate procedure can be used if needed or desirable:

1. First, perform steps *1* to *5* of the preceding procedure.

2. Use `wal_keep_segments`, or use replication slots (see later recipe).

3. Adjust `wal_keep_segments` on the master in `postgresql.conf`. Set this to a value no higher than the amount of free space on the drive on which the `pg_wal` directory is mounted, divided by 16 MB (note: this value is configurable from PG 10+).

4. If `pg_wal` isn't mounted on a separate drive, then don't assume that all of the current free space is available for transaction log files: `wal_keep_segments = 10000 #  160 GB`

5. Adjust the Hot Standby parameters if required (see the *Hot Standby and read scalability* recipe). Take a base backup, very similar to the process for taking a physical backup, as described in `Chapter 11`, *Backup and Recovery*.

6. Start the backup:

```
psql -c "select pg_start_backup('base backup for streaming
rep')"
```

7. Copy the data files (excluding the `pg_wal` directory):

```
rsync -cva --inplace --exclude=*pg_wal* \
${PGDATA}/ $STANDBYNODE:$PGDATA
```

8. Stop the backup:

```
psql -c "select pg_stop_backup(), current_timestamp"
```

9. Set the `recovery.conf` parameters on the standby. Note that `primary_conninfo` must not specify a database name, though it can contain any other PostgreSQL connection option. Note also that all options in `recovery.conf` are enclosed in quotes, whereas the `postgresql.conf` parameters need not be:

```
standby_mode = 'on'
primary_conninfo = 'host=alpha user=repuser'
trigger_file = '/tmp/postgresql.trigger.5432'
```

9. Start the standby server.

10. Carefully monitor the replication delay until the catch-up period is over. During the initial catch-up period, the replication delay will be much higher than we would normally expect it to be.

How it works...

Multiple standby nodes can connect to a single master. Set `max_wal_senders` to the number of standby nodes, plus at least one. If you are planning to use `pg_basebackup –wal-method=stream`, then allow for an additional connection per concurrent backup you plan for. You may wish to set up an individual user for each standby node, though it may be sufficient just to set the `application_name` parameter in `primary_conninfo`.

The architecture for streaming replication is this: on the master, one `WALSender` process is created for each standby that connects for streaming replication. On the standby node, a `WALReceiver` process is created to work cooperatively with the master. Data transfer has been designed and measured to be very efficient-data is typically sent in 8,192-byte chunks, without additional buffering at the network layer.

Both `WALSender` and `WALReceiver` will work continuously on any outstanding data to be replicated until the queue is empty. If there is a quiet period, then `WALReceiver` will sleep for a while.

The standby connects to the master using native PostgreSQL libpq connections. This means that all forms of authentication and security work for replication just as they do for normal connections. Note that, for replication sessions, the standby is the client and the master is the server, if any parameters need to be configured. Using standard PostgreSQL libpq connections also means that normal network port numbers are used, so no additional firewall rules are required. You should also note that if the connections use SSL, then encryption costs will slightly increase the replication delay and the CPU resources required.

There's more...

If the connection between the master and standby drops, it will take some time for that to be noticed across an indirect network. To ensure that a dropped connection is noticed as soon as possible, you may wish to adjust the timeout settings.

The standby will notice that the connection to the master has dropped after `wal_receiver_timeout` milliseconds. Once the connection is dropped the standby will retry the connection to the sending server every `wal_retrieve_retry_interval` milliseconds. Set these parameters in the `postgresql.conf` file on the standby.

A sending server will notice that the connection has dropped after `wal_sender_timeout` milliseconds, set in the `postgresql.conf` file on the sender. Once the connection is dropped the standby is responsible for re-establishing the connection.

You may also wish to increase `max_wal_senders` to one or two more than the current number of nodes so that it will be possible to reconnect even before a dropped connection is noted. This allows a manual restart to re-establish connections more easily. If you do this, then also increase the connection limit for the replication user. Changing that setting requires a restart.

Data transfer may stop if the connection drops or the standby server or the standby system is shut down. If replication data transfer stops for any reason, it will attempt to restart from the point of the last transfer. Will that data still be available? Let's see.

For streaming replication, the master keeps a number of files that is at least equal to `wal_keep_segments`. If the standby database server has been down for long enough, the master will have moved on and will no longer have the data for the last point of transfer. If that should occur, then the standby needs to be reconfigured using the same procedure with which we started.

You should plan to use `pg_basebackup  --wal-method=stream`. If you choose not to, you should note that the standby database server will not be streaming during the initial base backup. So, if the base backup is long enough, we might end up with a situation where replication will never start because the desired starting point is no longer available on the master. This is the error that you'll get:

> **FATAL: requested WAL segment 000000010000000000000002 has already been removed**

It's very annoying, and there's no way out of it—you need to start over. So start with a very high value of `wal_keep_segments`. Don't guess this randomly; set it to the available disk space on `pg_wal` divided by 16 MB, or less if it is a shared disk. If you still get that error, then you need to increase `wal_keep_segments` and try again, possibly also using techniques to speed up the base backup, which are discussed in `Chapter 11`, *Backup and Recovery*.

If you can't set `wal_keep_segments` high enough, there is an alternative. You must configure a third server or storage pool with increased disk storage capacity, which you can use as an archive. The master will need to have an `archive_command` that places files on the archive server, rather than the dummy command shown in the preceding procedure, in addition to parameter settings to allow streaming to take place. The standby will need to retrieve files from the archive using `restore_command`, as well as streaming using `primary_conninfo`. Thus, both the master and standby have two modes for sending and receiving, and they can switch between them should failures occur. This is the typical configuration for large databases. Note that this means that the WAL data will be copied twice, once to the archive and once directly to the standby. Two copies are more expensive, but also more robust.

Setting up streaming replication security

Streaming replication is at least as secure as normal user connections to PostgreSQL.

Replication uses standard libpq connections, so we have all the normal mechanisms for authentication and SSL support, and all the firewall rules are similar.

Replication must be specifically enabled on both the sender and standby sides. Cascading replication does not require any additional security.

When performing a base backup, the `pg_basebackup`, `pg_receivewal`, and `pg_recvlogical` utilities will use the same type of libpq connections as a running streaming standby. You can use other forms of base backup, such as `rsync`, though you'll need to manually set up the security configuration.

Standbys are identical copies of the master, so all users exist on all nodes with identical passwords. All of the data is identical (eventually) and all the permissions are the same too. If you wish to control access more closely, then you'll need different `pg_hba.conf` rules on each server to control this. Obviously, if your config files differ between nodes, then failover will be slightly more dramatic, unless you've given that some prior thought.

Getting ready

Identify or create a user/role to be used solely for replication. Decide what form of authentication will be used. If you are going across data centers or the wider internet, take this very seriously.

How to do it...

On the master, perform these steps:

1. Enable replication by setting a specific host access rule in `pg_hba.conf`.
2. Give the selected replication user/role the `REPLICATION` and `LOGIN` attributes:

    ALTER ROLE replogin REPLICATION;

3. Alternatively, create it using this command:

    CREATE ROLE replogin REPLICATION LOGIN;

On the standby, perform these steps:

1. Request replication by setting `primary_conninfo` in `recovery.conf`
2. If you are using SSL connections, use `sslmode=verify-full`
3. Enable per-server rules, if any, for this server in `pg_hba.conf`.

How it works...

Streaming replication connects to a virtual database called `replication`. We do this because the WAL data contains changes to objects in all databases, so in a way, we aren't just connecting to one database—we are connecting to all of them.

Streaming replication connects similar to a normal user, except that instead of a normal user process, we are given a `WALSender` process.

You can set a connection limit on the number of replication connections in two ways:

- At the role level by issuing the following command:

  ALTER ROLE replogin CONNECTION LIMIT 2;

- By limiting the overall number of `WALSender` processes via the `max_wal_senders` parameter

Always allow one more connection than you think is required, to allow for disconnections and reconnections.

There's more...

You may notice that the `WALSender` process may hit 100 percent CPU if you use SSL with compression enabled and write lots of data, or generate a large WAL volume from things such as DDL or vacuuming. You can disable compression on fast networks when you aren't paying per bandwidth charges, using `sslcompression=0` in the connection string specified for `primary_conninfo`.

Hot Standby and read scalability

Hot Standby (or read replicas) is the name for the PostgreSQL feature that allows us to connect to a standby node and execute read-only queries. Most importantly, Hot Standby allows us to run queries while the standby is being continuously updated through either file-based or streaming replication.

Hot Standby allows you to offload large or long running queries or parts of your read-only workload to the standby nodes. Should you need to switchover or failover to the standby node, your queries will keep executing during the promotion process to avoid any interruption of service.

You can add additional Hot Standby nodes to scale the read-only workload. There is no hard limit on the number of standby nodes, as long as you ensure enough server resources are available and parameters are set correctly – 10, 20, or more nodes are easily possible.

There are two main capabilities provided by a Hot Standby node. The first is that the standby node provides a secondary node in case the primary node fails. The second capability is that we can run queries on that node. In some cases, these two aspects can come into conflict with each other and can result in queries being cancelled. We need to decide ahead of time the importance we attach to each capability so that we can prioritize between them.

In most cases, the role of standby will take priority. Queries are good, but it's OK to cancel them to ensure that we have a viable standby. If we have more than one Hot Standby node, it may be possible to have one node nominated as standby and others dedicated to serving queries, without any regard for their need to act as standbys.

Standby nodes are started and stopped using the same server commands as master servers, which were covered in earlier chapters.

Getting ready

Hot Standby is usable with the following:

- File-based replication
- Streaming replication
- While performing a point-in-time recovery
- When using a permanently frozen standby

For the first two replication mechanisms, you will need to configure replication as described in earlier recipes. In addition, you will need to configure the following parameters:

On the master, set the following in `postgresql.conf`:

```
wal_level = 'replica'  #  PostgreSQL  9.6 and above, else hot_standby
```

On the standby, set the following in `postgresql.conf`:

```
hot_standby = on
```

Both of those settings are now the default in PostgreSQL 10. In earlier versions you will need to make these changes. You will need to do a clean restart of the database server on the master. Then, wait a few seconds and restart the standby for those changes to take effect. If you restart the standby too quickly, it will still keep reading the older transaction log data and fail to start. It will give a log message saying you need to enable Hot Standby, so be patient. You only need to configure this once, not every time you restart. See the *Delaying, pausing, and synchronizing replication* recipe to work out how to wait for actions on the master to arrive on the standby.

A permanently frozen standby can be created by specific settings in the `recovery.conf` file. Neither `restore_command` nor `primary_conninfo` should be set, in the case of `standby_mode = on`. In this mode, the server will start, but will always remain at the exact state of the database as it was when the `pg_stop_backup()` function completed.

Another point to note is that during the initial catch-up period, the replication delay will be much higher than we would normally expect it to be. You are advised to set `hot_standby = off` for the initial period immediately following the creation of the standby only. User connections during that initial period may use system resources or cause conflicts that could extend the catch-up delay. When the standby is fully caught up with the primary, then we can set `hot_standby = on` and restart, or simply prevent user access via `pg_hba.conf` until the standby catches up.

How to do it...

On the standby node, changes from the master are read from the transaction log and applied to the standby database. Hot Standby works by emulating running transactions from the master so that queries on the standby have the visibility information they need to fully respect MVCC. This makes the Hot Standby mode particularly suitable for serving a large workload of short or fast `SELECT` queries. If the workload is consistently short, then few conflicts will delay the standby, and the server will run smoothly.

Queries that run on the standby node see a version of the database that is slightly behind the primary node. We describe this as eventually consistent. *How long is eventually?* That time is exactly the replication delay plus the apply delay, as discussed in the *Replication concepts* section. You may also request that standby servers delay applying changes. See the *Delaying, pausing, and synchronizing replication* recipe later on in this section.

Resource contention (CPU, I/O, and so on) may increase apply delay. If the server is busy applying changes from the master, then you will have fewer resources to use for queries. This means that if there are no changes arriving, then you'll get more query throughput. If there are predictable changes in the write workload on the master, then you may need to throttle back your query workload on the standby when they occur.

Replication apply may also generate conflicts with running queries. Conflict may cause the replay to pause, and eventually queries on the standby may be canceled or disconnected. There are three main types of conflicts that can occur between the master and queries on the standby, which are as follows:

- Locks such as Access Exclusive locks
- Cleanup records
- Other special cases

If cancellations do occur, they will throw either error or fatal-level errors. These will be marked with SQLSTATE 40001 SERIALIZATION FAILURE. This could be trapped by an application, and the SQL can be resubmitted.

You can monitor the number of conflicts that occur in two places. The total number of conflicts in each database can be seen using this query:

```
SELECT datname, conflicts FROM pg_stat_database;
```

You can drill down further to look at the types of conflict seen using the following query:

```
    SELECT
  datname
, confl_tablespace
, confl_lock
, confl_snapshot
, confl_bufferpin
, confl_deadlock
FROM pg_stat_database_conflicts;
```

Tablespace conflicts are the easiest to understand. If you try to drop a tablespace that someone is still using, then you're going to get a conflict. Don't do that!

Lock conflicts are also easy to understand. If you wish to run a command on the master, such as ALTER TABLE ... DROP COLUMN, then you must lock the table first to prevent all types of access. The lock request is sent to the standby server as well, which will then cancel standby queries that are currently accessing that table after a configurable delay.

On high-availability systems, making DDL changes to tables that cause long periods of locking on the master can be difficult. You may want the tables on the standby to stay available for reads during the period in which the changes are being made on the master. To do that, temporarily set these parameters on the standby: `max_standby_streaming delay = -1` and `max_standby_archive_delay = -1`. Then, reload the server. As soon as the first lock record is seen on the standby, all further changes will be held. Once the locks on the master are released, you can reset the original parameter values on the standby, which will then allow the changes to be made there.

Setting the `max_standby_streaming_delay` and `max_standby_archive_delay` parameters to -1 is very timid and may not be useful for normal running if the standby is intended to provide High Availability. No user query will ever be canceled if it conflicts with applying changes. It will cause the apply process to wait indefinitely. As a result, the apply delay can increase significantly over time, depending on the frequency and duration of queries and the frequency of conflicts. To work out an appropriate setting for these parameters, you need to understand more about the other types of conflict, though there is also a simple way to avoid this problem entirely.

Snapshot conflicts require some understanding of the internal workings of MVCC, which many people find confusing. To avoid snapshot conflicts, you should set `hot_standby_feedback = on` in the standby's `postgresql.conf` file.

In some cases, this could cause table bloat on the master, so it is not set by default. If you don't wish to set `hot_standby_feedback = on`, then you have further options to consider. You can set an upper limit on the acceptable apply delay caused by conflicts by controlling two similar parameters: `max_standby_streaming_delay` and `max_standby_archive_delay`. As a last resort, you can also provide some protection against cancelled queries by setting `vacuum_defer_cleanup_age` to a value higher than 0. This parameter is fairly hard to set accurately, though I would suggest starting with a value of 1000 and then tune upwards. A vague and inaccurate assumption would be to say that each 1000 will be approximately one second of additional delay. This is probably helpful more often than it is wrong. Other conflict types (bufferpin, deadlocks, and so on) are possible, but they are rare.

If you want a completely static standby database with no further changes applied, then you can do this by stopping the server, modifying `recovery.conf` such that neither `restore_command` nor `primary_conninfo` are set but `standby_mode` is on, and then restarting the server. You can come back out of this mode, but only if the archive contains the required WAL files to catch up. Otherwise, you will need to reconfigure the standby from a base backup again.

If you attempt to run a non-read-only query, then you will receive an error marked with SQLSTATE 25006 READ ONLY TRANSACTION. That could be used to redirect SQL to the master, where it can execute successfully.

How it works...

Changes made by a transaction on the master will not be visible until the commit is applied onto the standby. So, for example, we have a master and a standby with a replication delay of four seconds between them. A long-running transaction may write changes to the master for one hour. How long does it take before those changes are visible on the standby? With Hot Standby, the answer is four seconds after the commit on the master. This is because the changes made during the transaction on the master are streamed while the transaction is still in progress, and in most cases, they are already applied on the standby when the commit record arrives.

You may also wish to use the remote_apply mode; see the *Delaying, pausing, and synchronizing replication* recipe later on this section.

Hot Standby can also be used when running a point-in-time recovery, so the WAL records applied to the database need not arrive immediately from a live database server. We can just use file-based recovery in that case, not streaming replication.

Finally, query performance has been dramatically improved in Hot Standby over time, so it's a good idea to upgrade for that reason alone.

Managing streaming replication

Replication is great, provided that it works. Replication works well if it's understood and works even better if it's tested.

Getting ready

You need to have a plan for the objectives for each individual server in the cluster. *Which standby server will be the failover target?*

How to do it...

Switchover is a controlled switch from the master to the standby. If performed correctly, there will be no data loss. To be safe, simply shut down the master node cleanly, using either the `smart` or `fast` shutdown modes. Do not use the `immediate` mode shutdown because you will almost certainly lose data that way.

Failover is a forced switch from the master node to a standby because of the loss of the master. So, in that case, there is no action to perform on the master; we presume it is not there anymore.

Next, we need to promote one of the standby nodes to be the new master. A standby node can be triggered into becoming a master node in one of two ways:

- pg_ctl promote
- Suppose you originally specified a `trigger_file` parameter like this:

```
trigger_file = '/tmp/postgresql.trigger.5432'
```

Then, you can create the `trigger` file by executing this:

```
touch /tmp/postgresql.trigger.5432
```

The `trigger_file` will be deleted when the transition is complete.

Note that the `trigger` file has nothing to do whatsoever with trigger-based replication. The `trigger` filename can be anything you like. We use a suffix of `5432` to ensure that we trigger only one server if there are multiple PostgreSQL servers operating on the same system.

The standby will become the master only once it has fully caught up. If you haven't been monitoring replication, this could take some time.

In versions before PostgreSQL 9.3, switching from standby to master may take some time while the database performs an immediate checkpoint, at least with database servers with large caches and high rate of changes being replicated from the master. From PostgreSQL 9.3 onwards, we can switch from the standby to the master very quickly, and then perform a smooth background checkpoint. There may still be significant I/O as writes begin on the new master.

Once the ex-standby becomes a master, it will begin to operate all normal functions, including starting to archive files if configured. Be careful to verify that you have all the correct settings for when this node begins to operate as a master.

It is likely that the settings will be different from those on the original master from which they were copied.

Note that I refer to this new server as **a master**, not **the master**. It is up to you to ensure that the previous master doesn't continue to operate a situation known as **split-brain**. You must be careful to ensure that the previous master stays down.

Management of complex failover situations is not provided with PostgreSQL, nor is automated failover. Situations can be quite complex with multiple nodes, and clusterware is used in many cases to manage this.

The role of the `recovery_end_command` is to clean up at the end of the switchover or failover process. You do not need to explicitly remove the `trigger` file, as was recommended in previous releases.

There's more...

Following a switchover from one node to another, it is common to think of performing a switchover back to the old master server, which is sometimes called failback or switchback.

Once a standby has become a master, it cannot go back to being a standby again. So, with log replication, there is no explicit switchback operation. This is a surprising situation for many people and is a repeated question, but it is quick to work around. Once you have performed a switchover, all you need to do is the following:

- Reconfigure the old master node again, repeating the same process as before to set up a standby node
- Switchover from the current to the old master node

The important part here is that if we perform the first step without deleting the files on the old master, it allows `rsync` to go much faster. When no files are present on the destination, `rsync` just performs a copy. When similarly named files are present on the destination, then `rsync` will compare the files and send only the changes. So, the `rsync` we perform on a switchback operation performs much less data transfer than in the original copy. It is likely that this will be enhanced in later releases of PostgreSQL. There are also ways to avoid this, as shown in the `repmgr` utility, which will be discussed later.

The `pg_rewind` utility has been developed as a way to perform an automated switchback operation. It performs a much faster switchback when there is a large database with few changes to apply. To allow correct operation, this program must run using the `wal_log_hints = on` parameter.

Using that parameter can cause more I/O on large databases, so while it improves performance for switchback it has a considerable overhead for normal running. If you think you would like to run `pg_rewind`, then make sure you work out how it behaves ahead of time. Trying to run it for the first time in a stress situation with a down server is a bad idea.

See also

Clusterware may provide additional features, such as automated failover, monitoring, or ease of management of replication:

- The `repmgr` utility is designed to manage PostgreSQL replication and failover. This is discussed in more detail in the *Using repmgr* recipe.
- The `pgpool` library is designed to allow session pooling and routing of requests to standby nodes.

Using repmgr

As said before, replication is great provided it works. It works well if it's understood and works even better if it's tested. This is a great reason to use `repmgr` utility.

`repmgr` 4.0 is an open source tool designed specifically for PostgreSQL replication. To get additional information about repmgr, visit `http://www.repmgr.org/`.

The `repmgr` utility provides a command-line interface and a management process (daemon) used to monitor and manage PostgreSQL servers involved in replication. The `repmgr` utility easily supports more than two nodes, with automatic failover detection.

Getting ready

Install `repmgr` utility from binary packages on each PostgreSQL node.

Set up replication security and network access between nodes according to the *Setting up streaming replication security* recipe.

How to do it...

The `repmgr` utility provides a set of single command-line actions that perform all the required activities on one node:

1. To start a new cluster with `repmgr` with the current node as its primary, use the following command:

   repmgr primary register

2. To add an existing standby to the cluster with `repmgr`, use the following command:

   repmgr standby register

3. Use the following command to request `repmgr` to create a new standby for you by copying `node1`. This will fail if you specify an existing `data` directory:

   repmgr standby clone node1 -D /path/of_new_data_directory

4. To reuse an old master as a standby, use the `rejoin` command:

   repmgr node rejoin -d 'host=node2 user=repmgr'

5. To switch from one primary to another one, run this command on the `standby` which you want to make a primary:

   repmgr standby switchover

6. To promote a `standby` to be the new primary, use the following command:

   repmgr standby promote

6. To request a `standby` to follow a new primary, use the following command:

   repmgr standby follow

7. Check the status of each registered node in the cluster, like this:

   repmgr cluster show

8. Request cleanup of monitoring data, as follows. This is relevant only if `--monitoring-history` is used:

   repmgr cluster cleanup

9. Create a `witness` server for use with auto-failover voting, like this:

```
repmgr witness create
```

The preceding commands are presented in a simplified form. Each command also takes one of these options:

- `--verbose`: This is useful when exploring new features
- `-f`: This specifies the path to the `repmgr.conf` file

For each node, create a `repmgr.conf` file containing at least the following parameters. Note that the `node_id` and `node_name` parameters need to be different on each node:

```
node_id=2
node_name=beta
conninfo='host=beta user=repmgr'
data_directory=/var/lib/pgsql/10/data
```

Once all the nodes are registered, you can start the `repmgr` daemon on each node, like this:

```
repmgrd -d -f /var/lib/pgsql/repmgr/repmgr.conf &
```

If you would like the daemon to generate monitoring information for that node, you should set `monitoring_history=yes` in the `repmgr.conf` file.

Monitoring data can be accessed using this:

```
repmgr=# select * from repmgr.replication_status;
-[ RECORD 1 ]-------------+---------------------------------
primary_node_id           | 1
standby_node_id           | 2
standby_name              | node2
node_type                 | standby
active                    | t
last_monitor_time         | 2017-08-24 16:28:41.260478+09
last_wal_primary_location | 0/6D57A00
last_wal_standby_location | 0/5000000
replication_lag           | 29 MB
replication_time_lag      | 00:00:11.736163
apply_lag                 | 15 MB
communication_time_lag    | 00:00:01.365643
```

How it works...

repmgr 4 works with PostgreSQL 9.3+ and PostgreSQL 10 and later versions. repmgr supports the latest features of PostgreSQL, such as cascading, synchronous replication, and replication slots. It uses `pg_basebackup`, allowing you to clone from a standby. The use of `pg_basebackup` also removes the need for `rsync` and key exchange between servers. Also, cascaded standby nodes no longer need to re-follow.

There's more...

The default behavior for `repmgr` utility is manual failover.

The `repmgr` utility also supports automatic failover capabilities. It can automatically detect failures of other nodes and then decide which server should become the new master by voting among all of the still available standby nodes. The `repmgr` utility supports a witness server to ensure that there are an odd number of voters in order to get a clear winner in any decision.

Using replication slots

Replication slots allow you to define your replication architecture explicitly. They also allow you to track details of nodes even when they are disconnected. Replication slots work with both PSR and LSR.

Replication slots ensure that data required by a downstream node persists until the node receives it. They are crash-safe, so if a connection is lost, the slot still continues to exist. By tracking data on downstream nodes, we avoid these problems:

- When a standby disconnects, the feedback data provided by `hot_standby_feedback` is lost. When the standby reconnects, it may be sent cleanup records that result in query conflicts. Replication slots remember the standby's `xmin` value even when disconnected, ensuring that cleanup conflicts can be avoided.
- When a standby disconnects, the knowledge of which WAL files were required is lost. When the standby reconnects, we may have discarded the required WAL files, requiring us to completely regenerate the downstream node (assuming that this is possible). Replication slots ensure that nodes retain the WAL files needed by all downstream nodes.

Replication slots are required by LSR and for any other use of logical decoding. Replication slots are optional with PSR.

Getting ready

This recipe assumes that you have already set up replication according to the earlier recipes so that `wal_level`, `max_wal_senders`, and other parameters are set.

A replication slot represents one link between two nodes. At any time, each slot can support one connection. If you draw a diagram of your replication architecture, then each connecting line is one slot. Each slot must have a unique name. The slot name must contain only lowercase letters, numbers, and underscores.

As discussed previously, each node should have a unique name. So a suggestion would be to construct the slot name from the two node names that it links. For various reasons, there may be a need for multiple slots between two nodes, so additional information is also required for uniqueness. For two servers called `alpha` and `beta`, an example of a slot name would be `alpha_beta_1`.

For LSR, each slot refers to a single database rather than the whole server. In that case, slot names could also include database names.

How to do it...

1. Set `max_replication_slots` > 0 on each sending node. This change requires a restart. Set the value to at least one more than the number of planned slots:

   ```
   max_replication_slots = 2
   ```

2. For PSR slots, you have to first create the slot on the sending node, like this:

   ```
   SELECT (pg_create_physical_replication_slot
   ('alpha_beta_1', true)).wal_position;
   wal_position
   ------------------
   0/5000060
   ```

3. Monitor it in use by using the following:

   ```
   SELECT * FROM pg_replication_slots;
   ```

4. In the `recovery.conf` file in the `data` directory on the standby, set the `primary_slot_name` parameter using the unique name that you assigned earlier:

```
primary_slot_name = 'alpha_beta_1'
```

Slots can be removed using the following query:

```
SELECT pg_drop_physical_replication_slot('alpha_beta_1');
```

There's more...

Replication slots can be used to support applications where downstream nodes are disconnected for extended periods of time. Replication slots prevent removal of WAL files, which are needed by disconnected nodes. Therefore, it is important to be careful that WAL files don't build up, causing *out of disk space* errors due to physical replication slots created with no currently connected standby.

See also

- See the *Logical replication* recipe for more details on using slots with LSR

Monitoring replication

Monitoring the status and progress of your replication is essential. We'll start by looking at the server status and then query the progress of replication.

Getting ready

You'll need to start by checking the state of your server(s).

Check whether a server is up using `pg_isready` or another program that uses the `PQping()` API call. You'll get one of the following responses:

- `PQPING_OK (return code 0)`: The server is running and appears to be accepting connections.

- `PQPING_REJECT` `(return code 1)`: The server is running, but is in a state that disallows connections (startup, shutdown, or crash recovery) or a standby that is not enabled with Hot Standby.
- `PQPING_NO_RESPONSE` `(return code 2)`: The server could not be contacted. This might indicate that the server is not running, there is something wrong with the given connection parameters (for example, wrong port number), or there is a network connectivity problem (for example, a firewall blocking the connection request).
- `PQPING_NO_ATTEMPT` `(return code 3)`: No attempt was made to contact the server, for example, invalid parameters.

 We don't differentiate between a master and a standby, though this may change in later releases. Neither do we say whether a server is accepting write transactions or only read-only transactions (a standby or a master connection in read-only mode).

You can know whether a server is a master or a standby by connecting and executing this query:

```
SELECT pg_is_in_recovery();
```

There are also two other states that may be important for backup and replication: paused and in-exclusive-backup. The paused state doesn't affect user queries, but replication will not progress at all when paused. Only one exclusive backup may occur at any one time.

You can also check whether replay is paused by executing this query:

```
SELECT pg_is_wal_replay_paused();
```

If you want to check whether a server is in-exclusive-backup mode, execute the following query:

```
SELECT pg_is_in_backup();
```

There is no supported function that shows whether a non-exclusive backup is in progress, though there isn't as much to worry about if there is. If you care about that, make sure you set the `application_name` of the backup program so that it shows up in the session status output of `pg_stat_activity`, as discussed in `Chapter 8`, *Monitoring and Diagnosis*.

How to do it...

The rest of this recipe assumes that you have enabled `hot_standby`. This is not an absolute requirement, but it makes things much, much easier.

Both `repmgr` and `pgpool` provide replication monitoring facilities. Munin plugins are available for graphing replication and apply delay.

Replication works by processing the WAL transaction log on other servers. You can think of WAL as a single, serialized stream of messages. Each message in the WAL is identified by an 8-byte integer known as a **Log Sequence Number** (**LSN**). For historical reasons, we show this as two separate hex numbers; for example, the LSN value X is shown as XXXX/YYYY.

You can compare any two LSNs using `pg_wal_lsn_diff()`. In some places, prior to PostgreSQL 10, an LSN was referred to as a "location", a term no longer in use.

To understand how to monitor progress, you need to understand a little more about replication as a transport mechanism. The stream of messages flows through the system like water through a pipe. You can work out how much progress has been made by measuring the LSN at different points in the pipe. You can also check for blockages in the pipe by measuring the relative progress between points.

New WAL records are inserted into the WAL files on the master. The current insert LSN can be found using this query:

```
SELECT pg_current_wal_insert_lsn();
```

However, WAL records are not replicated until they have been written and synced to the WAL files on the master. The LSN of the most recent WAL write is given by this query on the master:

```
SELECT pg_current_wal_lsn();
```

Once written, WAL records are then sent to the standby. The recent status can be found by running this query on the standby (this and the later functions return NULL on a master):

```
SELECT pg_last_wal_receive_lsn();
```

Once WAL records have been received, they are written to WAL files on the standby. When the standby has written those records, they can then be applied to it. The LSN of the most recent apply is found using this standby query:

```
SELECT pg_last_wal_replay_lsn();
```

Remember that there will always be timing differences if you run status queries on multiple nodes. What we really need is to see all of the information on one node. A view called `pg_stat_replication` provides the information that we need:

```
SELECT pid, application_name /* or other unique key */
,pg_current_wal_insert_lsn() /* WAL Insert lsn */
,sent_lsn /* WALSender lsn */
,write_lsn /* WALReceiver write lsn */
,flush_lsn /* WALReceiver flush lsn */
,replay_lsn /* Standby apply lsn */
,backend_start /* Backend start */
FROM pg_stat_replication;
-[ RECORD 1 ]------------------+----------------------------- pid |
16496
application_name               | pg_basebackup pg_current_wal_insert_lsn    |
0/80000D0
sent_lsn                       |
write_lsn                      |
flush_lsn                      |
replay_lsn                     |
backend_start                  | 2017-01-27  15:25:42.988149+00
-[ RECORD 2 ]------------------+-------------------pid
16497
application_name               | pg_basebackup pg_current_wal_insert_lsn    |
0/80000D0
sent_lsn                       | 0/80000D0
write_lsn                      | 0/8000000
flush_lsn                      | 0/8000000
replay_lsn |
backend_start                  | 2017-01-27  15:25:43.18958+00
```

Each row in this view represents one replication connection. The preceding snippet shows the output from a `pg_basebackup` that is using `--wal-method=stream`. The first connection shown is the base backup, while the second session is streaming WAL changes. Note that the `replay_lsn` is NULL, indicating that this is not a standby.

Standby nodes send regular status messages to let the sender know how far it has progressed. If you run this query on the master, you'll be able to see all the directly connected standbys. If you run this query on a standby, you'll see values representing any cascaded standbys, but nothing about the master or any of the other standbys connected to the master. Note that because the data has been sent from a remote node, it is very likely that processing will have progressed beyond the point being reported, but we don't know that for certain. That's just physics. Welcome to the world of distributed systems!

In PostgreSQL 10, replication delay times are provided directly using sampled message timings to provide the most accurate viewpoint of current delay times. Use this query:

```
SELECT pid, application_name /* or other unique key */
   ,write_lag, flush_lag, replay_lag
  FROM pg_stat_replication;
```

Another view called `pg_stat_wal_receiver` provides information about the standby that we may be interested in; this view returns zero rows on the master.

There's more...

The `pg_stat_replication` view shows only the currently connected nodes. If a node is supposed to be connected but it isn't, then there is no record of it at all, anywhere. If you don't have a list of the nodes that are supposed to be connected, then you'll just miss it.

Replication slots give you a way to define which connections are supposed to be present. If you have defined a slot and it is currently connected, then you will get one row in `pg_stat_replication` for the connection and one row in `pg_replication_slots` for the corresponding slot. To find out which slots don't have current connections, you can run this query:

```
SELECT slot_name, database, age(xmin), age(catalog_xmin)
  FROM pg_replication_slots
  WHERE NOT active;
```

To find the details of the currently connected slots, run something like this query:

```
SELECT slot_name
  FROM pg_replication_slots
  JOIN pg_stat_replication ON pid = active_pid;
```

Performance and synchronous replication

We usually refer to synchronous replication as simply **sync rep**. The sync rep allows us to offer a confirmation to the user that a transaction has been committed and fully replicated on at least one standby server. To do that, we must wait for the transaction changes to be sent to at least one standby, and then have that feedback returned to the master.

The additional time taken for the message's round trip will add elapsed time for write transactions, which increases in proportion to the distance between servers. PostgreSQL offers a choice to the user as to what balance they would like between durability and response time.

Getting ready

The user application must be connected to a master to issue transactions that write data. The default level of durability is defined by the `synchronous_commit` parameter. That parameter is user settable, so it can be set for different applications, sessions, or even individual transactions. For now, ensure that the user application is using this level:

```
SET synchronous_commit = on;
```

We must decide which standbys should take over from the master in the event of a failover. We do this by setting a parameter called `synchronous_standby_names`.

You will need to configure at least three nodes to use sync rep correctly.

How to do it...

Make sure you have set the `application_name` on each standby node. Decide the order of servers to be listed in the `synchronous_standby_names` parameter. Note that the standbys named must be directly attached standby nodes or else their names will be ignored. Synchronous replication is not possible for cascaded nodes, though cascaded standbys may be connected downstream. An example for a simple four node config of `nodeA` (master), `nodeB`, `nodeC`, and `nodeD` (standbys) would be set on `nodeA` as follows:

```
synchronous_standby_names = 'nodeB, nodeC, nodeD'
```

If you want to receive replies from the first two of the nodes in a list then we would specify this using the following special syntax:

```
synchronous_standby_names = '2 (nodeB, nodeC, nodeD)'
```

If you want to receive replies from any two nodes, known as quorum commit, then:

```
synchronous_standby_names = 'any 2 (nodeB, nodeC, nodeD)'
```

Set `synchronous_standby_names` on all of the nodes, not just the master.

You can see the `sync_state` of connected standbys using this query on the master:

```
SELECT
application_name
,state                    /* startup, backup, catchup or streaming */
,sync_priority            /* 0, 1 or more */
,sync_state               /* async, sync or potential */
FROM pg_stat_replication
ORDER BY sync_priority;
```

There are a few columns here with similar names, so be careful not to confuse them.

The `sync_state` column is just a human-readable form of `sync_priority`.
When `sync_state` is async, the `sync_priority` value will be zero (0). Standby nodes
mentioned in the `synchronous_standby_names` parameter will have a nonzero priority
that corresponds to the order in which they are listed. The standby node with a priority of
one (1) will be listed as having a `sync_state` value of sync. We refer to this node as the
sync standby. Other standby nodes configured to provide feedback are shown with a
`sync_state` value of potential and a `sync_priority` value more than 1.

If a server is listed in the `synchronous_standby_names` parameter, but is not currently
connected, then it will not be shown at all by the preceding query, so it is possible that the
node is shown with a lower actual priority value than the stated ordering in the parameter.
Setting `wal_receiver_status_interval` to 0 on the standby will disable status messages
completely, and the node will show as an async node, even if it is named in the
`synchronous_standby_names` parameter. You may wish to do this when you are
completely certain that a standby will never need to be a failover target, such as a test
server.

The state for each server is shown as one of startup, catchup, or streaming. When
another node connects, it will first show as startup, though only briefly before it moves to
catchup. Once the node has caught up with the master, it will move to streaming, and
only then will `sync_priority` be set to a nonzero value.

Catch-up typically occurs quickly after a disconnection or reconnection, such as when a standby node is restarted. When performing an initial base backup, the server will show as `backup`. After this, it will stay for an extended period at `catchup`. The delay at this point will vary according to the size of the database, so it could be a long period. Bear this in mind when configuring sync rep.

When a new standby node moves to the `streaming` mode, you'll see a message like this in the master node log:

```
LOG standby $APPLICATION_NAME is now the synchronous
standby with priority N
```

How it works...

Standby servers send feedback messages that describe the LSN of the latest transaction they have processed. Transactions committing on the master will wait until they receive feedback saying that their transaction has been processed. If there are no standbys available for sending feedback, then the transactions on the master will wait for standbys, possibly for a very long time. That is why we say that you must have at least three servers to sensibly use sync rep. It probably occurs to you that you could run with just two servers. You can, but such a configuration does not offer any transaction guarantees; it just appears to. Many people are confused on that point, but please don't listen to them!

Sync rep increases the elapsed time of write transactions (on the master). This can reduce performance of applications from a user perspective. The server itself will spend more time waiting than before, which may increase the required number of concurrently active sessions.

Remember that when using sync rep, the overall system is still eventually consistent. Transactions committing on the master are visible first on the standby, and a brief moment later those changes will be visible on the master (yes, standby, and then master). This means that an application that issues a write transaction on the master followed by a read transaction on the sync standby will be guaranteed to see its own changes.

You can increase performance somewhat by setting the `synchronous_commit` parameter to `remote_write`, though you will lose data if both master and standby crashes. You can also set the `synchronous_commit` parameter to `remote_apply` when you want to ensure that all changes are committed to the synchronous standbys and the master before we confirm back to the user. However, this is not the same thing as synchronous visibility—the changes become visible on the different standbys at different times.

There's more...

There is a small window of uncertainty for any transaction that is in progress just at the point the master goes down. This can be handled within the application by checking the return code following a commit operation, rather than just assuming that it has completed successfully, as developers often do.

If the commit fails, it is possible that the server committed the transaction successfully, but was unable to communicate that to the client, but we don't know for certain. We can resolve that uncertainty by rechecking a unique aspect of the transaction, such as reconfirming the existence of an object identifier that was inserted.

If such an object identifier doesn't exist, we can create a table for this purpose:

```
CREATE TABLE TransactionCheck
  (TxnId     SERIAL PRIMARY KEY);
```

During the transaction, we insert a row into that table using this query:

```
INSERT INTO TransactionCheck DEFAULT VALUES RETURNING TxnId;
```

Then, if the commit appears to fail, we can later reread this value to confirm the transaction state as committed or aborted.

Delaying, pausing, and synchronizing replication

Some advanced features and thoughts for replication are covered here.

Getting ready

If you have multiple standby servers, you may want to have one or more servers operating in a delayed apply state, for example, one hour behind the master. This can be useful to help recover from user errors such as mistaken transactions or dropped tables.

How to do it...

Normally, a standby will apply changes as soon as possible. When you set the `recovery_min_apply_delay` parameter in `recovery.conf`, the application of commit records will be delayed by the specified duration. Note that only commit records are delayed, so you may receive Hot Standby cancellations using this feature. You can prevent that by setting `hot_standby_feedback` to `on`, but use this with caution, since it can cause significant bloat on a busy master if `recovery_min_apply_delay` is large.

If something bad happens, then hit the **pause** button.

Hot Standby allows you to pause and resume replay of change:

1. To pause the replay, issue this query:

   SELECT pg_wal_replay_pause();

   Once paused, all queries will receive the same snapshot, allowing lengthy repeated analyses of the database, or retrieval of a dropped table.

2. To resume (un-pause) processing, use this query:

   SELECT pg_wal_replay_resume();

Be careful not to promote a delayed standby. If your delayed standby is the last server available, you should reset `recovery_min_apply_delay`, then restart the server, and allow it to catch up before issuing a promote action.

There's more...

A standby is an exact copy of the master. But how do you synchronize things so that the query results you get from a standby are guaranteed to be the same as you'd get from the master? Well, that in itself is not possible. It's just the physics of an eventually consistent system. We need it to be eventually consistent because otherwise, the synchronization would become a performance bottleneck.

What we can do is synchronize two requests on different servers, for example, if we wish to issue a write on the master and then later issue a read from a standby. Such a case is automatically handled by synchronous replication. If we aren't using sync rep, then we can wait for the standby to catch up with an action on the master, remembering that the master will have moved on by the time we've done this. To perform the wait you need to do the following:

1. On the master, perform an action that writes WAL. Just for testing purposes—not for real usage—we can issue a request like this:

    ```
    SELECT pg_create_restore_point('my action name')
    ```

2. On the master, commit the transaction using `commit;` with any setting other than `synchronous_commit = off`

3. On the master, find the current write LSN using this query:

    ```
    SELECT pg_current_wal_write_lsn();
    ```

4. On the standby, execute the following query repeatedly until the LSN value returned is equal to or higher than the LSN from the master:

    ```
    SELECT pg_last_wal_replay_lsn();
    ```

The following function performs such a wait:

```
CREATE OR REPLACE FUNCTION wait_for_lsn(lsn pg_lsn)
RETURNS VOID
LANGUAGE plpgsql
AS $$
BEGIN
    LOOP
        IF pg_last_wal_replay_lsn() IS NULL OR
           pg_last_wal_replay_lsn() >= lsn THEN
            RETURN;
        END IF;
        PERFORM pg_sleep(0.1);   /* 100ms */
    END LOOP;
END $$;
```

This isn't ideal since it can be cancelled while waiting. Later releases may contain better solutions.

See also

- Logical replication allows us to control the flow of data in various ways. For `pglogical` use these commands:

```
SELECT alter_subscription_disable();
SELECT alter_subscription_enable();
```

- We can also create a subscription with a parameter of `apply_delay`
- For PostgreSQL 10 subscriptions, use these commands:

```
ALTER SUBSCRIPTION mysub DISABLE;
ALTER SUBSCRIPTION mysub ENABLE;
```

Logical replication

Logical replication allows us to stream logical data changes between two nodes. By logical, we mean streaming changes to data without referring to specific physical attributes such as block number and row ID.

The main benefits of logical replication are as follows:

- Performance is roughly two times as better than that of the best trigger-based mechanisms
- Selective replication is supported, so we don't need to replicate the entire database (only available with pglogical at present)
- Replication can occur between different major releases, which can allow a zero-downtime upgrade

PostgreSQL 9.4 onwards provides a feature called logical decoding. This allows you to stream a set of changes out of a master server. This allows a master to become a sending node in logical replication. The receiving node requires a logical replication plugin to allow replication between two nodes.

Previously, we referred to physical replication as **streaming replication**. Now, we have to modify our descriptions so that we can refer to PSR and LSR. In terms of security, network data transfer, and general management, the two modes are very similar. Concepts used to monitor PSR can also be used to monitor LSR.

Since the target systems are fully writable masters in their own right, we can use the full power of PostgreSQL without restrictions. We can use temporary tables, triggers, different user accounts, and GRANT permissions differently. We can also define indexes differently, collect statistics differently, and run VACUUM on different schedules.

As a result, calling nodes just as sending and receiving nodes isn't enough. LSR works on a publish/subscribe model, so we refer to the nodes as publishers and subscribers.

LSR works on a per-database level, not a whole server level like PSR. One publishing node can feed multiple subscriber nodes without incurring additional disk write overhead.

PostgreSQL 10 contains native logical replication between servers for PostgreSQL 10 and above. Another option is the more flexible **pglogical** utility, which can send and receive data from PostgreSQL 9.4 and above, see (`https://2ndquadrant.com/en/resources/pglogical/`).

pglogical 2.1 allows you to perform the following actions:

- Full database replication
- Selective replication of subsets of tables using replication sets
- Selective replication of table rows at either the publisher or subscriber side
- Upgrades between major versions (see later recipe)
- Data forwarding to Postgres-XL or Postgres-BDR

Getting ready

To use `pglogical`, the publisher and subscriber must be running PostgreSQL 9.4 or higher and you must install the `pglogical` extension on both nodes.

The procedure is the following:

1. Identify all the nodes that will work together as parts of your replication architecture.
2. Each LSR link can replicate changes from a single database. If you have multiple databases in your PostgreSQL server, you will need one LSR link per database (not counting `template0` and `template1`).
3. Each LSR link will use one connection and one slot. Set the `max_replication_slots` and `max_connections` parameters to match those requirements.

4. Each LSR link requires one WAL sender on the publisher. Set `max_wal_senders` to match this requirement.

5. Each LSR link requires one apply process on the subscriber. Set `max_worker_processes` to match this requirement.

6. On each node do all of the following steps:

   ```
   CREATE EXTENSION pglogical;
   ```

7. If using PostgreSQL 9.4, then also install the following:

   ```
   CREATE EXTENSION pglogical_origin;
   ```

8. Any user-installed data types must be installed on both nodes.

9. Add this to `postgresql.conf shared_preload_libraries = 'pglogical'` `--add` to any existing list.

10. Set this parameter in `postgresql.conf`:

    ```
    wal_level = 'logical'
    ```

11. On each database, declare the node to `pglogical`:

    ```
    SELECT pglogical.create_node(
            node_name := 'nodeA',
            dsn := 'host=nodeA dbname=postgres');
    ```

An example of a `postgresql.conf` file on the source node for the preceding steps looks like this:

```
# Record data for Logical replication
wal_level = 'logical'
# Load the pglogical extension
shared_preload_libraries = 'pglogical'
# Allow replication slot creation (we need just one but it
does not hurt to have more)
max_replication_slots = 10
# Allow streaming replication (we need one for slot and
one for basebackup but again, it does not hurt to have more)
max_wal_senders = 10
max_worker_processes = 10
```

Logical replication supports selective replication, which means that you don't need to specify all the tables in the database. Identify the tables to be replicated. Define replication sets that correspond to groups of tables that should be replicated together. Ensure that all the transactions that touch any table in the set touch only a subset of the set, or the whole set.

Tables that will be replicated may need some preparatory steps as well. To allow logical replication to apply UPDATE and DELETE commands correctly on the target node, we need to define how we search for unique rows. This is known as the replica identity. By default, the replica identity will be the primary key of a table, so you need not take any action if you have already defined primary keys on your tables. In some cases, you may need to define the replica identity explicitly, using a command like this:

```
ALTER TABLE mytable REPLICA IDENTITY USING INDEX myuniquecol_idx;
```

Tables on the publisher and subscriber must have the same names and be in the same schema. Tables must also have the same columns with the same data types in each column. Tables must have the same PRIMARY KEY on both nodes. CHECK, NOT NULL, and UNIQUE constraints must be the same or weaker (more permissive) on the subscriber.

Logical replication also supports filtered replication, which means that only certain actions are replicated on the target node; for example, we can specify that INSERT commands are replicated while DELETE commands are filtered away. We can also specify a subset of the rows to be sent from the publisher or applied on the subscriber. This allows logical replication to support a greater range of data movement applications than was previously possible with trigger replication.

Replication requires superuser access for the roles providing replication.

How to do it...

Let's look at a few different examples of how to use logical replication:

1. To publish changes from all tables on a postgres database on nodeA, use the following:

```
SELECT pglogical.replication_set_add_all_tables(
            set_name := 'default',
            schema_names := ARRAY['public'],
            true);
```

And then, by issuing the following command on `nodeB`:

```
SELECT pglogical.create_subscription(
                 subscription_name := 'my_subscription_name',
                 provide_dsn := 'host=nodeA dbname=postgres'
                 );
```

2. Publish changes for `TableX` on the `MyApp` database on `nodeA` by using the following:

```
SELECT pglogical.create_replication_set(
                 set_name := 'SmallSet');
SELECT pglogical.replication_set_add_table(
                 set_name := 'SmallSet',
                 relation := 'TableX');
```

And then immediately copy all table data and then subscribe to changes for `TableX`:

```
SELECT pglogical.create_subscription(
                 subscription_name :=
'SmallSet_subscription',
                 replication_sets := ARRAY['SmallSet'],
                 provide_dsn := 'host=nodeA dbname=postgres'
                 );
```

3. Publish changes for rows on `TableY` where `status=7` on the `MyApp` database on `nodeA`, adding this into the existing replication set and immediately synchronizing data to all subscribing nodes:

```
SELECT pglogical.replication_set_add_table(
                 set_name := 'SmallSet',
                 relation := 'TableY',
                 row_filter := 'status = 7',
                 synchronize_data = true);
```

How it works...

Logical decoding is very efficient because it reuses the transaction log data (WAL) that was already being written for crash safety. Triggers are not used at all for this form of replication. Physical WAL records are translated into logical changes, which are then sent to the receiving node. Only real data changes are sent; no records are generated from changes to indexes, cleanup records from VACUUM, and so on. So bandwidth requirements are somewhat reduced, depending on the exact application.

Changes are discarded if the top-level transaction aborts (save points and other subtransactions are supported normally). Changes are applied in the order of the transactions committed, so replication never breaks because it sees an inconsistent sequence of activities, as can occur with other cruder replication techniques such as statement-based replication.

On the receiving side, changes are applied using direct database calls, leading to a very efficient mechanism. SQL is not re-executed, so volatile functions in the original SQL don't produce any surprises. For example, if you make an update like this:

```
UPDATE table
SET
 col1 = col1 + random()
,col2 = col2 + random()
WHERE key = value
```

Then, the final calculated values of `col1` and `col2` are sent, instead of repeating the execution of the functions when we apply the changes.

Triggers are fired on the subscribing node, so if you wish to filter the rows applied on the subscriber, you can define BEFORE ROW triggers that block or filter rows as you wish.

Logical replication will work even if you update one or more columns of the key (or any other replica identity), since it will detect that situation and send the old values of the columns with the changed row values. Statements that write many rows get turned into a stream of single row changes.

Locks taken at table-level (LOCK) or row-level (SELECT ... FOR...) are not replicated, nor are SET or NOTIFY commands.

Logical replication doesn't suffer from cancellations of queries on the apply node in the way Hot Standby does. There isn't any need for a feature such as `hot_standby_feedback`.

Both the publishing and subscribing nodes are masters, so it would be technically possible for writes (INSERT, UPDATE, and DELETE) and/or row-level locks (SELECT ... FOR...) to be made on the apply-side database. As a result, it is possible that local changes could lock out, slow down, or interfere with the application of changes from the source node. It is up to the user to enforce restrictions to ensure that this does not occur. You can do this by having a user role defined specifically for replication and then using REVOKE on all access apart from the SELECT privilege to replicated tables, rather than the user role applying the changes.

Data can be read on the apply side while changes are being made. That is just normal, and it's the beautiful power of PostgreSQL's MVCC feature.

The use of replication slots means that if the network drops, or if one of the nodes is offline, we can pick up the replication again from the precise point that we stopped.

There's more...

LSR can work alongside PSR. There are no conflicting parameters; just ensure that all requirements are met for both PSR and LSR.

With LSR and pglogical, neither DDL nor sequences are replicated; only the data changes (DML) are sent. Only the full version of Postgres-BDR provides these features at present.

Logical replication is one-way only, so if you want multi-master replication, see the *Bi-Directional Replication* recipe. Logical replication provides cascaded replication.

See also

In PostgreSQL 10, some aspects of LSR have been included with the core server. The same idea of publish and subscribe has been included as commands, allowing these to be dumped and restored between servers.

Let's look at the same examples as we saw earlier:

1. To publish changes from all tables on a postgres database on nodeA, use the following:

```
CREATE PUBLICATION pub_nodeA_postgres_all
    FOR ALL TABLES;
```

And then immediately copy all table data and then subscribe to changes from the default replication set on the `nodeA` database `postgres`, by issuing the following command on `nodeB`:

```
CREATE SUBSCRIPTION sub_nodeA_postgres_all
CONNECTION 'conninfo'
PUBLICATION pub_nodeA_postgres_all;
```

2. Publish changes for `TableX` on the `MyApp` database on `nodeA` by using the following:

```
CREATE PUBLICATION pub_nodeA_postgres_tablex
    FOR TABLE TableX;
```

And then immediately copy all table data and then subscribe to changes for `TableX`:

```
CREATE SUBSCRIPTION sub_nodeA_postgres_tablex
CONNECTION 'conninfo'
PUBLICATION pub_nodeA_postgres_tablex;
```

Publishing a subset of DML operations is possible, though it isn't yet possible to filter rows.

Creating a `PUBLICATION` requires `CREATE` privilege on current database. Creating a `SUBSCRIPTION` object will by default enable replication and have it start immediately, though it is often convenient to define these first with the option `WITH (enabled = off)` and then re-enable them later using `ALTER SUBSCRIPTION`. Subscriptions use normal user access security, so there is no need to enable *replication* via `pg_hba.conf`.

It is also possible to override the `synchronous_commit` parameter and demand that the server provides synchronous replication.

Bi-directional replication

Bi-directional replication (Postgres-BDR) is a project used to allow multi-master replication with PostgreSQL. There is a range of possible architectures. The first use case we support is all-nodes-to-all-nodes. Postgres-BDR will eventually support a range of complex architectures, which is discussed later.

Postgres-BDR aims for eventual inclusion within core PostgreSQL, though knowing that is a long and rigorous process, it also aims to provide working software solutions, now!

Postgres-BDR aims to allow the nodes of the cluster to be physically distributed, allowing worldwide access to data and allowing for disaster recovery. Each Postgres-BDR master node runs individual transactions; there is no globally distributed transaction manager. Postgres-BDR includes replication of data changes and data definition (DDL) changes. New tables are added automatically, ensuring that managing BDR is a low-maintenance overhead for applications.

Postgres-BDR also provides global sequences, if you wish to have a sequence that works across a distributed system. Normal local sequences are not replicated.

The key advantage of Postgres-BDR is that you can segregate your write workload across multiple nodes by application, user group, or geographical proximity. Each node can be configured differently, yet all work together to provide access to the same data. Some examples of use cases for this are as follows:

- Social media applications, where users need fast access to their local server, yet the whole database needs a single database view to cater for links and interconnections.
- Distributed businesses, where orders are taken by phone in one location and by websites in another location. Then, they are fulfilled via several other locations.
- Multinational companies that need fast access to data from many locations, yet wish to see a single, common view of their data.

Postgres-BDR builds upon the basic technology of logical replication, enhancing it in various ways. We refer heavily to the previous recipe, *Logical replication*.

Getting ready

Currently, Postgres-BDR can be deployed in the all-to-all architecture, which has been tested on clusters of up to 99 master nodes. Each of those nodes is a normal, fully functioning PostgreSQL server that can perform both reads and writes.

Postgres-BDR connects directly between each node, forming a mesh of connections. Changes flow directly to other nodes in constant time, no matter how many nodes are in use. This is quite different from circular replication used by other DBMS.

All Postgres-BDR nodes should have `pg_hba.conf` definitions to allow paths between each node. It would be easier to have these settings the same on all nodes, but that is not required.

Each node requires an LSR link to all other nodes for each replicated database. So, a 32-node Postgres-BDR cluster will require 31 LSR links per node. Ensure that the parameters are configured to allow for this and any possible future expansion. The parameters should be the same on all nodes to avoid confusion. Remember that these changes require restarting.

Postgres-BDR nodes also require configuring the mechanism for conflict detection:

```
track_commit_timestamps = on
```

Postgres-BDR 1 requires a modified version of PostgreSQL 9.4. Postgres-BDR 2 is available only as an interim measure as an extension for PostgreSQL 9.6. Postgres-BDR 3 will be available in 2018 for PostgreSQL 10 and above. For latest info, please consult https://www.2ndquadrant.com/en/resources/bdr/.

Future versions of PostgreSQL may contain multi-master replication, though this will not be until at least PostgreSQL 12 as we go to press.

How to do it...

To create a new node, we take a copy of one of the databases on the source nodes. This can be accomplished using either a physical base backup or a logical base backup. A physical copy includes all databases on the source node, so this mechanism is most suitable where there is only one active database on that node.

Command specifications are subject to change. Check out https://www.2ndquadrant.com/en/resources/bdr/ for the latest details on them.

How it works...

Postgres-BDR optimistically assumes that changes on one node do not conflict with changes on other nodes. Any conflicts are detected and then resolved automatically using a predictable last update wins strategy, though custom conflict handlers are supported to allow more precise definition for particular applications.

Applications that regularly cause conflicts won't run very well on Postgres-BDR. Having said that, such applications would also suffer from lock waits and resource contention on a normal database; the effects will be somewhat amplified by the distributed nature of Postgres-BDR, but only the existing problems are amplified. Applications that are properly designed to be scalable and contention free will work well on Postgres-BDR.

Postgres-BDR replicates changes at the row level, though work is underway to apply changes at column level and in a conflict-free manner. The current mechanism has some implications for applications:

- Suppose we perform two simultaneous updates on different nodes like this:

  ```
  UPDATE foo SET col1 = col1 + 1 WHERE key = value;
  ```

- Then, in the event of a conflict, we will keep only one of the changes (the last change). What we might like in this case is to make the changes additive. This requires a custom conflict handler.
- Two updates that change different columns on different nodes will still cause replication conflicts.

At the time of writing, Postgres-BDR supports only post-commit conflict resolution, though work is in progress to provide eager consistency (pre-commit resolution) in future releases.

Postgres-BDR provides tools to diagnose and correct contention problems. Conflicts are logged so that they can be identified and removed at the application level. You can log either the conflicting statement or the entire conflicting transaction. Optionally, they can be also saved in a table for easier analysis.

There's more...

If a node fails, there is no requirement for failover, so other nodes continue processing normally—there is no wait for failover, nor is there the need for complex voting algorithms to identify the best new master. Failed servers will need to rejoin the cluster.

Postgres-BDR will eventually support a range of complex architectures:

- **Cascading**: Postgres-BDR doesn't support cascading yet
- **Circular replication**: This reduces overhead of connections, but is brittle, and the delay for changes to propagate through the cluster increases as the number of nodes increases
- **Group to group**: This involves more complex regional or geographically disparate systems
- **Central rollup**: This involves central servers sending changes from remote nodes
- **Central broadcast**: This involves central servers sending changes out to remote nodes

Archiving transaction log data

PSR can send transaction log data to a remote node even if the node is not a full PostgreSQL server. This can be useful for archiving copies of transaction log data for various purposes.

PostgreSQL includes two client tools to stream data from the server to the client. The tools are designed using a pull model; that is, you run the tools on the node you wish the data to be saved on:

- `pg_receivewal` archives physical transaction log data (WAL files). This utility produces a straight copy of the original WAL files. Replication slots are recommended when using this tool from 9.4 onwards.
- `pg_recvlogical` archives the results of logical decoding of transaction log data. This utility produces a copy of the transformed data rather than physical WAL. Replication slots are required for this tool. You will need to use that with a logical decoding plugin.

Getting ready

This recipe assumes that you have already set up replication according to the earlier recipes so that `wal_level`, `max_wal_senders`, and other parameters are set. Remember that for `pg_recvlogical`, you must set `wal_level` to `logical`.

This recipe is a different way of archiving WAL files than using `archive_command`, so you will likely want to unset that parameter if you use this recipe.

You will need to configure security just as you did for replication. So, you will need a PostgreSQL connection string, just as before.

Decide where you want to put the data on the client. Remember that WAL files look the same for each server, so you need to put them in a directory with a useful name so that you don't confuse files from different servers. You don't need to do this step for normal replication because streaming replication normally copies the files to the downstream node's `pg_wal` directory.

How to do it...

To archive a physical WAL from a server called `alpha`, follow these steps:

1. If you decide to use replication slots, then create a slot using steps *1* to *3* of the *Using replication slots* recipe.
2. Execute the tool on the client:

```
pg_receivewal -D /pgarchive/alpha -d $MYCONNECTIONSTRING &
```

3. If using slots, also use the `--slot=slotname` parameter on the command line.

If the connection from the client tool to the server is lost, the default behavior is to loop indefinitely while trying to re-establish a connection. If you want the client tool to exit if the connection is lost, then specify the `-n` or `--no-loop` options.

The `pg_recvlogical` utility requires some form of logical decoding plugin, so look at the instructions for the plugin you are using to describe exactly how to use that.

There's more...

While playing with this feature for the first time, try the `--verbose` option.

For more detail on logical decoding plugins, we refer to the *Logical replication* recipe earlier in this chapter.

Replication monitoring will show `pg_receivewal` and `pg_recvlogical` in exactly the same way as it shows other connected nodes, so there is no additional monitoring required. The default `application_name` is the same as the name of the tool, so you may want to set that parameter to something more meaningful to you.

With `pg_receivewal` and `pg_recvlogical`, you can use the `--create-slot` and `--drop-slot` options to control replication slots.

You can archive WAL files using synchronous replication by specifying `pg_receivewal --synchronous`. This causes a disk flush (`fsync`) on the client so that WAL data is robustly saved to the disk. It then passes status information back to the server to acknowledge that the data is safe (regardless of the setting of the `-s` parameter).

See also

- If you want to browse the content of the WAL files, you'll need the `pg_waldump` program, which is an additional server-side utility

Upgrading minor releases

Minor release upgrades are released regularly by all software developers, and PostgreSQL has its share of corrections. When a minor release occurs, we bump the last number, usually by one. So the first release of a major release 10 is 10.0. The first set of bug fixes is 10.1, then 10.2, and so on.

This recipe is about moving from a minor release to minor release.

Getting ready

First, get hold of the new release, by downloading either the source or fresh binaries.

How to do it...

In most cases, PostgreSQL aims for minor releases to be simple upgrades. We make great efforts to keep the on-disk format the same for both data/index files and transaction log (WAL) files, but this isn't always the case; some files can change sometimes.

The upgrade process is as follows:

1. Read the release notes to see whether there are any special actions that need to be taken for this particular release. Make sure you consider steps required by all extensions that you have installed.
2. If you have professional support, talk to your support vendor to see whether additional safety checks over and above the upgrade instructions are required or recommended. Also, verify that the target release is fully supported by your vendor on your hardware, OS, and OS release level; it may not be, yet.
3. Apply any special actions or checks; for example, if the WAL format has changed, then you may need to reconfigure log-based replication following the upgrade. You may need to scan tables, rebuild indexes, or perform some other actions. Not every release has such actions, but watch closely for them, because if they exist, then they are important.

4. If you are using replication, test the upgrade by disconnecting one of your standby servers from the master.

5. Follow the instructions for your OS distribution and binary packager to complete the upgrade. These can vary considerably.

6. Start up the database server being used for this test, apply any post-upgrade special actions, and check that things are working for you.

7. Repeat steps 4 to 6 for other standby servers.

8. Repeat steps 4 to 6 for the primary server.

How it works...

Minor upgrades mostly affect the binary executable files, so it should be a simple matter of replacing those files and restarting. But check.

Major upgrades in-place

PostgreSQL provides an additional supplied program, called pg_upgrade, which allows you to migrate between major releases, such as from 9.2 to 9.6; or you can upgrade straight to the latest server version. These upgrades are performed in-place, meaning that we upgrade your database without moving to a new system. That does sound good, but pg_upgrade has a few things that you may wish to consider as potential negatives, which are as follows:

- The database server must be shut down while the upgrade takes place.
- Your system must be large enough to hold two copies of the database server: old and new copies. If it's not, then you have to use the link option of pg_upgrade, or use the *Major upgrades online* recipe later. If you use the link option on pg_upgrade, then there is no pg_downgrade utility. The only option in that case is a restore from backup, and that means extended unavailability while you restore.
- If you copy the database, then the upgrade time will be proportional to the size of the database.
- The pg_upgrade utility does not validate all your additional add-in modules, so you will need to set up a test server and confirm that these work, ahead of performing the main upgrade.

The pg_upgrade utility supports versions from PostgreSQL 8.4 onwards and allows you to go straight from your current release to the latest release in one hop.

Getting ready

Find out the size of your database (using the *How much disk space does a database use?* recipe in Chapter 2, *Exploring the Database*). If the database is large or you have an important requirement for availability, you should consider doing the major upgrade using replication tools as well. Then, check out the next recipe.

How to do it...

1. Read the release notes for the new server version to which you are migrating, including all of the intervening releases. Pay attention to the incompatibilities section carefully; PostgreSQL does change from release to release. Assume this will take some hours.

2. Set up a test server with the old software release on it. Restore one of your backups on it. Upgrade that system to the new release to verify that there are no conflicts from software dependencies. Test your application. Make sure you identify and test each add-in PostgreSQL module you were using to confirm that it still works at the new release level.

3. Back up your production server. Prepare for the worst; hope for the best!

4. Most importantly, work out who you will call if things go badly, and exactly how to restore from that backup you just took.

5. Install new versions of all the required software on the production server, and create a new database server.

6. Don't disable security during the upgrade. Your security team will do backflips if they hear about this. Keep your job!

7. Now, go and do that backup. Don't skip this step; it isn't optional. Check whether the backup is actually readable, accessible, and complete.

8. Shut down the database servers.

9. Run pg_upgrade -v and then run any required post-upgrade scripts. Make sure you check whether any were required.

10. Start up the new database server and immediately run a server-wide ANALYZE operation using `vacuumdb -analyze-in-stages`.

11. Run through your tests to check whether it worked or you need to start performing the contingency plan.

12. If all is OK, re-enable wide access to the database server. Restart the applications.

13. Don't delete your old server directory if you used the link method. The old `data` directory still contains the data for the new database server. Confusing! So don't get caught by this.

How it works...

The `pg_upgrade` utility works by creating a new set of database catalog tables, and then creating the old objects again in the new tables using the same identifiers as before.

The `pg_upgrade` utility works easily because the data block format hasn't changed between some releases. Since we can't (always) see the future, make sure you read the release notes.

Major upgrades online

Upgrading between major releases is hard, and it should be deferred until you have some good reasons and sufficient time to get it right.

You can use replication tools to minimize the downtime required for an upgrade, so we refer to this recipe as an **online upgrade**.

How to do it...

The following general steps should be followed, allowing at least a month for the complete process to ensure that everything is tested and everybody understands the implications:

1. Set up a new release of the software on a new test system.
2. Take a standalone backup from the main system and copy it to the test system.
3. Test the applications extensively against the new release on the test system.

When everything works and performs correctly, then do the following:

1. Set up a connection pooler to the main database (it may be there already).
2. Set up `pglogical` for all tables from old to new database servers. Make sure you wait until all the initial copy tasks have completed for all tables.

Retest the application extensively against the new release on live data, then when ready for the final cut-over, we can do the following:

1. Pause the connection pool.
2. Switch the config of the pool over to the new system, reload.
3. Resume the connection pool (so it now accesses a new server).

Downtime for the application is the length of time to these last three steps.

How it works...

The preceding recipe allows online upgrades with zero data loss because of the use of the clean switchover process. There's no need for lengthy downtime during the upgrade, and there's much reduced risk in comparison with an in-place upgrade. It works best with new hardware, and is a good way to upgrade the hardware or change the disk layout at the same time.

This procedure is also very useful for those cases where binary compatibility is not possible, such as changing server encoding, or migrating the database to a different operating system or architecture, where on-disk format will change as a result of low-level differences, such as endianness and alignment.

Other Books You May Enjoy

If you enjoyed this book, you may be interested in these other books by Packt:

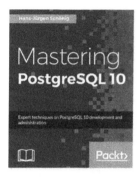

Mastering PostgreSQL 10
Hans-Jürgen Schönig

ISBN: 978-1-78847-229-6

- Get to grips with the advanced features of PostgreSQL 10 and handle advanced SQL
- Make use of the indexing features in PostgreSQL and fine-tune the performance of your queries
- Work with stored procedures and manage backup and recovery
- Master replication and failover techniques
- Troubleshoot your PostgreSQL instance for solutions to common and not-so-common problems
- Learn how to migrate your database from MySQL and Oracle to PostgreSQL without any hassle

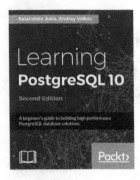

Learning PostgreSQL 10 - Second Edition
Salahaldin Juba, Andrey Volkov

ISBN: 978-1-78839-201-3

- Understand the fundamentals of relational databases, relational algebra, and data modeling
- Install a PostgreSQL cluster, create a database, and implement your data model
- Create tables and views, define indexes, and implement triggers, stored procedures, and other schema objects
- Use the Structured Query Language (SQL) to manipulate data in the database
- Implement business logic on the server side with triggers and stored procedures using PL/pgSQL
- Make use of advanced data types supported by PostgreSQL 10: Arrays, hstore, JSONB, and others
- Develop OLAP database solutions using the most recent features of PostgreSQL 10
- Connect your Python applications to a PostgreSQL database and work with the data efficiently
- Test your database code, find bottlenecks, improve performance, and enhance the reliability of the database applications

Leave a review - let other readers know what you think

Please share your thoughts on this book with others by leaving a review on the site that you bought it from. If you purchased the book from Amazon, please leave us an honest review on this book's Amazon page. This is vital so that other potential readers can see and use your unbiased opinion to make purchasing decisions, we can understand what our customers think about our products, and our authors can see your feedback on the title that they have worked with Packt to create. It will only take a few minutes of your time, but is valuable to other potential customers, our authors, and Packt. Thank you!

Index